An Introduction to Object-Oriented Programming

An Introduction to Object-Oriented Programming

Second Edition

Timothy Budd

Oregon State University

 **ADDISON-WESLEY**

An imprint of Addison Wesley Longman, Inc.

Reading, Massachusetts • Harlow, England • Menlo Park, California
Berkeley, California • Don Mills, Ontario • Sydney
Bonn • Amsterdam • Tokyo • Mexico City

Sponsoring Editor: Lynne Doran Cote
Associate Editor: Deborah Lafferty
Production Supervisor: Juliet Silveri
Production Services: Superscript Editorial Production Services
Cover Design Supervisor: Barbara Atkinson
Manufacturing Coordinator: Judy Sullivan

Library of Congress Cataloging-in-Publication Data

Budd, Timothy.
    An introduction to object-oriented programming / Timothy Budd. —
2nd ed.
      p.   cm.
    Includes bibliographical references and index.
    ISBN 0-201-82419-1
    1. Object-oriented programming (Computer science)   I. Title.
QA76.64.B83   1997
005.13—dc20   96-23738
                                                  CIP

This book was reproduced by Addison-Wesley from electronic files supplied by the author.

Preface

I started writing the first edition of this book in 1988, and it was finally published in the last days of 1990. The eight years between the original development of the book and the present have seen a series of changes in object-oriented programming, necessitating almost a complete rewriting of the text. Among these changes are the following:

- A better understanding of the distinction between subclasses and subtypes, and an appreciation of the fact that the two are often not the same.

- The rapid growth, evolution, and standardization of the language C++, including the introduction of templates, exceptions, Booleans, name spaces, strings, the RTTI (run-time type identification system), and the standard library.

- The introduction of the programming language Java, an exciting new tool for developing applications for the World Wide Web.

- The slow demise of the language Object Pascal after its abandonment by Apple as the primary language for application development on the Macintosh, only to be reborn as a new language with the same name as a tool for developing PC applications using Delphi.

- The equally slow decline in use of the language Objective-C. For those interested in languages this is an unfortunate loss, since the dynamically typed Objective-C is almost an ideal foil to the statically typed language C++. For this reason I have continued to discuss Objective-C in this edition.

- The development of interesting new object-oriented languages, such as Beta, CLOS, and Java, that incorporate both new ideas and old ideas in new guises.

- The development of new ways of thinking about *collections* of classes that work together, resulting in the refinement of ideas such as application frameworks and design patterns.

For these reasons and many more, almost every section of this edition has been revised. Nevertheless, I have attempted to retain the overall structure of the book, which can be described as a series of themes, as follows:

I. Introduction and Design. Chapter 1 introduces in an informal setting the basic concepts of object-oriented programming. Chapter 2 continues this by introducing the principle of designing by responsibility. These two chapters are fundamental, and their study should not be given short shrift. In particular, I strongly encourage at least one, if not several, group exercises in which CRC cards, introduced in Chapter 2, are used in problem solving. The manipulation of physical index cards in a group setting is one of the best techniques I have encountered for developing the notions of behavior, responsibility, and encapsulation.

II. Classes, Methods, and Messages. Chapters 3 and 4 introduce the basic syntax used by our example languages (Smalltalk, C++, Java, Objective-C, and Object Pascal) to create classes and methods and to send messages. Chapter 3 concentrates on the static features (classes and methods), while Chapter 4 describes the dynamic aspects (creating objects and sending messages). Chapters 5 and 6 reinforce these ideas with the first of a series of *case studies*–example programs developed in an object-oriented fashion and illustrating various features of the technique.

III. Inheritance and Software Reuse. Chapters 7, 8, and 9 introduce the concept of inheritance and the use of inheritance as a technique for software reuse. The case study in Chapter 8, written in the language Java, also illustrates the use of a standard API (application programming interface). Chapter 9 contrasts the use of inheritance and composition as dual techniques for software reuse.

IV. Inheritance in More Detail. Chapters 10 through 13 delve into the concept of inheritance in greater detail. The introduction of inheritance into a programming language has an impact on almost every other aspect of the language, and this impact is often not initially obvious to the student (or programmer). Chapter 10 discusses message lookup and the binding of methods to messages, illustrating the fact that subclasses and subtypes need not be the same. Chapter 11 discusses the semantics of method overriding, pointing out two very different interpretations found in almost all languages. Chapter 12 continues by exploring some of the further implications of inheritance on topics such as memory allocation, assignment, and testing for equality. Finally, Chapter 13 explores the idea of multiple inheritance.

V. Polymorphism. Much of the power of object-oriented programming comes through the application of various forms of polymorphism. Chapter 14 introduces the basic mechanisms used for attaining polymorphism in object-oriented languages, and follows with a pair of case studies that illustrate these points. The first, in Chapter 15, considers the creation of general-purpose container libraries. A specific library, the recently developed Standard Template Library in C++, is discussed in Chapter 16.

VI. Software Engineering. Chapter 17 discusses a number of standard software engineering topics in the context of object-oriented languages. Chapter 18 introduces some relatively new concepts in the field of object-oriented design, *application frameworks* and *design patterns*. Both are techniques for describing how collections of classes are used together in the solution of programming problems. Finally, Chapter 19 illustrates the design of an application framework by describing a specific example, the Little Application Framework.

VII. Advanced Topics. The concept of classes, on second examination, is not as simple as the development in Chapter 3 would lead us to believe. Chapter 20 briefly considers a number of advanced topics in object-oriented programming. Examples include delegation (object-oriented programming without classes) and metaclass programming (programming the language itself). Chapter 21 describes in general terms the variety of implementation techniques used in the execution of object-oriented languages.

In the ten-week course I teach at Oregon State University I devote approximately one week to each of the major areas described above. At the same time students work on moderate-sized projects using an object-oriented language of their choice, and the term ends with student presentations of project designs and outcomes.

In the first edition I concluded with a chapter titled "Further Information." Unfortunately, the field moved so quickly that this information was almost immediately out of date. Rather than placing this information in the second edition, I will try to maintain a Web site with recent information.

Obtaining the Source

Source code for the case studies presented in the book can be accessed via the mechanism of anonymous ftp from the machine `ftp.cs.orst.edu`, in the directory `/pub/budd/oopintro`. This directory will also be used to maintain a number of other items, such as an errata list, study questions for each chapter, and copies of the overhead slides I use in my course. This information can also be accessed via the World Wide Web, from my personal home pages at `http://www.cs.orst.edu/~budd/oopintro`. Requests for further information can be forwarded to the electronic mail address `budd@cs.orst.edu`, or to Professor Timothy A. Budd, Department of Computer Science, Oregon State University, Corvallis, Oregon, 97331.

Necessary Background

I have presented the material in this book assuming only that the reader is knowledgeable in some conventional programming language, such as Pascal or C. In my courses, the material has been used successfully at the upper-division (junior or senior) undergraduate level and at the first-year graduate level. In some cases (particularly in the last quarter of the book), further knowledge may be helpful but is not assumed. For example, a student who has taken a course in software engineering may find some of the material in Chapter 17 more relevant, and one who has had a course in compiler construction will find Chapter 21 more intelligible. Both chapters can be simplified in presentation if necessary.

Preface to First Edition

The inspiration to write this book arose, as it did for my earlier book on Smalltalk [Budd 1987], when I was faced with teaching a course and was not able to find a suitable existing text. I had for some years taught a seminar on Smalltalk and object-oriented programming, using my own book as the text. Starting in the late 1980s, I received an increasing number of requests for a course structured around C++. At the same time, the popularity of the Macintosh computer brought with it a slightly smaller call for instruction in Object Pascal. Finally, the announcement of the NeXT computer resulted in inquiries about how best to learn Objective-C.

Since I did not wish to teach four different courses, each dealing with a specific object-oriented language, I resolved to teach a single course in which I would lay out the principles of object-oriented programming, illustrating these principles with examples from each of the four languages. Participants would learn a little about each language and would complete a project in a language of their choice.

I then set out to find a textbook for such a course. What I discovered, to my surprise, was that existing texts, although in many ways quite admirable, were all oriented around a single language. Books I considered included Cox [Cox 1986], Goldberg and Robson [Goldberg 1983], Kaehler and Patterson [Kaehler 1986], Keene [Keene 1989], Meyer [Meyer 1988a], Pinson and Wiener [Pinson 1988] and its companion, Wiener and Pinson [Wiener 1988], Stroustrup [Stroustrup 1986], and Pohl [Pohl 1989]. Although in the end I selected a few of these as optional texts, I rejected all of them as a primary text for the simple reason that each, to a greater or lesser extent, gives the impression that "object-oriented programming" is synonymous with "object-oriented programming in X," where X is whatever programming language happens to be the author's favorite. Instead, I started writing my own lecture notes to use as a primary text. Over the course of the next year, I revised and extended these notes; this book is the result.

Various participants in my course (which turned out to be much more popular and hence much larger than I had anticipated), in addition to completing projects in the four languages that I mentioned above, successfully completed projects in Actor [Actor 1987], Turbo Pascal [Turbo 1988], and CLOS [Keene 1989]. Since my objective was to convey the principles of object-oriented programming independent of a specific language, I inquired of these individuals whether the material discussed in my lecture notes was applicable and useful in their work. On the basis of their positive response, I believe I have at least partially succeeded in achieving a measure of language independence.

This book should *not* be considered a substitute for either a language tutorial or a language reference manual for any of the four languages discussed. In each of the languages, there are numerous subtle but language-specific or implementation-specific features that I did not believe were relevant to the discussions in this text, but that are certainly important as practical matters to the programmer.

Acknowledgments

I am certainly grateful to the 65 students in my course, CS589, at Oregon State University who, in the fall of 1989, suffered through the development of the first draft of this text. They received one chapter at a time, often only a day or two before I lectured on the material. Their patience in this regard is appreciated. Their specific comments, corrections, critiques, and criticisms were most helpful. In particular, I wish to acknowledge the detailed comments provided by Thomas Amoth, Kim Drongesen, Frank Griswold, Rajeev Pandey, and Phil Ruder.

The solitaire game developed in Chapter 8 was inspired by the project completed by Kim Drongesen, and the billiards game in Chapter 6 was based on the project by Guenter Mamier and Dietrich Wettschereck. In both cases, however, the code itself has been entirely rewritten and is my own. In fact, in both cases my code is considerably stripped down for the purposes of exposition and is in no way comparable to the greatly superior projects completed by those students.

I am also grateful to the people who provided comments, corrections, critiques, and criticisms on subsequent drafts of the manuscript. These individuals include Michael Adar, Jerrie Andreas, Lynn Cochran, Brad Cox, Graham Dumpleton, Peter Grogono, Nola Hague, Marcia Horton, Ralph Johnson, Doug Lea, Ted Lewis, Stanley Lippman, Darcy McCallum, Lindsay Marshall, Makku Sakkinen, Michael Share, Dave Taenzer, Nabil Zamel, and several reviewers—including Ed Gehringer, James Heliotis, Karl Lieberherr, Jeff Parker, Justin Smith, and Daniel Sterms.

The source listings were printed with Latex macros based on C program formatting macros originally written by Éamonn McManus of Trinity College, Dublin.

For an author it is always useful to have others provide an independent perspective on ones work, and I admit to gaining useful insights into the first edition from a study guide prepared by Arina Brintz, Louise Leenen, Tommie Meyer, Helene Rosenblatt, and Anel Viljoen of the Department of Computer Science and Information Systems at the University of South Africa, in Pretoria.

Countless people have provided assistance by pointing out errors or omissions in the first edition and offering improvements. I am grateful to them all and sorry I cannot name more people here. Reviewers for the second edition included Thomas Bonnick, Northeastern University; M. A. Sridhar, University of South Carolina; and Walter C. Daugherity, Texas A & M University.

For the second edition my capable, competent, and patient editors at Addison-Wesley have been Lynne Doran Cote and Deborah Lafferty. Production assistance has been provided by Ann Knight of Superscript.

Contents

Chapter 1

Thinking Object-Oriented

Object-oriented programming (OOP) has become exceedingly popular in the past few years. Software producers rush to release object-oriented versions of their products. Countless books and special issues of academic and trade journals have appeared on the subject. Students strive to list "experience in object-oriented programming" on their résumés. To judge from this frantic activity, object-oriented programming is being greeted with even more enthusiasm than we saw heralding earlier revolutionary ideas, such as "structured programming" or "expert systems."

My intent in this first chapter is to investigate and explain the basic principles of object-oriented programming, and in doing so to illustrate the following two propositions:

- OOP is a revolutionary idea, totally unlike anything that has come before in programming.

- OOP is an evolutionary step, following naturally on the heels of earlier programming abstractions.

1.1 Why Is OOP Popular?

To judge from much of the popular press, the following represent a few of the possible reasons that object-oriented programming has, in the past decade, become so popular:

- The hope that it will quickly and easily lead to increased productivity and improved reliability (help solve the software crisis).

- The desire for an easy transition from existing languages.

- The resonant similarity to techniques of thinking about problems in other domains.

1

Object-oriented programming is just the latest in a long series of solutions that have been proposed to help solve the "software crisis." At heart, the software crisis simply means that our imaginations, and the tasks we would like to solve with the help of computers, almost always outstrip our abilities.

But while object-oriented techniques *do* facilitate the creation of complex software systems, it is important to remember that OOP is not a "silver bullet" (a term made popular by Fred Brooks [Brooks 1987]). Programming a computer is still one of the most difficult tasks ever undertaken by humans; becoming proficient in programming requires talent, creativity, intelligence, logic, the ability to build and use abstractions, and experience–even when the best of tools are available.

I suspect another reason for the particular popularity of languages such as C++ and Object Pascal (as opposed to languages such as Smalltalk and Beta) is that managers and programmers alike hope that a C or Pascal programmer can be changed into a C++ or Object Pascal programmer with no more effort than the addition of a few characters to the job title. Unfortunately, this hope is a long way from being realized. Object-oriented programming is a new way of thinking about what it means to compute, about how we can structure information inside a computer. To become proficient in object-oriented techniques requires a complete reevaluation of traditional software development.

1.2   Language and Thought

Human beings do not live in the objective world alone, nor alone in the world of social activity as ordinarily understood, but are very much at the mercy of the particular language which has become the medium of expression for their society. It is quite an illusion to imagine that one adjusts to reality essentially without the use of language and that language is merely an incidental means of solving specific problems of communication or reflection. The fact of the matter is that the 'real world' is to a large extent unconsciously built up on the language habits of the group.... We see and hear and otherwise experience very largely as we do because the language habits of our community predispose certain choices of interpretation.

Edward Sapir (quoted in [Whorf 1956])

This quote emphasizes the fact that the languages we speak directly influence the way in which we view the world. This is true not only for natural languages, such as the kind studied by the early twentieth century American linguists Edward Sapir and Benjamin Lee Whorf, but also for artificial languages such as those we use in programming computers.

1.2.1   Eskimos and Snow

An almost universally cited example of the phenomenon of language influencing thought, although also an erroneous one (see [Pullum 1991]) is the "fact" that Eskimo (or Inuit) languages have many words to describe various types of snow— wet, fluffy, heavy, icy, and so on. This is not surprising. Any community with common interests will naturally develop a specialized vocabulary for concepts they wish to discuss.

What is important is not to overgeneralize the conclusion we can draw from this simple observation. It is not that the Eskimo eye is in any significant respect different from my own, or that Eskimos can see things I cannot perceive. With time and training I could do just as well at differentiating types of snow. But the language I speak (namely, English) does not *force* me into doing so, and so it is not natural to me. Thus, different language (such as Inuktitut) can *lead* one (but does not *require* one) to view the world in a different fashion.

To make effective use of object-oriented principles requires one to view the world in a new way. But simply using an object-oriented language (such as C++) does not, by itself, force one to become an object-oriented programmer. While the use of an object-oriented language will simplify the development of object-oriented solutions, it is true, as it has been quipped, that "FORTRAN programs can be written in any language."

1.2.2   An Example from Computer Languages

The relationship we noted between language and thought for natural languages is even more pronounced in artificial computer languages. That is, the language in which a programmer thinks a problem will be solved will color and alter, fundamentally, the way in which an algorithm is developed.

An example will illustrate this relationship between computer language and problem solution. Several years ago a student working in genetic research was faced with a task in the analysis of DNA sequences. The problem could be reduced to relatively simple form. The DNA is represented as a vector of N integer values, where N is very large (on the order of tens of thousands). The problem was to discover whether any pattern of length M, where M was a fixed and small constant (say five or ten) is ever repeated in the vector of values.

ACTCGGATCTTGCATTTCGGCAATTGGACCCTGACTTGGCCA ...

The programmer dutifully sat down and wrote a simple and straightforward FORTRAN program something like the following:

```
      DO 10 I = 1, N-M
      DO 10 J = 1, N-M
      FOUND = .TRUE.
      DO 20 K = 1, M
20    IF X[I+K-1] .NE. X[J+K-1] THEN FOUND = .FALSE.
```

```
      IF FOUND THEN ...
10    CONTINUE
```

He was somewhat disappointed when trial runs indicated his program would need many hours to complete. He discussed his problem with a second student, who happened to be proficient in the programming language APL, who said that she would like to try writing a program for this problem. The first student was dubious; after all, FORTRAN was known to be one of the most "efficient" programming languages–it was compiled, and APL was only interpreted. So it was with a certain amount of incredulity that he discovered that the APL programmer was able to write an algorithm that worked in a matter of minutes, not hours.

What the APL programmer had done was to rearrange the problem. Rather than working with a vector of N elements, she reorganized the data into a matrix with roughly N rows and M columns:

A	C	T	C	G	G	positions 1 to M
C	T	C	G	G	A	positions 2 to $M+1$
T	C	G	G	A	T	positions 3 to $M+2$
C	G	G	A	T	T	positions 4 to $M+3$
G	G	A	T	T	C	positions 5 to $M+4$
G	A	T	T	C	T	positions 6 to $M+5$
	.	.	.			
T	G	G	A	C	C	
G	G	A	C	C	C	
	.	.	.			

She then sorted this matrix by rows. If any pattern was repeated, then two adjacent rows in the sorted matrix had identical values.

	.	.	.		
T	G	G	A	C	C
T	G	G	A	C	C
	.	.	.		

It was a trivial matter to check for this condition. The reason the APL program was faster had nothing to do with the speed of APL versus FORTRAN; it was simply that the FORTRAN program employed an algorithm that was $O(M \times N^2)$, whereas the sorting solution used by the APL programmer required approximately $O(M \times N \log N)$ operations.

The point of this story is not that APL is in any way a "better" programming language than FORTRAN, but that the APL programmer was naturally led to discover a better solution. The reason, in this case, is that loops are very difficult to write in APL whereas sorting is trivial–it is a built-in operator defined as part of the language. Thus, because the sorting operation is so easy to perform, good APL programmers tend to look for novel applications for it. It is in this manner that the programming language in which the solution is to be written directs the programmer's mind to view the problem in a certain way.

1.2.3 Church's Conjecture and the Whorf Hypothesis

The assertion that the language in which an idea is expressed can influence or direct a line of thought is relatively easy to believe. However, a stronger conjecture, known in linguistics as the Sapir-Whorf hypothesis, goes much further and remains controversial [Pullum 1991].

The Sapir-Whorf hypothesis asserts that it may be possible for an individual working in one language to imagine thoughts or to utter ideas that cannot in any way be translated, cannot even be understood, by individuals operating in a different linguistic framework. According to advocates of the hypothesis, this can occur when the language of the second individual has no equivalent words and lacks even concepts or categories for the ideas involved in the thought. It is interesting to compare this idea with an almost directly opposite concept from computer science–namely, Church's conjecture.

Starting in the 1930s and continuing through the 1940s and 1950s there was a great deal of interest within the mathematical and nascent computing community in a variety of formalisms that could be used for the calculation of functions. Examples are the notations proposed by Church [Church 1936], Post [Post 1936], Markov [Markov 1951], Turing [Turing 1936], Kleene [Kleene 1936] and others. Over time a number of arguments were put forth to demonstrate that many of these systems could be used in the simulation of other systems. Often, such arguments for a pair of systems could be made in both directions, effectively showing that the systems were identical in computation power. The sheer number of such arguments led the logician Alonzo Church to pronounce a conjecture that is now associated with his name:

> **Church's Conjecture:** Any computation for which there exists an effective procedure can be realized by a Turing machine.

By nature this conjecture must remain unproven and unprovable, since we have no rigorous definition of the term "effective procedure." Nevertheless, no counterexample has yet been found, and the weight of evidence seems to favor affirmation of this claim.

Acceptance of Church's conjecture has an important and profound implication for the study of programming languages. Turing machines are wonderfully simple mechanisms, and it does not require many features in a language to simulate such a device. In the 1960s, for example, it was demonstrated that a Turing machine could be emulated in any language that possessed at least a conditional statement and a looping construct [Böhm 1966]. (This greatly misunderstood result was the major ammunition used to "prove" that the infamous goto statement was unnecessary.)

If we accept Church's conjecture, any language in which it is possible to simulate a Turing machine is sufficiently powerful to perform *any* realizable algorithm. (To solve a problem, find the Turing machine that produces the desired result, which by Church's conjecture must exist; then simulate the execution of the Turing machine in your favorite language.) Thus, arguments about the relative "power" of programming languages–if by power we mean "ability to solve problems"–are generally vacuous. The late Alan Perlis had a term for such arguments, calling them a "Turing Tarpit" because they are often so difficult to extricate oneself from, and so fundamentally pointless.

Note that Church's conjecture is, in a certain sense, almost the exact opposite of the Sapir-Whorf hypothesis. Church's conjecture states that in a fundamental way all programming languages are identical. Any idea that can be expressed in one language can, in theory, be expressed in any language. The Sapir-Whorf hypothesis, you will recall, claimed that it was possible to have ideas that could be expressed in one language that could not be expressed in another.

Many linguists reject the Sapir-Whorf hypothesis and instead adopt a sort of "Turing-equivalence" for natural languages. By this we mean that, with a sufficient amount of work, any idea can be expressed in any language. For example, while the language spoken by a native of a warm climate may not make it instinctive to examine a field of snow and categorize it by type or use, with time and training it certainly can be learned. Similarly, object-oriented techniques do not provide any new computational power that permits problems to be solved that cannot, *in theory*, be solved by other means. But object-oriented techniques *do* make it *easier* and more natural to address problems in a fashion that tends to favor the management of large software projects.

Thus, for both computer and natural languages the language will *direct* thoughts but cannot *proscribe* thoughts.

1.3   A New Paradigm

Object-oriented programming is frequently referred to as a new programming *paradigm*. Other programming paradigms include the imperative-programming paradigm (languages such as Pascal or C), the logic programming paradigm (Prolog), and the functional-programming paradigm (FP or Haskell).

It is interesting to examine the definition of the word "paradigm": The following is from the *American Heritage Dictionary of the English Language*:

> **par a digm** *n.* **1.** A list of all the inflectional forms of a word taken as an illustrative example of the conjugation or declension to which it belongs. **2.** Any example or model. [Late Latin *paradīgma*, from Greek *paradeigma*, model, from *paradeiknunai*, to compare, exhibit.]

At first blush, the conjugation or declension of Latin words would seem to have little to do with computer programming languages. To understand the connection, we must note that the word was brought into the modern vocabulary through an influential book, *The Structure of Scientific Revolutions*, by the historian of science Thomas Kuhn [Kuhn 1970]. Kuhn used the term in the second form, to describe a set of theories, standards, and methods that together represent a way of organizing knowledge–that is, a way of viewing the world. Kuhn's thesis was that revolutions in science occur when an older paradigm is reexamined, rejected, and replaced by another.

It is in this sense, as a model or example and as an organizational approach, that Robert Floyd used the term in his 1979 ACM Turing Award lecture [Floyd 1979], "The Paradigms of Programming." A programming paradigm is a way of conceptualizing what it means to perform computation and how tasks to be carried out on a computer should be structured and organized.

Although new to computation, the organizing technique that lies at the heart of object-oriented programming can be traced back at least as far as Linnæus (1707–1778), if not further back to Plato. Paradoxically, the style of problem solving embodied in the object-oriented technique is frequently the method used to address problems in everyday life. Thus, computer novices are often able to grasp the basic ideas of object-oriented programming easily, whereas people who are more computer literate are often blocked by their own preconceptions. Alan Kay, for example, found that it was usually easier to teach Smalltalk to children than to computer professionals [Kay 1977].

In trying to understand exactly what is meant by the term *object-oriented programming*, it is useful to examine the idea from several perspectives. The next few sections outline three aspects of object-oriented programming; each illustrates a particular reason that this technique should be considered an important new tool.

1.4   A Way of Viewing the World

To illustrate some of the major ideas in object-oriented programming, let us consider first how we might go about handling a real-world situation and then ask how we could make the computer more closely model the techniques employed.

Suppose I wish to send some flowers to my grandmother (who is named Elsie) for her birthday. She lives in a city many miles away, so my picking the flowers and carrying them to her door myself is out of the question. Nevertheless, sending her the flowers is an easy enough task; I merely go down to my local florist (who happens to be named Flo), tell her the kinds and numbers of flowers I want sent and my grandmother's address, and I can be assured the flowers will be delivered expediently and automatically.

1.4.1   Agents, Responsibility, Messages, and Methods

At the risk of belaboring a point, let me emphasize that the mechanism I used to solve my problem was to find an appropriate *agent* (namely, Flo) and to pass to her a *message* containing my request. It is the *responsibility* of Flo to satisfy my request. There is some *method*–some algorithm or set of operations–used by Flo to do this. I do not need to know the particular method she will use to satisfy my request; indeed, often I do not want to know the details. This information is usually *hidden* from my inspection.

If I investigated however, I might discover that Flo delivers a slightly different message to another florist in my grandmother's city. That florist, in turn, makes the arrangement and passes it, along with yet another message, to a delivery person, and so on. In this manner my request is finally satisfied by a sequence of requests from one agent to another.

So, our first principle of object-oriented problem solving is the vehicle by which activities are initiated:

> Action is initiated in object-oriented programming by the transmission of a *message* to an agent (an *object*) responsible for the action. The message encodes the request for an action and is accompanied by any additional information (arguments) needed to carry out the request. The *receiver* is the agent to whom the message is sent. If the receiver accepts the message, it accepts the responsibility to carry out the indicated action. In response to a message, the receiver will perform some *method* to satisfy the request.

We have noted the important principle of *information hiding* in regard to message passing–that is, the client sending the request need not know the actual means by which the request will be honored. There is another principle, all too human, that we see is implicit in message passing. If there is a task to perform, the first thought of the client is to find somebody else he or she can ask to do the work. This second reaction often becomes atrophied in many programmers with extensive experience in conventional techniques. Frequently, a difficult hurdle to overcome is the idea in the programmer's mind that he or she must write everything and not use the services of others. An important part of object-oriented programming is the development of reusable components, and an important first step in the use of reusable components is a willingness to try one.

Information hiding is also an important aspect of programming in conventional languages. In what sense is a message different from, say, a procedure call? In both cases, there is a set of well-defined steps that will be initiated following the request. But, there are two important distinctions.

The first is that in a message there is a designated *receiver* for that message; the receiver is some agent to which the message is sent. In a procedure call, there is no designated receiver. (Although we could adopt a convention of, for example, always referring to the first argument to a procedure as the receiver, something that is very close to how receivers are actually implemented.)

The second is that the *interpretation* of the message (that is, the method used to respond to the message) is dependent on the receiver and can vary with different receivers. I can give a message to my wife Beth, for example, and she will understand it and a satisfactory outcome will be produced (that is, flowers will be delivered to my grandmother). However, the method Beth uses to satisfy the request (in all likelihood, simply passing the request on to Flo) will be different from that used by Flo in response to the same request. If I ask Ken, my dentist, to send flowers to my grandmother, he may not have a method for solving that problem. If he understands the request at all, he will probably issue an appropriate error diagnostic.

Let us move our discussion back to the level of computers and programs. There, the distinction between message passing and procedure calling is that, in message passing, there is a designated receiver, and the interpretation–the selection of a method to execute in response to the message–may vary with different receivers. Usually, the specific receiver for any given message will not be known until run time, so the determination of which method to invoke cannot be made until then. Thus, we say there is late *binding* between the message (function or procedure name) and the code fragment (method) used to respond to the message. This situation is in contrast to the very early (compile-time or link-time) binding of name to code fragment in conventional procedure calls.

1.4.2 Responsibilities

A fundamental concept in object-oriented programming is to describe behavior in terms of *responsibilities*. My request for action indicates only the desired outcome (flowers for my grandmother). The florist is free to pursue any technique that achieves the desired objective and is not hampered by interference on my part.

By discussing a problem in terms of responsibilities we increase the level of abstraction. This permits greater *independence* between agents, a critical factor in solving complex problems. In Chapter 2 we will investigate in more detail how we can use an emphasis on responsibility to drive the software design process. The entire collection of responsibilities associated with an object is often described by the term *protocol*.

The difference between viewing software in traditional, structured terms and viewing it from an object-oriented perspective can be summarized by a twist on a well-known quote:

> Ask not what you can do *to* your data structures,
> but rather ask what your data structures can do *for* you.

1.4.3 Classes and Instances

Although I have only dealt with Flo a few times, I have a rough idea of the behavior I can expect when I go into her shop and present her with my request. I am able to make certain assumptions because I have some information about florists in general, and I expect that Flo, being an instance of this category, will fit the general pattern. We can use the term Florist to represent the category (or *class*) of all florists. Let us incorporate these notions into our second principle of object-oriented programming:

> All objects are *instances* of a *class*. The method invoked by an object
> in response to a message is determined by the class of the receiver.

> All objects of a given class use the same method in response to similar messages.

One current problem in the object-oriented community is the proliferation of different terms for similar ideas. Thus, a class is known in Object Pascal as an *object type*, and a *super class* (which we will describe shortly) is known as an *ancestor class* or a *parent class*, and so on. The glossary at the end of this book should be of some help with unusual terms. We will use the convention, common in object-oriented languages, of always designating classes by a name beginning with an uppercase letter. Although commonly used, this convention is not enforced by most language systems.

1.4.4   Class Hierarchies–Inheritance

I have more information about Flo–not necessarily because she is a florist but because she is a shopkeeper. I know, for example, that I probably will be asked for money as part of the transaction, and that in return for payment I will be given a receipt. These actions are true of grocers, stationers, and other shopkeepers. Since the category Florist is a more specialized form of the category Shopkeeper, any knowledge I have of Shopkeepers is also true of Florists and hence of Flo.

One way to think about how I have organized my knowledge of Flo is in terms of a hierarchy of categories (see Figure 1.1). Flo is a Florist, but Florist is a specialized form of Shopkeeper. Furthermore, a Shopkeeper is also a Human; so I know, for example, that Flo is probably bipedal. A Human is a Mammal (therefore they nurse their young), and a Mammal is an Animal (therefore it breathes oxygen), and an Animal is a Material Object (therefore it has mass and weight). Thus, quite a lot of knowledge that I have that is applicable to Flo is not directly associated with her, or even with her category Florist.

The principle that knowledge of a more general category is also applicable to a more specific category is called *inheritance*. We say that the class Florist will inherit attributes of the class (or category) Shopkeeper.

There is an alternative graphical technique often used to illustrate this relationship, particularly when there are many individuals with differing lineages. This technique shows classes listed in a hierarchical tree-like structure, with more abstract classes (such as Material Object or Animal) listed near the top of the tree, and more specific classes, and finally individuals, are listed near the bottom. Figure 1.2 shows this class hierarchy for Flo. This same hierarchy also includes Beth, my dog Flash, Phyl the platypus who lives at the zoo, and the flowers I am sending to my grandmother.

Information that I possess about Flo because she is an instance of class Human is also applicable to my wife Beth, for example. Information that I have about her because she is a Mammal is applicable to Flash as well. Information about all members of Material Object is equally applicable to Flo and to her flowers. We capture this in the idea of inheritance:

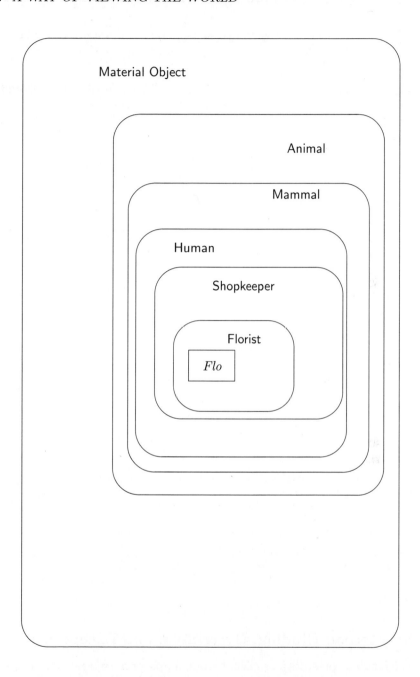

Figure 1.1 – The categories surrounding Flo.

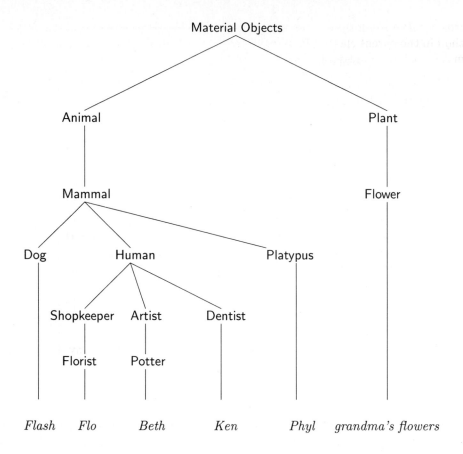

Figure 1.2 – A class hierarchy for various material objects.

Classes can be organized into a hierarchical *inheritance* structure.
A *child class* (or *subclass*) will inherit attributes from a *parent class*
higher in the tree. An *abstract parent class* is a class (such as **Mammal**) for which there are no direct instances; it is used only to create
subclasses.

1.4.5   Method Binding, Overriding, and Exceptions

Phyl the platypus presents a problem for our simple organizing structure. I know
that mammals give birth to live children, and Phyl is certainly a **Mammal**, yet
Phyl (or rather his mate Phyllis) lays eggs. To accommodate this, we need to
find a technique to encode *exceptions* to a general rule.

We do this by decreeing that information contained in a subclass can *override*
information inherited from a parent class. Most often, implementations of this

approach takes the form of a method in a subclass having the same name as a method in the parent class, combined with a rule for how the search for a method to match a specific message is conducted:

> The search for a method to invoke in response to a given message begins with the *class* of the receiver. If no appropriate method is found, the search is conducted in the *parent class* of this class. The search continues up the parent class chain until either a method is found or the parent class chain is exhausted. In the former case the method is executed; in the latter case, an error message is issued. If methods with the same name can be found higher in the class hierarchy, the method executed is said to *override* the inherited behavior.

Even if the compiler cannot determine which method will be invoked at run time, in many object-oriented languages it can determine whether there will be an appropriate method and issue an error message as a compile-time error diagnostic rather than as a run-time message. We will discuss the mechanism for overriding in various computer languages in Chapter 11.

That my wife Beth and my florist Flo will respond to my message by different methods is an example of one form of *polymorphism*. We will discuss this important part of object-oriented programming in Chapter 14. As explained, that I do not, and need not, know exactly what method Flo will use to honor my message is an example of *information hiding*, which we will discuss in Chapter 17.

1.4.6 Summary of Object-Oriented Concepts

Alan Kay, considered by some to be the father of object-oriented programming, identified the following characteristics as fundamental to OOP [Kay 1993]:

1. Everything is an *object*.

2. Computation is performed by objects communicating with each other, requesting that other objects perform actions. Objects communicate by sending and receiving *messages*. A message is a request for action bundled with whatever arguments may be necessary to complete the task.

3. Each object has its own *memory*, which consists of other objects.

4. Every object is an *instance* of a *class*. A class simply represents a grouping of similar objects, such as integers or lists.

5. The class is the repository for *behavior* associated with an object. That is, all objects that are instances of the same class can perform the same actions.

6. Classes are organized into a singly rooted tree structure, called the *inheritance hierarchy*. Memory and behavior associated with instances of a class are automatically available to any class associated with a descendant in this tree structure.

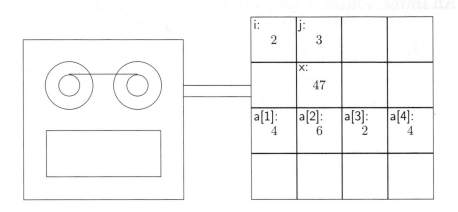

Figure 1.3 – Visualization of imperative programming.

1.5   Computation as Simulation

The view of programming represented by the example of sending flowers to my grandmother is very different from the conventional conception of a computer. The traditional model describing the behavior of a computer executing a program is a *process-state* or *pigeon-hole* model. In this view, the computer is a data manager, following some pattern of instructions, wandering through memory, pulling values out of various slots (memory addresses), transforming them in some manner, and pushing the results back into other slots (see Figure 1.3). By examining the values in the slots, we can determine the state of the machine or the results produced by a computation. Although this model may be a more or less accurate picture of what takes place inside a computer, it does little to help us understand how to solve problems using the computer, and it is certainly not the way most people (pigeon handlers and postal workers excepted) go about solving problems.

In contrast, in the object-oriented framework we never mention memory addresses, variables, assignments, or any of the conventional programming terms. Instead, we speak of objects, messages, and responsibility for some action. In Dan Ingalls's memorable phrase:

> Instead of a bit-grinding processor...plundering data structures, we have a universe of well-behaved objects that courteously ask each other to carry out their various desires [Ingalls 1981].

Another author has described object-oriented programming as "animistic": a process of creating a host of helpers that form a community and assist the programmer in the solution of a problem [Actor 1987].

This view of programming as creating a "universe" is in many ways similar to a style of computer simulation called "discrete event-driven simulation." In brief, in a discrete event-driven simulation the user creates computer models of the various elements of the simulation, describes how they will interact with one another, and sets them moving. This is almost identical to the average object-oriented program, in which the user describes what the various entities in the universe for the program are, and how they will interact with one another, and finally sets them in motion. Thus, in object-oriented programming, we have the view that *computation is simulation* [Kay 1977].

1.5.1 The Power of Metaphor

An easily overlooked benefit to the use of object-oriented techniques is the power of *metaphor*. When programmers think about problems in terms of behaviors and responsibilities of objects, they bring with them a wealth of intuition, ideas, and understanding from their everyday experience. When envisioned as pigeon holes, mailboxes, or slots containing values, there is little in the programmer's background to provide insight into how problems should be structured.

Although anthropomorphic descriptions such as the quote by Ingalls may strike some people as odd, in fact they are a reflection of the great expositive power of metaphor. Journalists make use of metaphor every day, as in the following description of object-oriented programming from *Newsweek:*

> Unlike the usual programming method–writing software one line at a time–NeXT's "object-oriented" system offers larger building blocks that developers can quickly assemble the way a kid builds faces on Mr. Potato Head.

Possibly this feature, more than any other, is responsible for the frequent observation that it is often easier to teach object-oriented programming concepts to computer novices than to computer professionals. Novice users quickly adapt the metaphors with which they are already comfortable from their everyday life, whereas seasoned computer professionals are blinded by an adherence to more traditional ways of viewing computation.

1.5.2 Avoiding Infinite Regression

Of course, objects cannot always respond to a message by politely asking another object to perform some action. The result would be an infinite circle of requests, like two gentlemen each politely waiting for the other to go first before entering a doorway, or like a bureaucracy of paper pushers, each passing on all papers to some other member of the organization. At some point, at least a few objects need to perform some work besides passing on requests to other agents. This work is accomplished differently in various object-oriented languages.

In blended object-oriented/imperative languages, such as C++, Object Pascal, and Objective-C, it is accomplished by methods written in the base (non-object-oriented) language. In pure object-oriented languages, such as Smalltalk or Java, it is accomplished by "primitive" or "native" operations that are provided by the underlying system.

1.6   Coping with Complexity

When computing was in its infancy, most programs were written in assembly language, by a single individual, and would not be considered large by today's standards. Even so, as programs became more complex, programmers found it difficult to remember all the information they needed to know in order to develop or debug their software. Which values were contained in what registers? Did a new identifier name conflict with any previously defined name? What variables needed to be initialized before control could be transferred to another section of code?

The introduction of higher-level languages, such as FORTRAN, Cobol, and Algol, solved some difficulties (such as automatic management of local variables and implicit matching of arguments to parameters) while simultaneously raising people's expectations of what a computer could do. As programmers attempted to solve ever more complex problems using a computer, tasks exceeding the grasp of even the best programmers became the norm. Thus, teams of programmers working together on major programming efforts became commonplace.

1.6.1   The Nonlinear Behavior of Complexity

As programming projects became larger, an interesting phenomenon was observed. A task that would take one programmer two months to perform could not be accomplished by two programmers working for one month. In Fred Brooks's memorable phrase, "The bearing of a child takes nine months, no matter how many women are assigned to the task" [Brooks 1975].

The reason for this nonlinear behavior was complexity–in particular, the interconnections between software components were complicated, and large quantities of information had to be communicated among the various members of the programming team. Brooks also said:

> Since software construction is inherently a systems effort–an exercise in complex interrelationships–communication effort is great, and it quickly dominates the decrease in individual task time brought about by partitioning. Adding more men then lengthens, not shortens, the schedule [Brooks 1975].

What brings about this complexity? It is not simply the sheer size of the tasks undertaken, because size by itself would not be a hindrance to partitioning each into several pieces. The unique feature of software systems developed using conventional techniques–one that makes them among the most complex systems developed by people–is their high degree of interconnectedness. Interconnectedness means the dependence of one portion of code on another portion.

Consider that any portion of a software system must be performing an essential task, or it would not be there. Now, if this task is useful to the other parts of the program, there must be some communication of information either into or out of the component under consideration. Because of this, a complete understanding of what is going on requires a knowledge of both the portion of code we are considering and the code that uses it. In short, an individual section of code cannot be understood in isolation.

1.6.2 Abstraction Mechanisms

Programmers have had to deal with the problem of complexity for a long time. To understand more fully the importance of object-oriented techniques, we should review the variety of mechanisms programmers have used to control complexity. Chief among these is *abstraction*, the ability to encapsulate and isolate design and execution information. In one sense, object-oriented techniques are not at all revolutionary, but can be seen as a natural outcome of a long historical progression from procedures, to modules, to abstract data types, and finally to objects.

Procedures

Procedures and functions were two of the first abstraction mechanisms to be widely used in programming languages. Procedures allowed tasks that were executed repeatedly, or executed with only slight variations, to be collected in one place and reused rather than being duplicated several times. In addition, the procedure gave the first possibility for *information hiding*. One programmer could write a procedure, or a set of procedures, that was used by many others. The other programmers did not need to know the exact details of the implementation–they needed only the necessary interface. But procedures were not an answer to all problems. In particular, they were not an effective mechanism for information hiding, and they only partially solved the problem of multiple programmers making use of the same names.

Example–A Stack

To illustrate these problems, we can consider a programmer who must write a set of routines to implement a simple stack. Following good software engineering principles, our programmer first establishes the visible interface to her work–say, a set of four routines: init, push, pop, and top. She then selects some suitable implementation technique. There are many choices here, such as an array with a top-of-stack pointer, a linked list, and so on. Our intrepid programmer selects from among these choices, then proceeds to code the utilities, as shown in Figure 1.4.

It is easy to see that the data contained in the stack itself cannot be made local to any of the four routines, since they must be shared by all. But if the only choices are local variables or global variables (as they are in FORTRAN, or

```
int datastack[100];
int datatop = 0;

void init()
{
    datatop = 0;
}

void push(int val)
{
    if (datatop < 100)
        datastack [datatop++] = val;
}

int top()
{
    if (datatop > 0)
        return datastack [datatop - 1];
    return 0;
}

int pop()
{
    if (datatop > 0)
        return datastack [--datatop];
    return 0;
}
```

Figure 1.4 – Failure of procedures in information hiding.

in C prior to the introduction of the **static** modifier), then the stack data must be maintained in global variables. However, if the variables are global, there is no way to limit the accessibility or visibility of these names. For example, if the stack is represented in an array named **datastack**, this fact must be made known to all the other programmers since they may want to create variables using the same name and should be discouraged from doing so. This is true even though these data values are important only to the stack routines and should not have any use outside of these four procedures. Similarly, the names **init**, **push**, **pop**, and **top** are now reserved and cannot be used in other portions of the program for other purposes, even if those sections of code have nothing to do with the stack routines.

Block Scoping

The block-scoping mechanism of Algol and its successors, such as Pascal, offers slightly more control over name visibility than does a simple distinction between local and global names. At first, we might hope that this ability solves the information-hiding problem. Unfortunately, it does not. Any scope that permits access to the four named procedures must also permit access to their common data. To solve this problem, a different structuring mechanism had to be developed.

```
begin
    var
        datastack : array [ 1 .. 100 ] of integer;
        datatop : integer;

    procedure init; ...
    procedure push(val : integer); ...
    function pop : integer; ...
...
end;
```

Modules

In one sense, modules can be viewed simply as an improved technique for creating and managing collections of names and their associated values. Our stack example is typical, in that there is some information (the interface routines) that we want to be widely and publicly available, whereas there are other data values (the stack data themselves) that we want restricted. Stripped to its barest form, a *module* provides the ability to divide a name space into two parts. The *public* part is accessible outside the module; the *private* part is accessible only within the module. Types, data (variables), and procedures can all be defined in either portion.

David Parnas, who in [Parnas 1972] popularized the notion of modules, described the following two principles for their proper use:

1. One must provide the intended user with all the information needed to use the module correctly, and *nothing more*.

2. One must provide the implementor with all the information needed to complete the module, and *nothing more*.

The philosophy is much like the military doctrine of "need to know"; if you do not need to know some information, you should not have access to it. This explicit and intentional concealment of information is known as *information hiding*.

Modules solve some, but not all, of the problems of software development. For example, they will permit our programmer to hide the implementation details of her stack, but what if the other users want to have two (or more) stacks?

As a more extreme example, suppose a programmer announces that he has developed a new type of numeric abstraction, called **Complex**. He has defined the arithmetic operations for complex numbers–addition, subtraction, multiplication, and so on, and has defined routines to convert numbers from conventional to complex. There is just one small problem: Only one complex number can be manipulated.

The complex number system would not be useful with this restriction, but this is just the situation in which we find ourselves with simple modules. Modules by themselves provide an effective method of information hiding, but they do not allow us to perform *instantiation*, which is the ability to make multiple copies of the data areas. To handle the problem of instantiation, computer scientists needed to develop a new concept.

Abstract Data Types

An *abstract data type* is a programmer-defined data type that can be manipulated like the system-defined data types. As with system-defined types, an abstract data type corresponds to a set (perhaps infinite in size) of legal data values and a number of primitive operations that can be performed on those values. Users can create variables with values that range over the set of legal values and can operate on those values using the defined operations. For example, our intrepid programmer could define his stack as an abstract data type and the stack operations as the only legal operations allowed on instances of the stack.

Modules are frequently used as an implementation technique for abstract data types, although we emphasize that modules are an implementation technique and that the abstract data type is a more theoretical concept. The two are related but are not identical. To build an abstract data type, we must be able to:

1. Export a type definition.

2. Make available a set of operations that can be used to manipulate instances of the type.

3. Protect the data associated with the type so that they can be operated on only by the provided routines.

4. Make multiple instances of the type.

As we have defined them, modules serve only as an information-hiding mechanism and thus directly address only list items 2 and 3, although the others can be accommodated via appropriate programming techniques. *Packages*, found in languages such as CLU and Ada, are an attempt to address more directly the issues involved in defining abstract data types.

In a certain sense, an object is simply an abstract data type. People have said, for example, that Smalltalk programmers write the most "structured" of all programs because they cannot write anything but definitions of abstract data types. It is true that an object definition is an abstract data type, but the notions of object-oriented programming build on the ideas of abstract data types and add to them important innovations in code sharing and reusability.

Objects–Messages, Inheritance, and Polymorphism

Object-oriented programming adds several important new ideas to the concept of the abstract data type. Foremost among these is *message passing*. Activity is initiated by a *request* to a specific object, not by the invoking of a function. In large part, this is merely a change of emphasis; the conventional view places primary emphasis on the operation, whereas the object-oriented view emphasizes the value itself. (Do you call the push routine with a stack and a data value, or do you ask a stack to push a value onto itself?) If this were all there is to object-oriented programming, the technique would not be considered a major innovation. But added to message passing are powerful mechanisms for overloading names and reusing software.

Implicit in message passing is the idea that the *interpretation* of a message can vary with different objects. That is, the behavior and response that the message elicit will depend upon the object receiving it. Thus, push can mean one thing to a stack, and a very different thing to a mechanical-arm controller. Since names for operations need not be unique, simple and direct forms can be used, leading to more readable and understandable code.

Finally, object-oriented programming adds the mechanisms of *inheritance* and *polymorphism*. Inheritance allows different data types to share the same code, leading to a reduction in code size and an increase in functionality. Polymorphism allows this shared code to be tailored to fit the specific circumstances of individual data types. The emphasis on the independence of individual components permits an incremental development process in which individual software units are designed, programmed, and tested before being combined into a large system.

We will describe all of these ideas in more detail in subsequent chapters.

1.7 Reusable Software

People have asked for decades why the construction of software cannot mirror more closely the construction of material objects. When we construct a building, a car, or an electronic device, for example, we typically piece together a number of off-the-shelf components rather than fabricate each new element from scratch. Can software be constructed in the same fashion?

Software reusability has been a much sought-after and seldom-achieved goal. A major reason for this is the tight interconnectedness of most software constructed in a conventional manner. As we discussed in an earlier section, it is difficult to extract from one project elements of software that can be easily used in an unrelated project, because each portion of code typically has interdependencies with all other portions. These interdependencies may be a result of data definitions or may be functional dependencies.

For example, organizing records into a table and performing indexed lookup operations on the table are very common in programming. Yet table-lookup routines are almost always written over again for each new application. Why? Because, in conventional languages the record format for the elements is tightly bound with the more general code for insertion and lookup. It is difficult to write code that can work for arbitrary data, for any record type.

Object-oriented techniques provide a mechanism for cleanly separating the essential information (insertion and retrieval) from the inconsequential information (the format for particular records). Thus, by using object-oriented techniques we can construct large reusable software components. Many packages of commercial software components are now available, and the development of reusable components is a rapidly growing part of the commercial software industry.

1.8   Summary

- Object-oriented programming is not simply a few new features added to programming languages. Rather, it is a new way of *thinking* about the process of decomposing problems and developing programming solutions.

- Object-oriented programming views a program as a collection of loosely connected agents, termed *objects*. Each object is responsible for specific tasks. It is by the interaction of objects that computation proceeds. In a certain sense, therefore, programming is nothing more or less than the simulation of a model universe.

- An object is an encapsulation of *state* (data values) and *behavior* (operations). Thus, an object is in many ways similar to a module or an abstract data type.

- The behavior of objects is dictated by the object *class*. Every object is an instance of some class. All instances of the same class will behave in a similar fashion (that is, invoke the same method) in response to a similar request.

- An object will exhibit its behavior by invoking a method (similar to executing a procedure) in response to a message. The interpretation of the message (that is, the specific method used) is decided by the object and may differ from one class of objects to another.

- Objects and classes extend the concept of abstract data types by adding the notion of *inheritance*. Classes can be organized into a hierarchical inheritance tree. Data and behavior associated with classes higher in the tree can also be accessed and used by classes lower in the tree. Such classes are said to inherit their behavior from the parent classes.

- By reducing the interdependency among software components, object-oriented programming permits the development of reusable software systems. Such components can be created and tested as independent units, in isolation from other portions of a software application.

- Reusable software components permit the programmer to deal with problems on a higher level of abstraction. We can define and manipulate objects simply in terms of the messages they understand and a description of the tasks they perform, ignoring implementation details.

Further Reading

I noted earlier that many consider Alan Kay to be the father of object-oriented programming. Like most simple assertions, this one is only somewhat supportable. Kay himself [Kay 1993] traces much of the influence on his development of Smalltalk to the earlier computer programming language Simula, developed in Scandinavia in the early 1960s [Dahl 1966, Kirkerud 1989]. A more accurate history would be that most of the principles of object-oriented programming were fully worked out by the developers of Simula, but that these would have been largely ignored by the profession had they not been rediscovered by Kay in the creation of the Smalltalk programming language. A widely read 1981 issue of *Byte* magazine did much to popularize the concepts developed by Kay and his team at Xerox PARC.

The term "software crisis" seems to have been coined by Doug McIlroy at a 1968 NATO conference on software engineering. It is curious that we have been in a state of crisis now for more than half the life of computer science as a discipline. Despite the end of the Cold War, the end of the software crisis seems to be no closer now than it was in 1968. See, for example, Gibb's article "Software's Chronic Crisis" in the September 1994 issue of *Scientific American* [Gibbs 1994].

To some extent, the software crisis may be largely illusory. For example, tasks considered exceedingly difficult five years ago seldom seem so daunting today. It is only the tasks that we wish to solve *today* that seem, in comparison, to be nearly impossible, which seems to indicate that the field of software development has, indeed, advanced steadily year by year.

The quote from the American linguist Edward Sapir is taken from "The Relation of Habitual Thought and Behavior to Language," reprinted in *Language, Thought and Reality* [Whorf 1956]. This book contains several interesting papers on the relationships between language and our habitual thinking processes. I urge any serious student of computer languages to read these essays; some of them have surprising relevance to artificial languages.

Another interesting book along similar lines is *The Alphabet Effect* by Robert Logan [Logan 1986], which explains in terms of language why logic and science developed in the West while for centuries China had superior technology. In a more contemporary investigation of the effect of natural language on computer science, J. Marshall Unger [Unger 1987] describes the influence of the Japanese language on the much-heralded Fifth Generation project.

The commonly held observation that Eskimo languages have many words for snow was debunked by Geoffrey Pullum in his book of essays on linguistics [Pullum 1991]. In an article in the *Atlantic Monthly* ("In Praise of Snow" January 1995), Cullen Murphy pointed out that the vocabulary used to discuss snow among English speakers for whom a distinction between types of snow is important–namely, those who perform research on the topic–is every bit as large or larger than that of the Eskimo.

In any case, the point is irrelevant to our discussion. It is certainly true that groups of individuals with common interests tend to develop their own specialized vocabulary, and once developed, the vocabulary itself tends to direct their thoughts along paths that may not be natural to those outside the group. Such is the case with OOP. While object-oriented ideas can, with discipline, be used without an object-oriented language, the use of object-oriented terms helps direct the programmer's thought along lines that may not have been obvious without the OOP terminology.

My history is slightly imprecise with regard to Church's conjecture and Turing machines. Church actually conjectured about partial functions [Church 1936]; which were later shown to be equivalent to computations performed with Turing machines [Turing 1936]. Kleene described the conjecture in the form we have here, also giving it the name by which it has become known. Rogers gives a good summary of the arguments for the equivalence of various computational models [Rogers 1967].

It was the Swedish botanist Carolus Linnæus, you will recall, who developed the ideas of genus, species, and so forth. This is the prototypical hierarchical organization scheme exhibiting inheritance, since abstract classifications describe features that are largely common to all subclassifications. Most inheritance hierarchies closely follow the model of Linnæus.

The criticism of procedures as an abstraction technique, because they fail to provide an adequate mechanism for information hiding, was first stated by William Wulf and Mary Shaw [Wulf 1973] in an analysis of many of the problems surrounding the use of global variables. These arguments were later expanded upon by David Hanson [Hanson 1981].

Like most terms that have found their way into the popular jargon, *object-oriented* is used more often than it is defined. Thus, the question What is object-oriented programming? is surprisingly difficult to answer. Bjarne Stroustrup has quipped that many arguments appear to boil down to the following syllogism:

- X is good.

- Object-oriented is good.

- *Ergo,* X is object-oriented [Stroustrup 1988].

Roger King argued [Kim 1989], that his cat is object-oriented. After all, a cat exhibits characteristic behavior, responds to messages, is heir to a long tradition of inherited responses, and manages its own quite independent internal state.

Many authors have tried to provide a precise description of the properties a programming language must possess to be called *object-oriented*. See, for example, the analysis by Josephine Micallef [Micallef 1988], or Peter Wegner [Wegner 1986]. Wegner, for example, distinguishes *object-based* languages, which support only abstraction (such as Ada), from *object-oriented* languages, which must also support inheritance.

Other authors–notably Brad Cox [Cox 1990]–define the term much more broadly. To Cox, object-oriented programming represents the *objective* of programming by assembling solutions from collections of off-the-shelf subcomponents, rather than any particular *technology* we may use to achieve this objective. Rather than drawing lines that are divisive, we should embrace any and all means that show promise in leading to a new software Industrial Revolution. Cox's book on OOP [Cox 1986], although written early in the development of object-oriented programming and now somewhat dated in details, is nevertheless one of the most readable manifestos of the object-oriented movement.

Exercises

1. In an object-oriented inheritance hierarchy, each level is a more specialized form of the preceding level. Give an example of a hierarchy found in everyday life that has this property. Some types of hierarchy found in everyday life are not inheritance hierarchies. Give an example of a noninheritance hierarchy.

2. Look up the definition of *paradigm* in at least three dictionaries. Relate these definitions to computer programming languages.

3. Take a real-world problem, such as the task of sending flowers described earlier, and describe its solution in terms of agents (objects) and responsibilities.

4. If you are familiar with two or more distinct computer programming languages, give an example of a problem showing how one language would direct the programmer to one type of solution, and a different language would encourage an alternative solution.

5. If you are familiar with two or more distinct natural languages, describe a situation that illustrates how one language directs the speaker in a certain direction, and the other language encourages a different line of thought.

6. Argue either for or against the position that computing is basically simulation. (You may want to read the article by Alan Kay in *Scientific American* [Kay 1977].)

Chapter 2

Object-Oriented Design

When programmers ask other programmers, "What exactly is this object-oriented programming all about, anyway?" the response often tends to emphasize the syntactic features of languages such as C++ or Object Pascal, as opposed to their older, non object-oriented versions, C or Pascal. Thus, discussion usually turns rather quickly to issues such as classes and inheritance, message passing, and virtual and static methods. But such conversations miss the most important point of object-oriented programming, which has nothing to do with syntax.

Working in an object-oriented language (that is, one that supports inheritance, message passing, and classes) is neither a necessary nor sufficient condition for doing object-oriented programming. As we emphasized in Chapter 1, the most important aspect of OOP is a design technique driven by the determination and delegation of responsibilities. This technique has been called *responsibility-driven design* [Wirfs-Brock 1989b, Wirfs-Brock 1990].

2.1   Responsibility Implies Noninterference

As anyone can attest who can remember being a child, or who has raised children, responsibility is a sword that cuts both ways. When you make an object (be it a child or a software system) responsible for specific actions, you expect a certain behavior, at least when the rules are observed. But just as important, responsibility implies a degree of independence or noninterference. If you tell a child that she is responsible for cleaning her room, you do not normally stand over her and watch while that task is being performed–that is not the nature of responsibility. Instead, you expect that, having issued a directive in the correct fashion, the desired outcome will be produced.

Similarly, in the flowers example from Chapter 1, I give the request to deliver flowers to my florist without stopping to think about how my request will be serviced. The florist, having taken on the responsibility for this service, is free to operate without interference on my part.

27

The difference between conventional programming and object-oriented programming is in many ways the difference between actively supervising a child while she performs a task, and delegating to the child responsibility for that performance. Conventional programming proceeds largely by doing something *to* something else–modifying a record or updating an array, for example. Thus, one portion of code in a software system is often intimately tied, by control and data connections, to many other sections of the system. Such dependencies can come about through the use of global variables, through use of pointer values, or simply through inappropriate use of and dependence on implementation details of other portions of code. A responsibility-driven design attempts to cut these links, or at least make them as unobtrusive as possible.

This notion might at first seem no more subtle than the notions of information hiding and modularity, which are important to programming even in conventional languages. But responsibility-driven design elevates information hiding from a technique to an art. This principle of information hiding becomes vitally important when one moves from programming in the small to programming in the large.

One of the major benefits of object-oriented programming occurs when software subsystems are reused from one project to the next. For example, a simulation manager (such as the one we will develop in Chapter 6) might work for both a simulation of balls on a billiards table and a simulation of fish in a fish tank. This ability to reuse code implies that the software can have almost no domain-specific components; it must totally delegate responsibility for domain-specific behavior to application-specific portions of the system. The ability to create such reusable code is not one that is easily learned–it requires experience, careful examination of case studies (paradigms, in the original sense of the word), and use of a programming language in which such delegation is natural and easy to express. In subsequent chapters, we will present several such examples.

2.2   Programming in the Small and in the Large

The difference between the development of individual projects and of more sizable software systems is often described as programming in the small versus programming in the large.

Programming in the small characterizes projects with the following attributes:

- Code is developed by a single programmer, or perhaps by a very small collection of programmers. A single individual can understand all aspects of a project, from top to bottom, beginning to end.

- The major problem in the software development process is the design and development of algorithms for dealing with the problem at hand.

Programming in the large, on the other hand, characterizes software projects with features such as the following:

- The software system is developed by a large team of programmers. Individuals involved in the specification or design of the system may differ from those involved in the coding of individual components, who may differ as well from those involved in the integration of various components in the final product. No single individual can be considered responsible for the entire project, or even necessarily understands all aspects of the project.

- The major problem in the software development process is the management of details and the communication of information between diverse portions of the project.

While the beginning student will usually be acquainted with programming in the small, aspects of many object-oriented languages are best understood as responses to the problems encountered while programming in the large. Thus, some appreciation of the difficulties involved in developing large systems is a helpful prerequisite to understanding OOP.

2.3   Why Begin with Behavior?

Why begin the design process with an analysis of behavior? The simple answer is that the behavior of a system is usually understood long before any other aspect.

Earlier software development techniques concentrated on ideas such as characterizing the basic data structures or the overall structure of function calls, often within the creation of a formal specification of the desired application. But structural elements of the application can be identified only after a considerable amount of problem analysis. Similarly, a formal specification often ended up as a document understood by neither programmer nor client. But *behavior* is something that can be described almost from the moment an idea is conceived, and (often unlike a formal specification) can be described in terms meaningful to both the programmers and the client.

We will illustrate the application of Responsibility-Driven Design (RDD) with a case study.

2.4   A Case Study in RDD

Imagine you are the chief software architect in a major computer firm. One day your boss walks into your office with an idea that, it is hoped, will be the next major success in your product line. Your assignment is to develop the *Interactive Intelligent Kitchen Helper* (Figure 2.1).

The task given to your software team is stated in very few words (written on what appears to be the back of a slightly-used dinner napkin, in handwriting that appears to be your boss's).

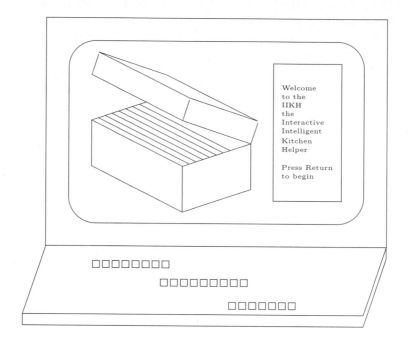

Figure 2.1 – View of the Interactive Intelligent Kitchen Helper.

2.4.1   The Interactive Intelligent Kitchen Helper

Briefly, the Interactive Intelligent Kitchen Helper (IIKH) is a PC-based application that will replace the index-card system of recipes found in the average
kitchen. But more than simply maintaining a database of recipes, the kitchen
helper assists in the planning of meals for an extended period, say a week. The
user of the IIKH can sit down at a terminal, browse the database of recipes,
and interactively create a series of menus. The IIKH will automatically scale the
recipes to any number of servings and will print out menus for the entire week,
for a particular day, or for a particular meal. And it will print an integrated
grocery list of all the items needed for the recipes for the entire period.

As is usually true with the initial descriptions of most software systems,
the specification for the IIKH is highly ambiguous on a number of important
points. It is also true that, in all likelihood, the eventual design and development
of the software system to support the IIKH will require the efforts of several
programmers working together. Thus, the initial goal of the software team must
be to clarify the ambiguities in the description and to outline how the project
can be divided into components to be assigned for development to individual
team members.

The fundamental cornerstone of object-oriented programming is to characterize software in terms of *behavior*; that is, actions to be performed. We will see this repeated on many levels in the development of the IIKH. Initially, the team will try to characterize, at a very high level of abstraction, the behavior of the entire application. This then leads to a description of the behavior of various software subsystems. Only when all behavior has been identified and described will the software design team proceed to the coding step. In the next several sections we will trace the tasks the software design team will perform in producing this application.

2.4.2   Working through Scenarios

The first task is to refine the specification. As we have already noted, initial specifications are almost always ambiguous and unclear on anything except the most general points. There are several goals for this step. One objective is to get a better handle on the "look and feel" of the eventual product. This information can then be carried back to the client (in this case, your boss) to see if it is in agreement with the original conception. It is likely, perhaps inevitable, that the specifications for the final application will change during the creation of the software system, and it is important that the design be developed to easily accommodate change and that potential changes be noted as early as possible. (See Section 2.6.2; "Preparing for Change.") Equally important, at this point very high level decisions can be made concerning the structure of the eventual software system. In particular, the activities to be performed can be mapped onto components.

2.4.3   Identification of Components

The engineering of a complex physical system, such as a building or an automobile engine, is simplified by dividing the design into smaller units. So, too, the engineering of software is simplified by the identification and development of software components. A *component* is simply an abstract entity that can perform tasks–that is, fulfill some responsibilities. At this point, it is not necessary to know exactly the eventual representation for a component or how a component will perform a task. A component may ultimately be turned into a function, a structure or class, or a collection of other components (a *pattern*). At this level of development there are just two important characteristics:

- A component must have a small well-defined set of responsibilities.

- A component should interact with other components to the minimal extent possible.

We will shortly discuss the reasoning behind the second characteristic. For the moment we are simply concerned with the identification of component responsibilities.

2.5   CRC Cards–Recording Responsibility

In order to discover components and their responsibilities, the programming team walks through scenarios. That is, the team acts out the running of the application just as if it already possessed a working system. Every activity that must take place is identified and assigned to some component as a responsibility.

Component Name	Collaborators
	List of
Description of the	*other components*
responsibilities assigned	
to this component	

As part of this process, it is often useful to represent components using small index cards. Written on the face of the card is the name of the software component, the responsibilities of the component, and the names of other components with which the component must interact. Such cards are sometimes known as CRC (Component, Responsibility, Collaborator) cards [Beck 1989], and are associated with each software component. As responsibilities for the component are discovered, they are recorded on the face of the CRC card.

2.5.1   Give Components a Physical Representation

While working through scenarios, it is useful to assign CRC cards to different members of the design team. The member holding the card representing a component records the responsibilities of the associated software component, and acts as the "surrogate" for the software during the scenario simulation. He or she describes the activities of the software system, passing "control" to another member when the software system requires the services of another component.

An advantage of CRC cards is that they are widely available, inexpensive, and erasable. This encourages experimentation, since alternative designs can be tried, explored, or abandoned with little investment. The physical separation of the cards encourages an intuitive understanding of the importance of the logical separation of the various components, helping to emphasize the cohesion and coupling (which we will describe shortly). The constraints of an index card are also a good measure of approximate complexity–a component that is expected to perform more tasks than can fit easily in this space is probably too complex, and the team should find a simpler solution, perhaps by moving some responsibilities elsewhere to divide a task between two or more new components.

2.5.2   The What/Who Cycle

As we noted at the beginning of this discussion, the identification of components takes place during the process of imagining the execution of a working system. Often this proceeds as a cycle of what/who questions. First, the programming team identifies *what* activity needs to be performed next. This is immediately followed by answering the question of *who* performs the action. In this manner, designing a software system is much like organizing a collection of people, such as a club. Any activity that is to be performed must be assigned as a responsibility to some component.

A popular bumper sticker states that phenomena can and will spontaneously occur. (The bumper sticker uses a slightly shorter phrase.) We know, however, that in real life this is seldom true. If any action is to take place, there must be an agent assigned to perform it. Just as in the running of a club any action to be performed must be assigned to some individual, in organizing an object-oriented program all actions must be the responsibility of some component. The secret to good object-oriented design is to first establish an agent for each action.

2.5.3   Documentation

At this point the development of documentation should begin. Two documents should be essential parts of any software system: the user manual and the system design documentation. Work on both of these can commence even before the first line of code has been written.

The user manual describes the interaction with the system from the user's point of view; it is an excellent means of verifying that the development team's conception of the application matches the client's. Since the decisions made in creating the scenarios will closely match the decisions the user will be required to make in the eventual application, the development of the user manual naturally dovetails with the process of walking through scenarios.

Before any actual code has been written, the mindset of the software team is most similar to that of the eventual users. Thus, it is at this point that the developers can most easily anticipate the sort of questions to which a novice user will need answers.

The second essential document is the design documentation. The design documentation records the major decisions made during software design, and should thus be produced when these decisions are fresh in the minds of the creators, and not after the fact when many of the relevant details will have been forgotten. It is often far easier to write a general global description of the software system early in the development. Too soon, the focus will move to the level of individual components or modules. While it is also important to document the module level, too much concern with the details of each module will make it difficult for subsequent software maintainers to form an initial picture of the larger structure.

CRC cards are one aspect of the design documentation, but many other important decisions are not reflected in them. Arguments for and against any major design alternatives should be recorded, as well as factors that influenced the final decisions. A log or diary of the project schedule should be maintained. Both the user manual and the design documents are refined and evolve over time in exactly the same way the software is refined and evolves.

2.6   Components and Behavior

To return to the IIKH, the team decides that when the system begins, the user will be presented with an attractive informative window (see Figure 2.1). The responsibility for displaying this window is assigned to a component called the **Greeter**. In some as yet unspecified manner (perhaps by pull-down menus, button or key presses, or use of a pressure-sensitive screen), the user can select one of several actions. Initially, the team identifies just five actions:

1. Casually browse the database of existing recipes, but without reference to any particular meal plan.

2. Add a new recipe to the database.

3. Edit or annotate an existing recipe.

4. Review an existing plan for several meals.

5. Create a new plan of meals.

These activities seem to divide themselves naturally into two groups. The first three are associated with the recipe database; the latter two are associated with menu plans. As a result, the team next decides to create components corresponding to these two responsibilities. Continuing with the scenario, the team elects to ignore the meal plan management for the moment and move on to refine the activities of the **Recipe Database** component. Figure 2.2 shows the initial CRC card representation of the **Greeter**.

Broadly speaking, the responsibility of the recipe database component is simply to maintain a collection of recipes. We have already identified three elements of this task: The recipe component database must facilitate browsing the library of existing recipes, editing the recipies, and including new recipes in the database.

Greeter

Display Informative Initial Message

Offer User Choice of Options

Pass Control to either

    Recipe Database Manager

    Plan Manager for processing

Collaborators

Database Manager

Plan Manager

Figure 2.2 – CRC card for the Greeter.

2.6.1 Postponing Decisions

There are a number of decisions that must eventually be made concerning how best to let the user browse the database. For example, should the user first be presented with a list of categories, such as "soups," "salads," "main meals," and "desserts"? Alternatively, should the user be able to describe keywords to narrow a search, perhaps by providing a list of ingredients, and then see all the recipes that contain those items ("Almonds, Strawberries, Cheese"), or a list of previously inserted keywords ("Bob's favorite cake")? Should scroll bars be used or simulated thumb holes in a virtual book? These are fun to think about, but the important point is that such decisions do not need to be made at this point (see Section 2.6.2, "Preparing for Change"). Since they affect only a single component, and do not affect the functioning of any other system, all that is necessary to continue the scenario is to assert that by some means the user can select a specific recipe.

2.6.2 Preparing for Change

It has been said that all that is constant in life is the inevitability of uncertainty and change. The same is true of software. No matter how carefully one tries to develop the initial specification and design of a software system, it is almost certain that changes in the user's needs or requirements will, sometime during the life of the system, force changes to be made in the software. Programmers and software designers need to anticipate this and plan accordingly.

- The primary objective is that changes should affect as few components as possible. Even major changes in the appearance or functioning of an application should be possible with alterations to only one or two sections of code.

- Try to predict the most likely sources of change and isolate the effects of such changes to as few software components as possible. The most likely sources of change are interfaces, communication formats, and output formats.

- Try to isolate and reduce the dependency of software on hardware. For example, the interface for recipe browsing in our application may depend in part on the hardware on which the system is running. Future releases may be ported to different platforms. A good design will anticipate this change.

- Reducing coupling between software components will reduce the dependence of one upon another, and increase the likelihood that one can be changed with minimal effect on the other.

- In the design documentation maintain careful records of the design process and the discussions surrounding all major decisions. It is almost certain that the individuals responsible for maintaining the software and designing future releases will be at least partially different from the team producing the initial release. The design documentation will allow future teams to know the important factors behind a decision and help them avoid spending time discussing issues that have already been resolved.

2.6.3   Continuing the Scenario

Each recipe will be identified with a specific recipe component. Once a recipe is selected, control is passed to the associated recipe object. A recipe must contain certain information. Basically, it consists of a list of ingredients and the steps needed to transform the ingredients into the final product. In our scenario, the recipe component must also perform other activities. For example, it will display the recipe interactively on the terminal screen. The user may be given the ability to annotate or change either the list of ingredients or the instruction portion. Alternatively, the user may request a printed copy of the recipe. All of these actions are the responsibility of the Recipe component. (For the moment, we will continue to describe the Recipe in singular form. During design we can think of this as a prototypical recipe that stands in place of a multitude of actual recipes. We will later return to a discussion of singular versus multiple components.)

Having outlined the actions that must take place to permit the user to browse the database, we return to the recipe database manager and pretend the user has indicated a desire to add a new recipe. The database manager somehow decides in which category to place the new recipe (again, the details of how this is done are unimportant for our development at this point), requests the name of the new recipe, and then creates a new recipe component, permitting the user to edit this new blank entry. Thus, the responsibilities of performing this new task are a subset of those we already identified in permitting users to edit existing recipes.

Having explored the browsing and creation of new recipes, we return to the Greeter and investigate the development of daily menu plans, which is the Plan Manager's task. In some way (again, the details are unimportant here) the user can save existing plans. Thus, the Plan Manager can either be started by retrieving an already developed plan or by creating a new plan. In the latter case, the user is prompted for a list of dates for the plan. Each date is associated with a separate Date component. The user can select a specific date for further investigation, in which case control is passed to the corresponding Date component. Another activity of the Plan Manager is printing out the recipes for the planning period. Finally, the user can instruct the Plan Manager to produce a grocery list for the period.

The Date component maintains a collection of meals as well as any other annotations provided by the user (birthday celebrations, anniversaries, reminders, and so on). It prints information on the display concerning the specified date. By some means (again unspecified), the user can indicate a desire to print all the information concerning a specific date or choose to explore in more detail a specific meal. In the latter case, control is passed to a Meal component.

The Meal component maintains a collection of augmented recipes, where the augmentation refers to the user's desire to double, triple, or otherwise increase a recipe. The Meal component displays information about the meal. The user can add or remove recipes from the meal, or can instruct that information about the meal be printed. In order to discover new recipes, the user must be permitted at this point to browse the recipe database. Thus, the Meal component must interact with the recipe database component. The design team will continue in this fashion, investigating every possible scenario. The major category of scenarios we have not developed here is exceptional cases. For example, what happens if a user selects a number of keywords for a recipe and no matching recipe is found? How can the user cancel an activity, such as entering a new recipe, if he or she decides not to continue? Each possibility must be explored, and the responsibilities for handling the situation assigned to one or more components.

Having walked through the various scenarios, the software design team eventually decides that all activities can be adequately handled by six components (Figure 2.3). The Greeter needs to communicate only with the Plan Manager and the Recipe Database components. The Plan Manager needs to communicate only with the Date component; and the Date agent, only with the Meal component. The Meal component communicates with the Recipe Manager and, through this agent, with individual recipes.

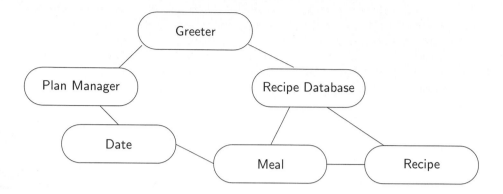

Figure 2.3 – Communication between the six components in the IIKH.

2.6.4   Interaction Diagrams

While a description such as that shown in Figure 2.3 may describe the static relationships between components, it is not very good for describing their dynamic
interactions during the execution of a scenario. A better tool for this purpose is
an *interaction diagram*. Figure 2.4 shows the beginning of an interaction diagram
for the interactive kitchen helper. In the diagram, time moves forward from the
top to the bottom. Each component is represented by a labeled vertical line. A
component sending a message to another component is represented by a horizontal arrow from one line to another. Similarly, a component returning control
and perhaps a result value back to the caller is represented by an arrow. (Some
authors use two different arrow forms, such as a solid line to represent message
passing and a dashed line to represent returning control.) The commentary on
the right side of the figure explains more fully the interaction taking place.

   With a time axis, the interaction diagram is able to describe better the sequencing of events during a scenario. For this reason, interaction diagrams can
be a useful documentation tool for complex software systems.

2.7   Software Components

In this section we will explore a software component in more detail. As is true
of all but the most trivial ideas, there are many aspects to this seemingly simple
concept.

2.7.1   Behavior and State

We have already seen how components are characterized by their behavior, that
is, by what they can do. But components may also hold certain information.

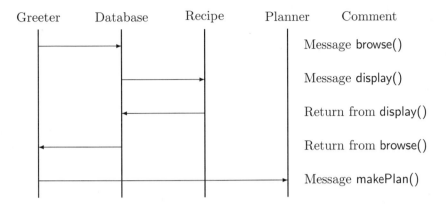

Figure 2.4 – An Example interaction diagram.

Let us take as our prototypical component a Recipe structure from the IIKH. One way to view such a component is as a pair consisting of *behavior* and *state*.

- The *behavior* of a component is the set of actions it can perform. The complete description of all the behavior for a component is sometimes called the *protocol*. For the Recipe component this includes activities such as editing the preparation instructions, displaying the recipe on a terminal screen, or printing a copy of the recipe.

- The *state* of a component represents all the information held within it. For our Recipe component the state includes the ingredients and preparation instructions. Notice that the state is not static and can change over time. For example, by editing a recipe (a behavior) the user can make changes to the preparation instructions (part of the state).

It is not necessary that all components maintain state information. For example, it is possible that the Greeter component will not have any state since it does not need to remember any information during the course of execution. However, most components will consist of a combination of behavior and state.

2.7.2 Instances and Classes

The separation of state and behavior permits us to clarify a point we avoided in our earlier discussion. Note that in the real application there will probably be many different recipes. However, all of these recipes will *perform* in the same manner. That is, the behavior of each recipe is the same; it is only the state– the individual lists of ingredients and instructions for preparation–that differs between individual recipes. In the early stages of development our interest is in characterizing the behavior common to all recipes; the details particular to any one recipe are unimportant.

The term *class* is used to describe a set of objects with similar behavior. We will see in later chapters that a class is also used as a syntactic mechanism in almost all object-oriented languages. An individual representative of a class is known as an *instance*. Note that behavior is associated with a class, not with an individual. That is, all instances of a class will respond to the same instructions and perform in a similar manner. On the other hand, state is a property of an individual. We see this in the various instances of the class Recipe. They can all perform the same actions (editing, displaying, printing) but use different data values. We will investigate the class concept in more detail in Chapter 3.

2.7.3   Coupling and Cohesion

Two important concepts in the design of software components are coupling and cohesion. Cohesion is the degree to which the responsibilities of a single component form a meaningful unit. High cohesion is achieved by associating in a single component tasks that are related in some manner. Probably the most frequent way in which tasks are related is through the necessity to access a common data area. This is the overriding theme that joins, for example, the various responsibilities of the Recipe component.

Coupling, on the other hand, describes the relationship between software components. In general, it is desirable to reduce the amount of coupling as much as possible, since connections between software components inhibit ease of development, modification, or reuse.

In particular, coupling is increased when one software component must access data values–the state–held by another component. Such situations should almost always be avoided in favor of moving a task into the list of responsibilities of the component that holds the necessary data. For example, one might conceivably first assign responsibility for editing a recipe to the Recipe Database component, since it is while performing tasks associated with this component that the need to edit a recipe first occurs. But if we did so, the Recipe Database agent would need the ability to directly manipulate the state (the internal data values representing the list of ingredients and the preparation instructions) of an individual recipe. It is better to avoid this tight connection by moving the responsibility for editing to the recipe itself.

We will discuss coupling and cohesion, and other software engineering issues, in more detail in Chapter 17.

2.7.4   Interface and Implementation–Parnas's Principles

The emphasis on characterizing a software component by its behavior has one extremely important consequence. It is possible for one programmer to know how to *use* a component developed by another programmer, without needing to know how the component is *implemented*. For example, suppose each of the six components in the IIKH is assigned to a different programmer. The programmer developing the Meal component needs to allow the IIKH user to browse the database of recipes and select a single recipe for inclusion in the meal. To do this, the Meal component can simply invoke the browse behavior associated with the Recipe Database component, which is defined to return an individual Recipe. This description is valid regardless of the particular implementation used by the Recipe Database component to perform the actual browsing action.

The purposeful omission of implementation details behind a simple interface is known as *information hiding*. We say the component *encapsulates* the behavior, showing only how the component can be used, not the detailed actions it performs. This naturally leads to two different views of a software system. The interface view is the face seen by other programmers. It describes *what* a software component can perform. The implementation view is the face seen by the programmer working on a particular component. It describes *how* a component goes about completing a task.

The separation of interface and implementation is perhaps *the* most important concept in software engineering. Yet it is difficult for students to understand, or to motivate. Information hiding is largely meaningful only in the context of multiperson programming projects. In such efforts, the limiting factor is often not the amount of coding involved, but the amount of communication required between the various programmers and between their respective software systems. As we will describe shortly, software components are often developed in parallel by different programmers, and in isolation from each other.

There is also an increasing emphasis on the reuse of general-purpose software components in multiple projects. For this to be successful, there must be minimal and well-understood interconnections between the various portions of the system. As we noted in the last chapter, these ideas were captured by computer scientist David Parnas in a pair of rules, known as **Parnas's principles:**

- The developer of a software component must provide the intended user with all the information needed to make effective use of the services provided by the component, and should provide *no* other information.

- The developer of a software component must be provided with all the information necessary to carry out the given responsibilities assigned to the component, and should be provided with *no* other information.

A consequence of the separation of interface from implementation is that a programmer can experiment with several different implementations of the same structure without affecting other software components.

2.8   Formalize the Interface

We continue with the description of the IIKH development. In the next several steps the descriptions of the components will be refined. The first step in this process is to formalize the patterns and channels of communication.

A decision should be made as to the general structure that will be used to implement each component. A component with only one behavior and no internal state may be made into a function–for example, a component that simply takes a string of text and translates all capital letters to lowercase. Components with many tasks are probably more easily implemented as classes. Names are given to each of the responsibilities identified on the CRC card for each component, and these will eventually be mapped onto function or procedure names. Along with the names, the types of any arguments to be passed to the function are identified. Next, the information maintained within the component itself should be described. All information must be accounted for. If a component requires some data to perform a specific task, the source of the data, either through argument or global value, or maintained internally by the component, must be clearly identified.

2.8.1   Coming up with Names

Careful thought should be given to the names associated with various activities. Shakespeare said that a name change does not alter the object being described,[1] but certainly not all names will conjure up the same mental images in the listener. As government bureaucrats have long known, obscure and idiomatic names can make even the simplest operation sound intimidating. The selection of useful names is extremely important, as names create the vocabulary with which the eventual design will be formulated. Names should be internally consistent, meaningful, preferably short, and evocative in the context of the problem. Often a considerable amount of time is spent finding just the right set of terms to describe the tasks performed and the objects manipulated. Far from being a barren and useless exercise, proper naming early in the design process greatly simplifies and facilitates later steps.

The following general guidelines have been suggested [Keller 1990]:

- Use pronounceable names. As a rule of thumb, if you cannot read a name out loud, it is not a good one.

- Use capitalization (or underscores) to mark the beginning of a new word within a name, such as "CardReader" or "Card_reader," rather than the less readable "cardreader."

- Examine abbreviations carefully. An abbreviation that is clear to one person may be confusing to the next. Is a "TermProcess" a terminal process, something that terminates processes, or a process associated with a terminal?

---

[1] "What's in a name? That which we call a rose, by any other name would smell as sweet; So Romeo would, were he not Romeo call'd, retain that dear perfection which he owes without that title." *Romeo and Juliet*, Act II, Scene 2.

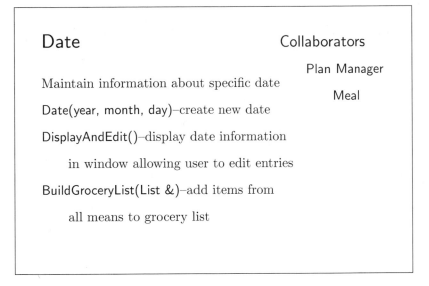

Figure 2.5 – Revised CRC card for the Date component.

- Avoid names with several interpretations. Does the empty function tell whether something is empty, or empty the values from the object?

- Avoid digits within a name. They are easy to misread as letters (0 as O, 1 as l, 2 as Z, 5 as S).

- Name functions and variables that yield Boolean values so they describe clearly the interpretation of a true or false value. For example, "PrinterIsReady" clearly indicates that a true value means the printer is working, whereas "PrinterStatus" is much less precise.

- Take extra care in the selection of names for operations that are costly and infrequently used. By doing so, errors caused by using the wrong function can be avoided.

Once names have been developed for each activity, the CRC cards for each component are redrawn, with the name and formal arguments of the function used to elicit each behavior identified. An example of a CRC card for the Date is shown in Figure 2.5. What is not yet specified is how each component will perform the associated tasks.

Once more, scenarios or role playing should be carried out at a more detailed level to ensure that all activities are accounted for, and that all necessary information is maintained and made available to the responsible components.

2.9   Designing the Representation

At this point, if not before, the design team can be divided into groups, each responsible for one or more software components. The task now is to transform the description of a component into a software system implementation. The major portion of this process is designing the data structures that will be used by each subsystem to maintain the state information required to fulfill the assigned responsibilities.

It is here that the classic data structures of computer science come into play. The selection of data structures is an important task, central to the software design process. Once they have been chosen, the code used by a component in the fulfillment of a responsibility is often almost self-evident. But data structures must be carefully matched to the task at hand. A wrong choice can result in complex and inefficient programs, while an intelligent choice can result in just the opposite.

It is also at this point that descriptions of behavior must be transformed into algorithms. These descriptions should then be matched against the expectations of each component listed as a collaborator, to ensure that expectations are fulfilled and necessary data items are available to carry out each process.

2.10   Implementing Components

Once the design of each software subsystem is laid out, the next step is to implement each component's desired behavior. If the previous steps were correctly addressed, each responsibility or behavior will be characterized by a short description. The task at this step is to implement the desired activities in a computer language. In a later section we will describe some of the more common heuristics used in this process.

If they were not determined earlier (say, as part of the specification of the system), then decisions can now be made on issues that are entirely self-contained within a single component. An decision we saw in our example problem was how best to let the user browse the database of recipes.

As multiperson programming projects become the norm, it becomes increasingly rare that any one programmer will work on all aspects of a system. More often, the skills a programmer will need to master are understanding how one section of code fits into a larger framework and working well with other members of a team.

Often, in the implementation of one component it will become clear that certain information or actions might be assigned to yet another component that will act "behind the scene," with little or no visibility to users of the software abstraction. Such components are sometimes known as *facilitators*. We will see examples of facilitators in some of the later case studies.

An important part of analysis and coding at this point is characterizing and documenting the necessary preconditions a software component requires to complete a task, and verifying that the software component will perform correctly when presented with legal input values. This is establishing the correctness aspect of the algorithms used in the implementation of a component.

2.11 Integration of Components

Once software subsystems have been individually designed and tested, they can be integrated into the final product. This is often not a single step, but part of a larger process. Starting from a simple base, elements are slowly added to the system and tested, using *stubs*–simple dummy routines with no behavior or with very limited behavior–for the as yet unimplemented parts.

For example, in the development of the IIKH, it would be reasonable to start integration with the Greeter component. To test the Greeter in isolation, stubs are written for the Recipe Database manager and the daily Meal Plan manager. These stubs need not do any more than print an informative message and return. With these, the component development team can test various aspects of the Greeter system (for example, that button presses elicit the correct response). Testing of an individual component is often referred to as *unit testing*.

Next, one or the other of the stubs can be replaced by more complete code. For example, the team might decide to replace the stub for the Recipe Database component with the actual system, maintaining the stub for the other portion. Further testing can be performed until it appears that the system is working as desired. (This is sometimes referred to as *integration testing*.)

The application is finally complete when all stubs have been replaced with working components. The ability to test components in isolation is greatly facilitated by the conscious design goal of reducing connections between components, since this reduces the need for extensive stubbing.

During integration it is not uncommon for an error to be manifested in one software system, and yet to be caused by a coding mistake in another system. Thus, testing during integration can involve the discovery of errors, which then results in changes to some of the components. Following these changes the components should be once again tested in isolation before an attempt to reintegrate the software, once more, into the larger system. Reexecuting previously developed test cases following a change to a software component is sometimes referred to as *regression testing*.

2.12 Maintenance and Evolution

It is tempting to think that once a working version of an application has been delivered the task of the software development team is finished. Unfortunately, that is almost never true. The term *software maintenance* describes activities subsequent to the delivery of the initial working version of a software system. A wide variety of activities fall into this category.

- Errors, or *bugs*, can be discovered in the delivered product. These must be corrected, either in *patches* to existing releases or in subsequent releases.

- Requirements may change, perhaps as a result of government regulations or standardization among similar products.

- Hardware may change. For example, the system may be moved to different platforms, or input devices, such as a pen-based system or a pressure-sensitive touch screen, may become available. Output technology may change–for example, from a text-based system to a graphical window-based arrangement.

- User expectations may change. Users may expect greater functionality, lower cost, and easier use. This can occur as a result of competition with similar products.

- Better documentation may be requested by users.

A good design recognizes the inevitability of changes and plans an accommodation for them from the very beginning.

Exercises

1. Describe the responsibilities of an organization that includes at least six types of members. Examples of such organizations are a school (students, teachers, principal, janitor), a business (secretary, president, worker), and a club (president, vice-president, member). For each member type, describe the responsibilities and the collaborators.

2. Create a scenario for the organization you described in Exercise 1 using an interaction diagram.

3. For a common game such as solitaire or twenty-one, describe a software system that will interact with the user as an opposing player. Example components include the deck and the discard pile.

4. Describe the software system to control an ATM (Automated Teller Machine). Give interaction diagrams for various scenarios that describe the most common uses of the machine.

Chapter 3

Classes and Methods

Although the terms they use may be different, all object-oriented languages have in common the concepts of *classes*, *instances*, *message passing*, *methods*, and *inheritance*, as introduced in Chapter 1. As noted already, the use of different terms for similar concepts is rampant in object-oriented programming languages. We will use a consistent and, we hope, clear terminology for all languages, and we will note in language-specific sections the various synonyms for our terms. Refer to the Glossary for explanations of unfamiliar terms.

This chapter will describe the static attributes of classes, and Chapter 4 will outline their dynamic use. Here we will illustrate the mechanics of declaring a class and defining methods associated with instances of the class. In Chapter 4 we will examine how instances of classes are created and how messages are passed to those instances. We will defer an explanation of the mechanics of inheritance until Chapter 7.

An important issue to clarify is the distinction between a class or object *declaration* and an object *instantiation*. The former, the topic of this chapter, is a *type* definition. It specifies the data values and behavior to be associated with a new type of value, but does not actually create any new data values. *Instantiation*, the creation of new instances of a class, can be considered a form of variable declaration, and will be the topic of the next chapter. (The distinction is made somewhat confusing by the fact that in strongly typed languages, such as C++, an instantiation of a *variable*, as opposed to a class, is performed by a declaration statement).

3.1 Encapsulation

In Chapter 1, we noted that object-oriented programming, and objects in particular, can be viewed from many perspectives. In this chapter, we wish to view objects as examples of *abstract data types*.

Programming that makes use of data abstractions is a methodological approach to problem solving where information is consciously hidden in a small

47

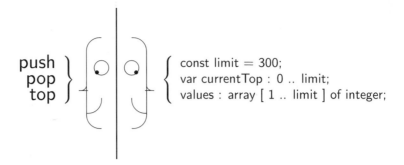

Figure 3.1 – The interface and implementation faces of a stack.

part of a program. In particular, the programmer develops a series of abstract data types, each of which can be viewed as having two faces. This is similar to the dichotomy in Parnas's principles, discussed in Chapter 2. From the outside, a client (user) of an abstract data type sees only a collection of operations that define the behavior of the abstraction. On the other side of the interface, the programmer defining the abstraction sees the data variables that are used to maintain the internal state of the object.

For example, in an abstraction of a **stack** data type, the user would see only the description of the legal operations–say, **push**, **pop**, and **top**. The implementor, on the other hand, needs to know the actual concrete data structures used to implement the abstraction (Figure 3.1). The concrete details are encapsulated within a more abstract framework.

We have been using the term *instance* to mean a representative, or example, of a class. We will accordingly use the term *instance variable* to mean an internal variable maintained by an instance. Each instance has its own collection of instance variables. These values should not be changed directly by clients, but rather should be changed only by methods associated with the class.

A simple view of an object is, then, a combination of *state* and *behavior*. The state is described by the instance variables, whereas the behavior is charac- terized by the methods. From the outside, clients can see only the behavior of objects; from the inside, the methods provide the appropriate behavior through modifications of the state as well as by interacting with other objects.

3.2   Varieties of Classes

Classes in object-oriented programming can have several different forms of re- sponsibility, and thus, not surprisingly, are used for many different purposes. The following categories cover a large number of cases:

- Data managers

- Data sinks or data sources

- View or observer classes

- Facilitator or helper classes

These categories represent the most common uses of classes, so they are useful as a guide in the design phase of object-oriented programming. However, the list is not complete. Most object-oriented applications include examples of each of these categories as well as some that do not seem to fit into any group. If a class appears to span two or more of these categories, it can often be broken up into two or more classes.

Data Managers, sometimes called **Data**, or **State**, classes, are classes with the principal responsibility of maintaining data or state information of one sort or another. For example, in an abstraction of a playing card, a major task for the class **Card** is simply to maintain the data values that describe rank and suit. Data Manager classes are often recognizable as the nouns in a problem description and are usually the fundamental building blocks of a design.

Data Sinks or **Data Sources**, are classes that generate data, such as a random number generator, or that accept data and then process them further, such as a class performing output to a disk or file. Unlike a data manager, a data sink or data source does not hold the data for any period of time, but generates it on demand (for a data source) or processes it when called upon (for a data sink).

View or **Observer** classes. An essential portion of most applications is the display of information on an output device such as a terminal screen. Because the code for performing this activity is often complex, frequently modified, and largely independent of the actual data being displayed, it is good programming practice to isolate display behavior in classes other than those that maintain the data being displayed.

Because one can separate the object being viewed (often called the *model*) from the view that displays the visual representation of that object, the design of a system for providing graphical display of information can often be greatly simplified. Ideally, the model neither requires nor contains any information about the view. This facilitates code reuse, since a model can then be used in several applications. It is not uncommon for a single model to have more than one view. For example, financial information could be displayed as bar charts, pie charts, or tables of figures, all without changing the underlying model.

Facilitator, or **Helper** classes. These are classes that maintain little or no state information themselves but assist in the execution of complex tasks. For example, in displaying a playing card image we use the services of a facilitator class that handles the drawing of lines and text on the display device. Another facilitator class might help maintain linked lists of cards.

3.3   Example: A Playing Card

We will use a software abstraction of a common playing card to illustrate the various object-oriented programming languages we consider in this book. In a subsequent chapter we will use this class in the development of a program to play solitaire. The class Card itself, however, like a real playing card, has little knowledge of its intended use and can be incorporated into any type of card game.

In Figure 3.2 we show a CRC card that describes the behavior of a card. The responsibilities of the class Card are very limited. Basically a card is simply a data manager, which holds and returns the rank and suit values and draws itself.

Card

Maintain suit and rank
Return color
Maintain face-up or face-down status
Draw card on playing surface
Erase card on playing surface

Figure 3.2 – A CRC card for the class Card.

As we noted in Chapter 2, CRC cards are refined and redrawn frequently, slowly evolving from a natural-language to a more code-like form. The next step in this process is to provide names and argument lists for each method. At this step the length of the description can exceed the size of a card, and several cards can be stapled together (or the card format can be abandoned altogether in favor of a more report-like description).

The card image shown in Figure 3.3 shows this next step in refinement. Notice that even when the responsibilities require nothing more than returning a value (such as deciding whether a card is face up or face down, or discovering the suit and rank), we have nevertheless defined a function to mediate the request. There are practical as well as theoretical reasons for doing so, which we will return to in Chapter 17.

Card

---

suit – return card suit
rank – return card rank
color – return card color
erase, draw – erase or draw card image
faceUp, flip – test or flip card

Figure 3.3 – Revision of CRC card for class Card.

As suggested earlier, at this point the data values to be maintained by each instance of the playing card can be identified and recorded on the back side of the CRC card. The next step is to translate the behavior and state described on the front and back of the CRC card into executable code. We will consider this step after first exploring the dichotomy between description and definition.

3.4 Interface and Implementation

In Chapter 1, we traced some of the evolution of the ideas of object-oriented programming, noting that the ideas build on and extend earlier concepts of modularization and information hiding. In the course of this evolutionary process, some ideas and concepts are discarded when they prove to be at odds with object-oriented design and other notions are retained and even extended. In particular, Parnas's principles are as applicable to object-oriented techniques as they are to modules. We could rephrase Parnas's ideas in terms of objects as follows:

- A class definition must provide the intended user with all the information necessary to manipulate an instance of the class correctly, and *nothing more*.

- A method must be provided with all the information necessary to carry out its given responsibilities, and *nothing more*.

Parnas's principles divide the world of an object into two spheres. There is the world as seen by the user of an object (or, more precisely, by the user of the services provided by an object); we will call this view the *interface*, since it describes how the object is interfaced to the world at large. The second view, the view from within the object, we will call the *implementation*. The user of an object is permitted to access no more than what is described in the interface. The implementation describes how the responsibility promised by the interface is achieved.

With the exception of Smalltalk, all the languages we are considering support, to some degree, the division into interface and implementation. We will describe the mechanics of this division in the sections specific to each language. Note that this separation of interface and implementation is not exactly the same as the encapsulation of data discussed earlier. One is an abstract concept; the other is an implementation mechanism. Another way to phrase this idea is to say that modules can be used in the process of implementing objects or abstract data types, but a module by itself is not an abstract data type.

3.5   Classes and Methods

In the following sections we describe in detail the mechanics of defining classes and methods in each of the languages we are considering. As you read these descriptions, note how some object-oriented languages treat classes as a specialized form of records whereas other languages take a different approach.

3.5.1   Classes and Methods in Object Pascal

At least two very different languages carry the name *Object Pascal*. The original is the language defined by Larry Tesler of Apple Computer [Tesler 1985], built on top of the original module facilities of Apple Pascal. The second is the language originally known as Turbo Pascal [Turbo 1988, O'Brian 1989], which was designed and is distributed by Borland International. The first is most often found on Macintosh computers; the second is most often associated with PCs. The Borland language has received renewed attention because of its use as the underlying language in the Delphi application development environment [Borland 1995], which has introduced new features not found in the original Turbo Pascal. In the presentations in this book we will try to describe both versions of the language, noting where and how they differ.

In Object Pascal, a module is called a *unit*. Unlike in C++ and Objective-C, the unit is maintained in a single file rather than split into two separate files. Nevertheless, the unit is divided into interface and implementation components. Units can import other units, a process that makes available to the importer the features described in the interface section of the imported unit.

A portion of the unit for the class Card in the Apple version of Object Pascal is shown in Figure 3.4. The body of the interface section is similar to a function

```
unit card;

interface

type
    suits = (Heart, Club, Diamond, Spade);

    colors = (Red, Black);

    Card = object
            (* data fields *)
        suitValue : suits;
        rankValue : integer;
        faceUp    : boolean;

            (* initialization *)
        procedure setRankAndSuit (c : integer; s : suits);

            (* manipulation *)
        function    color    : colors;
        procedure   draw (win : window; x, y: integer);
        function    faceUp   : boolean;
        procedure   flip;
        function    rank     : integer;
        function    suit     : suits;
    end;

implementation
    ...
end.
```

Figure 3.4 – The interface portion of a unit in Apple Object Pascal.

body in Pascal and can contain const, type and var sections, including declarations of non-object-oriented data types, such as the enumerated types suits and colors.

The description of a class is similar to a record description, except that it can contain procedure and function headings as well as data fields. The data fields must be listed first, before any function definitions. A name cannot denote both a data field and a method, and thus we use the name suitValue for the data field, which is distinct from the function suit that returns this value. Multiple classes can be defined in a single unit.

The declaration of a class is examined by clients to discover how a class is manipulated much more frequently than the actual code is examined. For this reason, comments can be used to facilitate the rapid retrieval of information. The data declarations should be separated from the declaration of methods. Methods should be grouped and labeled according to the more abstract classifications of behavior. Within each group, methods should be listed in alphabetical order. Tab stops should be used to line up each method name, so the names can be scanned quickly as a table.

Although judicious use of comments can improve readability, the programmer should avoid overuse. Assuming that methods are provided with meaningful names, there is no reason to comment every method declaration, for example. Too many comments can complicate, rather than simplify, the readability of the code.

A declaration of an object variable does not actually create a new instance of the variable, but merely sets aside space for a pointer to the value. Variables or fields declared with an object type can contain either value data or, as with variables declared to be of type pointer in Pascal, the special value nil.

The Delphi language, shown in Figure 3.5, differs in many ways from the Apple dialect. It borrows several features from C++ as well as a few from Smalltalk. In place of the keyword object, new classes are declared using the keyword class. A parent class, from which the new class will inherit, must be specified following this term. Most often this parent is simply the system class TObject, as shown here. (The initial T stands for *type*. It is conventional in the Delphi Pascal community that all class names begin with this letter, and many of the tools in the Borland programming environment depend on this property. Hence the name TCard rather than Card.) A constructor is a special type of method, invoked when a new instance of the class is created. We will discuss constructors in more detail in Chapter 4. Finally, the keywords public and private are used to divide the class description into the interface portion (those fields accessible to users of the class) and the implementation portion (those fields used only internally in the class). This is similar to C++, which we will describe shortly. The Apple language provides no similar mechanism for hiding either data or methods from users of the class abstraction.

The implementation section of a module, like the interface section, can contain const, type, and var sections, as well as function and procedure bodies. Any types and variables declared in the implementation section are useful only within

```
unit card;

interface

type
    suits = (Heart, Club, Diamond, Spade);

    colors = (Red, Black);

    TCard = class (TObject)
        public
                (* creation *)
            constructor Create (c : integer; s : suits);

                (* manipulation *)
            function     color    : colors;
            procedure    draw (win : TWindow; x, y: integer);
            function     faceUp    : boolean;
            procedure    flip;
            function     rank    : integer;
            function     suit    : suits;

        private
            suitValue : suits;
            rankValue : integer;
            faceUp : boolean;
        end;

implementation
    ...
end.
```

Figure 3.5 – The interface portion of a unit in Delphi Object Pascal.

```
implementation

const
    CardWidth = 65;
    CardHeight = 75;

function Card.color : colors;
begin
    case suit of
        Diamond:      color := Red;
        Heart:        color := Red;
        Spade:        color := Black;
        Club:         color := Black;
    end
end;
...
end.
```

Figure 3.6 – The implementation portion of a unit in Object Pascal.

the unit. Figure 3.6 shows a portion of the implementation unit for the class Card. Unlike procedure names in conventional languages, method names need not be unique and the same method name can be used in several different classes, even within the same module. Thus, when a method is defined, a special syntax is needed to indicate the class for which the definition of the method is being provided. In Object Pascal, this syntax is the class name followed by a period and finally the method name.

3.5.2   Classes and Methods in Smalltalk

An explanation of Smalltalk is almost inextricably tied to at least a simple understanding of the Smalltalk user interface. Thus, an explanation of how new classes are created in Smalltalk must necessarily begin with an explanation of the Smalltalk *browser*. Not only is the browser somewhat complex, but the exact details differ between implementations, so our discussion must be somewhat superficial. The reader interested in learning more should consult a reference specifically devoted to the Smalltalk system he or she is using, such as [Goldberg 1984, LaLonde 1990b, Korienek 1993, Smith 1995].

To the user, the view of a browser is that of a window divided into five panes–four small ones over one large one (Figure 3.7). Each upper pane scrolls over lists of textual material; the bottom pane is used for displaying and editing information. The browser is manipulated by means of a mouse, which must have three buttons: the left button indicates editing operations and selection; the middle and right buttons produce menus of operations.

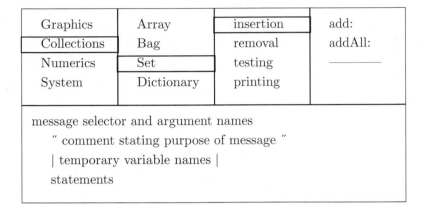

Graphics	Array	insertion	add:
Collections	Bag	removal	addAll:
Numerics	Set	testing	———
System	Dictionary	printing	

message selector and argument names
      ″ comment stating purpose of message ″
      | temporary variable names |
      statements

Figure 3.7 – A view of the Smalltalk browser.

Classes in Smalltalk are grouped into categories. The first pane scrolls over all the categories known to the Smalltalk system. Although it is possible to create a new category, it suffices for our purposes to select an existing category and create our new class in it. Selecting "Graphics-Primitives" in the first pane produces two actions: The first displays, in the second pane, the list of all the classes currently organized under the selected category; the second displays, in the large editing pane, the text of a message used to create new classes.

Using a point-and-click editor, the user can change the message to this:

```
Object subclass: #Card
    instanceVariableNames: 'suit rank'
    classVariableNames: ''
    poolDictionaries: ''
    category: 'Graphics-Primitives'
```

For the moment, we will treat this as merely a descriptive device that indicates the class Card is to be made a subclass of the class Object. (As in Delphi Pascal all classes in Smalltalk must be subclasses of an existing class. The class Object is the most common class used for this purpose.) Each instance of the class Card maintains two data values.

Notice that the names of these values are not tied to any particular data type. Smalltalk does not have any type-declaration statements, and variables can take on any value whatsoever. (We will have more to say about typed versus untyped languages later in our discussion of message passing.) There are no class or pool variables associated with our class. (Class and pool variables are advanced topics. The former will be discussed in a later chapter; the latter is beyond the scope of this book.)

The pound (#) sign in front of the word Card identifies the item as a *symbol*. The most important property of a symbol is the one-to-one correspondence between its value and its name; that is, each named symbol may have a different value, but every symbol with the same name shares the same value. Thus, symbols are commonly used as keys and place holders for categories.

Having defined the characteristics of the new class, the user selects accept from a menu of operations. The new class having been entered, the third pane describes groups of permitted operations (initially empty).

Selecting a group pane brings into play the final pane of the upper group, which selects individual methods. As with the category pane, when a group pane is selected the existing methods in the group are displayed in the fourth pane; simultaneously a template that can be edited to generate new methods is displayed in the bottom window. This edit template is as shown in the earlier figure.

To create a new method, the user edits this template and selects accept from a menu when complete. The following code shows the method used to initialize the suit and rank of a card.

```
setSuit: s rank: r
      " set the suit and rank instance variables "
      suit := s.
      rank := r
```

In Smalltalk, arguments are separated by keywords, which can be recognized because they end in a colon (identifiers cannot end in a colon). Thus, the name of the method defined here is setSuit:rank:, which takes two arguments that are known to the method as s and r. On some versions of Smalltalk the assignment arrow is the left arrow character, ←, on most other versions the more conventional two-character sequence is employed. Finally, you should notice that the period is used as a statement separator (it is optional on the last statement of the method).

Access to instance variables from outside of the methods associated with a class is not permitted in Smalltalk. Therefore, to provide such access we must define explicit *accessor functions*. The method suit, shown below, returns the value of the instance variable of the same name.

```
suit
      " return the suit of the current card "
      ↑ suit
```

The up arrow is the same as the return keyword in many languages. It indicates that the expression that follows the operator is to be returned as the result of executing the method. Notice that methods can have the same names as instance variables and no confusions can arise (at least to the system–we will say nothing of the programmer).

The integers between 1 and 13 are logical values that represent the rank field. We will use symbols to represent the suit value. Similarly, a method such as color can return a symbol as a result. The following shows this method.

```
color

    " return the color of the current card "

    (suit = #diamond) ifTrue: [ ↑ #red ].
    (suit = #club)    ifTrue: [ ↑ #black ].
    (suit = #spade)   ifTrue: [ ↑ #black ].
    (suit = #heart)   ifTrue: [ ↑ #red ].
```

Notice that conditional statements in Smalltalk are written as though they were messages sent to the conditional part (indeed they are). The brackets create what are known as blocks and can be thought of in this circumstance as similar to the begin-end pairs of Pascal. (The reality is slightly more complex. In fact, a block is itself an object, which is being passed as an argument with the message ifTrue: to a Boolean object. This detail can be largely ignored by the beginning Smalltalk programmer.)

3.5.3 Classes and Methods in Objective-C

Objective-C is an object-oriented extension of the imperative programming language C, and so it inherits much of the structure and use of that language. In particular, the implementation of modules is based on the common C convention that divides files into two categories: interface (normally given a ".h" extension) and implementation (in C normally given the extension ".c", which in Objective-C is changed to ".m"). The assumption is that a user of a class (the first person in Parnas's dichotomy) needs to see only the interface file.

The interface file, such as that for our card abstraction (Figure 3.8), serves two purposes. To the programmer, it is an important aid in documenting the purpose and functionality of a class. To the system, it conveys information such as types and storage requirements. Occasionally these two uses are in conflict with each other. For example, in Objective-C, as in Smalltalk, users of a class are not permitted access to the instance information–the internal state–of an object. Only the methods associated with a class can access or modify the instance data, but to determine storage requirements, the system must know the size of each object. Thus, instance variables are described in the interface file not for the benefit of the user (although they may provide some descriptive information, they are inaccessible) but rather for the benefit of the compiler.

The first several lines of the interface file consist of code that would be the same in C and Objective-C. The "import" directive is similar to the "include" directive in C, except that it ensures that the file is included only once. In this case, the file being imported is the interface description of the class Object. The

```
/*
    interface description for the class Card
    in Objective-C
    written by Tim Budd, 1995
*/

# import <objc/Object.h>

    /* define symbolic constants for the suits */
# define    Heart    0
# define    Club     1
# define    Diamond    2
# define    Spade    3

    /* define symbolic constants for the colors */
# define    Red     0
# define    Black    1

    /* the interface for the class Card */
@ interface Card : Object
{
    int    suit;
    int    rank;
    int    faceup;
}

    /* methods for class Card */
- (void)    suit: (int) s rank: (int) c;
- (int)     color;
- (int)     rank;
- (int)     suit;
- (void)    flip;
- (void)    drawAt: (int) and: (int);
@ end
```

Figure 3.8 – An Objective-C interface file.

"define" directives construct several symbolic constants, which we will use for the suits and colors.

The at sign (@) indicates the beginning of Objective-C-specific code. In this case, the code describes the interface to objects of class Card. It is possible to place interfaces for several classes in the same interface file, although each class normally has a separate file. In Objective-C, as in Smalltalk and Delphi Pascal, every class must be a subclass of an existing class, with the class Object serving as the most common value.

The list enclosed in braces that follows the class indication represents the declaration of the instance variables (data) that will be associated with the class. Each instance of the class will have a separate data area. Objective-C distinguishes between conventional C values–integers, reals, structures, and the like–and objects. The latter are declared as the data type id. As with pointer values in C, a variable declared as type id can contain either a legal value or the special value Null.

The lines following the data description define the methods that will be associated with this class. Each method description begins with a minus sign (−) in the first column, which can be followed by an optional type expression, similar to a cast expression in C. This expression indicates the type of value the method will return. An object type (id) is the default assumption if no explicit alternative is given. Thus, the method suit (notice that methods can have the same name as instance values) returns a value of type integer. The method flip is described by the type void, which is the C way of indicating it returns no value that is, it is a procedure, not a function. Once again, tab stops, comments, and alphabetic ordering can improve the readability of the description.

Methods that take arguments, such as the method to move a card or to test a point for inclusion within the area bounded by a card, are written in the Smalltalk fashion with keywords separating the arguments. Unlike in Smalltalk, however, each argument must be given a declaration of type, with the object type id being assumed if no alternative is provided. This declaration is given in the same cast-like syntax used to indicate the result type.

The implementation file (Figure 3.9) begins by importing the interface file for our playing-card abstraction. Once more, Objective-C code can be freely mixed with ordinary C code; in this case, the next two lines define symbolic constants for the length and width of our playing card.

The implementation directive defines the actual code for the methods associated with the class. Both the parent-class name and the instance-variable definitions can be omitted from the implementation part; they will then be taken from the interface description.

It is not necessary for the order of methods in the implementation section to match the order of methods in the interface section. To simplify finding a specific method body, methods are often listed in alphabetical order. The method headings are repeated, just as in the interface file, only now they are followed by the body of the methods. This body is enclosed in braces, as in C.

```
/*
    implementation of class Card
    in Objective-C
    written by Tim Budd, 1995
*/

# import "card.h"

# define cardWidth 68
# define cardHeight 75

@ implementation Card

- (int) color
{
    return suit % 2;
}

- (int) rank
{
    return rank;
}

- (void) suit: (int) s rank: (int) c
{
    suit = s;
    rank = c;
    faceup = 0;
}

    // ... some material omitted

@ end
```

Figure 3.9 – An Objective-C implementation file.

3.5.4   Classes and Methods in C++

C++, like Objective-C, is an object-oriented extension of the imperative programming language C. As in C, it is useful to distinguish between interface files (conventionally given a ".h" extension) and implementation files (the extension varies across systems).

As in Objective-C, an interface file, such as that for our playing-card abstraction, can contain descriptions of more than one class, although usually only if the classes are closely related. Since C and C++ do not support the import keyword (see the discussion of Objective-C), the conditional inclusion facility can be used to the same effect; the first time the file card.h is included, the symbol cardh (which presumably does not occur elsewhere) is not defined, and thus the ifndef (if not defined) statement is satisfied (since the value cardh is *not* defined) and the file will be read. On all subsequent readings of the file within the module, the symbol will be known and the file will be skipped.

```
# ifndef CARDH // make certain file is read only once
# define CARDH
   ...
# endif
```

Class descriptions begin with the keyword class (Figure 3.10). In C++ a class description is much like a C structure definition, except that it is permitted to have procedure headings as well as data values. The keyword private: precedes those portions that can be accessed only by the methods in the class itself, whereas the keyword public: indicates the true interface–those elements that are accessible outside the class. As in Objective-C, the description of the private instance variables is given only for the benefit of the compiler, so that the compiler can determine the memory requirements for an object. To a user of a class, these fields remain inaccessible (it is a violation of the first clause in Parnas's principles).

Because users are most often interested in the public interface, it should always be listed first. Similarly, comments, tab stops, grouping, and alphabetizing should be used to make the declaration more readable.

The function card(suits, int) in the class description is unique in several respects. Not only is its name the same as the class name, but it has no return type. This function is called a *constructor* and is used in the initialization of a newly created instance of the class. We will discuss constructors in more detail in Chapter 4.

The keyword void indicates, as in Objective-C, the absence of a type. When used as the return type for a method, it means the method is used like a procedure for its side effect and not for a functional result.

The methods draw and halfdraw illustrate the declaration of parameter types as part of the declaration of a function. This style of function declaration is known as a *prototype* and has now been adopted as part of the ANSI standard

```
enum suits {diamond, club, heart, spade};
enum colors {red, black};

    //
    //      playing card abstraction
    //      used in solitare game
    //      written by Tim Budd, 1995
    //

class card {
public:
        // constructor
    card (suits, int);

        // access attributes of card
    colors    color ();
    bool      faceUp();
    int       rank();
    suits     suit();

        // perform actions
    void      draw     (window &, int x, int y);
    void      flip     ();
    void      halfdraw (window &, int x, int y);

private:
    bool      faceup;
    int       r;    // rank
    suits     s;    // suit
};
```

Figure 3.10 – A class description in C++.

C language as well as C++. Notice that the prototype is similar to an argument list, although the arguments are provided with types and names are optional.

The argument of type **window**, being manipulated in the member function **draw**, is being passed by *reference*. This is indicated by the ampersand in the argument list. Large structures, such as window descriptions, are often passed by reference.

Since methods are treated simply as special types of fields in an object and are otherwise not distinguished from data fields, it is not possible for a method and a data field to share a common name. Thus, the field **s** stores the value representing the suit of the card, whereas the method **suit** returns this value. Similarly, **r** and **rank** store and return the rank field, respectively.

An implementation file for a class must provide definitions for the methods described in the interface file. The beginning of an implementation file for our playing-card abstraction is shown below.

```
//
//      implementation file
//      for playing card abstraction
//

# include "card.h"

card::card (suits sv, int rv)
{
    s = sv;             // initialize suit
    r = rv;             // initialize rank
    faceup = true;      // initially face up
}

int card::rank()
{
    return r;
}
```

The body of a method is written as a conventional C function, but the class name and two colons precede the method name. Instance variables (fields) defined by a class can be referenced within a method as variables. The combination of class name and method name to produce the fully qualified function name can be thought of as analogous to the combination of given name and family name to identify an individual.

To encourage programmers to make use of the design principles of abstraction and encapsulation, C++ provides the ability to define *inline functions*. An inline function looks to the caller exactly like a non-inline function, using the same syntax for parameters and arguments. The only difference is that the compiler can choose to expand inline functions into code directly at the point of call, avoiding the overhead of procedure call and return instructions. (As is the case with the register directive, the inline directive is a suggestion to the compiler, which the compiler is free to ignore.)

```
inline int Card::rank ()
{
    return r;
}
```

Abstraction and encapsulation often encourage large numbers of functions that perform little work and thus have small function bodies. By defining these as inline functions, programmers can maintain the benefits of encapsulation while avoiding some of the run-time costs of function invocation. Although overconcern with efficiency can be detrimental to the development of reliable code, programmers are often justly uneasy when a function body consists of perhaps only a single return statement, meaning that the execution time overhead of the procedure call may be larger than the execution time of the procedure body. By use of an inline function these problems can be avoided. If the function being defined is part of the public interface for a class, the entire inline function definition is given in the interface file, not the implementation file.

As the name suggests, an inline function will be expanded into direct code when called, thus eliminating the overhead of a procedure call. On the other hand, multiple copies of the function body can be created, so the feature should be used only with functions in which the function body is very small or that are called very rarely. Although they provide an efficiency advantage over conventional procedures, inline functions continue to enforce the protection policies of the class designer. For example, clients cannot have direct access to data values that are declared private.

When extensive use is made of inline functions, it is not uncommon for the implementation file to be shorter than the interface file.

It is also possible to write inline definitions by defining the body of the method directly in the class definition, as shown in Figure 3.11. However, such use tends to make the class definition more difficult to read and so should be employed only when there are very few methods and the method bodies are very short. In addition, some compilers require that data fields and inline functions be defined before they are used. This forces the private data fields to be listed before the public interface, and forces the rearrangement of the functions. By separating the body of the inline function from the class definition, methods can be listed in a logical order for exposition in the class definition, and a different order dictated by the implementation in the text following the class definition.

3.5.5   Classes and Methods in Java

It is difficult to know if one should describe Java as a dialect of C++. Although the two have superficial surface similarities, the underlying differences are substantial

```
//
//      playing card abstraction
//      used in solitare game
//      written by Tim Budd, 1995
//

class card {
public:
        // constructors
    card (suits, int);
    card ();
    card (const card & c);

        // access attributes of card
    int       rank()
                { return r;}
    suits     suit()
                { return s;}
    colors    color ();
    bool      faceUp()
                { return faceup; }

        // perform actions
    void    draw (window & w, int x, int y);
    void    halfdraw (window & w, int x, int y);
    void    flip()
                { faceup = ! faceup; }

private:
    bool     faceup;
    int      r;     // rank
    suits    s;     // suit
};
```

Figure 3.11 – A class description with inline method bodies.

enough to warrant calling Java an entirely new language. On the one hand, Java does not have pointers, references, structures, unions, the **goto** statement, functions (as opposed to methods), or operator overloading. On the other hand, it does support strings as a primitive data type (which C++ does not) and uses garbage collection for memory management.

Although Java is a general-purpose programming language in its own right, recent interest in it has been tied to it use as a means of programming World Wide Web browsers. Here we will ignore many of the issues related to this use and instead concentrate on Java as a programming languages.

A class declaration in Java (such as the one shown in Figure 3.12) is very similar to the declaration in C++, with the following differences:

- There is no preprocessor, global variables, or enumerated data types. Symbolic values can be created by declaring and initializing a local variable by use of the keyword **final**. Final values cannot be subsequently reassigned and are thus the equivalent of constant values.

- Method implementations are provided directly in the class definition rather than at a separate location. (This is optionally permitted in C++ but required in Java).

- Rather than separating the class declaration into private and public portions, the keywords **public** and **private** are applied individually to every instance variable or method definition.

- The Boolean data type is named **boolean**, as opposed to **bool** in C++.

- With the exception of constructors (which, as in C++, are distinguished by the fact that the function name is the same as the class name), all methods must specify a return type.

In Chapter 8 we will present a case study of an application written entirely in Java.

```
class Card {
        // static values for colors and suits
    final public int red = 0;
    final public int black = 1;
    final public int spade = 0;
    final public int heart = 1;
    final public int diamond = 2;
    final public int club = 3;
        // data fields
    private boolean faceup;
    private int  r;
    private int s;

        // constructor
    Card (int sv, int rv) { s = sv; r = rv; faceup = false; }

        // access attributes of card
    public int     rank() { return r; }

    public int     suit() { return s; }

    public int     color () {
        if (suit() == heart || suit() == diamond)
            return red;
        return black ; }

    public boolean     faceUp() { return faceup; }

        // perform actions
    public void     draw (Graphics g, int x, int y) {
        ... /* omitted */ ...
        }

    public void     flip() { faceup = ! faceup; }
};
```

Figure 3.12 – A typical Java class declaration.

Exercises

1. Suppose you were required to program in a non-object-oriented language, such as Pascal or C. How would you simulate the notion of classes and methods?

2. In Smalltalk and Objective-C, methods that take multiple arguments are described using a keyword to separate each argument; in C++ the argument list follows a single method name. Describe some of the advantages and disadvantages of each approach; in particular, explain the effect on readability and understandability.

3. A digital counter is a bounded counter that turns over when its integer value reaches a certain maximum. Examples include the numbers in a digital clock and the odometer in a car. Define a class description for a bounded counter. Provide the ability to set maximum and minimum values, to increment the counter, and to return the current counter value.

4. Write a class description for complex numbers. Write methods for addition, subtraction, and multiplication of complex numbers.

5. Write a class description for a fraction, a rational number composed of two integer values. Write methods for addition, subtraction, multiplication, and division of fractions. How do you handle the reduction of fractions to lowest-common-demoninator form?

6. Consider the following two combinations of class and function in C++. Explain the difference in using the function addi as the user would see it.

```
class example1 {
public:
     int i;
};

int addi(example1 & x, int j)
{
    x.i = x.i + j;
    return x.i;
}


class example2 {
public:
     int i;
     int addi(int j)
         { i = i + j; return i; }
};
```

7. In both the C++ and Objective-C versions of the playing card abstraction, the modular division instruction is used to determine the color of a card based on the suit value. Is this a good practice? Discuss a few of the advantages and disadvantages. Rewrite the methods to remove the dependency on the particular values associated with the suits.

8. Do you think it is better to have the access modifiers private and public associated with every individual object, as in Java, or used to create separate areas in the declaration, as in C++, Objective-C, and Delphi Pascal? Give reasons to support your view.

9. Contrast the encapsulation provided by the class mechanism with the encapsulation provided by the module facility. How are they different? How are they the same?

Chapter 4

Messages, Instances, and Initialization

In Chapter 3 we outlined the *static* features of object-oriented programming. That is, we described how to create new types, new classes, and new methods. In this chapter, we continue our exploration of the mechanics of object-oriented programming by examining the *dynamic* features. Dynamic features include how values are instantiated (or created), how they are initialized, and how they communicate with each other by message passing.

In the first section, we will explore the mechanics of message passing. Then we will investigate creation and initialization. By *creation* we mean the allocation of memory space for a new object and the binding of that space to a name. By *initialization* we mean not only the setting of initial values in the data area for the object, similar to the initialization of fields in a record, but also the more general process of establishing the initial conditions necessary for the manipulation of an object. The degree to which this latter task can be hidden from clients who use an object in most object-oriented languages is an important aspect of *encapsulation*, which we identified as one of the principle advantages of object-oriented techniques over other programming styles.

4.1   Message-Passing Syntax

We are using the term *message passing* (sometimes also called *method lookup*) to mean the dynamic process of asking an object to perform a specific action. In Chapter 1 we informally described message passing and noted how a message differs from an ordinary procedure call. In particular:

- A *message* is always given *to* some object, called the *receiver*.

73

- The action performed in response to the message is not fixed, but may differ depending upon the class of the receiver. That is, different objects may accept the same message, and yet perform different actions.

There are three identifiable parts to any message-passing expression. These are the *receiver* (the object to which the message is being sent), the *message selector* (the text that indicates the particular message being sent), and the *arguments* used in responding to the message.

Although the concept is central to object-oriented programming, the terms used in the various languages and the syntax employed to represent the ideas vary widely. In the following sections, we will describe the features particular to each of the languages we are considering, as well as the vocabulary used in the different programming communities.

4.1.1   Message Passing Syntax in Object Pascal

Unlike the rest of the OOP community, Delphi Pascal programmers use the term *message* to refer to a specialized form of window management command. The more conventional message is known as a *method lookup*.

A *method lookup* in Object Pascal is simply a request sent to an object to invoke one of the objects' methods. As we noted in Chapter 3, a method is described in an object declaration in a manner similar to a data field in a record declaration. Analogously, the conventional dot notation used to represent access to a data field is extended to mean invocation of a method. The message selector–the text that follows the dot–must match one of the methods defined in the class (or inherited from a parent class; we will explore inheritance in Chapter 7). Thus, if aCard has been declared to be an object of class Card, the following command instructs the card to draw itself on the given window at the given location.

```
aCard.draw (win, 25, 37);
```

The object to the left of the period is known as the *receiver* for the message. Notice that, with the exception of the designation of a receiver, the syntax used for a message is identical to the syntax used in a conventional function or procedure call. If no arguments are specified, the parenthetical list is omitted. For example, the following message instructs the card to flip itself over:

```
aCard.flip;
```

If the method specified is declared as a procedure, the expression must be used as a procedure. Similarly, if the method is declared as a function, it must be used as a function.

The compiler checks the validity of all message-passing expressions. Attempting to pass a message that is not known in the class description of the receiver produces an error indication.

Within a method, the pseudo-variable self is used to refer to the receiver of the message. This variable is not declared, but can be used as an argument or as the receiver in further messages. For example, the method color, which returns the color of a card, could be written as follows:

```
function Card.color : colors;
begin
    if (self.suit = Heart) or (self.suit = Diamond) then
        color := Red
    else
        color := Black;
end;
```

Here, the method suit is being invoked to obtain the suit value. This is considered better programming practice than giving the method direct access to the data field suitValue. (Delphi Pascal also permits specifying the result of a function by assigning to the special variable Result, rather than the name of the function.)

4.1.2 Message-Passing Syntax in C++

As we noted in Chapter 3, although the *concepts* of methods and messages are applicable to C++, methods and messages as terms are seldom used in C++ texts. Instead, a method is described as a *member function*, and passing a message to an object is referred to as *invoking a member function*.

Just as a class declaration looks similar, in many ways, to a structure declaration, the syntax used to invoke a member function is similar to that used to access data members (what we are calling instance variables.) The notation states the receiver, followed by a period, and then the message selector (which must correspond to a member function name in the class of the receiver), and finally the arguments in a parenthesized list.

If theCard is declared as an instance of the class Card, the following statement instructs the card to print itself on a given window at the coordinates 25 and 37:

```
theCard.draw (win, 25, 37);
```

Even when no arguments are required, parentheses are still necessary to distinguish the invocation of a member function from the accessing of member data. Thus, the following code might be used to determine whether the card is face up:

```
if ( theCard.faceUp() )
    { ... }
else
    { ... }
```

As in Object Pascal, the compiler checks the validity of a message-passing expression by referring to the declared class of the receiver. An attempt to invoke messages that are not listed as part of this class are flagged as compiler errors.

A member function that is declared to yield a value of type void can be used only as a statement–that is, as a procedure call. Member functions that yield other values can be used, in C fashion, as either statements (like procedures) or functions (like a function call).

There is a pseudo-variable associated with every method that holds the receiver for the message that invoked the method. In C++, this variable is called this and is a *pointer* to the receiver, not the receiver value itself. Thus, pointer indirection ($-$ >) must be used to send subsequent messages to the receiver. For example, the method color, used to determine the face color of a card, could have been written as follows if we had wished to avoid direct access to the private field maintaining the suit value:

```
colors Card::color ()
{      switch ( this->suit() ) {
          case heart:
          case diamond:
              return red;
          }
      return black;
}
```

The variable this is also frequently used when, from within a method, it is necessary to pass the receiver of a message as an argument to another function.

```
void aClass::aMessage(bClass b, int x)
{      // pass ourselves as argument
      b->doSomething(this, x);
}
```

In C++ the use of this as a receiver can often be avoided. Within the body of a method, a call to another method made without a receiver specified is interpreted as a message to the current receiver. Thus, the method color could (and usually would) be written as follows:

```
colors Card::color ()
{      switch ( suit() ) {
          case heart:
          case diamond:
              return red;
          }
      return black;
}
```

4.1.3 Message-Passing Syntax in Java

The syntax for message passing in Java is almost identical to that used by C++. The only notable exception concerns the pseudo-variable this, which in C++ is a pointer but in Java represents an object (since Java does not have pointer values!).

4.1.4 Message-Passing Syntax in Smalltalk

The syntax used to represent a message in Smalltalk is different from that used in C++ or Object Pascal. It is still the case that the first part of the message-passing expression describes the *receiver*–the object to which the message is being given. Instead of this part being followed by a period, a space is used to separate the receiver from the message selector.

As in C++, the selector must match one of the methods defined in the class of the receiver. Unlike C++, however, Smalltalk is a *dynamically typed* language. This means that the check to determine if the receiver class understands the selector is performed at run time, not at compile time.

If aCard is a variable of class Card, the following instructs the associated card to be marked as flipped over:

```
aCard flip
```

As we noted in Chapter 3, arguments to methods are indicated by *keyword selectors*. Each keyword is followed by a colon, and a keyword must precede each argument. The following would be used to request the card described by aCard to draw itself at the location given by the coordinates 25 and 37:

```
aCard drawOn: win at: 25 and: 37
```

In Smalltalk, even binary operators, such as + and *, are interpreted as messages, with the receiver being taken from the left hand value and the argument being represented by the right hand value.[1] As with keyword and unary messages (messages with no arguments), classes are free to provide whatever meaning they want to associate with binary messages. There is a precedence ordering, with unary messages having highest precedence, binary messages having next-highest precedence, and keyword messages having lowest precedence.

In Smalltalk the pseudo-variable self denotes the receiver of a message within a method. This value is frequently used as a target for yet another message, indicating that an object desires to send a message to itself. For example, the method color described earlier could be rewritten in the following to avoid direct access to the instance variable suit:

---

[1] C++ provides a similar ability to overload the meaning of binary operators, such as +, −, or <, and even the assignment operator. This topic is beyond the scope of this book, although we will briefy mention the overloading of assignment in Chapter 12.

```
color
    " return color of current card "
    (self suit = #diamond)    ifTrue: [ ↑ #red ].
    (self suit = #club)       ifTrue: [ ↑ #black ].
    (self suit = #spade)      ifTrue: [ ↑ #black ].
    (self suit = #heart)      ifTrue: [ ↑ #red ].
```

4.1.5   Message-Passing Syntax in Objective-C

The syntax and terminology for message passing in Objective-C closely follows the Smalltalk model. There are keyword and unary messages, but unlike in Smalltalk, classes in Objective-C cannot redefine binary operators.

Message passing in Objective-C can occur only within *message expressions*. A message expression is an expression enclosed in square brackets [...]. So, for example, if aCard is an instance of class Card, the following message instructs the card to flip over. Note the use of the semicolon to end the statement.

```
[ aCard flip ];
```

Like Smalltalk, Objective-C is a *dynamically typed* language. This means that the test to determine if the receiver will understand a message is performed at run time, not at compile time. A run-time error message is generated if the receiver fails to recognize the message.

The Smalltalk syntax is used for messages that take arguments. For example, the following directs aCard to draw itself on a given window at the coordinates 25 and 36:

```
[ aCard drawOn: win at: 25 and: 36 ];
```

Brackets are necessary only around the message-passing expression. If the message-passing expression results in a value to be used with an assignment statement, the assignment operator must be placed outside the brackets. Thus, the following expression assigns to the variable newCard a copy of the card aCard:

```
newCard = [ aCard copy ];
```

Message-passing expressions can be used anywhere ordinary C expressions are legal. For example, the following C statement tests whether the card aCard is face up:

```
if ( [ aCard faceUp ] ) ...
```

As in Object Pascal, inside a method Objective-C uses the name self to refer to the receiver for the current message. Unlike in the other languages, however, self is a true variable that be modified by the user. We will see in Section 4.3.3, "*factory methods*," that such modification can be useful.

4.2 Issues in Creation and Initialization

Before examining in detail the mechanics of creation and initialization in each of the programming languages we are considering, we will examine in an abstract way some of the issues associated with these functions. By considering the various alternatives in the design space, the reader will be better prepared to appreciate the features that have and have not been selected in each language. The features we will investigate include stack versus heap storage allocation, memory recovery, pointers, and immutable creation.

4.2.1 Stack versus Heap Storage Allocation

The question of stack versus heap storage allocation concerns how storage for variables is allocated and released and what explicit steps the programmer must take in these processes. We can distinguish variables that are *automatic* from those that are *dynamic*.

The essential difference between automatic and dynamic variables is that storage for an automatic variable is created when the procedure (or block) containing the variable declaration is entered, and is released (again automatically) when the procedure (or block) is exited. Many programming languages use the term *static* to describe variables allocated automatically on the stack. We will use the alternative term *automatic* because it is more descriptive and because static is a keyword that means something (in fact, several things) quite different in C and C++. At the time the space is created for an automatic variable, the name and the created space are linked, and they cannot change during the time the variable is in existence.

Now consider dynamic variables. In many conventional languages, such as Pascal, a dynamic variable is created by the system-provided procedure new(x), which takes as its argument a variable declared as a pointer. An example follows:

```
type
    shape: record
        form : (triangle, square);
        side : integer;
    end;
var
    aShape : ↑ shape;
begin
    new(aShape);
    ...
end.
```

The newly created space is allocated, and as a side effect the value of the variable argument is changed to point to this new space. Thus, the processes of *allocation* and *naming* are tied together.

In other languages, such as C, allocation and naming are not tied together. In C, for example, memory is allocated by the system library function malloc, which takes as its argument the amount of memory to allocate. The malloc call returns a pointer to a block of memory, which is then assigned to a pointer variable by a normal assignment operator. The following illustrates this process:

```
struct shape {
    enum { triangle, square } form;
    int side;
    };

shape * aShape;
...

aShape = (struct shape *)
    malloc(sizeof(struct shape));
```

The essential difference between stack-based and heap-based storage allocation is that storage is allocated for an automatic (stack-resident) variable without any explicit directive from the user, whereas space is allocated for a dynamic variable only when requested. The way in which memory is released is also different in the two techniques. The programmer almost never needs to consider the release of automatic variables, whereas he or she may need to consider the release of heap-based storage. This is the topic of the next section.

4.2.2   Memory Recovery

When heap-based storage allocation techniques are employed, some means must be provided to recover storage that is no longer being used. Generally, languages fall into two broad categories. Pascal, C, and C++ require the user to keep track of values, to determine when they are no longer useful, and explicitly to free their space by calling a system-supplied library routine. This routine is called dispose in Pascal, for example, and free in C.

Other languages, such as Java and Smalltalk, can automatically detect when values are no longer accessible and hence can no longer contribute to any future computations. Such values are then automatically collected, and their space is recovered and recycled in future memory allocations. This process is known as *garbage collection*. Several well-known algorithms can be used to perform such recovery. The description of these algorithms is beyond the scope of this book; but a good overview is given by Cohen [Cohen 1981].

As with the arguments for and against dynamic typing (which we will investigate in Chapter 10), the arguments for and against garbage collection tend to pit efficiency against flexibility. Automatic garbage collection can be expensive, and it necessitates a run-time system to manage memory. On the other hand, in languages in which the programmer is required to manage the dynamic memory area, the following errors are common:

- An attempt is made to use a memory area that has not yet been allocated.

- Memory that is allocated dynamically is never released, a problem known as *memory leak.*

- An attempt is made to use memory that has been already freed.

- Memory is freed by two different procedures, leading to the same memory location being freed twice.

To avoid these problems it is often necessary to ensure that every dynamically allocated memory object has a designated *owner.* The owner of the memory is responsible for ensuring that the memory location is used properly and is freed when it is no longer required. In large programs, as in real life, disputes over the ownership of shared resources can be a source of difficulty.

4.2.3 Pointers

Pointers are an efficient and effective means of dealing with dynamic information and are therefore used in almost all implementations of object-oriented languages. Whether pointers represent an abstraction suitable for use by most programmers is a topic of considerable debate in the programming languages community, reflected in the fact that not all object-oriented languages provide pointers.

In some languages (such as Java, Smalltalk, and Object Pascal), objects are represented internally as pointers but are not used as pointers by the programmer. In other languages (such as C++), the user must explicitly distinguish between variables holding values and variables holding pointers to values. As we will see in the case studies in C++ presented elsewhere, when the object-oriented features of the language are used, explicit pointers are frequently employed. In Objective-C, variables declared as id are in fact pointers, but this is largely hidden from the user. When objects are declared with an explicit class in Objective-C, it is necessary for the programmer to distinguish between objects and explicit pointers to objects.

4.2.4 Immutable Creation

In Chapter 3, we presented a description of the class Card and noted one property we would like our playing-card abstraction to possess–namely, that the values associated with the suit and rank of the card be set once and thereafter not altered. Variables, such as the suit and rank instance variables, that do not alter their values during the course of execution are known as *single-assignment,* or *immutable.* An object for which all instance variables are immutable is, in turn, known as an immutable object.

Immutable values should be distinguished from program constants, although in large part the distinction is one of scope and binding time. A constant in most languages (C or Pascal, for example), must be known at compile time, has global scope, and remains fixed. An immutable value can be assigned, but only once; the value is not determined until execution time, when the object containing the value is created.

Immutable objects, of course, can always be constructed by convention. For example, we can provide the message to set the suit and rank value for our playing-card abstraction, and simply trust that the client will use this facility only once during the process of initializing a new object and not subsequently to alter the values of an existing object. More cautious object-oriented developers prefer to not leave themselves dependent on the good will of their clients, and so use a linguistic mechanism that ensures proper use. The languages we are examining differ in the degree to which they provide such services.

4.3   Mechanisms for Creation and Initialization

We have described some of the possible options in the design of mechanisms for creation and initialization in programming languages. In the following sections we will outline the exact mechanisms used in each of the programming languages we are considering.

4.3.1   Creation and Initialization in C++

C++ follows C (as well as Pascal and other Algol-like languages) in having both automatic and dynamic variables. An automatic variable is assigned space when the block containing the declaration is entered, and space is freed when control exits from the block. One change from C is that a declaration need not appear at the beginning of a block; the only requirement is that it appear prior to the first use of the declared variable. Thus, declarations can be moved closer to the point where the variables are used.

Implicit initialization is facilitated in C++ through the use of object *constructors.* As we noted in Chapter 3, a constructor is a method with the same name as that of the object class. Although the definition of a constructor is part of the class description, the constructor is used as part of the initialization process. Thus, we will discuss it here. In particular, a constructor method is automatically and implicitly invoked any time an object of the associated class is created. This is typically when a variable is declared, although it also occurs when objects are created dynamically with the new operator and when temporaries are created in a number of different circumstances.

For example, consider the following class declaration, which could be used as part of a complex number abstract data type:

```
class Complex {
public:
     // constructor
     Complex ();
     Complex (double);
     Complex (double, double);

     // operations
          ...
private:
     // data areas
     double realPart;
     double imaginaryPart;
};
```

There are three constructor functions associated with the class. The one invoked depends upon the arguments used when a value is created. A declaration with no arguments, such as the following:

```
Complex numberOne;
```

invokes the first form of the constructor. The function body for the constructor might be something like this:

```
Complex::Complex()
{
     // initialize both parts to zero
     realpart = 0.0;
     imaginaryPart = 0.0;
}
```

Note that the constructor body differs from a normal method definition in that a constructor does not explicitly name a return type. The mechanism of constructors is made considerably more powerful when combined with the ability in C++ to overload function names. A function name is said to be *overloaded* when there are two or more function bodies known by the same name. In C++, overloaded functions are disambiguated by differences in parameter lists.

This capability is often used by constructors to provide more than one style of initialization. For example, we might want to initialize a complex number by providing only the real part and sometimes by providing both a real and an imaginary value. The class definition shown earlier provided these capabilities. A series of declarations invoking these constructors might appear as follows:

```
Complex pi = 3.14159;
Complex e (2.71);
Complex i (0, 1);
```

The first two values invoke the constructor which takes only one argument. A definition for this function might be:

```
Complex::Complex(int rp)
{          // assign the real part
    realPart = rp;
          // set the imaginary part to zero
    imaginaryPart = 0.0;
}
```

Constructors that take two or more arguments must be written in the third form shown above, where the arguments appear as an argument list with the declaration.

The body of a constructor is often simply a sequence of assignment statements. These statements can be replaced by *initializers* in the function heading, as in the following variation of the class body given above. Each initializer clause simply names an instance variable and in parentheses lists the value to be used to initialize the variable.

```
Complex::Complex(int rp) : realPart(rp), imaginaryPart(0.0)
    { /* no further initialization necessary */ }
```

Variables declared within a block are created automatically when the block is entered and released automatically when the block is exited. Dynamic values are created with the keyword new, followed by the name of the object and arguments to be used with the constructor for the object. The result is a *pointer* to a newly created object. The following, for example, might create a new complex number.

```
Complex * c;
```

```
c = new Complex(3.14159, -1.0);
```

The parentheses are unnecessary if no arguments are being passed.

```
Complex * d = new Complex;
```

An array of values can be created by a size given in square brackets. The size argument is computed at run time, and can be any integer expression. Values created in this fashion are initialized using the default constructor (the constructor that takes no arguments).

```
Complex * carray = new Complex[27];
```

Memory for dynamically allocated values must be explicitly released by the programmer, using the operator **delete** (or **delete** [ ] for an array of objects).

Values can be declared as immutable in C++ through the use of the **const** keyword. Such values are declared as constant and are not allowed to change. Instance variables declared as constant must be initialized with an initializer clause, as a constant value cannot be the target of an assignment statement.

Although less commonly needed, a function can be defined in C++ that is invoked automatically whenever memory for an object is released. This function is called the *destructor*. For automatic variables, space is released when the procedure containing the declaration for the variable is exited. For dynamically allocated variables, space is released with the operator **delete**. The destructor function is written as the name of the class preceded by a tilde (∼). It does not take any arguments and is seldom directly invoked by the user.

A simple but clever function will illustrate the use of constructors and destructors. The class **Trace** defines a simple class that can be used to trace the flow of execution. The constructor class takes as argument a descriptive string and prints a message when space for the associated variable is allocated (which is when the procedure containing the declaration is entered). A second message is printed when space for the variable is released, which is when the procedure is exited.

```
class Trace {
public:
    // constructor and destructor
    Trace      (char *)
    ∼Trace     ();
private:
    char * text;
};

Trace::Trace (char * t) : text(t)
{    printf("entering %s\n", text); }

Trace::∼Trace ()
{    printf("exiting %s\n", text); }
```

To trace the flow of execution, the programmer simply creates a declaration for a dummy variable of type **Trace** in each procedure to be traced. Consider the following pair of routines:

```
void procedureA ()
{
    Trace ("procedure A");
```

```
    procedureB (7);
}

void procedureB (int x)
{
    Trace ("procedure B");
    if (x < 5) {
        Trace ("Small case in Procedure B");
        ...
    }
    else {
        Trace ("Large case in Procedure B");
        ...
    }
}
```

By their output, the values of type Trace will trace out the flow of execution. A typical output might be:

```
entering procedure A
entering procedure B
entering Large case in Procedure B
...
exiting Large case in Procedure B
exiting procedure B
exiting procedure A
```

4.3.2   Creation and Initialization in Java

A major difference between Java and C++ is that Java uses automatic garbage collection, thus freeing the programmer from having to deal with memory management. All values are automatically recovered when they are no longer accessible in the environment of the running program.

All variables of object type in Java are initially assigned the value null. Object values are created with the operator new. Unlike in C++, in Java parentheses must be used with this operator even if no arguments are necessary.

```
    // create a five of spades
Card aCard = new Card(Card.spade, 5);
    // create another card
Card bCard = new Card();
```

The concept of constructors is similar in Java to that in C++, with the exception that constructors in Java do not support initializer clauses. Unlike in C++, one constructor in Java can invoke another constructor, which often allows common behavior to be factored out of several constructors. For this to happen, the constructor must be invoked with the keyword this.

```
class newClass {
    newClass (int i) {
        // do some initialization
        // ...
        }
    newClass (int i, int j) {
        // first, invoke one argument constructor
        this(i);
        // then do some more initialization
        // ...
        }
    }
```

Destructors are slightly different in Java than in C++. The destructor concept in Java is represented by a function named finalize, taking no argument and returning no result. Finalize is automatically invoked by the system after memory has been recovered by the garbage collection, and before such memory is recycled for a new use. The programmer is provided with no guarantees of when, if ever, a finalize method will be called; thus, these methods should not be relied on for program correctness but should rather be considered an optimization.

An unusual feature of Java is its use of a string as argument to the new operator to determine at run time the type of object that will be allocated. Most generally, the string is an expression that is built up at run time. The constructor with no arguments will be invoked to initialize the newly created object.

```
        // build an instance of Complex
    a = new ("Comp" + "lex");
```

As we saw in Chapter 3, variables that cannot be reassigned can be created by the keyword final. Such values are not truly immutable, however, as nothing prevents the programmer from passing a message to such a value that will result in the alteration of the internal state of the variable. Thus, finalized values are not equivalent to const values in C++, which are guaranteed to be immutable.

```
    final aCard = new Card(Card.spade, 3);
    aCard.flip(); // changes state of the card
```

4.3.3   Creation and Initialization in Objective-C

Objective-C combines Smalltalk syntax and C declarations. Typically, objects are declared to be instances of type id, so more precise type information may not be known until run time. The actual object allocation is performed, as in Smalltalk, by passing the message new to a class object. (Note that id is defined via a typedef, and in fact a variable of type id is a pointer to the actual object.)

Variables declared as id are always dynamic. As we will see in Chapter 7, it is also possible to declare Objective-C variables using a class name directly. Such variables are automatic, having space allocated for them on the stack when the procedure in which they are contained is entered; this storage is released when the enclosing procedure is exited.

Variations in initialization in Objective-C are provided through the use of *factory methods*. Like class methods in Smalltalk, factory methods define functionality for a specific class. (This is in contrast to normal methods, which define functionality for *instances* of a class. One of the more difficult aspects of object-oriented programming is differentiating attributes of instances and attributes of classes. We will return to this in a later chapter.)

A method definition preceded by a plus sign (+) is a factory method; a method preceded by a minus sign (−) is an *instance method*. Multiple factory methods can be defined in a class. The following example illustrates the definition of a factory method that creates and initializes an instance of the class Card.

```
@ implementation Card {

+ suit: (int) s rank: (int) r {
    self = [ Card new ];
    suit = s;
    rank = r;
    return self;
}

@end
```

Notice that the message new is used to create a new instance of a class, as in Smalltalk. The Objective-C compiler does not issue any warning when instance variables are used within factory methods. If such references are made, it is assumed (although this assumption is not checked) that the value of the variable self is a valid instance of the class. Since normally in a factory method, self refers to the class itself and not to an instance, the user must first alter the value of self before referencing instance fields. (The fact that the type of self is not checked for validity before references are made to instance variables can be a source of subtle errors in Objective-C programs.) In the preceding method, it is only after self has been changed that references to the instance fields suit and rank refer to the correct locations.

Although objects are allocated dynamically in Objective-C, the system does not perform automatic storage management. The user can alert the system that storage for an object is no longer being used by means of the message **free**, which is defined in class **Object** and thus understood by all objects:

```
[ aCard free ];
```

Objective-C does not provide any direct mechanism for the creation of immutable or constant values.

4.3.4   Creation and Initialization in Object Pascal

In Object Pascal, all objects are dynamic and must be created explicitly by use of the system function **new**. The argument to **new** is an object identifier. Similarly, the system routine **dispose** is used to reclaim the space occupied by an object when the latter is no longer needed. It is up to the user to manage storage using **new** and **dispose**; the language provides only minimal support. A run-time error occurs if there is insufficient memory available to honor a request for allocation. It may or may not occur if an attempt is made to use a object that has not been properly allocated.

```
type
    Complex : object
        rp : real;
        ip : real;
        procedure initial (r, i : real);
        ...
        end;
var
    aNumber : Complex;

procedure Complex.initial (r, i : real);
begin
    rp := r;
    ip := i;
end;

begin
    new (aNumber);
    aNumber.initial(3.1415926, 2.4);
    ...
    dispose(aNumber);
end.
```

Notice that the dereferencing operator is not needed when object values are manipulated, despite their close similarity to pointers. In other words, references to objects, although they are dynamic, are not indicated in the same manner as are explicit pointer values.

Apple Object Pascal differs from other object-oriented languages in providing no support for implicit object initialization. Instead, once an object is created (via new), it is common to call an explicit initialization method. The example above illustrates this behavior.

Support for protection is weak in Apple Object Pascal. For example, there is no way to prevent direct access to the fields rp and ip in an instance of Complex, and there is no way to ensure that the initial message is not invoked more than once.

The Delphi version of Object Pascal is much closer to C++. We have seen how fields in a class definition can be hidden from users by the private directive. Delphi Pascal also supports constructors. As we saw in Section 3.5.1, these are declared in the class description with the constructor keyword. Values are then created by use of a constructor method as a message passed to the class itself.

```
aCard := Card.Create(spade, 5);
```

Storage for a new value will be created and the value automatically initialized by invocation of the constructor function. Unlike C++, Delphi Pascal does not allow overloaded versions of the same function name but does permit multiple different constructors.

Delphi Pascal also supports a form of destructor. A destructor function (usually called Destroy) is declared by the keyword destructor. When a dynamically allocated object is freed, the free method tests self for nil, and, if non-nil, calls the destructor function.

```
type
    TClass = class (TObject)
        constructor Create (arg : integer);
        procedure doTask(value : integer);
        destructor Destroy;
    end;

destructor Destroy;
begin
        (* whatever housekeeping is necessary *)
    ...
end;
```

Although Delphi Pascal does not support immutable or constant data fields directly, such values can be simulated through use of a construct called a *property*. A property is declared and manipulated like an data field–the field is set by being made a target for an assignment statement and is accessed by name. However, the syntax actually hides the real access mechanism, which is most often a function but can be a simple alias for another data field. An example declaration of a property is shown in the following code. Properties that define only a read clause are read-only, while those that define only a write clause are write-only. (Note that read-only values can be set from within the constructor or other methods that have access to the private portions of the class description.)

```
type
    TnewClass = class (TObject)
        property readOnly : Integer read internalValue;
        property realValue : Real read internalReal
                    write checkArgument;
    private
        internalValue : Integer;
        internalReal : Real;
        procedure checkArgument (arg : Real);
    end;
```

4.3.5   Creation and Initialization in Smalltalk

Smalltalk variables are dynamically typed. Thus, a variable can potentially hold a value of any class. An instance of a given class is created by the passing of the message new to the *class object* associated with the class. We will discuss class objects in more detail in Chapter 18; for now, it suffices to say that a class object is simply an object that encapsulates information about a class, including how to create new instances.

The value returned by the class object exists independently of any name, but is usually almost immediately assigned a name either by assignment or by being passed as an argument. The following, for example, creates a new instance of our class Card.

```
    aCard := Card new.
```

The user does not take explicit action to deallocate memory in Smalltalk. Values that are no longer accessible to the running program are recovered automatically by the garbage-collection system. A run-time error occurs if, after garbage collection has been performed, it is still not possible to honor a request for storage allocation.

Smalltalk provides several mechanisms to assist in object initialization. *Class methods* are methods that can be associated with a specific class object. We will discuss class objects and class methods in more detail in Chapter 18; for the moment, it is sufficient to know that class methods can be used only as messages to a class object, and are thus used in place of the message new. Frequently, these methods invoke new to create the new object and then perform some further initialization code. Since class methods cannot directly access instance variables, they must typically invoke instance messages to perform initialization.

For example, a class method suit:rank: is shown below. It creates a new instance of the Card object and then calls the method suit:rank: (presumably defined as a method in the class Card) to establish the values of the instance variables.

```
suit: s rank: r | newCard |
      " first create the card "
      newCard := Card new.
      " then initialize it "
      newCard suit: s rank: r.
      " finally return it "
      ↑ newCard
```

To create a new instance of class Card–for example, the four of diamonds–the user would type the following:

```
aCard := Card suit: #diamond rank: 4.
```

A feature to note in the method just presented is the use of a local variable (called a temporary variable in Smalltalk.) The programmer can declare temporary variables simply by listing their names between vertical bars between the method heading and the method body. This is true for both class and normal methods. The scope of temporary variables includes only the method in which they are declared.

Smalltalk provides no direct mechanism for initializing immutable fields. Frequently, methods, such as suit:rank: used here, will be marked as "private." The understanding is that private methods should not be invoked directly by clients, but this limitation is honored only by convention, and no enforcement is attempted.

Another technique for initializing objects in Smalltalk is the *cascaded message* (or simply a *cascade*), which is handy when multiple messages are to be sent to the same receiver, as is frequently the case during initialization. The cascaded message is written as the receiver, followed by the list of messages, which are separated by semicolons. For example, the following expression creates a new Set and initializes it with the values 1, 2, and 3. The result assigned to the variable aSet is the newly initialized set. The use of cascades often eliminates the need for temporary variables.

```
aSet := Set new add: 1 ; add: 2 ; add: 3.
```

Exercises

1. Write a method copy for the class Card of Chapter 3. This method should return a new instance of the class Card with the suit and rank fields initialized to be the same as the receiver.

2. In a language that does not provide direct support for immutable instance variables, how might you design a software tool that would help to detect violations of access? (Hint: The programmer can provide directives in the form of comments that tell the tool which variables should be considered immutable.)

3. We have seen two styles for invoking methods. The approach used in C++ is similar to a conventional function call. The Smalltalk and Objective-C approaches separate arguments with keyword identifiers. Which do you think is more readable? Which is more descriptive? Which is more error-prone? Present short arguments to support your opinions.

4. How might you design a tool to detect the different types of memory allocation and free problems described in Section 4.2.2?

5. Andrew Appel [Appel 1987] argues that under certain circumstances heap-based memory allocation can be more efficient than stack-based memory allocation. Read this article and summarize the points of Appel's argument. Are the situations in which this is true likely to be encountered in practice?

6. Write a short (two- or three-paragraph) essay arguing for or against automatic memory-management (garbage-collection) systems.

Chapter 5

A Case Study: The Eight Queens Puzzle

This chapter presents the first of several case studies (or paradigms, in the original sense of the word) of programs developed by object-oriented methods. The programs will be rather small so that we can present versions in each of the languages we discuss in this book. Later case studies will be presented in only one language.

After first describing the problem, we will discuss how an object-oriented solution would differ from another type of solution. The chapter then concludes with a solution written in each language.

5.1 The Eight-Queens Puzzle

In the game of chess, the queen can attack any piece that lies on the same row, on the same column, or along a diagonal. The **eight-queens** is a classic logic puzzle. The task is to place eight queens on a chessboard in such a fashion that no queen can attack any other queen. A solution is shown in Figure 5.1, but this solution is not unique. The eight-queens puzzle is often used to illustrate problem-solving or backtracking techniques (see [Griswold 1983, Budd 1987, Berztiss 1990], for example).

How would an object-oriented solution to the eight-queens puzzle differ from a solution written in a conventional imperative programming language? In a conventional solution, some sort of data structure would be used to maintain the positions of the pieces. A program would then solve the puzzle by systematically manipulating the values in these data structures, testing each new position to see whether it satisfied the property that no queen can attack any other.

We can provide an amusing but nevertheless illustrative metaphor for the difference between a conventional and an object-oriented solution. A conventional program is like a human being sitting above the board, and moving the chess

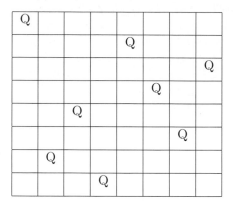

Figure 5.1 – One solution to the eight-queens puzzle.

pieces, which have no animate life of their own. In an object-oriented solution, on the other hand, we will empower the *pieces* to solve the problem themselves. That is, instead of a single monolithic entity controlling the outcome, we will distribute responsibility for finding the solution among many interacting agents. It is as if the chess pieces themselves are animate beings who interact with each other and take charge of finding their own solution.

Thus, the essence of our object-oriented solution will be to create objects that represent each of the queens, and to provide them with the abilities to discover the solution. With the computing-as-simulation view of Chapter 1, we are creating a model universe, defining behavior for the objects in this universe, then setting the universe in motion. When the activity of the universe stabilizes, the solution has been found.

5.1.1   Creating Objects That Find Their Own Solution

How might we define the behavior of a queen object so that a group of queens working together can find a solution on their own? The first observation is that, in any solution, no two queens can occupy the same column, and consequently no column can be empty. At the start we can therefore assign a specific column to each queen and reduce the problem to the simpler task of finding an appropriate row.

To find a solution it is clear that the queens will need to communicate with each other. Realizing this, we can make a second important observation that will greatly simplify our programming task–namely, each queen needs to know only about the queens to her immediate left. Thus, the data values maintained for each queen will consist of three values: a **column value**, which is *immutable*; a **row value**, which is altered in pursuit of a solution; and the **neighboring queen** to the immediate left.

Let us define an *acceptable solution for column n* to be a configuration of columns 1 through *n* in which no queen can attack any other queen in those columns. Each queen will be charged with finding acceptable solutions between herself and her neighbors on her left. We will find a solution to the entire puzzle by asking the right most queen to find an acceptable solution. A CRC-card description of the class Queen, including the data managed by each instance (recall that this information is described on the back side of the card), is shown in Figure 5.2.

5.2 Using Generators

As with many similar problems, the solution to the eight-queens puzzle involves two interacting steps: generating possible partial solutions and filtering out solutions that fail to satisfy some later goal. This style of problem solving is sometimes known as the generate and test paradigm (see [Hanson 1981], [Berztiss 1990]).

Let us consider the filter step first, as it is easier. For the system to test a potential solution it is sufficient for a queen to take a coordinate (row-column) pair and produce a Boolean value that indicates whether that queen, or any queen to her left, can attack the given location. A pseudo code algorithm that checks to see whether a queen can attack a specific position is given below. The procedure canAttack uses the fact that, for a diagonal motion, the differences in rows must be equal to the differences in columns.

```
function queen.canAttack(testRow , testColumn) -> boolean
    /* test for same row */
    if row = testRow then
        return true

    /* test diagonals */
    columnDifference := testColumn - column
    if (row + columnDifference = testRow) or
       (row - columnDifference = testRow)
            then return true

    /* we can't attack, see if neighbor can */
    return neighbor.canAttack(testRow, testColumn)
end
```

5.2.1 Initialization

We will divide the task of finding a solution into parts. The method initialize establishes the initial conditions necessary for a queen object, which in this case simply means setting the data values. This is usually followed immediately by a

Queen
---

initialize – initialize row, then find
    first acceptable solution for self and
    neighbor
advance – advance row and find next
    acceptable solution
canAttack – see whether a position can
    be attacked by self or neighbors

Queen – data values
---

row – current row number (changes)
column – column number (fixed)
neighbor – neighbor to left (fixed)

Figure 5.2   Front and back sides of the Queen CRC card.

call on findSolution to discover a solution for the given column. Because such a solution will often not be satisfactory to subsequent queens, the message advance is used to advance to the next solution.

A queen in column n is initialized by being given a column number, and the neighboring queen (the queen in column $n - 1$). At this level of analysis, we will leave unspecified the actions of the leftmost queen, who has no neighbor. We will explore various alternative actions in the example problems we subsequently present. We will assume the neighbor queens (if any) have already been initialized, which includes their having found a mutually satisfactory solution. The queen in the current column simply places herself in row 1. A pseudo-code description of the algorithm is shown below.

```
function queen.initialize(col, neigh) -> boolean

        /* initialize our column and neighbor values */
    column := col
    neighbor := neigh

        /* start in row 1 */
    row := 1
end
```

5.2.2 Finding a Solution

To find a solution, a queen simply asks its neighbors if they can attack. If so, then the queen advances herself, if possible (returning failure if she cannot). When the neighbors indicate they cannot attack, a solution has been found.

```
function queen.findSolution -> boolean

        /* test positions */
    while neighbor.canAttack (row, column) do
        if not self.advance then
            return false

        /* found a solution */
    return true
end
```

As we noted in Chapter 4, the pseudo-variable self denotes the receiver for the current message. In this case we want the queen who is being asked to find a solution to pass the message advance to herself.

5.2.3   Advancing to the Next Position

The procedure advance divides into two cases. If we are not at the end, the
queen simply advances the row value by 1. Otherwise, she has tried all positions
and not found a solution, so nothing remains but to ask her neighbor for a new
solution and start again from row 1.

```
function queen.advance -> boolean

        /* try next row */
    if row < 8 then begin
        row := row + 1
        return self.findSolution
        end

        /* cannot go further */
        /* move neighbor to next solution */
    if not neighbor.advance then
        return false

        /* start again in row 1 */
    row := 1
    return self.findSolution
end
```

The one remaining task is to print out the solution. This is most easily
accomplished by a simple method, print that is rippled down the neighbors.

```
procedure print
    neighbor.print
    write row, column
end
```

5.3   The Eight-Queens Puzzle in Each Language

In this section we present solutions to the eight-queens puzzle in each of the
programming languages we are considering. Examine each variation, and compare how the basic features provided by the language make subtle changes to
the final solution. In particular, examine the solutions written in Smalltalk and
Objective-C, which use a special class for a sentinel value, and contrast this
with the solutions given in Object Pascal, C++, or Java, all of which use a null
pointer for the leftmost queen and thus must constantly test the value of pointer
variables.

5.3.1 The Eight-Queens Puzzle in Object Pascal

The class definition for the eight-queens puzzle in Apple Object Pascal is shown below. A subtle but important point is that this definition is recursive; objects of type Queen maintain a data field that is itself of type Queen. This is sufficient to indicate that declaration and storage allocation are not necessarily linked; if they were, an infinite amount of storage would be required to hold any Queen value. We will contrast this with the situation in C++ when we discuss that language, and we will consider the relationship between declaration and storage allocation in more detail in Chapter 12.

```
type
    Queen = object
            (* data fields *)
        row :        integer;
        column :     integer;
        neighbor :   Queen;

            (* initialization *)
        procedure initialize (col : integer; ngh : Queen);

            (* operations *)
        function    canAttack
                    (testRow, testColumn : integer) : boolean;
        function    findSolution : boolean;
        function    advance : boolean;
        procedure   print;
    end;
```

The class definition for the Delphi language differs only slightly, as shown below. The Borland language allows the class declaration to be broken into public and private sections, and it includes a constructor function, which we will use in place of the initialize routine.

```
TQueen = class (TObject)
public
    constructor Create (initialColumn : integer; nbr : TQueen);
    function findSolution : boolean;
    function advance : boolean;
    procedure print;

private
    function canAttack (testRow, testColumn : integer) : boolean;
    row : integer;
    column : integer;
```

```
        neighbor : TQueen;
end;
```

The pseudo-code presented in the earlier sections is reasonably close to the Pascal solution, with two major differences. The first is the lack of a return statement in Pascal, and the second is the necessity to first test whether a queen has a neighbor before passing a message to that neighbor. The functions findSolution and advance, shown below, illustrate these differences. (Note that Delphi Pascal differs from standard Pascal in permitting short-circuit interpretation of the and and or directives (as C++ does). Thus, the code for the Delphi language could in a single expression combine the test for neighbor being non-null and the passing of a message to the neighbor).

```
function Queen.findSolution : boolean;
var
    done : boolean;
begin
    done := false;
    findsolution := true;

        (* test positions *)
    if neighbor <> nil then
        while not done and neighbor.canAttack(row, column) do
            if not self.advance then begin
                findSolution := false;
                done := true;
            end;
end;

function Queen.advance : boolean;
begin
    advance := false;
        (* try next row *)
    if row < 8 then begin
        row := row + 1;
        advance := self.findSolution;
    end
    else begin
            (* cannot go further *)
            (* move neighbor to next solution *)
        if neighbor <> nil then
            if not neighbor.advance then
                advance := false
            else begin
                row := 1;
```

```
            advance := self.findSolution;
        end;
    end;
end;
```

The main program allocates space for each of the eight queens and initializes the queens with their column number and neighbor value. Since during initialization the first solution will be discovered, it is only necessary for the queens to print their solution. The code to do this in Apple Object Pascal is shown below. Here, neighbor and i are temporary variables used during initialization and lastQueen is the most recently created queen.

```
begin
    neighbor := nil;
    for i := 1 to 8 do begin
            (* create and initialize new queen *)
        new (lastQueen);
        lastQueen.initial (i, neighbor);
        if not lastQueen.findSolution then
            writeln('no solution');
            (* newest queen is next queen neighbor *)
        neighbor := lastQueen;
    end;

        (* print the solution *)
    lastQueen.print;

    end;
end.
```

By providing explicit constructors that combine new object creation and initialization, the Delphi language allows us to eliminate one of the temporary variables. The main program for the Delphi language is as follows:

```
begin
    lastQueen := nil;
    for i := 1 to 8 do begin
            // create and initialize new queen
        lastQueen := Queen.create(i, lastQueen);
        lastQueen.findSolution;
        end;

        // print the solution
    lastQueen.print;
end;
```

5.3.2   The Eight-Queens Puzzle in C++

The most important difference between the pseudo-code description of the algorithm presented earlier and the eight-queens puzzle as actually coded in C++ is the explicit use of pointer values. The class description for the class Queen is shown below. Each instance maintains, as part of its data area, a pointer to another queen value. Note that, unlike the Object Pascal solution, in C++ this value must be declared explicitly as a pointer rather than an object value.

```
class Queen {
public:
        // constructor
    Queen (int, Queen *);

        // find and print solutions
    bool findSolution();
    bool advance();
    void print();

private:
        // data fields
    int row;
    const int column;
    Queen * neighbor;

        // internal method
    bool canAttack (int, int);
};
```

As in the Delphi Pascal solution, we have subsumed the behavior of the method initialize in the constructor. We will describe this shortly.

There are three data fields. The integer data field column has been marked as const. This identifies the field as an immutable value, which cannot change during execution. The third data field is a pointer value, which either contains a null value (that is, points at nothing) or points to another queen.

Since initialization is performed by the constructor, the main program can simply create the eight queen objects, and then print their solution. The variable lastQueen will point to the most recent queen created. This value is initially a null pointer–it points to nothing. A loop then creates the eight values, initializing each with a column value and the previous queen value. When the loop completes, the leftmost queen holds a null value for its neighbor field while every other queen points to its neighbor, and the value lastQueen points to the rightmost queen.

```
void main() {
    Queen * lastQueen = 0;

    for (int i = 1; i <= 8; i++) {
        lastQueen = new Queen(i, lastQueen);
        if (! lastQueen->findSolution())
            cout << "no solution\n";
    }

    lastQueen->print();
}
```

We will describe only those methods that illustrate important points. The complete solution can be examined in Appendix A.

The constructor method must use the initialization clauses on the heading to initialize the constant value column, as it is not permitted to use an assignment operator to initialize instance fields that have been declared const. An initialization clause is also used to assign the value neighbor, although we have not declared this field as constant.

```
Queen::Queen(int col, Queen * ngh)
    : column(col), neighbor(ngh)
{
    row = 1;
}
```

Because the value of the neighbor variable can be either a queen or a null value, a test must be performed before any messages are sent to the neighbor. This is illustrated in the method findSolution. The use of short-circuit evaluation in the logical connectives and the ability to return from within a procedure simplify the code in comparison to the Object Pascal version, which is otherwise very similar.

```
bool Queen::findSolution()
{
    while (neighbor && neighbor->canAttack(row, column))
            if (! advance())
                return false;
    return true;
}
```

The advance method must similarly test to make certain there is a neighbor before trying to advance the neighbor to a new solution. When passing a message to oneself, as in the recursive message findSolution, it is not necessary to specify a receiver.

```
bool Queen::advance()
{
    if (row < 8) {
        row++;
        return findSolution();
        }

    if (neighbor && ! neighbor->advance())
        return false;

    row = 1;
    return findSolution();
}
```

5.3.3   The Eight-Queens Puzzle in Java

The solution in Java is in many respects similar to the C++ solution. However, in Java the bodies of the methods are written directly in place, and public or private designations are placed on the class definitions themselves. The following is the class description for the class Queen, with some of the methods omitted.

```
class Queen {
        // data fields
    private int row;
    private int column;
    private Queen neighbor;

        // constructor
    Queen (int c, Queen n) {
            // initialize data fields
        row = 1;
        column = c;
        neighbor = n;
        }

    public boolean findSolution() {
        while (neighbor != null &&
                neighbor.canAttack(row, column))
            if (! advance())
                return false;
        return true;
        }

    public boolean advance() {
```

```
                ...
        }

    private boolean canAttack(int testRow, int testColumn) {
                ...
        }

    public void paint (Graphics g) {
                ...
        }
}
```

Unlike in C++, in Java the link to the next queen is simply declared as an object of type Queen and not as a pointer to a queen. Before a message is sent to the neighbor instance variable, an explicit test is performed to see if the value is null.

Since Java provides a rich set of graphics primitives, this solution will differ from the others in actually drawing the final solution as a board. The method paint will draw an image of the queen, then print the neighbor images.

```
class Queen {
    ...
    public void paint (Graphics g) {
            // x, y is upper left corner
        int x = (row - 1) * 50;
        int y = (column - 1) * 50;
        g.drawLine(x+5, y+45, x+45, y+45);
        g.drawLine(x+5, y+45, x+5, y+5);
        g.drawLine(x+45, y+45, x+45, y+5);
        g.drawLine(x+5, y+35, x+45, y+35);
        g.drawLine(x+5, y+5, x+15, y+20);
        g.drawLine(x+15, y+20, x+25, y+5);
        g.drawLine(x+25, y+5, x+35, y+20);
        g.drawLine(x+35, y+20, x+45, y+5);
        g.drawOval(x+20, y+20, 10, 10);
            // then draw neighbor
        if (neighbor != null)
            neighbor.paint(g);
        }
}
```

The graphics routines draw a small crown, which looks like this:

Java does not have global variables nor functions that are not member functions. As we will describe in more detail in Chapter 8, a program is created by the defining of a subclass of the system class Applet, and then the overriding of certain methods. Notably, the method init is used to provide any initialization for the application, while the method paint is used to redraw the screen. We will also define the method mouseDown, which is invoked when a mouse button press occurs, advancing to the next solution on each mouse click. We name the application class QueenSolver and define it as follows:

```java
public class QueenSolver extends Applet {

    private Queen lastQueen;

    public void init() {
        lastQueen = null;
        for (int i = 1; i <= 8; i++) {
            lastQueen = new Queen(i, lastQueen);
            lastQueen.findSolution();
            }
        }

    public void paint(Graphics g) {
            // draw board
        for (int i = 0; i <= 8; i++) {
            g.drawLine(50 * i, 0, 50*i, 400);
            g.drawLine(0, 50 * i, 400, 50*i);
            }
            // draw queens
        lastQueen.paint(g);
        }

    public boolean mouseDown(java.awt.Event evt, int x, int y) {
            // find next solution, print it
        lastQueen.advance();
        repaint();
        return true;
        }
}
```

Note that the application class must be declared as public, because it must be accessible to the main program.

5.3.4   The Eight-Queens Puzzle in Objective-C

The interface description for our class Queen is as follows:

```
@interface Queen : Object
{     /* data fields */
    int row;
    int column;
    id neighbor;
}

    /* methods */
- (void) initialize: (int) c neighbor: ngh;
- (int)   advance;
- (void) print;
- (int)   canAttack: (int) testRow column: (int) testColumn;
- (int)   findSolution;

@end
```

Each queen will maintain three data fields: a row value, a column, and the neighbor queen. The last is declared with the data type id. This declaration indicates that the value being held by the variable is an object type, although not necessarily a queen.

In fact, we can use this typeless nature of variables in Objective-C to our advantage. We will employ a technique that is not possible, or at least not as easy, in a more strongly typed language such as C++ or Object Pascal. Recall that the leftmost queen does not have any neighbor. In the C++ solution, this was indicated by the null, or empty value, in the neighbor pointer variable in the leftmost queen. In the current solution, we will instead create a new type of class, a *sentinel value*. The leftmost queen will point to this sentinel value, thereby ensuring that every queen has a valid neighbor.

Sentinel values are frequently used as endmarkers and are found in algorithms that manipulate linked lists, such as our linked list of queen values. The difference between an object-oriented sentinel and a more conventional value is that an object-oriented sentinel value can be *active*–it can have *behavior*–which means it can respond to requests.

What behaviors should our sentinel value exhibit? Recall that the neighbor links in our algorithm were used for two purposes. The first was to ensure that a given position could not be attacked; our sentinel value should always respond negatively to such requests, since it cannot attack any position. The second use of the neighbor links was in a recursive call to print the solution. In this case our sentinel value should simply return, since it does not have any information concerning the solution.

Putting these together yields the following implementation for our sentinel queen.

```
@implementation SentinelQueen : Object
- (int) advance
{
    /* do nothing */
    return 1;
}

- (int) findSolution
{
    /* do nothing */
    return 1;
}

- (void) print
{
    /* do nothing */
}

- (int) canAttack: (int) testRow column: (int) testColumn;
{
    /* cannot attack */
    return 0;
}
@end
```

In the full solution there is an implementation section for SentinelQueen, but no interface section. This omission is legal, although the compiler will provide a warning since it is somewhat unusual.

The use of the sentinel allows the methods in class Queen to simply pass messages to their neighbor without first determining whether or not she is the leftmost queen. The method for canAttack, for example, illustrates this use:

```
- (int) canAttack: (int) testRow column: (int) testColumn
{    int columnDifference;

    /* can attack same row */
    if (row == testRow)
        return 1;

    columnDifference = testColumn - column;
```

```
      if ((row + columnDifference == testRow) ||
         (row - columnDifference == testRow))
              return 1;

      return [ neighbor canAttack:testRow column: testColumn ];
}
```

Within a method, a message sent to the receiver is denoted by a message sent to the pseudo-variable self.

```
- (void) initialize: (int) c neighbor: ngh
{
      /* set the constant fields */
      column = c;
      neighbor = ngh;
      row = 1;
}


- (int) findSolution
{
      /* loop until we find a solution */
      while ([neighbor canAttack: row and: column ])
          if (! [self advance])
              return 0; /* return false */
      return 1; /* return true */
}
```

Other methods are similar, and are not described here.

5.3.5   The Eight-Queens Puzzle in Smalltalk

The solution to the eight-queens puzzle in Smalltalk is in most respects very similar to the solution given in Objective-C. Like Objective-C, Smalltalk handles the fact that the leftmost queen does not have a neighbor by defining a special *sentinel* class. The sole purpose of this class is to provide a target for the messages sent by the leftmost queen.

The sentinel value is the sole instance of the class SentinelQueen, a subclass of class Object, which implements the following three methods:

advance

```
      " sentinels do not attack "
      ↑ false
```

```
canAttack: row column: column
        " sentinels cannot attack "
    ↑ false
```

```
result
        " return empty list as result "
    ↑ List new
```

One difference between the Objective-C and Smalltalk versions is that the Smalltalk code returns the result as a list of values rather than printing it on the output. The techniques for printing output are rather tricky in Smalltalk and vary from implementation to implementation. By returning a list we can isolate these differences in the calling method.

The class Queen is a subclass of class Object. Instances of class Queen maintain three instance variables: a row value, a column value, and a neighbor. Initialization is performed by the method setColumn:neighbor:

```
setColumn: aNumber neighbor: aQueen
        " initialize the data fields "
    column := aNumber.
    neighbor := aQueen.
    row := 1.
```

The canAttack method differs from the Objective-C counterpart only in syntax:

```
canAttack: testRow column: testColumn | columnDifference |
    columnDifference := testColumn - column.
    (((row = testRow) or:
        [ row + columnDifference = testRow]) or:
        [ row - columnDifference = testRow])
            ifTrue: [ ↑ true ].
    ↑ neighbor canAttack: testRow column: testColumn
```

Rather than testing for the negation of a condition, Smalltalk provides an explicit ifFalse statement, which is used in the method advance:

```
advance
        " first try next row "
    (row < 8)
        ifTrue: [ row := row + 1. ↑ self findSolution ].
        " cannot go further, move neighbor "
    (neighbor advance)
        ifFalse: [ ↑ false ].
        " begin again in row 1 "
```

```
    row := 1.
    ↑ self findSolution
```

The while loop in Smalltalk must use a block as the condition test, as in the following:

```
findSolution
    [ neighbor canAttack: row column: column ]
        whileTrue: [ self advance ifFalse: [ ↑ false ] ].
    ↑ true
```

A recursive method is used to obtain the list of answer positions. Recall that an empty list is created by the sentinel value in response to the message result.

```
result
    ↑ neighbor result; addLast: row
```

A solution can be found by invocation of the following method, which is not part of class Queen but is instead attached to some other class, such as Object.

```
solvePuzzle | lastQueen |
    lastQueen := SentinelQueen new.
    1 to: 8 do: [:i | lastQueen := (Queen new)
        setColumn: i neighbor: lastQueen.
        lastQueen findSolution ].
    ↑ lastQueen result
```

A solution to the eight-queens puzzle constructed without the use of a sentinel value was described in my earlier book on Smalltalk [Budd 1987].

Exercises

1. Modify any one of the programs to produce all possible solutions rather than just one. How many possible solutions are there for the eight-queens puzzle? How many of these are rotations of other solutions? How might you filter out rotations?

2. Can you explain why the sentinel class in the Objective-C and Smalltalk versions of the eight-queens puzzle do not need to provide an implementation for the method findSolution, despite the fact that this message is passed to the neighbor value in the method advance?

3. Suppose we generalize the eight-queens problem to the N-queens problem, where the task is to place N queens on an N by N chessboard. How must the programs be changed?

It is clear that there are values for N for which no solution exists (consider N=2 or N=3, for example). What happens when your program is executed for these values? How might you produce more meaningful output?

4. Using whatever graphics facilities your system has, alter one of the programs to display dynamically on a chessboard the positions of each queen as the program advances. What portions of the program need to know about the display?

Chapter 6

A Case Study: A Billiards Game

In our second case study, we will develop a simple simulation of a billiard table. The program is written in Object Pascal and designed to be executed on a Macintosh.[1] As with the eight-queens program, the design of this program will stress the creation of autonomous interacting agents working together to produce the desired outcome.

6.1 The Elements of Billiards

The billiard table as the user sees it consists of a window containing a rectangle with holes (pockets) in the corners, 15 colored balls, and 1 white cue ball. By clicking the mouse the user simulates striking the cue ball, imparting a certain amount of energy to it. The direction of motion for the cue ball will be opposite to that of the mouse position in relation to the cue. Once a ball has energy it will start to move, reflecting off of walls, falling into holes, and potentially striking other balls. When a ball strikes another ball some of the energy of the first is given to the second, while the direction of movement of the two balls is changed by the collision.

---

[1] The billiards program was developed on a PowerPC Macintosh using the CodeWarrior Pascal compiler, version 1.1. In the powerPC version of the game the motion is so rapid that I found it useful to insert a loop that slowed the action down by repeating a number of times the call on draw in the Ball.update routine.

The game implemented by the program described in this chapter does not correspond to any actual game. It is not pool, it is not billiards, it is simply balls moving around a table consisting of walls and holes.

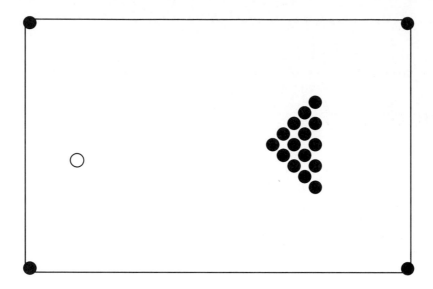

6.2   Graphical Objects

The heart of the simulation is three linked lists of *graphical objects*, which comprise the walls, holes, and balls. Each graphical object will include a link field and a field indicating the region of the screen occupied by the object.[2]

A simplifying assumption we have made is that all graphical objects occupy rectangular regions. This is, of course, quite untrue for a round object such as a ball. A more realistic alternative would have been to write a procedure that determined whether two balls have intersected based on the geometry of the ball rather than on the intersection of their regions. Once again, the complexity of the procedure would only have detracted from the issues we wish to address in our case study.

The primary objective in this case study is the way in which responsibility for behavior has been vested in the objects themselves. Every graphical object knows not only how to draw itself but how to move and how to interact with the other objects in the simulation.

---

[2]There are clear conflicts in ordering in the presentation of this case study. On the one hand, it is important for the reader to see examples of object-oriented principles as soon as possible; thus, placing this particular case study early in the book is desirable. On the other hand, this program, like almost all object-oriented programs, would benefit from more advanced techniques, which we will not discuss until later. In particular, the graphical objects might be better described by an inheritance hierarchy, such as we will describe in Chapter 7. Similarly, it is generally considered poor programming practice for the objects being maintained on a linked list to hold the link fields as part of their data area; a better design would separate the container from the elements in the list. Solving this problem is non-trivial and introduces complications not particularly relevant to the points addressed here. We will discuss container classes in Chapter 15.

6.2.1   The Wall Graphical Object

The first of our three graphical objects is a wall. It is defined by the following class description:

```
Wall = object
        (* data fields *)
    link : Wall;
    region : Rect;
        (* factor used to reflect striking balls *)
    convertFactor : real;

        (* initialization function *)
    procedure initialize
        (left, top, right, bottom : integer; cf : real);

        (* draw wall *)
    procedure draw;

        (* notify wall that a ball has struck *)
    procedure hitBy (aBall : Ball);
end;
```

The link field maintains a linked list of wall objects. The initialization method simply defines the region of the wall and sets the convert factor:

```
procedure Wall.initialize
    (left, top, right, bottom : integer; cf : real);
begin
        (* initialize conversion factor *)
    convertFactor := cf;

        (* set up region for wall *)
    SetRect (region, left, top, right, bottom);
end;
```

A wall can be drawn simply by printing a solid rectangle. A Macintosh toolbox routine performs this task:

```
procedure Wall.draw;
begin
    PaintRect (region);
end;
```

The most interesting behavior of a wall occurs when it has been struck by a ball. The direction of the ball is modified by use of the convert factor for the wall. (Convert factors are either zero or pi, depending upon whether the wall is horizontal or vertical). The ball subsequently moves off in a new direction.

```
procedure Wall.hitBy (aBall : Ball);
begin
        (* bounce the ball off the wall *)
    aBall.setDirection(convertFactor - aBall.direction);
end;
```

6.2.2   The Hole Graphical Object

A hole is defined by the following class description:

```
Hole = object
        (* data fields *)
    link : Hole;
    region : Rect;

        (* initialize location of hole *)
    procedure initialize (x, y : integer);

        (* draw the hole *)
    procedure draw;

        (* notify hole that it has received a ball *)
    procedure hitBy (aBall : Ball);
end;
```

As with walls, the initialization and drawing of holes is largely a matter of invoking the correct toolbox routines:

```
procedure Hole.initialize (x, y : integer);
begin
        (* identify region centered around x, y *)
    SetRect (region, x - 5, y - 5, x + 5, y + 5);
end;
```

```
procedure hole.draw;
begin
    PaintOval (region);
end;
```

Of more interest is what happens when a hole is struck by a ball. There are two cases. If the ball happens to be the cue ball (which is identified with a global variable, CueBall), it is placed back into play at a fixed location. Otherwise, all the energy is drained from the ball and it is moved off the table to a special display area.

```
procedure Hole.hitBy (aBall : Ball);
begin
        (* drain energy from ball, remove it *)
    aBall.energy := 0.0;
    aBall.erase;

        (* move ball *)
    if aBall = CueBall then
        aBall.setCenter(50, 100)
    else begin
        saveRack := saveRack + 1;
        aBall.setCenter (10 + saveRack * 15, 250);
    end;

    (* redraw ball *)
    aBall.draw;
end;
```

6.2.3   The Ball Graphical Object

Our final graphical object is the ball, defined by the following class description:

```
Ball = object
        (* data values maintained by balls *)
    link : Ball;
    region : Rect;
    direction : real; (* direction measured in radians *)
    energy : real;

        (* initialization routine *)
    procedure initialize (x, y : integer);

        (* basic methods *)
    procedure draw;
    procedure erase;
    procedure update;
    procedure hitBy (aBall : Ball);
    procedure setDirection (newDirection : real);
```

```
      (* return x, y coordinate center of ball *)
    function x : integer;
    function y : integer;
end;
```

In addition to the link and rectangle regions common to the other objects, a ball maintains two new data fields; a direction, measured in radians, and an energy, which is an arbitrary real value. Like a hole, a ball is initialized by arguments that specify the center of the ball. Initially a ball has no energy and a direction of zero.

```
procedure Ball.initialize (x, y : integer);
begin
    SetRect (region, x - 5, y - 5, x + 5, y + 5);
    setDirection (0.0);
    energy := 0.0;
end;
```

```
procedure Ball.setDirection (newDirection : real);
begin
    direction := newDirection;
end;
```

A ball is drawn either as a frame or as a solid circle, depending upon whether or not it represents the cue ball.

```
procedure Ball.draw;
begin
    if self = CueBall then
            (* draw an open circle *)
        FrameOval (region)
    else
            (* draw a filled circle *)
        PaintOval (region)
end;
```

```
procedure Ball.erase;
begin
    EraseRect (region);
end;
```

The method **update** is used to update the position of the ball. If the ball has a nontrivial amount of energy, it moves slightly, then checks to see if it has hit another object. A global variable named **ballMoved** is set true if any ball on the table has moved. If the ball has hit another object, it notifies the second object that it has been struck. This notification process is divided into three steps, corresponding to hitting holes, walls, and other balls. Inheritance, which we will study in Chapter 7, will provide a means by which these three tests can be combined into a single loop.

```
procedure Ball.update;
var
    hptr : Hole;
    wptr : Wall;
    bptr : Ball;
    dx, dy : integer;
    theIntersection : Rect;
begin
    if energy > 0.5 then begin
        ballMoved := true;
            (* erase ball *)
        erase;
            (* decrease energy *)
        energy := energy - 0.05;
            (* move ball *)
        dx := trunc(5.0 * cos(direction));
        dy := trunc(5.0 * sin(direction));
        offsetRect(region, dx, dy);
            (* redraw ball *)
        draw;
            (* see if we hit a hole *)
        hptr := listOfHoles;
        while (hptr <> nil) do
            if SectRect (region, hptr.region,
                theIntersection) then begin
                hptr.hitBy(self);
                hptr := nil;
            end
            else
                hptr := hptr.link;

            (* see if we hit a wall *)
        wptr := listOfWalls;
        while (wptr <> nil) do
            if SectRect (region, wptr.region,
                theIntersection) then begin
                wptr.hitBy(self);
                wptr := nil;
            end
```

```
            else
                wptr := wptr.link;

            (* see if we hit a ball *)
        bptr := listOfBalls;
        bhit := nil;
        while (bptr <> nil) do
            if (bptr <> self) and
                SectRect (region, bptr.region,
                theIntersection) then begin
                bptr.hitBy(self);
                bptr := nil;
            end
            else
                bptr := bptr.link;
    end;
end;
```

When one ball strikes another ball, the energy of the first one is split and half is given to the second one. The angles of both are also changed.

```
procedure Ball.hitBy (aBall : Ball);
var
    da : real;
begin
        (* cut the energy of the hitting ball in half *)
    aBall.energy := aBall.energy / 2;

        (* and add it to our own *)
    energy := energy + aBall.energy;

        (* set our new direction *)
    setDirection(hitAngle(self.x - aBall.x, self.y - aBall.y));

        (* and set the hitting balls direction *)
    da := aBall.direction - direction;
    aBall.setDirection (aBall.direction + da);
end;

function hitAngle (dx, dy : real) : real;
    const
        PI = 3.14159;
    var
        na : real;
begin
```

```
    if (abs(dx) < 0.05) then
        na := PI / 2
    else
        na := arctan (abs(dy / dx));
    if (dx < 0) then
        na := PI - na;
    if (dy < 0) then
        na := - na;
    hitAngle := na;
end;
```

6.3   The Main Program

The previous section described the static characteristics of the program. The dynamic characteristics are set in motion when a mouse press occurs, at which time the following function is invoked:

```
procedure mouseButtonDown (x, y : integer);
var
    bptr : Ball;
begin
        (* give the cue ball some energy *)
    CueBall.energy := 20.0;
        (* and a direction *)
    CueBall.setDirection(hitAngle (cueBall.x - x, cueBall.y - y));
        (* then update as long as any ball moves *)
    ballMoved := true;
    while ballMoved do begin
        ballMoved := false;
        bptr := listOfBalls;
        while bptr <> nil do begin
            bptr.update;
            bptr := bptr.link;
        end;
    end;
end;
```

The remainder of the program is relatively straight forward and will not be presented here. The complete source is given in Appendix B. The majority of the code is concerned with the initialization of the new objects and with the event loop that waits for the user to perform an action.

To stress the point we made at the beginning of this chapter, the most important feature of this case study is the fashion in which control has been decentralized and the objects themselves have been given the power to control and direct the flow of execution. When a mouse press occurs, all that happens is that the cue ball is provided with a certain amount of energy. Thereafter, the interaction of the balls drives the simulation.

6.4   Using Inheritance

In Chapter 1 we informally introduced inheritance, and in Chapter 7 we will discuss how inheritance works in each of the languages we are considering. In this section we will describe how inheritance can be used to simplify the billiards simulation. The reader may wish to return to this section after reading the general treatment of inheritance in the next chapter.

The first step in using inheritance in our billiards simulation is to define a general class for "graphical objects." This class includes all three items: balls, walls, and holes. The parent class is defined as follows:

```
GraphicalObject = object
        (* data fields *)
    link : GraphicalObject;
    region : Rect;

        (* initialization function *)
    procedure setRegion (left, top,  right, bottom : integer);

        (* operations that graphical objects perform *)
    procedure draw;
    procedure erase;
    procedure update;
    function intersect (anObj : GraphicalObject) :  boolean;
    procedure hitBy (anObj : GraphicalObject);
end;
```

The setRegion initialization function simply sets up the region for the object. The draw and update functions do nothing, as the actual behavior they exhibit is provided by child classes. The erase routine erases the region of the object. The intersect routine returns true if the argument object intersects with the receiver. Lastly, the hitBy routine is also overridden by child classes. Although only balls will move, and thus the argument to this function is always a ball, the fact that the class Ball has not yet been defined means we must declare the argument as the more general type GraphicalObject.

```
procedure GraphicalObject.setRegion
    (left, top, right, bottom : integer);
```

```
begin
    SetRect (region, left, top, right, bottom);
end;

procedure GraphicalObject.draw;
begin (* redefined in child classes *)
end;

procedure GraphicalObject.erase;
begin
    EraseRect (region);
end;

procedure GraphicalObject.update;
begin      (* redefined in child classes *)
end;

procedure GraphicalObject.hitBy (anObject : GraphicalObject);
begin      (* redefined in child classes *)
end;

function GraphicalObject.intersect
    (anObject : GraphicalObject) : boolean;
var
    theIntersection : Rect;
begin
    intersect := SectRect
        (region, anObject.region, theIntersection);
end;
```

The classes Ball, Wall, and Hole are then declared as subclasses of the general class GraphicalObject and need not repeat the declarations for data areas or functions, unless they are being overridden.

```
Hole = object (GraphicalObject)
        (* initialize location of hole *)
    procedure initialize (x, y : integer);
        (* draw the hole *)
    procedure draw; override;
        (* notify hole that it has received a ball *)
    procedure hitBy (anObject : GraphicalObject); override;
end;
```

The procedure hitBy must use a cast to convert the argument into the type Ball. It is prudent to test the type of the argument before issuing the cast.

```
procedure Wall.hitBy (anObj : GraphicalObject)
var
    aBall : Ball;
begin
    if Member(anObj, Ball) then begin
        aBall := Ball(anObj);
        aBall.setDirection(convertFactor - aBall.direction);
    end;
end;
```

By making CueBall a subclass of Ball, we can eliminate the conditional statement in the routine that draws the ball's image.

```
CueBall = object (Ball)
    procedure draw; override;
end;
```

```
procedure Ball.draw;
begin
        (* draw a filled circle *)
    PaintOval (region);
end;
```

```
procedure CueBall.draw;
begin
        (* draw an open circle *)
    FrameOval (region);
end;
```

The greatest simplification comes from the fact that it is now possible to keep all graphical objects on a single linked list. Thus, the routine that draws the entire screen, for example, can be written as follows:

```
procedure drawBoard;
var
    gptr : GraphicalObject;
begin
    SetPort (theWindow);
    gptr := listOfObjects;
    while gptr <> nil do begin
        gptr.draw;
        gptr := gptr.link;
    end;
end;
```

The most important point in this code concerns the invocation of the function draw within the loop. Despite the fact that there is only one function call written here, sometimes the function invoked will be from class Ball; at other times it will be from class Wall, or class Hole. The fact that one function call might result in many different function bodies being invoked is a form of *polymorphism*. We will discuss this important topic in more detail in Chapter 14.

The routine that tests to see if a moving ball has hit anything in the function Ball.update is similarly simplified. This can be seen in the complete source listing provided in Appendix B.

Exercises

1. Suppose you want to perform a certain action every time the billiards program executes the event loop task. Where is the best place to insert this code?

2. Suppose you want to make the balls colored. What portions of the program do you need to change?

3. Suppose you want to add pockets on the side walls, as on a conventional pool table. What portions of the program do you need to change?

4. The billiards program uses a "breadth-first" technique, cycling repeatedly over the list of balls, moving each a little as long as any ball has energy. An alternative, and in some ways more object-oriented, approach is to have each ball continue to update itself as long as it possesses any energy, and update any ball that it hits. With this technique, it is only necessary to start the cue ball moving in order to put the simulation in motion. Revise the program to use this approach. Which do you think provides a more realistic simulation? Why?

Chapter 7

Inheritance

The first step in learning object-oriented programming is understanding the basic philosophy of organizing the performance of a task as the interaction of loosely coupled software components. This organizational approach was the central lesson in the case studies of Chapters 5 and 6.

The *next* step in learning object-oriented programming is organizing classes into a hierarchical structure based on the concept of inheritance. By *inheritance*, we mean the property that instances of a child class (or subclass) can access both data and behavior (methods) associated with a parent class (or superclass).

7.1 An Intuitive Description of Inheritance

Let us return to Flo the florist from the first chapter. There is a certain behavior we expect florists to perform, not because they are florists but simply because they are shopkeepers. For example, we expect Flo to request money for the transaction and in turn give us a receipt. These activities are not unique to florists, but are common to bakers, grocers, stationers, car dealers, and other merchants. It is as though we have associated certain behavior with the general category Shopkeeper, and as Florists are a specialized form of shopkeepers, the behavior is automatically identified with the subclass.

In programming languages, inheritance means that the behavior and data associated with child classes are always an *extension* (that is, a larger set) of the properties associated with parent classes. A subclass must have all the properties of the parent class, and other properties as well. On the other hand, since a child class is a more specialized (or restricted) form of the parent class, it is also, in a certain sense, a *contraction* of the parent type. This tension between inheritance as expansion and inheritance as contraction is a source for much of the power inherent in the technique, but at the same time it causes much confusion as to its proper employment. We will see this when we examine a few of the uses of inheritance in a subsequent section.

Inheritance is always transitive, so that a class can inherit features from superclasses many levels away. That is, if class Dog is a subclass of class Mammal, and class Mammal is a subclass of class Animal, then Dog will inherit attributes both from Mammal and from Animal.

A complicating factor in our intuitive description of inheritance is the fact that subclasses can *override* behavior inherited from parent classes. For example, the class Platypus overrides the reproduction behavior inherited from class Mammal, since platyupuses lay eggs. We will briefly mention the mechanics of overriding in this chapter, then return to a more detailed discussion of the semantics of overriding in Chapter 11.

7.2   Subclass, Subtype, and Substitutability

Consider the relationship of the data type associated with a parent class to the data type associated with a derived, or child, class. The following argument can be made:

- Instances of the subclass must possess all data areas associated with the parent class.

- Instances of the subclass must implement, through inheritance at least (if not explicitly overridden) all functionality defined for the parent class. (They can also define new functionality, but that is unimportant for the present argument).

- Thus, an instance of a child class can mimic the behavior of the parent class and should be *indistinguishable* from an instance of the parent class if substituted in a similar situation.

We will see later in this chapter, when we examine the various ways in which inheritance can be used, that this is not always a valid argument. Nevertheless, it is a good description of our idealized view of inheritance. We will therefore formalize this ideal in what is called the *principle of substitutability*.

The principle of substitutability says that if we have two classes, A and B, such that class B is a subclass of class A (perhaps several times removed), it should be possible to substitute instances of class B for instances of class A in *any situation* with *no observable effect*.

As we will see in Chapter 10, the term *subtype* often refers to a subclass relationship in which the principle of substitutability is maintained, to distinguish such forms from the general *subclass* relationship, which may or may not satisfy this principle.

We saw a use of the principle of substitutability in Chapter 6. Section 6.4 described the following procedure:

```
procedure drawBoard;
var
    gptr : GraphicalObject;
begin
    SetPort (theWindow);
        (* draw each graphical object *)
    gptr := listOfObjects;
    while gptr <> nil do begin
        gptr.draw;
        gptr := gptr.link;
    end;
end;
```

The global variable listOfObjects maintains a list of graphical objects, which can be any of three types. The variable gptr is declared to be simply a graphical object, yet during the course of executing the loop it takes on values that are, in fact, derived from each of the subclasses. Sometimes gptr holds a ball, sometimes a hole, and sometimes a wall. In each case, when the draw function is invoked, the correct method for the current value of gptr will be executed–not the method in the declared class GraphicalObject. For this code to operate correctly it is imperative that the functionality of each of these subclasses match the expected functionality specified by the parent class; that is, the subclasses must also be subtypes.

7.2.1 Subtypes and Strong Typing

Statically typed languages (such as C++ and Object Pascal) place much more emphasis on the principle of substitutability than do dynamically typed languages (such as Smalltalk and Objective-C). The reason for this is that statically typed languages tend to characterize objects by their class, whereas dynamically typed languages tend to characterize objects by their behavior. For example, a polymorphic function (a function that can take objects of various classes) in a statically typed language can ensure a certain level of functionality only by insisting that all arguments be subclasses of a given class. Since in a dynamically typed language arguments are not typed at all, the same requirement would be simply that an argument must be able to respond to a certain set of messages. We will discuss static and dynamic typing more in Chapter 10, and polymorphism in more detail in Chapter 14.

7.3 Forms of Inheritance

Inheritance is used in a surprising variety of ways. In this section we will describe a few of its more common uses. Note that the following list represents general abstract categories and is not intended to be exhaustive. Furthermore, it sometime happens that two or more descriptions are be applicable to a single situation, because some methods in a single class use inheritance in one way while others use it in another.

In the following list,[1] pay careful attention to which uses of inheritance support the subtyping relationship and which do not.

7.3.1   Subclassing for Specialization (Subtyping)

Probably the most common use of inheritance and subclassing is for specialization. In subclassing for specialization, the new class is a specialized form of the parent class but satisfies the specifications of the parent in all relevant respects. Thus, in this form the principle of substitutability is explicitly upheld. Along with the following category (subclassing for specification) this is the most ideal form of inheritance, and something that a good design should strive for.

Here is an example of subclassing for specialization. A class Window provides general windowing operations (moving, resizing, iconification, and so on). A specialized subclass TextEditWindow inherits the window operations and *in addition*, provides facilities that allow the window to display textual material and the user to edit the text values. Because the text edit window satisfies all the properties we expect of a window in general (thus, a TextEditWindow window is a subtype of Window in addition to being a subclass), we recognize this situation as an example of subclassing for specialization.

7.3.2   Subclassing for Specification

Another frequent use for inheritance is to guarantee that classes maintain a certain common interface–that is, they implement the same methods. The parent class can be a combination of implemented operations and operations that are deferred to the child classes. Often, there is no interface change of any sort between the parent class and the child class–the child merely implements behavior described, but not implemented, in the parent.

This is actually a special case of subclassing for specialization, except that the subclasses are not refinements of an existing type but rather realizations of an incomplete abstract specification. In such cases the parent class is sometimes known as an *abstract specification class*.

In the billards simulation example presented in the Chapter 6, the class GraphicalObject was an abstract class since it described, but did not implement, the methods for drawing the object and responding to a hit by a ball. The subsequent classes Ball, Wall, and Hole then used subclassing for specification when they provided meanings for these methods.

In general, subclassing for specification can be recognized when the parent class does not implement actual behavior but merely defines the behavior that will be implemented in child classes.

---

[1]The categories described here are adopted from [Halbert 1987], although I have added some new categories of my own. The editable-window example is from [Meyer 1988a].

7.3.3 Subclassing for Construction

A class can often inherit almost all of its desired functionality from a parent class perhaps changing only the names of the methods used to interface to the class, or modifying the arguments in a certain fashion. This may be true even if the new class and the parent class fail to share the *is-a* relationship.

For example, the Smalltalk class hierarchy implements a generalization of an array called Dictionary. A dictionary is a collection of key-value pairs, like an array, but the keys can be arbitrary values. A *symbol table*, such as might be used in a compiler, can be considered a dictionary indexed by symbol names in which the values have a fixed format (the symbol-table entry record). A class SymbolTable can therefore be made a subclass of the class Dictionary, with new methods defined that are specific to the use as a symbol table. Another example might be forming a *set* data abstraction on top of a base class which provides *list* methods. In both these cases, the child class is not a more specialized form of the parent class, because we would never think of substituting an instance of the child class in a situation where an instance of the parent class is being used.

A common use of subclassing for construction occurs when classes are created to write values to a binary file, for example, in a persistent storage system. A parent class may implement only the ability to write raw binary data. A subclass is constructed for every structure that is saved. The subclass implements a save procedure for the data type, which uses the behavior of the parent type to do the actual storage.[2]

```
class Storable {
    void writeByte(unsigned char);
    };

class StoreMyStruct : public Storable {
    void writeStruct (MyStruct & aStruct);
    };
```

Subclassing for construction tends to be frowned upon in statically typed languages, since it often directly breaks the principle of substitutability (forming subclasses that are not subtypes). On the other hand, because it is often a fast and easy route to developing new data abstractions, it is widely employed in dynamically typed languages. Many instances of subclassing for construction can be found in the Smalltalk standard library.

We will investigate an example of subclassing for construction in Chapter 8. We will also see that C++ provides an interesting mechanism, *private inheritance*, which permits subclassing for construction without breaking the principle of substitutability.

---

[2]This example illustrates the blurred lines between categories. If the child class implements the storage using a different method name, we say it is subclassing for construction. If, on the other hand, the child class uses the same name as the parent class, we might say the result is subclassing for specification.

7.3.4   Subclassing for Generalization

Using inheritance to subclass for generalization is, in a certain sense, the opposite of subclassing for specialization. Here, a subclass extends the behavior of the parent class to create a more general kind of object. Subclassing for generalization is often applicable when we build on a base of existing classes that we do not wish to modify, or cannot modify.

Consider a graphics display system in which a class Window has been defined for displaying on a simple black-and-white background. You could create a subtype ColoredWindow that lets the background color be something other than white by adding an additional field to store the color and overriding the inherited window display code that specifies the background be drawn in that color.

Subclassing for generalization frequently occurs when the overall design is based primarily on data values and only secondarily on behavior. This is shown in the colored window example, since a colored window contains data fields that are not necessary in the simple window case.

As a rule, subclassing for generalization should be avoided in favor of inverting the type hierarchy and using subclassing for specialization. However, this is not always possible.

7.3.5   Subclassing for Extension

While subclassing for generalization modifies or expands on the existing functionality of an object, subclassing for extension adds totally new abilities. Subclassing for extension can be distinguished from subclassing for generalization in that the latter must override at least one method from the parent and the functionality is tied to that of the parent. Extension simply adds new methods to those of the parent, and the functionality is less strongly tied to the existing methods of the parent.

An example of subclassing for extension is a StringSet class that inherits from a generic Set class but is specialized for holding string values. Such a class might provide additional methods for string-related operations–for example, "search by prefix," which returns a subset of all the elements of the set that begin with a certain string value. These operations are meaningful for the subclass, but are not particularly relevant to the parent class.

As the functionality of the parent remains available and untouched, subclassing for extension does not contravene the principle of substitutability and so such subclasses are always subtypes.

7.3.6   Subclassing for Limitation

Subclassing for limitation occurs when the behavior of the subclass is smaller or more restrictive than the behavior of the parent class. Like subclassing for generalization, subclassing for limitation occurs most frequently when a programmer is building on a base of existing classes that should not, or cannot, be modified.

For example, an existing class library provides a double-ended-queue, or *deque*, data structure. Elements can be added or removed from either end of the deque, but the programmer wishes to write a stack class, enforcing the property that elements can be added or removed from only one end of the stack.

In a manner similar to subclassing for construction, the programmer can make the Stack class a subclass of the existing Deque class, and can modify or override the undesired methods so that they produce an error message if used. These methods override existing methods and eliminate their functionality, which characterizes subclassing for limitation. (Overriding, by which a subclass changes the meaning of a method defined in a parent class, will be discussed in a subsequent chapter).

Because subclassing for limitation is an explicit contravention of the principle of substitutability, and because it builds subclasses that are not subtypes, it should be avoided whenever possible.

7.3.7 Subclassing for Variance

Subclassing for variance is employed when two or more classes have similar implementations but do not seem to possess any hierarchical relationships between the abstract concepts represented by the classes. The code necessary to control a mouse, for example, may be nearly identical to the code required to control a graphics tablet. Conceptually, however, there is no reason why class Mouse should be made a subclass of class Tablet, or the other way. One of the two classes is then arbitrarily selected to be the parent, with the common code being inherited by the other and device-specific code being overridden.

Usually, however, a better alternative is to factor out the common code into an abstract class, say PointingDevice, and to have both classes inherit from this common ancestor. As with subclassing for generalization, this choice may not be available if you are building on a base of existing classes.

7.3.8 Subclassing for Combination

A common situation is a subclass that represents a *combination* of features from two or more parent classes. A teaching assistant, for example, may have characteristics of both a teacher and a student, and can therefore logically behave as both. The ability of a class to inherit from two or more parent classes is known as *multiple inheritance*; it is sufficiently subtle and complex that we will devote an entire chapter to the concept.

7.3.9 Summary of the Forms of Inheritance

We can summarize the various forms of inheritance by the following table:

- **Specialization.** The child class is a special case of the parent class; in other words, the child class is a subtype of the parent class.

- **Specification.** The parent class defines behavior that is implemented in the child class but not in the parent class.

- **Construction.** The child class makes use of the behavior provided by the parent class, but is not a subtype of the parent class.

- **Generalization.** The child class modifies or overrides some of the methods of the parent class.

- **Extension.** The child class adds new functionality to the parent class, but does not change any inherited behavior.

- **Limitation.** The child class restricts the use of some of the behavior inherited from the parent class.

- **Variance.** The child class and parent class are variants of each other, and the class-subclass relationship is arbitrary.

- **Combination.** The child class inherits features from more than one parent class. This is multiple inheritance and will be the subject of a later chapter.

7.4   Inheritance in Various Languages

In the following sections we will describe in detail the syntax used to describe inheritance in each of the languages we are considering. Note the differences between the languages that require all classes to be subclasses of a common parent class (often named Object, as in Smalltalk and Objective-C) and those that permit a number of different independent class hierarchies.

The advantage of the single inheritance structure is that the functionality provided in the root of the tree, in class Object, is inherited by all objects. Thus, every object is guaranteed to possess a common minimal level of functionality. Its disadvantage is that it combines all classes into a tightly coupled unit.

By having several independent inheritance hierarchies, an application is not forced to carry a large library of classes, only a few of which may be used in any one program. Of course, that means there is no programmer-defined functionality that *all* objects are guaranteed to possess.

In part, the differing views of objects are one more distinction between languages that use dynamic typing and those that use static typing (a topic we will return to in Chapter 12). In dynamic languages, objects are characterized chiefly by the messages they understand. If two objects understand the same set of messages and react in similar ways, they are, for all practical purposes, indistinguishable regardless of the relationships of their respective classes. Under these circumstances, it is useful to have all objects inherit a large portion of their behavior from a common base class.

7.4.1 Inheritance in Object Pascal

In Apple Object Pascal, inheritance from a parent class is indicated by placement of the name of the parent class inside parentheses after the object keyword. For example, suppose we had decided to make the classes Ball, Wall, and Hole in our billiard simulation inherit from a common GraphicalObject class. We would have indicated this as shown in Figure 7.1

As illustrated by the figure, child classes can add both new data fields and new behavior. They can also override existing behavior by redefining methods, indicated by the keyword override, as in the draw method. The arguments to an overridden method must match in type and number the arguments for the parent class.

The Delphi version of Object Pascal differs in two important respects. First, as we saw in earlier chapters, the keyword class is used in place of the keyword object in the class definition, and classes must always inherit from another class. The class TObject is ultimately the root class for all objects. Second, in addition to the keyword override, the keyword virtual is appended to those methods in the parent class that are allowed to be overridden, much as in C++ (to be described shortly). An example illustrating these changes in shown in Figure 7.2. (Omitting the override is a common source of error, since the declaration is legal but the interpetation is incorrect. We will discuss this in more detail in Chapter 10.)

A more radical difference between Delphi Pascal and Apple Object Pascal is the introduction of dynamic methods. A dynamic method uses a different run-time lookup mechanism (closer to that used by Objective-C than by C++; see Chapter 21 for an explanation of these mechanisms). This makes dynamic methods slightly slower than virtual methods, but they also use less space. The keyword dynamic in place of virtual indicates that a dynamic method is being declared. Many of the methods associated with operating-system windows-related activity is implemented with dynamic methods. The term *message* is often restricted to mean only these windows-related actions.

7.4.2 Inheritance in Smalltalk

As we noted in Chapter 3, in Smalltalk inheritance is intrinsic to creating new classes. A new class cannot be defined without first specifying an existing class from which it will inherit. In fact, a new class is created through the sending of a *message* to the parent class from which the new class will inherit.

```
List subclass: #Set
     instanceVariables: #( )
     classVariables: #( )
```

There is a single ancestor class, named Object, from which all other classes ultimately descend. Class Object provides all objects with a consistent and common functionality. Examples of methods provided by this class are the ability to

```
type
    GraphicalObject = object
            (* data fields *)
        region : Rect;
        link : GraphicalObject;
            (* operations *)
        procedure draw;
        procedure update;
        procedure hitBy (aBall : Ball);
    end;

    Ball = object (GraphicalObject)
            (* data fields *)
        direction : real;
        energy : real;

            (* initialization *)
        procedure initialize (x, y : integer);

            (* overridden methods *)
        procedure draw; override;
        procedure update; override;
        procedure hitBy (aBall : Ball); override;

            (* ball-specific methods *)
        procedure erase;
        procedure setCenter (newx, newy : integer);
        function x : integer;
        function y :integer;
    end;
```

Figure 7.1 – An example of inheritance in Apple Object Pascal.

```
type
    GraphicalObject = class (TObject)
            (* data fields *)
        region : Rect;
        link : GraphicalObject;
            (* operations *)
        procedure draw; virtual;
        procedure update; virtual;
        procedure hitBy (aBall : Ball); virtual;
    end;

    Ball = class (GraphicalObject)
            (* data fields *)
        direction : real;
        energy : real;

            (* initialization *)
        procedure initialize (x, y : integer);

            (* overridden methods *)
        procedure draw; override;
        procedure update; override;
        procedure hitBy (aBall : Ball); override;

            (* ball-specific methods *)
        procedure erase;
        procedure setCenter (newx, newy : integer);
        function x : integer;
        function y :integer;
    end;
```

Figure 7.2 – An example of inheritance in Delphi Pascal.

compare one object against another, the ability to print a string representation of an object, and so on.

Only single inheritance is supported by Smalltalk. That is, each class inherits from only one parent class. A method can override a method from a parent class simply by being named the same.

7.4.3 Inheritance in Objective-C

As in Smalltalk, in Objective-C inheritance is an intrinsic part of forming a new class. The interface description of every new class must define the parent class from which the new class will inherit. The following indicates that class Card will inherit from class Object.

```
@interface Card : Object
{
  ...
}
...
@end
```

As in Smalltalk, there is a single ancestor class, Object, from which all other classes ultimately descend. Class Object provides all objects with a consistent and common functionality, and it is frequently used as a parent for new classes.

Only single inheritance is permitted. That is, a class cannot inherit from two or more parent classes. As in Smalltalk, a method having the same name as one found in a parent class overrides the inherited method.

7.4.4 Inheritance in C++

In C++, unlike in Smalltalk and Objective-C, a new class need not inherit from an existing class. Inheritance is indicated in the class heading by the keyword public followed by the name of the parent class. The following example, from a program similar to the one we will examine in Chapter 8, illustrates this syntax. Here the new class, TablePile, inherits from the more general class, CardPile, which represents an abstraction for a pile of cards.

```
    class TablePile : public CardPile {
      ...
    };
```

The keyword public can be replaced by the keyword private to indicate subclassing for construction; that is, a form of inheritance that does not create a subtype relationship. We will see an example of this in Chapter 11.

As we noted in an earlier chapter, an advantage of object-oriented languages is that they tend to join the creation of a new value to the initialization for the value. Inheritance complicates this process somewhat, since both the parent class and a new class may have initialization code to perform. To allow this, the constructor in the child class must explicitly invoke the constructor in the parent class; it does so using an initialization clause in the constructor for the child class, as in the following:

```
TablePile::TablePile(int x, int y, int c)
    : CardPile(x, y) // initialize parent
{
    // then initialize child class
    ...
}
```

C++ supports multiple inheritance; that is, a new child class can be specified as inheriting from two or more parent classes. We will investigate the implications of this in more detail in a later chapter.

In an earlier chapter we introduced the keywords **private** and **public**, indicating that one describes the interface for the class an the other describes implementation details. A third keyword, **protected**, can be used with classes formed by inheritance. Protected fields are part of the implementation, but are accessible to subclasses as well as to the implementation of the class itself.

When the keyword **virtual** is used preceding the description of a member function, it indicates that the member function is likely to be overridden in a subclass, or is in fact overriding a similarly function in the parent class. (The keyword is optional in the child class, but it is good practice to retain it). However, the semantics of overriding in C++ are subtle and depend upon how the receiver has been declared. We will postpone a discussion of this point until Chapter 11.

7.4.5   Inheritance in Java

Of all the languages we are considering in this book, Java goes the farthest in separating the concepts of subclass and subtype. Subclasses are declared using the keyword **extends**, as in the following example:

```
class window {
    // ...
    };

class textEditWindow extends window {
    // ...
    };
```

Subclasses are assumed to be subtypes (although, as with C++, this assumption is not always valid). This means that an instance of a subclass can be assigned to a variable declared as the parent class type. Methods in the child class that have the same name as those in the parent class override the inherited behavior. As in C++, the keyword protected can be used to designate methods and data fields that are accessible only within the class or within subclasses but are not part of the more general interface.

All classes are derived from a single root class, Object. If no parent class is explicitly provided, the class Object is assumed. Thus, the class declaration for window shown above is the same as the following:

```
class window extends Object {
    // ...
    };
```

An alternative form of subtyping involves an *interface*. An interface defines the protocol for certain behavior but no implementation. In this respect it is similar to an abstract parent class. The following is an example interface, describing objects that can read from and write to an input/output stream.

```
public interface Storing {
    void writeOut(Stream s);
    void readFrom(Stream s);
    };
```

An interface defines a new type. This means that variables can be declared simply by the interface name. A class can then indicate that it implements the protocol defined by an interface. Instances of the class can be assigned to variables declared as the interface type, just as instances of a child class can be assigned to variables declared as the parent class type.

```
public class BitImage implements Storing {
    void writeOut (Stream s) {
        // ...
        };
    void readFrom (Stream s) {
        // ...
        }:
    };
```

Although Java only supports single inheritance (inheritance from only one parent class), a class can indicate that it supports multiple interfaces. Many problems for which multiple inheritance might be used in C++ can be solved in Java by the use of multiple interfaces. Interfaces are allowed to extend other interfaces and are even permitted to extend multiple interfaces.

The idea of subclassing for specification is formalized in Java through the abstract modifier. If a class is declared as abstract, it must be subclassed. It is not permitted to create an instance of an abstract class, only subclasses.

Methods as well can be declared to be abstract and, if so, need not have an implementation. Thus, defining a class as abstract ensures that it will be used only as a specification of behavior, not an implementation.

```
abstract class storable {

    public abstract writeOut();

}
```

An alternative modifier, final, indicates that the class (or method) cannot be subclassed or modified. Thus, the user is guaranteed that the behavior of the class will be as defined and not modified by a later subclass.

```
final class newClass extends oldClass {
    ...
    }
```

7.5 The Benefits of Inheritance

In this section we will describe some of the many important benefits of the proper use of inheritance.

7.5.1 Software Reusability

When behavior is inherited from another class, the code that provides that behavior does not have to be rewritten. This may seem obvious, but the implications are important. Many programmers spend much of their time rewriting code they have written many times before–for example, to search for a pattern in a string or to insert a new element into a table. With object-oriented techniques, these functions can be written once and reused.

Other benefits of reusable code include increased reliability (the more situations in which code is used, the greater the opportunities for discovering errors) and the decreased maintenance cost because of sharing by all users of the code.

7.5.2 Code Sharing

Code sharing can occur on several levels with object-oriented techniques. On one level, many users or projects can use the same classes. (Brad Cox [Cox 1986] calls these software-ICs, in analogy to the integrated circuits used in hardware design). Another form of sharing occurs when two or more classes developed by a single programmer as part of a project inherit from a single parent class. For example, a Set and an Array may both be considered a form of Collection. When this happens, two or more types of objects will share the code that they inherit.

This code needs to be written only once and will contribute only once to the size of the resulting program.

7.5.3   Consistency of Interface

When two or more classes inherit from the same superclass, we are assured that the behavior they inherit will be the same in all cases. Thus, it is easier to guarantee that interfaces to similar objects are in fact similar, and that the user is not presented with a confusing collection of objects that are almost the same but behave, and are interacted with, very differently.

7.5.4   Software Components

In Chapter 1, we noted that inheritance provides programmers with the ability to construct reusable software components. The goal is to permit the development of new and novel applications that nevertheless require little or no actual coding. Already, several such libraries are commercially available, and we can expect many more specialized systems to appear in time.

7.5.5   Rapid Prototyping

When a software system is constructed largely out of reusable components, development time can be concentrated on understanding the new and unusual portion of the system. Thus, software systems can be generated more quickly and easily, leading to a style of programming known as *rapid prototyping* or *exploratory programming*. A prototype system is developed, users experiment with it, a second system is produced that is based on experience with the first, further experimentation takes place, and so on for several iterations. Such programming is particularly useful in situations where the goals and requirements of the system are only vaguely understood when the project begins.

7.5.6   Polymorphism and Frameworks

Software produced conventionally is generally written from the bottom up, although it may be *designed* from the top down. That is, the lower-level routines are written, and on top of these slightly higher abstractions are produced, and on top of these even more abstract elements are generated. This process is like building a wall, where every brick must be laid on top of an already laid brick.

Normally, code portability decreases as one moves up the levels of abstraction. That is, the lowest-level routines may be used in several different projects, and perhaps even the next level of abstraction may be reused, but the higher-level routines are intimately tied to a particular application. The lower-level pieces can be carried to a new system and generally make sense standing on their own; the higher-level components generally make sense (because of declarations or data dependencies) only when they are built on top of specific lower-level units.

Polymorphism in programming languages permits the programmer to generate high-level reusable components that can be tailored to fit different applications by changes in their low-level parts. We will have much more to say about this topic in subsequent chapters.

7.5.7 Information Hiding

A programmer who reuses a software component needs only to understand the nature of the component and its interface. It is not necessary for the programmer to have detailed information concerning matters such as the techniques used to implement the component. Thus, the interconnectedness between software systems is reduced. We earlier identified the interconnected nature of conventional software as being one of the principle causes of software complexity.

7.6 The Costs of Inheritance

Although the benefits of inheritance in object-oriented programming are great, almost nothing is without cost of one sort or another. For this reason, we must consider the cost of object-oriented programming techniques, and in particular the cost of inheritance.

7.6.1 Execution Speed

It is seldom possible for general-purpose software tools to be as fast as carefully hand-crafted systems. Thus, inherited methods, which must deal with arbitrary subclasses, are often slower than specialized code.

Yet, concern about efficiency is often misplaced.[3] First, the difference is often small. Second, the reduction in execution speed may be balanced by an increase in the speed of software development. Finally, most programmers actually have little idea of how execution time is being used in their programs. It is far better to develop a working system, monitor it to discover where execution time is being used, and improve those sections, than to spend an inordinate amount of time worrying about efficiency early in a project.

7.6.2 Program Size

The use of any software library frequently imposes a size penalty not imposed by systems constructed for a specific project. Although this expense may be substantial, as memory costs decrease the size of programs becomes less important. Containing development costs and producing high-quality and error-free code rapidly are now more important than limiting the size of programs.

---

[3]The following quote from an article by Bill Wulf offers some apt remarks on the importance of efficiency: "More computing sins are committed in the name of efficiency (without necessarily achieving it) than for any other single reason—including blind stupidity" [Wulf 1972].

7.6.3 Message-Passing Overhead

Much has been made of the fact that message passing is by nature a more costly operation than simple procedure invocation. As with overall execution speed, however, overconcern about the cost of message passing is frequently penny-wise and pound-foolish. For one thing, the increased cost is often marginal–perhaps two or three additional assembly-language instructions and a total time penalty of 10 percent. (Timing figures vary from language to language. The overhead of message passing will be much higher in dynamically bound languages, such as Smalltalk, and much lower in statically bound languages, such as C++.) This increased cost, like others, must be weighed against the many benefits of the object-oriented technique.

A few languages, notably C++, make a number of options available to the programmer that can reduce the message-passing overhead. These include eliminating the polymorphism from message passing (qualifying invocations of member functions by a class name, in C++ terms) and expanding inline procedures. Similarly, the Delphi Pascal programmer can choose **dynamic** methods, which use a run-time lookup mechanism, or **virtual** methods, which use a slightly faster technique. Dynamic methods are inheritantly slower, but require less space.

7.6.4 Program Complexity

Although object-oriented programming is often touted as a solution to software complexity, in fact, overuse of inheritance can often simply replace one form of complexity with another. Understanding the control flow of a program that uses inheritance may require several multiple scans up and down the inheritance graph. This is what is known as the *yo-yo* problem, which we will discuss in more detail in a later chapter.

Exercises

1. Suppose you were required to program a project in a non-object oriented language, such as Pascal or C. How would you simulate the notion of classes and methods? How would you simulate inheritance? Could you support multiple inheritance? Explain your answer.

2. We noted that the execution overhead associated with message passing is typically greater than the overhead associated with a conventional procedure call. How might you measure these overheads? For a language that supports both classes and procedures (such as C++ or Object Pascal), devise an experiment to determine the actual performance penalty of message passing.

3. Consider the three geometric concepts of a line (infinite in both directions), a ray (fixed at a point, infinite in one direction), and a segment (a portion

of a line with fixed end points). How might you structure classes representing these three concepts in an inheritance hierarchy? Would your answer differ if you concentrated more on the data representation or more on the behavior? Characterize the type of inheritance you would use. Explain the reasoning behind your design.

4. Why is the example used in the following explanation not a valid illustration of inheritance?

> Perhaps the most powerful concept in object-oriented programming systems is inheritance. Objects can be created by inheriting the properties of other objects, thus removing the need to write any code whatsoever! Suppose, for example, a program is to process complex numbers consisting of real and imaginary parts. In a complex number, the real and imaginary parts behave like real numbers, so all of the operations (+, -, /, *, sqrt, sin, cos, etc.) can be inherited from the class of objects call REAL, instead of having to be written in code. This has a major impact on programmer productivity.

Chapter 8

A Case Study: Solitaire

A program for playing the card game *solitaire* will illustrate the utility and power of inheritance and overriding. In Chapters 3 and 4 we examined portions of this program, specifically the abstraction of the playing card represented by the class Card. The language for this case study will be Java.

Our major emphasis will be on the class CardPile, which represents the abstract notion of a pile of playing cards. Since moving cards from one pile to another is the major component of solitaire, the subclasses of class CardPile are the major data structures used in implementing the solitaire program. There are a variety of card piles, and inheritance and overriding are used extensively to simplify the development of these components and ensure that they can all be manipulated in a similar fashion.

8.1   The Class Card

In earlier chapters we discussed the abstraction represented by the class Card. Here, we reiterate some of the important points about this class.

Each instance of Card (Figure 8.1) maintains a suit and rank value. To prevent modification of these values, the instance variables maintaining them are declared **private** and access is mediated through *accessor functions*.

The value of the suit and rank fields are set by the *constructor* for the class. In addition, a separate function permits the user to determine the color of the card. Integer constant values (in Java defined by the use of **final static** constants) are defined for the colors red and black as well as for the suits. Another pair of integer constants represent the height and width of a card.

There are important reasons that data values representing suit and rank should be returned through an accessor function rather than users of the Card abstraction having direct access to the data field. One of the most important is that it ensures that the rank and suit fields can be read but not modified. (The corresponding function used primarily to modify the value of a data field is often termed a *mutator*.)

```
class Card {
        // constructor
    Card (int sv, int rv) { s = sv; r = rv; faceup = false; }

        // access attributes of card
    public int          rank ()        { return r; }

    public int           suit()        { return s; }

    public boolean      faceUp()      { return faceup; }

    public void         flip()        { faceup = ! faceup; }

    public int          color()
        {
        if (suit() == heart || suit() == diamond)
            return red;
        return black;
        }

    public void         draw (Graphics g, int x, int y) { ... }

        // static data fields for colors and suits
    final static int width = 50;
    final static int height = 70;
    final static int red = 0;
    final static int black = 1;
    final static int heart = 0;
    final static int spade = 1;
    final static int diamond = 2;
    final static int club = 3;

        // data fields
    private boolean faceup;
    private int r;
    private int s;
}
```

Figure 8.1 – Description of the class card.

The only other actions a card can perform, besides setting and returning the state of the card, are to flip over and to display itself. The function flip() is a one-line function that simply reverses the value held by a instance variable. The drawing function is more complex, making use of the drawing facilities provided by the Java standard application library. The application library provides a data type called **Graphics** that provides a variety of methods for drawing lines and common shapes, as well as for coloring. An argument of this type is passed to the **draw** function, as are the integer coordinates representing the upper left corner of the card.

The card images are simple line drawings, as shown below. Diamonds and hearts are drawn in red, spades and clubs in black. The hash marks on the back are drawn in yellow. A portion of the procedure for drawing a playing card is shown in Figure 8.2.

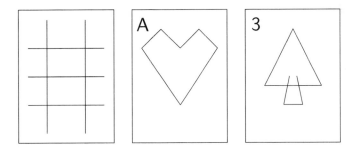

The most important feature of the playing-card abstraction is the manner in which each card is responsible for maintaining within itself all card-related information and behaviors. The card knows both its value and how to draw itself. In this manner the information is encapsulated and isolated from the application using the playing card. If, for example, one were to move the program to a new platform using different graphics facilities, only the **draw** method within the class itself would need to be altered.

8.2 Linked Lists

The container a card pile uses to hold the card values is a *linked list*. By separating the container class from the card, and from the card pile, we allow each class to be concerned with a limited set of issues.

This is an improvement over the case study presented in Chapter 6 in which, you will recall, each graphical object maintained a link field to the next graphical object. The simple design of Chapter 6 is problematic on a number of grounds. Not only is this link field not particularly important to the object held in the container, but such a design prevents an object from appearing in two or more lists. By creating separate classes for the linked-list abstraction, we permit much more flexibility in the use of containers.

```
class Card {
    ...
    public void        draw (Graphics g, int x, int y) {
        String names[] = {"A", "2", "3", "4", "5", "6",
                "7", "8", "9", "10", "J", "Q", "K"};
            // clear rectangle, draw border
        g.clearRect(x, y, width, height);
        g.setColor(Color.black);
        g.drawRect(x, y, width, height);
            // draw body of card
        if (faceUp()) {
            if (color() == red) g.setColor(Color.red);
            else g.setColor(Color.blue);
            g.drawString(names[rank()], x+3, y+15);
            if (suit() == heart) {
                g.drawLine(x+25, y+30, x+35, y+20);
                g.drawLine(x+35, y+20, x+45, y+30);
                g.drawLine(x+45, y+30, x+25, y+60);
                g.drawLine(x+25, y+60, x+5, y+30);
                g.drawLine(x+5, y+30, x+15, y+20);
                g.drawLine(x+15, y+20, x+25, y+30);
                }
            else if (suit() == spade) { ... }
            else if (suit() == diamond) { ... }
            else if (suit() == club) {
                g.drawOval(x+20, y+25, 10, 10);
                g.drawOval(x+25, y+35, 10, 10);
                g.drawOval(x+15, y+35, 10, 10);
                g.drawLine(x+23, y+45, x+20, y+55);
                g.drawLine(x+20, y+55, x+30, y+55);
                g.drawLine(x+30, y+55, x+27, y+45);
                }
            }
        else { // face down
            g.setColor(Color.yellow);
            g.drawLine(x+15, y+5, x+15, y+65);
            g.drawLine(x+35, y+5, x+35, y+65);
            g.drawLine(x+5, y+20, x+45, y+20);
            g.drawLine(x+5, y+35, x+45, y+35);
            g.drawLine(x+5, y+50, x+45, y+50);
            }
        }
}
```

Figure 8.2 – Procedure to draw a playing card.

```
class Link {
    public Link (Object newValue, Link next)
        { valueField = newValue; nextLink = next; }

    public Object value ()
        { return valueField; }

    public Link next ()
        { return nextLink; }

    private Object valueField;
    private Link nextLink;
}

class LinkedList {
    public LinkedList () { firstLink = null; }

    public void add (Object newValue)
        { firstLink = new Link(newValue, firstLink); }

    public boolean empty ()
        { return firstLink == null; }

    public Object front ()
        {   if (firstLink == null)
               return null;
          return firstLink.value(); }

    public void pop ()
        { if (firstLink != null)
             firstLink = firstLink.next(); }

    public ListIterator iterator ()
        { return new ListIterator (firstLink); }

    private Link firstLink;
}
```

Figure 8.3 – The classes Link and LinkedList.

```
class ListIterator {
    public ListIterator (Link firstLink)
        { currentLink = firstLink; }

    public boolean atEnd ()
        { return currentLink == null; }

    public void next ()
        { if (currentLink != null)
            currentLink = currentLink.next();}

    public Object current ()
        { if (currentLink == null)
            return null;
          return currentLink.value(); }

    private Link currentLink;
}
```

Figure 8.4 – The class ListIterator.

Two classes are used in the linked-list abstraction. LinkedList is the front of the list, the class with which users interact. Behind the scenes, the values are actually maintained by instances of a class Link. Normally users would not even be aware that the class Link even exists. Both these classes are shown in Figure 8.3.

Because the linked-list container is a general-purpose abstraction and does not know the type of object it will contain, the type associated with the elements is the root class type Object. A value declared as Object, such as the value field in the Link class, is *polymorphic*–it can hold any sort of value.

The LinkedList class provides operations for adding an element to a list, testing whether or not the list is empty, accessing the first element in the list, and removing the first element from the list.

More generally, we want a way for a user of the linked-list abstraction to loop over the values held by a list without removing them from the list and without requiring detailed information about the lists internal structure (that is, without needing to know about the class Link). As we will see in Chapter 16, such abilities are frequently provided by the designer of the list class making available a type of object termed an *iterator*. An iterator hides the details of the representation for the container and provides a simple interface for accessing the values one by one. An iterator for the linked list is shown in Figure 8.4. By use of an iterator, a loop can be written in the following fashion:

```
ListIterator itr = aList.iterator();
while (! itr.atEnd() ) {
    ... do something list itr.current() ...
    itr.next();
    }
```

Note how the list itself returns an iterator as the result of a member function and how the use of the iterator avoids any mention of the link fields of the list.

8.3 The Game

The version of solitaire we will describe is known as klondike. The countless variations on this game make it probably the most common version of solitaire; so much so that when you say "solitaire," most people think of klondike. The version we will use is that described in [Morehead 1949]; in the exercises we will explore some of the common variations.

The layout of the game is shown in Figure 8.5. A single standard pack of 52 cards is used. The *tableau*, or playing table, consists of 28 cards in 7 piles. the first pile has 1 card, the second 2, and so on up to 7. The top card of each pile is initially face up; all other cards are face down.

The suit piles (sometimes called *foundations*) are built up from aces to kings in suits. They are constructed above the tableau as the cards become available. The object of the game is to build all 52 cards into the suit piles.

The cards that are not part of the tableau are initially all in the *deck*. Cards in the deck are face down, and are drawn one by one from the deck and placed, face up, on the *discard pile*. From there, they can be moved onto either a tableau pile or a foundation. Cards are drawn from the deck until the pile is empty; at this point, the game is over if no further moves can be made.

Cards can be placed on a tableau pile only on a card of next-higher rank and opposite color. They can be placed on a foundation only if they are the same suit and next higher card or if the foundation is empty and the card is an ace. Spaces in the tableau that arise during play can be filled only by kings.

The topmost card of each tableau pile and the topmost card of the discard pile are always available for play. The only time more than one card is moved is when an entire collection of face-up cards from a tableau (called a *build*) is moved to another tableau pile. This can be done if the bottommost card of the build can be legally played on the topmost card of the destination. Our initial game will not support the transfer of a build, but we will discuss this as a possible extension. The topmost card of a tableau is always face up. If a card is moved from a tableau, leaving a face-down card on the top, the latter card can be turned face up.

From this short description, it is clear that the game of solitaire mostly involves manipulating piles of cards. Each type of pile has many features in common with the others and a few aspects unique to the particular type. In

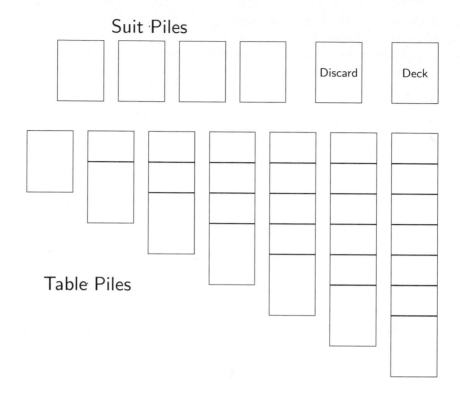

Figure 8.5 – Layout for the solitaire game.

the next section, we will investigate in detail how inheritance can be used in such circumstances to simplify the implementation of the various card piles by providing a common base for the generic actions and permitting this base to be redefined when necessary.

8.4   Card Piles–Inheritance in Action

Much of the behavior we associate with a card pile is common to each variety of pile in the game. For example, each pile maintains a linked list of the cards in the pile, and the operations of inserting and deleting elements from this linked list are common. Other operations are given default behavior in the class CardPile, but they are sometimes overridden in the various subclasses. The class CardPile is shown in Figure 8.6.

Each card pile maintains the coordinate location for the upper left corner of the pile, as well as a linked list containing the cards in the pile. All these values are set by the constructor for the class. The data fields are declared as

```
class CardPile {
    CardPile (int xl, int yl)
        { x = xl; y = yl; cardList = new LinkedList(); }

    public Card top() { return (Card) cardList.front(); }

    public boolean empty() { return cardList.empty(); }

    public Card pop() {
        Card result = (Card) cardList.front();
        cardList.pop();
        return result; }

        // the following are sometimes overridden

    public boolean includes (int tx, int ty) {
        return x <= tx && tx <= x + Card.width &&
            y <= ty && ty <= y + Card.height; }

    public void select (int tx, int ty) { }

    public void addCard (Card aCard) { cardList.add(aCard); }

    public void display (Graphics g) {
        g.setColor(Color.black);
        if (cardList.empty())
            g.drawRect(x, y, Card.width, Card.height);
        else
            top().draw(g, x, y); }

    public boolean canTake (Card aCard) { return false; }

        // coordinates of the card pile
    protected int x;
    protected int y;
    protected LinkedList cardList;
}
```

Figure 8.6 – Description of the class CardPile.

protected and thus accessible to member functions associated with this class and to member functions associated with subclasses.

The three functions top(), pop(), and empty() manipulate the list of cards, using functions provided by the LinkedList class. A new card is added to the list by addCard(Card), which is one of the functions modified by subclasses. Note that the linked-list member function front() returns an Object. This must be converted to a Card by the functions top() and pop().

The remaining five operations are common to the abstract notion of our card piles, but they differ in details in each case. For example, the function canTake(Card) asks whether it is legal to place a card on the given pile. A card can be added to a foundation pile, for instance, only if it is an ace and the foundation is empty, or if the card is of the same suit as the current topmost card in the pile and has the next-higher value. A card can be added to a tableau pile, on the other hand, only if the pile is empty and the card is a king, or if it is of the opposite color as the current topmost card in the pile and has the next lower value.

The actions of the five virtual functions defined in CardPile can be characterized as follows:

includes –Determines if the coordinates given as arguments are contained within the boundaries of the pile. The default action simply tests the topmost card; this is overridden in the tableau piles to test all card values.

canTake –Tells whether a pile can take a specific card. Only the tableau and suit piles can take cards, so the default action is simply to return no; this is overridden in the two classes mentioned.

addCard –Adds a card to the card list. It is redefined in the discard pile class to ensure that the card is face up.

display –Displays the card deck. The default method merely displays the topmost card of the pile, but is overridden in the tableau class to display a column of cards. The top half of each hidden card is displayed. So that the playing surface area is conserved, only the topmost and bottommost face-up cards are displayed (this permits us to give definite bounds to the playing surface).

select –Performs an action in response to a mouse click. It is invoked when the user selects a pile by clicking the mouse in the portion of the playing field covered by the pile. The default action does nothing, but is overridden by the table, deck, and discard piles to play the topmost card, if possible.

The following table illustrates the important benefits of inheritance. Given five operations and five classes, there are 25 potential methods we might have had to define. By making use of inheritance we need to implement only 13. Furthermore, we are guaranteed that each pile will respond in the same way to similar requests.

```
class SuitPile extends CardPile {

    SuitPile (int x, int y) { super(x, y); }

    public boolean canTake (Card aCard) {
        if (empty())
            return aCard.rank() == 0;
        Card topCard = top();
        return (aCard.suit() == topCard.suit()) &&
            (aCard.rank() == 1 + topCard.rank());
    }
}
```

Figure 8.7 – The class SuitPile.

	CardPile	SuitPile	DeckPile	DiscardPile	TableauPile
includes	×				×
canTake	×	×			×
addCard	×			×	
display	×				×
select	×		×	×	×

8.4.1   The Suit Piles

We will examine each of the subclasses of CardPile in detail, pointing out various uses of object-oriented features as they are encountered. The simplest subclass is the class SuitPile, shown in Figure 8.7, which represents the pile of cards at the top of the playing surface, the pile being built up in suit from ace to king.

The class SuitPile defines only two methods. The constructor for the class takes two integer arguments and does nothing more than invoke the constructor for the parent class CardPile. Note the use of the keyword super to indicate the parent class. The method canTake determines whether or not a card can be placed on the pile. A card is legal if the pile is empty and the card is an ace (that is, has rank zero) or if the card is the same suit as the topmost card in the pile and of the next higher rank (for example, a three of spades can only be played on a two of spades).

All other behavior of the suit pile is the same as that of our generic card pile. When selected, a suit pile does nothing. When a card is added it is simply inserted into the linked list. To display the pile only the topmost card is drawn.

8.4.2   The Deck Pile

The DeckPile (Figure 8.8) maintains the original deck of cards. It differs from the generic card pile in two ways. When constructed, rather than creating an empty pile of cards, it creates the complete deck of 52 cards, inserting them in random order into the linked list. Another member of the Java run-time library provides a random double-precision value between 0 and 1; this is converted into a random integer value during the course of shuffling the deck.

The method select is invoked when the mouse button is used to select the card deck. If the deck is empty, it does nothing. Otherwise, the topmost card is removed from the deck and added to the discard pile.

Java does not have global variables. Where a value is shared between multiple instances of similar classes, such as the various piles used in our solitaire game, an instance variable can be declared static. As we will see in Chapter 20, one copy of a static variable is created and shared between all instances. In our present program, static variables will be used to maintain all the various card piles. These will be held in an instance of class Solitaire, which we will subsequently describe. To access these values we use a complete qualified name, which includes the name of the class as well as the name of the variable. This is shown in the select method in Figure 8.8, which refers to the variable Solitare.discardPile to access the discard pile.

8.4.3   The Discard Pile

The class DiscardPile (Figure 8.9) is interesting in that it exhibits two very different forms of inheritance. The select method *overrides* or *replaces* the default behavior provided by class CardPile, replacing it with code that when invoked (when the mouse is pressed over the card pile) checks to see if the topmost card can be played on any suit pile or, alternatively, on any tableau pile. If the card cannot be played, it is kept in the discard pile.

The method addCard is a different sort of overriding. Here the behavior is a *refinement* of the default behavior in the parent class. That is, the behavior of the parent class is completely executed, and, in addition, new behavior is added. In this case, the new behavior ensures that when a card is placed on the discard pile it is always face up. After satisfying this condition, the code in the parent class is invoked to add the card to the pile by passing the message to the pseudo-variable named super.

Another form of refinement occurs in the constructors for the various subclasses. Each must invoke the constructor for the parent class to guarantee that the parent is properly initialized before the constructor performs its own actions. The parent constructor is invoked by the pseudo-variable super being used as a function inside the constructor for the child class. In Chapter 11 we will have much more to say about the distinction between replacement and refinement in overriding.

8.4.4   The Tableau Piles

The most complex of the subclasses of CardPile is that used to hold a tableau, or table pile. It is shown in Figures 8.10 and 8.11. Table piles differ from the generic card pile in the following ways:

```
class DeckPile extends CardPile {

    DeckPile (int x, int y) {
            // first initialize parent
        super(x, y);
            // then create the new deck
            // first put them into a local pile
        CardPile pileOne = new CardPile(0, 0);
        CardPile pileTwo = new CardPile(0, 0);
        int count = 0;
        for (int i = 0; i < 4; i++)
            for (int j = 0; j <= 12; j++) {
                pileOne.addCard(new Card(i, j));
                count++;
                }
            // then pull them out randomly
        for (; count > 0; count--) {
            int limit = ((int)(Math.random() * 1000)) % count;
                // move down to a random location
            for (int i = 0; i < limit; i++)
                pileTwo.addCard(pileOne.pop());
                // then add the card found there
            addCard(pileOne.pop());
                // then put the decks back together
            while (! pileTwo.empty())
                pileOne.addCard(pileTwo.pop());
            }
        }

    public void select(int tx, int ty) {
        if (empty())
            return;
        Solitare.discardPile.addCard(pop());
        }
}
```

Figure 8.8 – The class DeckPile.

```
class DiscardPile extends CardPile {

    DiscardPile (int x, int y) { super (x, y); }

    public void addCard (Card aCard) {
        if (! aCard.faceUp())
            aCard.flip();
        super.addCard(aCard);
        }

    public void select (int tx, int ty) {
        if (empty())
            return;
        Card topCard = pop();
        for (int i = 0; i < 4; i++)
            if (Solitare.suitPile[i].canTake(topCard)) {
                Solitare.suitPile[i].addCard(topCard);
                return;
                }
        for (int i = 0; i < 7; i++)
            if (Solitare.tableau[i].canTake(topCard)) {
                Solitare.tableau[i].addCard(topCard);
                return;
                }
        // nobody can use it, put it back on our list
        addCard(topCard);
        }
}
```

Figure 8.9 – The class DiscardPile.

- When initialized (by the constructor), the table pile removes a certain number of cards from the deck, placing them in its pile. The number of cards so removed is determined by an additional argument to the constructor. The topmost card of this pile is then displayed face up.

- A card can be added to the pile (method canTake) only if the pile is empty and the card is a king, or if the card is the opposite color from that of the current topmost card and one smaller in rank.

- When a mouse press is tested to determine if it covers this pile (method includes) only the left, right, and top bounds are checked; the bottom bound is not tested since the pile may be of variable length.

```
class TablePile extends CardPile {

    TablePile (int x, int y, int c) {
            // initialize the parent class
        super(x, y);
            // then initialize our pile of cards
        for (int i = 0; i < c; i++) {
            addCard(Solitare.deckPile.pop());
            }
            // flip topmost card face up
        top().flip();
        }

    public boolean canTake (Card aCard) {
        if (empty())
            return aCard.rank() == 12;
        Card topCard = top();
        return (aCard.color() != topCard.color()) &&
            (aCard.rank() == topCard.rank() - 1);
        }

    public boolean includes (int tx, int ty) {
            // don't test bottom of card
        return x <= tx && tx <= x + Card.width &&
            y <= ty;
        }

    private int stackDisplay(Graphics g, ListIterator itr) {
        int localy;
        if (itr.atEnd())
            return y;
        Card aCard = (Card) itr.current();
        itr.next();
        localy = stackDisplay(g, itr);
        aCard.draw(g, x, localy);
        return localy + 35;
        }

        ...
```

Figure 8.10 – The class TablePile, part 1.

```
class TablePile extends CardPile {
    ...

    public void select (int tx, int ty) {
        if (empty())
            return;

            // if face down, then flip
        Card topCard = top();
        if (! topCard.faceUp()) {
            topCard.flip();
            return;
            }

            // else see if any suit pile can take card
        topCard = pop();
        for (int i = 0; i < 4; i++)
            if (Solitare.suitPile[i].canTake(topCard)) {
                Solitare.suitPile[i].addCard(topCard);
                return;
                }
            // else see if any other table pile can take card
        for (int i = 0; i < 7; i++)
            if (Solitare.tableau[i].canTake(topCard)) {
                Solitare.tableau[i].addCard(topCard);
                return;
                }
            // else put it back on our pile
        addCard(topCard);
        }

    public void display (Graphics g)
        { stackDisplay(g, cardList.iterator()); }
}
```

Figure 8.11 – The class TablePile, part 2.

- When the pile is selected, the topmost card is flipped if it is face down. If it is face up, an attempt is made to move the card first to any available suit pile, and then to any available table pile. Only if no pile can take the card is it left in place.

- To display the pile, each card in the pile is drawn in turn, each moving down slightly. To do this from the bottom of the pile to the top a small private recursive routine traverses the linked list, printing the cards as control returns from the recursive call. This function uses an iterator to cycle through the elements of the list.

8.5 Playing the Polymorphic Game

As we saw already in the eight queens-program (Chapter 5), a framework for all Java applications is provided by the class **Applet**. To create a new application the programmer subclasses from this class, redefining various methods. The class **Solitaire**, which is the central class for this application, is shown in Figure 8.12.

We noted earlier that the variables maintaining the different piles, which are shared in common between all classes, are declared as **static** data fields in this class. These data fields are initialized in the **init** method for the class.[1]

Arrays in Java are somewhat different from arrays in most languages. Java distinguishes the three activities of array declaration, array allocation, and assignment to an array location. Note that the declaration statements indicate only that the named objects are an array and not that they have any specific bound. One of the first steps in the initialization routine is to allocate space for the three arrays (the suit piles, the tableau, and the array **allPiles** we will discuss shortly). The **new** command allocates space for the arrays, but does not assign any values to the array elements.

The next step is to create the deck pile. Recall that the constructor for this class creates and shuffles the entire deck of 52 cards. The discard pile is similarly constructed. A loop then creates and initializes the four suit piles, and a second loop creates and initializes the tableau piles. Recall that as part of the initialization of the tableau, cards are removed from the deck and inserted in the tableau pile.

The array **allPiles** is used to represent all 13 card piles. Note that as each pile is created it is also assigned a location in this array, as well as in the appropriate static variable. We will use this array to illustrate yet another aspect of inheritance. The principle of substitutability is used here: The array **allPiles** is declared as an array of **CardPile**, but in fact is maintaining a variety of card piles.

This array of all piles is used in situations where it is not important to distinguish between various types of card piles; for example, in the repaint procedure. To repaint the display, each different card pile is simply asked to display itself.

---

[1] Because they are static, they could also have been initialized in a static block. We will introduce static blocks in Chapter 20.

```
public class Solitaire extends Applet {
    static DeckPile deckPile;
    static DiscardPile discardPile;
    static TablePile tableau [ ];
    static SuitPile suitPile [ ];
    static CardPile allPiles [ ];

    public void init() {
            // first allocate the arrays
        allPiles = new CardPile[13];
        suitPile = new SuitPile[4];
        tableau = new TablePile[7];
            // then fill them in
        allPiles[0] = deckPile = new DeckPile(335, 5);
        allPiles[1] = discardPile = new DiscardPile(268, 5);
        for (int i = 0; i < 4; i++)
            allPiles[2+i] = suitPile[i] =
                new SuitPile(15 + 60 * i, 5);
        for (int i = 0; i < 7; i++)
            allPiles[6+i] = tableau[i] =
                new TablePile(5 + 55 * i, 80, i+1);
        }

    public void paint(Graphics g) {
        for (int i = 0; i < 13; i++)
            allPiles[i].display(g);
        }

    public boolean mouseDown(Event evt, int x, int y) {
        for (int i = 0; i < 13; i++)
            if (allPiles[i].includes(x, y)) {
                allPiles[i].select(x, y);
                repaint();
                return true;
                }
        return true;
        }
}
```

Figure 8.12 – The class Solitaire.

Similarly, when the mouse is pressed, each pile is queried to see if it contains the given position; if so, the card is selected. Remember, of the piles being queried here seven are tableau piles, four are foundations, and the remaining are the discard pile and the deck. Furthermore, the actual code executed in response to the invocation of the includes and select routines may be different in each call, depending upon the type of pile being manipulated.

The use of a variable declared as an instance of the parent class holding a value from a subclass is one aspect of *polymorphism*, a topic we will return to in more detail in a subsequent chapter.

8.6 Building a More Complete Game

The solitaire game described here is minimal and exceedingly hard to win. A more realistic game would include at least a few of the following variations:

- The method select in class TablePile would be extended to recognize builds. That is, if the topmost card could not be played, the bottommost face-up card in the pile should be tested against each tableau pile; if it could be played, the entire collection of face-up cards should be moved.

- Our game halts after one series of moves through the deck. An alternative would be that when the user selected the empty deck pile (by clicking the mouse in the area covered by the deck pile) the discard pile would be reshuffled and copied back into the deck, allowing execution to continue.

Various other alternatives are described in the exercises.

Exercises

1. The solitaire game has been designed to be as simple as possible. A few features are somewhat annoying, but can be easily remedied with more coding. These include the following:

   (a) The topmost card of a tableau pile should not be moved to another tableau pile if there is another face-up card below it.

   (b) An entire build should not be moved if the bottommost card is a king and there are no remaining face-down cards.

   For each, describe what procedures need to be changed, and give the code for the updated routine.

2. The following are common variations of klondike. For each, describe which portions of the solitaire program need to be altered to incorporate the change.

(a) If the user clicks on an empty deck pile, the discard pile is moved (perhaps with shuffling) back to the deck pile. Thus, the user can traverse the deck pile multiple times.

(b) Cards can be moved from the suit pile back into the tableau pile.

(c) Cards are drawn from the deck three at a time and placed on the discard pile in reverse order. As before, only the topmost card of the discard pile is available for playing. If fewer than three cards remain in the deck pile, all the remaining cards (as many as that may be) are moved to the discard pile. (In practice, this variation is often accompanied by variation 1, permitting multiple passes through the deck).

(d) The same as variation 3, but any of the three selected cards can be played. (This requires a slight change to the layout as well as an extensive change to the discard pile class).

(e) Any royalty card, not simply a king, can be moved onto an empty tableau pile.

3. The game "thumb and pouch" is similar to klondike except that a card may be built on any card of next-higher rank, of any suit but its own. Thus, a nine of spades can be played on a ten of clubs, but not on a ten of spades. This variation greatly improves the chances of winning. (According to Morehead [Morehead 1949], the chances of winning Klondike are 1 in 30, whereas the chances of winning thumb and pouch are 1 in 4.) Describe what portions of the program need to be changed to accommodate this variation.

Chapter 9

Mechanisms for Software Reuse

Object-oriented programming has been billed as the technology that will finally permit software to be constructed from general-purpose reusable components. Writers such as Brad Cox have even gone so far as to describe object orientation as heralding the "industrial revolution" in software development [Cox 1986]. While the reality may not quite match the expectations of OOP pioneers (a topic we will address more at the end of this chapter), it *is* true that object-oriented programming makes possible a level of software reuse that is orders of magnitude more powerful than that permitted by previous software construction techniques. In this chapter, we will investigate the two most common mechanisms for software reuse, which are known as *inheritance* and *composition*.

But a mechanism for reuse is only the first step. Inheritance and composition provide the means for software reuse, but to be effective they must, in general, be applied within a *framework* that lays out a pattern for reuse. Patterns and frameworks will be examined in Chapter 18.

9.1   Inheritance and Substitutability

Inheritance and composition as techniques for software reuse are perhaps best understood in relation to the principle of substitutability. Recall from Chapter 8 that the principle of substitutability referred to the relation between a *variable* declared as one class and a *value* derived from another class. The principle of substitutability claims that it should be legal to assign the value to the variable if the class of the value is the same as, or a subclass of, the class of the variable.

We saw an illustration of substitability in the billiards simulation in Chapter 6. In the procedure to draw the screen image, a variable was declared as a GraphicalObject, but in fact it held a succession of different objects, that are all instances of classes declared as subclasses of GraphicalObject.

In this section we will discuss, not actual classes, but abstract concepts. Under what conditions does substitutability hold for two abstract ideas? That is, under what conditions can an instance of some abstract idea be substituted in a situation where we expecte to use an instance of another abstract idea? One classic rule of thumb that has become central to object-oriented design is known as the *is-a* rule.

9.1.1   The Is-a Rule and the Has-a Rule

An understanding of two different forms of relationship is fundamental to knowing how and when to apply object-oriented software reuse techniques. These two relationships are known colloquially as *is-a* and *has-a* (or *part-of*).

The *is-a* relationship holds between two concepts when the first is a specialized instance of the second. That is, for all practical purposes the behavior and data associated with the more specific idea form a subset of the behavior and data associated with the more abstract idea. For example, all the examples of inheritance we described in the early chapters satisfy the *is-a* relationship (a Florist *is-a* Shopkeeper, a Dog *is-a* Mammal, a Ball *is-a* GraphicalObject, and so on).

The relationship derives its name from a simple rule of thumb that tests the relationship. To determine if concept X is a specialized instance of concept Y, simply form the English sentence "*An* X *is a* Y". If the assertion "sounds correct," that is, if it seems to match your everyday experience, you may judge that X and Y have the *is-a* relationship.

The *has-a* relationship, on the other hand, holds when the second concept is a component of the first but the two are not in any sense the same thing, no matter how abstract the generality. For example, a Car *has-a* Engine, although clearly it is not the case that a Car *is-a* Engine or that an Engine *is-a* Car. A Car, however, *is-a* Vehicle, which in turn *is-a* MeansOfTransportation.

Once again, the test for the *has-a* relationship is to simply form the English sentence "*An* X *has a* Y", and let common sense tell you whether the result sounds reasonable.

Most of the time, the distinction is clear-cut. But, sometimes it may be subtle or may depend on circumstances. In the next section we will use one such gray-area case to illustrate the two software development techniques that are naturally tied to these two relationships.

9.2   Composition and Inheritance Described

To illustrate composition and inheritance, we will use the construction of a set abstraction by making use of an existing class List, which maintains a list of integer values. Imagine we have already developed a class List with the following interface:

```
class List {
public:
        // constructor
    List    ();

        // methods
    void    addToFront    (int);
    int     firstElement  ();
    int     length        ();
    int     includes      (int)
    void    remove        (int);


    ...
};
```

That is, our list abstraction permits us to add a new element to the front of the
list, to return the first element of the list, to compute the number of elements in
the list, to see if a value is contained in the list, and to remove an element from
the list.

We want to develop a set abstraction, to perform operations such as adding a
value to the set, determining the number of elements in the set, and determining
whether a specific value occurs in the set.

9.2.1   Using Composition

We will first investigate how the set abstraction can be formed with composition.
Recall from our earlier discussion that an object is simply an encapsulation of
data (data values) and behavior. When composition is employed to reuse an
existing data abstraction in the development of a new data type, a portion of the
state of the new data structure is simply an instance of the existing structure.
This is illustrated below, where the data type Set contains an instance field
named theData, which is declared to be of type List.

```
class Set {
public:
    Set    ();    // constructor

        // operations
    void    add         (int);
    int     size        ();
    int     includes    (int)

private:    // data area for set values
    List    theData;
};
```

Because the List abstraction is stored as part of the data area for our set, it must be initialized in the constructor. As with the initialization of data fields in classes (Chapter 4), the initializer clause in the constructor provides the arguments used to initialize the data field. In this case the constructor we invoke for class List is the constructor with no arguments.

```
    // initialize list
Set::Set() : theData()
{
    // no further initialization
}
```

Operations that manipulate the new structure are implemented by use of the existing operations provided for the earlier data type. For example, the implementation of the includes operation for our set data structure simply invokes the similarly named function already defined for lists.

```
int Set::size ()
{
    return theData.length();
}

int Set::includes (int newValue)
{
    return theData.includes(newValue);
}
```

The only operation that is slightly more complex is addition, which must first check to ensure that the value is not already contained in the collection (since values can appear in a set no more than once).

```
void Set::add (int newValue)
{
        // if not already in set
    if (! includes (newValue))
            // then add
        theData.addToFront(newValue);

        // otherwise do nothing
}
```

The important point is the fact that composition provides a way to leverage off an existing software component in the creation of a new application. By use of the existing List class, the majority of the difficult work in managing the data values for our new component have already been addressed.

On the other hand, composition makes no explicit or implicit claims about substitutability. When formed in this fashion, the data types Set and List are entirely distinct and neither can be substituted in situations where the other is required.

Composition in Other Languages

Composition can be applied in any of the object-oriented languages we consider in this book; indeed, it can be applied in non-object-oriented languages as well. The only significant difference in the various langauges is in the way in which the encapsulated data abstraction is initialized. In Smalltalk this is generally performed with a *class method*; in Objective-C, with a *factory method*; and in Java and Object Pascal, with a constructor.

9.2.2 Using Inheritance

An entirely different mechanism for software reuse in object-oriented programming is the concept of inheritance; with which a new class can be declared a *subclass*, or *child class*, of an existing class. In this way, all data areas and functions associated with the original class are automatically associated with the new data abstraction. The new class can, in addition, define new data values or new functions; it can also *override* functions in the original class, simply by defining new functions with the same names as those of functions that appear in the parent class.

These possibilities are illustrated in the class description below, which implements a different version of the Set abstraction. By naming the class List in the class heading, we indicate that our Set abstraction is an extension, or a refinement, of the existing class List. Thus, all operations associated with lists are immediately applicable to sets as well.

```
class Set : public List {
public:
        // constructor
    Set    ();

        // operations
    void    add    (int);
    int     size   ();
};
```

Notice that the new class does not define any new data fields. Instead, the data fields defined in the List class will be used to maintain the set elements, but they must still be initialized. This is performed by invocation of the constructor for the parent class as part of the constructor for the new class.

```
Set::Set()   : List()
{     // no further initialization
}
```

Similarly, functions defined in the parent class can be used without any further effort, so we need not bother to define the includes method, because the inherited method from List uses the same name and shares the same purpose. The addition of an element to a set, however, requires slightly more work and is handled as follows:

```
void    Set::add     (int newValue)
{
        // add only if not already in set
    if (! includes(newValue))
        addToFront (newValue);
}
```

Compare this function with the earlier version. Both techniques are powerful mechanisms for code reuse, but unlike composition, inheritance carries an implicit assumption that subclasses are, in fact, subtypes. This means that instances of the new abstraction should react similarly to instances of the parent class.

Inheritance in Other Languages

In Chapter 7 we outlined the syntax used to indicate inheritance in each of the languages we are considering. As with composition, the major issue is ensuring that the parent abstraction is properly initialized.

9.2.3   Private Inheritance in C++

C++ provides an interesting compromise between the software reuse mechanisms of composition and of inheritance. It does so by using the keyword private in place of the keyword public in the heading of a class definition. In this way, the programmer indicates that inheritance should be used in the *construction* of the new data abstraction, but the new abstraction should *not* be considered a specialized form of the parent class.

```
class Set : private List {
public:
        // constructor
    Set    () : List() { }

        // operations
    void    add          (int);
```

```
    int     includes    (int x)
            { return List::includes(x); }
    int     size        ()
            { return List::length(); }
};
```

In the vocabulary we will discuss in more detail in Chapter 10, private inheritance creates a subclass that is not a subtype. That is, private inheritance uses inheritance mechanism, but explicitly breaks the principle of substitutability. Operations and data areas inherited from the parent class can be used in the methods for the new abstraction, but they do not "flow through" to become available to users of the new abstraction. For this reason any methods that the programmer wants to export, such as the includes method in the set abstraction, must be redefined in the new class, even if all they do is invoke the method from the parent class. (As illustrated, inline method bodies can often be used to avoid the overhead of the procedure call in these simple routines.)

Private inheritance is an interesting idea and is most useful when (as in this case) an object is composed largely of one other data abstraction and the majority of work invoked in processing the new object is performed by the encapsulated abstraction, yet the two concepts fail to satisfy the *is-a* relationship necessary for a public inheritance.

9.3   Composition and Inheritance Contrasted

Having illustrated two mechanisms for software reuse, and having seen that they are both applicable to the implementation of sets, we can comment on some of the advantages and disadvantages of the two approaches.

- Composition is the simpler of the two techniques. Its advantage is that it more clearly indicates exactly what operations can be performed on a particular data structure. Looking at the declaration for the Set data abstraction, it is clear that the only operations provided for the data type are addition, the inclusion test, and size. This is true regardless of what operations are defined for lists.

- In inheritance the operations of the new data abstraction are a superset of the operations of the original data structure on which the new object is built. Thus, to know exactly what operations are legal for the new structure the programmer must examine the declaration for the original. An examination of the Set declaration, for example, does not immediately indicate that the includes test can be legally applied to sets. It is only by examination of the declaration for the earlier List data abstraction that the entire set of legal operations can be ascertained.

  The difficulty that occurs when, to understand a class constructed using inheritance, the programmer must frequently flip back and forth between two (or more) class declarations has been labelled the "yo-yo" problem [Taenzer 1989].

- The brevity of data abstractions constructed with inheritance is, in another light, an advantage. Using inheritance it is not necessary to write any code to access the functionality provided by the class on which the new structure is built. For this reason, implementations using inheritance are almost always, as in the present case, considerably shorter in code than are implementations constructed with composition, and they often provide greater functionality. For example, the inheritance implementation makes available not only the includes test for sets but also the function remove.

- Inheritance does not prevent users from manipulating the new structure using methods from the parent class, even if these are not appropriate. For example, when we use inheritance to derive the class Set from the class List, nothing prevents users from adding new elements to the set using the inherited method addToFront.

- In composition the fact that the class List is used as the storage mechanism for our sets is merely an implementation detail. With this technique it would be easy to reimplement the class to make use of a different technique (such as a hash table), with minimal impact on the users of the Set abstraction. If users counted on the fact that a Set is merely a specialized form of List, such changes would be more difficult to implement.

- Inheritance may allow us to use the new abstraction as an argument in an existing *polymorphic* function. We will investigate this possibility in more detail in Chapter 14. Because composition does not imply substitutability, it usually precludes polymorphism.

- Understandability and maintainability are difficult to judge. Inheritance has the advantage of brevity of code but not of protocol. Composition code, although longer, is the only code that another programmer must understand to use the abstraction. A programmer faced with understanding the inheritance version needs to ask whether any behavior inherited from the parent class was necessary for proper utilization of the new class, and would thus have to understand both classes.

- Data structures implemented through inheritance tend to have a very small advantage in execution time over those constructed with composition, since one additional function call is avoided (although techniques such as inline functions in C++ can be used to eliminate much of this overhead).

Of the two possible implementation techniques, can we say which is better in this case? One answer involves the substitution principle. Ask yourself whether, in an application that expected to use a List data abstraction, it is correct to substitute instead an instance of class Set. While the technical answer might be yes (the Set abstraction does implement all the List operations), the more common sense answer is no. For this reason it appears that, *in this case*, composition is the better approach.

The bottom line is that the two techniques are very useful, and an object-oriented programmer should be familiar with both of them.

9.4 Will Widespread Software Reuse Become Reality?

In the early days of object-oriented programming, it was said that composition and inheritance had finally provided a way to create software from general-purpose interchangeable components. However, while certain progress has been made (there are now a large number of commercial vendors who market general-purpose object-oriented software libraries for various applications, such as user interfaces and container classes), the overall process has not lived up to the early expectations. There are a variety of reasons for this:

- Inheritance and composition provide the *means* for producing reusable components, but they do not, by themselves, provide *guidelines* for how such a task should be performed. It turns out that producing good and useful software components is, if anything, almost always more difficult than developing special purpose software to solve the task at hand.

- Because producing reusable components is difficult, the benefits cannot usually be realized within a single project. Indeed, they may slow down project development. Rather than creating immediate benefits, the cost of such development must be amortized over many programming projects. But as each projects usually has its own budget and schedule, there is often no management mechanism to support such amortization.

- Because the benefits of developing reusable components do not immediately improve a project, there is usually little incentive for programmers to strive toward reusability.

- Because each new problem typically requires a slightly different set of behaviors, it is often difficult to design a truly useful and general-purpose software component the first time. Rather, useful reusable software components evolve slowly over many projects until they finally reach a stable state.

- Many programmers and managers are leery of software that has not been developed "in-house." This wariness is called the "not-invented-here" syndrome. Because mangers pride themselves on the quality of their programmer teams, they naturally believe they can do better than whatever team developed the reusable software.

- Because many programmers have little formal training, or have not kept pace with recent programming innovations (such as object-oriented techniques), they may not be aware of the mechanisms available for the development of reusable software components.

In short, development of software mechanisms for reuse does not, by itself, guarantee the development of a technological and management *culture* that will support and encourage reuse. Human organizations tend to move much more slowly than does technological change, so it may be many years before we see the true benefits promised by the object-oriented approach. Nevertheless, even though object reuse is probably not anywhere as frequent as claimed, it does occur and has been proven many times to be useful and cost-saving when applied correctly. For this reason it is inevitable that reuse will eventually become the norm for software development.

Several recent books provide guidelines for developing reusable components include [Carroll 1995, McGregor 1992, Meyer 1994, Goldberg 1995].

Exercises

1. There are various ways to implement a *stack* data structure–for example, with lists, or with an array. Suppose we have both a class List and a class Array. For each base class, illustrate how one could build a stack using both inheritance and composition. You can imagine whatever methods you wish for the base classes. Which implementation technique seems more appropriate in this case?

2. Suppose again that we have an existing List data structure, and want to build an abstraction representing an *ordered list*, where elements are inserted in sequence, rather than simply at the front of the list. Do we use inheritance or composition as an implementation technique in this case? Provide a short argument to justify your answer.

Chapter 10

Subclasses and Subtypes

One of the most interesting features of object-oriented languages is that the *value* held by a variable may not match exactly the *declaration* for that variable. We saw this near the end of the billiard simulation program in Chapter 6, where a variable declared as a GraphicalObject in fact held a value of type Ball, Wall, or Hole. This property is one aspect of *polymorphism*, a topic we will discuss in more detail in Chapter 14. In a more conventional language, such as Pascal or C, if a variable is declared as maintaining a value of type integer, no matter what happens we are guaranteed that the bit pattern in the memory assigned to the variable will be interpreted as an integer value. In an object-oriented language, on the other hand, a value declared as maintaining a Window value may, in fact, be maintaining a GraphicWindow, a TextEditWindow, or some other window type.

A few vocabulary terms will help in understanding the implications of this change. We will use the term *static type* to refer to the type assigned to a variable through a declaration statement. The term *dynamic type* will refer to the type associated with a value. The fact that a variable may hold a value with a dynamic type that differs from the static type associated with the variable is the source for much of the power provided by object-oriented techniques. A variable for which the dynamic type need not match the static type is said to be *polymorphic*.

Two other terms are relevant to our discussion. The concept of *subclass* was introduced already in Chapter 7. Subclassing provides a way of constructing new software components using existing components. The concept of *subtype* is more abstract. A subtype is defined in terms of behavior, not structure. We say a type, B, is a subtype of another type, A, if one can substitute an instance of class B wherever an instance of class A is called for with no observable change in behavior.

Notice that the notion of a subtype corresponds to our idealized principle of substitutability introduced in Chapter 9. Abstractly, however, there is no reason why the concepts of subtype and subclass should have any relation. Indeed, in dynamically typed languages such as Smalltalk, they are not related. Two classes can share common behavior–for example, responding to the same set of messages–without any common implementation or common ancestor (other than the class Object, common to all values in Smalltalk). If their responses to these common messages are sufficiently similar, one class could easily substitute for the other. Imagine creating a sparse array class that implements the various subscript operations provided by the class Array. Without need for recoding, one can substitute an instance of this sparse array class in an algorithm designed to work with arrays.

Most strongly typed object-oriented languages, such as Object Pascal and C++, blur the distinction between subtypes and subclasses in two ways. First, they only permit variables to hold values of different type when the dynamic type of the value is a subclass of the static type of the variable. Second, they make the assumption that all subclasses are, in fact, subtypes. This assumption is not always valid. Since subclasses can override methods and replace the behavior of the parent with arbitrary new behavior, there is generally no guarantee that a subclass will also be a subtype.

10.1   Issues in Binding and Message Lookup

In a subsequent section we will discuss mechanisms to deal with the subclass and subtype distinction found in the various programming languages we are considering. First, however, we must discuss, in general terms, two problems. The first is the question of *method binding*–that is, whether one should bind a message to a method based on the static or the dynamic type of a variable. The second is the question of reverse polymorphism–whether it is possible to *undo* the separation of static and dynamic types and reassign a value to a variable based on its dynamic, rather than static, type. A third, related, question, the exact meaning attached to method overriding, is sufficiently complex that we will defer its discussion to a later chapter.

10.1.1   Method Binding

The existence of a polymorphic variable naturally implies two different views (see Figure 10.1). We can consider the variable from the point of view of the declaration statement (the static view) or from the point of view of its current value (the dynamic view). This distinction is brought into focus when we consider a method that is defined in the parent class and overridden in the child class. In Figure 10.1, for example, we have a method, mouseDown, that is associated both with a general parent class (the class Window) and with a child class (the class TextEditWindow). When the variable that holds this value is used as the receiver for a message, should the message bind to the method associated with the static type, or to that associated with the dynamic type?

There is no right answer to this question. Most of the time binding the message to the dynamic type is what we expect, but there are situations where

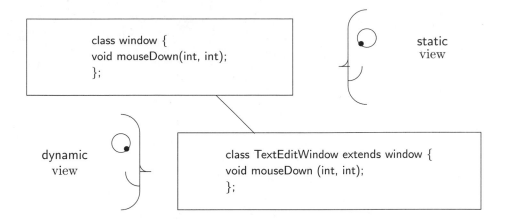

Figure 10.1 – Two views of a polymorphic variable.

the opposite is also useful. In the language specific sections that follow we will note how different languages deal with this problem.

10.1.2   The Reverse Polymorphism Problem

The principle of substitutability says that, to a variable declared as a parent class type, we can assign a value constructed from a child class type. Can we go in the other direction? That is, having assigned a variable of type TextEditWindow to a variable declared as maintaining a value of type Window, can we then assign the contents of the variable back to another instance of class TextEditWindow?

There are actually two related problems involved in this question. To illustrate, suppose we define a class, Ball, and two subclasses, BlackBall and WhiteBall. Next, we construct the software equivalent of a box into which we can drop two instances of class Ball, and one of those instances (selected randomly) will fall out and be returned (Figure 10.2). We drop a BlackBall and a WhiteBall into the box and recover the result.

Now, the resulting object can certainly be considered a Ball and can thus be assigned to a variable declared as that type. But is it a BlackBall? The two questions we can ask are (1) Can I tell whether or not it is a BlackBall? and (2) What mechanisms are necessary to assign the value to an instance of the child class?

Although the BlackBall/WhiteBall example may seem contrived, the underlying problem is quite common. Consider the development of classes for frequently used data structures: sets as sets, stacks, queues, lists, and the like, which are used to maintain collections of objects. A touted benefit of object-oriented programming is the production of reusable software components, and collection containers are candidates for such components. However, a collection container

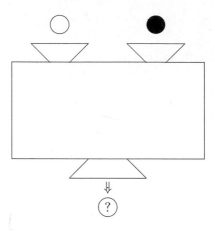

Figure 10.2 – A ball losing its identity.

is in some circumstances exactly like the ball machine. If a programmer places two different objects in a set and later takes one out, how does he or she know which type of object will result?

These problems are not trivial, but they are solvable. In the language-specific sections of this chapter, we will describe the mechanisms to solve the reverse polymorphism problem, if such facilities are available. In a subsequent chapter, we will consider the container class problem in more detail.

10.2   Binding in Programming Languages

In the following sections, we describe binding of types and methods in the languages we are considering. In particular, contrast how method binding is performed in statically typed languages (Object Pascal, C++, and Java), and in dynamically typed languages (Smalltalk and Objective-C).

10.2.1   Binding and Message Lookup in Object Pascal

Object Pascal is statically typed: Every identifier must be declared. Also, the concepts of subclass and subtype are combined. It is implicitly assumed that subclasses are subtypes, and an identifier declared as an object type can hold values of that type or of any type derived by inheritance from it.

Although the *language* is statically typed, objects nevertheless carry with them knowledge of their own dynamic type. In Apple Object Pascal a system-defined predicate, Member, can be used to determine whether an identifier is an instance of a specific class. The Member function takes an object-reference expression (usually a simple identifier) and a class name (in Object Pascal terminology an object type name). It returns the value true if the object-reference is an object of the given type, and false otherwise. For example, given a class Animal, we can determine whether a variable, fido, of type Animal is an instance of the more specialized subclass Mammal, using the following test:

```
if Member (fido, Mammal) then
    writeln ('fido is a mammal')
else
    writeln ('fido is not a mammal');
```

Note that Member returns true even if fido is an instance of a more specialized class, such as Dog.

When coupled with the ability to perform type casts, the Member function can be used to partly solve the reverse polymorphism problem. When the ball is taken from the box, the programmer can use Member to determine whether the result is a BlackBall or a WhiteBall and can cast the ball to the right type accordingly.

In Delphi Pascal the class of an object can be tested with the is operator. This operator returns true when the class of the left argument is an instance of, or inherits from, the class of the right argument. The operator as performs a type-safe dynamic cast. If the left argument is not an instance of the right argument, an exception is raised; otherwise, the value is converted to the right hand type. These mechanisms can be used to perform reverse polymorphism.

```
if aBall is BlackBall then
    bBall := aBall as BlackBall
else
    writeln('cannot convert ball to black ball');
```

If we want to test the class of an object exactly (that is, the exact class and not whether the class is or derives from another class), we can compare the ClassInfo field to a class value. Every object in Delphi Pascal holds an ClassInfo field.

```
if aBall.ClassInfo = BlackBall then
    . . .
```

Although Object Pascal is statically typed, it always uses dynamic binding to match a method to a message. Thus, if the method hasLiveYoung is defined in class Mammal and overridden in class Platypus, the subclass will be searched even when the receiver is declared as class (object type) Mammal.

Methods are dynamically bound in Object Pascal, but the legality of any message-passing expression is determined by the static class of the receiver. Only if this class understands the message being invoked will the compiler generate code to perform the message. To illustrate, the variable phyl is declared as an

instance of class Animal, but clearly holds a value of type Mammal. Despite this,
the compiler will object to the message hasLiveYoung, which we assume is defined
for Mammals, not for all animals.

```
var
     phyl : Animal;
     newPlat : Platypus;

begin
     new (newPlat);
     phil := newPlat;
         (* compiler will give error on following *)
     if   phil.hasLiveYoung then
         ...
```

10.2.2   Binding and Message Lookup in Smalltalk

Smalltalk is a dynamically typed language. Instance variables, as we saw in
earlier chapters, are declared only by name and not by type. As with all dynamically typed languages, substitutability and reverse polymorphism are not
at issue, since any variable can be assigned any value.

It *is* possible to inquire as to the class of any object. All objects respond to
the message class by returning an object representing their class. Thus, if fido is
a variable suspected of holding a value of type Dog, the test

```
( fido class == Dog ) ifTrue: [ ... ]
```

will tell us if our suspicions are correct. But, the test will fail if we replace Dog
with Mammal. Thus, in Smalltalk (and in Objective-C) two tests can be used on
objects. The first, isMemberOf:, takes a class name as argument and is equivalent
to the test just shown. The second, isKindOf:, is similar to the Member function
in Object Pascal; it tells us whether the receiver is an instance, either directly or
by inheritance, of the argument class. Thus, if fido is a Dog, the following test
succeeds, but the test with isMemberOf: fails:

```
( fido isKindOf: Mammal ) ifTrue: [ ... ]
```

The use of isKindOf: is considered poor programming practice because it
tightly binds the code to values from a specific class. We are usually interested
less in the class of an object than in whether the object will understand a specific
message. In other words, we are interested less in subclasses than in subtypes.
Thus, both Seal and Dog might implement a method bark. Given a particular
object, say fido, we can use the following technique to determine whether the
object will respond to the message bark:

```
( fido respondsTo: #bark ) ifTrue: [ ... ]
```

Notice that the method selector is represented by a symbol.

In Smalltalk the notions of subclass and subtype are clearly separate. Since static types are not available, dynamic binding is always used to match methods to messages. If a receiver does not understand a particular message, a run-time error diagnostic is produced.

The standard library in Smalltalk (called the *standard image*) provides a rich set of container classes that makes extensive use of the late-binding features of the language.

10.2.3 Binding and Message Lookup in Objective-C

Objective-C is fundamentally a dynamically typed language. This should not be surprising, given the opinions of the developer, Brad Cox, noted at the end of the chapter. In large part, everything about binding and message lookup in Smalltalk holds as well for Objective-C, including the fact that all objects understand the messages class, isKindOf:, and isMemberOf:. Dynamic binding is always used when the receiver is a dynamically typed object.

To determine whether a given object understands a specific message, we can use the system-provided routine @selector to convert the textual form of a message selector into an internal encoding, as in the following:

```
if ( [ fido respondsTo: @selector(bark) ] ) { ... }
```

An interesting feature of Objective-C is the optional use of statically typed variables in combination with dynamically typed quantities. In contradiction to what we said in Chapter 3, objects can be statically declared in one of two ways. Given a class declaration, such as class Mammal, the declaration

```
Mammal anAnimal;
```

defines a new identifier named anAnimal and allocates space for it. As in C++, message passing will then be static, based on the class Mammal, and such values do not support substitutability (that is, if you try to assign to such a value an instance of a subclass, such as Dog, the value will still be considered only a Mammal).

Alternatively, a declaration can be phrased in terms of explicit pointers. Such a declaration does not declare space for the object, and substitutability will in this case be honored. Space is allocated for values, as it is with normal dynamic variables, through the message new. However, when static class names are used to define receivers, method binding, although still dynamic, will be slightly faster.

```
Mammal * fido;
fido = [ Dog new ];
```

Because of the late-bound nature of the language, it is relatively easy to write container classes in Objective-C; in fact, a large set of such data structures is provided in the standard Objective-C library.

10.2.4   Binding and Message Lookup in C++

Two primary objectives in the design of the C++ programming language were space and time efficiency (see [Ellis 1990, Stroustrup 1994]). It was intended as an improvement over C for both object-oriented and non-object-oriented applications. A basic tenet of C++ is that no feature should incur a cost (either in space or execution time) unless it is used. For example, if the object-oriented features of C++ are ignored, the remainder of the language should execute as fast as does conventional C. Thus, it is not surprising that most features in C++ are statically, rather than dynamically, bound.

As noted in Chapter 7, C++ does *not* support the principle of substitutability, except when using pointers or references. We will see the reason for this in Chapter 12 when we examine memory management in C++ programs.

Method binding is relatively complicated in C++. For ordinary variables (not pointers or references), it is performed statically. But when objects are denoted through pointers or references, dynamic binding is used. In the latter case, whether the method lookup is based on the static or the dynamic type of the value is determined by whether the associated method is declared using the keyword virtual in the static class. If it is so declared, lookup is based on the dynamic class. If it is not, lookup is based on the static class. Even when dynamic binding is used, the *legality* of any message-passing expression is determined by the compiler on the basis of the static class of the receiver.

Consider, for example, the following classes and a global variable declaration:

```
class Mammal {
public:
    void speak() { printf("can't speak"); }
};

class Dog : public Mammal {
public:
    void speak() { printf("wouf wouf"); }
    void bark() { printf("wouf wouf, as well"); }
};

Mammal fred;
Dog    lassie;
Mammal * fido = new Dog;
```

As given, the expression fred.speak() yields "can't speak" and the expression lassie.speak() yields a bark. However, the expression fido→speak() also yields the expression "can't speak" because the method in class Mammal is not declared as virtual. The expression fido→bark() is not permitted by the compiler, even though we (i.e., the programmer) know that the dynamic type of the value associated with fido is class Dog. Nevertheless, the static type is only class Mammal, and generally mammals don't bark.

If we change the declaration by adding the virtual designation, as follows:

```
class Mammal {
public:
    virtual void speak() { printf("can't speak"; }
};
```

the expected outcome for the expression fido→speak() (namely, fido will bark) is produced.

A relatively recent change in the C++ language is the addition of facilities for discovering the dynamic class of an object. These make up the RTTI (*run-time type identification*) system.

In the RTTI system, every class has an associated structure of type typeinfo, which encodes various bits of information about the class. One field, name, contains the name of the class as a string. The function typeid can be used to discover the type information associated with a value. Hence, the following will print out the string "Dog" which is the run-time type being held in the variable named fido. It is necessary to dereference the pointer variable fido so that the argument is the value the pointer references and not the pointer value itself.

```
    cout << "fido is a " << typeid(*fido).name() << endl;
```

It is also possible to ask if one type-information structure represents a subclass of another type-information structure, using the member function before. For example, the following two calls produce true and false, respectively.

```
    if (typeid(*fido).before(typeid(fred))) ....
    if (typeid(fred).before(typeid(lassie))) ...
```

Before the introduction of RTTI, one common programmers trick was to encode explicit *is-a* methods in class hierarchies. For example, to test animal values to see if they represent a dog or cat, we can write methods such as the following:

```
class Mammal {
public:
    virtual int  isaDog() { return 0; }
    virtual int  isaCat() { return 0; }
};
```

```
class Dog : public Mammal {
public:
    virtual int  isaDog() { return 1; }
};

class Cat : public Mammal {
public:
    virtual int  isaCat() { return 1; }
};

Mammal * fido;
```

A test, such as fido→isaDog(), can then be used to determine if the variable fido is currently holding a value of type Dog. If so, a cast can be used to convert the quantity into the correct type.

By returning a pointer rather than an integer, we can extend this trick to combine both the test for subclass type and the conversion. This is similar to another part of RTTI, called dynamic_cast, which we will describe shortly. Since a function in the class Mammal is returning a pointer to a Dog, the class Dog must have a forward reference. The result of the assignment is either a null pointer or a valid reference to a Dog; so, the test on the result must still be performed but we have eliminated the need for the cast. This is shown as follows:

```
class Dog;      // forward reference
class Cat;

class Mammal {
public:
    virtual Dog *  isaDog() { return 0; }
    virtual Cat *  isaCat() { return 0; }
};

class Dog : public Mammal {
public:
    virtual Dog *  isaDog() { return this; }
};

class Cat : public Mammal {
public:
    virtual Cat *  isaCat() { return this; }
};

Mammal * fido;
Dog * lassie;
```

A statement such as

```
lassie = fido->isaDog();
```

can then *always* be performed. It will result in the variable lassie holding a non-null value only if fido indeed held a value of class Dog. If fido did *not* hold a dog value, then a null pointer value will be assigned to the variable lassie.

```
if (lassie)
      ... fido was indeed a dog
else
      ... assignment did not work
      ... fido was not a dog
```

While it is possible for the programmer to implement this, the disadvantage of this technique for performing reverse polymorphism is that it requires adding methods to both the parent and the child classes. If there are many child classes inheriting from one common parent class, the mechanism can become unwieldy. If making changes to the parent class is not permitted this technique is not possible.

Because similar problems occur frequently, a general solution has been added to C++. The template function dynamic_cast takes a type as an argument and, like the function just defined, returns either the argument value (if the cast is legal) or a null value (if the cast is not legal). An assignment equivalent to the one in the preceding example could be written in the following form:

```
      // convert only if fido is a dog
lassie = dynamic_cast<Dog *> (fido);
      // then check to see if cast worked
if (lassie) ...
```

Three other types of cast (static_cast, const_cast, and reinterpret_cast) have also been added to C++, but their use is uncommon and they will not be described here. However, programmers are encouraged to use these newer, more type-safe facilities instead of the older cast mechanism.

10.2.5   Binding and Message Lookup in Java

Although Java is superficially similar to C++, its method binding and message lookup are considerably simpler than in C++. In Java all variables know their dynamic type. It is assumed that subclasses are subtypes, and therefore a value can be assigned to a parent class type with no explicit conversion. The reverse assignment (reverse polymorphism) is permitted with an explicit cast. A run-time test is performed to determine if the assignment is valid, and, if not, an exception is produced.

```
Ball aBallValue;
    // ... missing code
    // perform reverse polymorphism assignment
BlackBall bball = (BlackBall) aBallValue;
```

It is also possible to test the dynamic type of a value using the operator instanceOf.

```
if (aBallValue instanceOf BlackBall)
    ...
else
    ...
```

Messages are always bound to methods on the basis of the dynamic type of the receiver; there is no virtual keyword, as in C++. An interesting feature of Java is that data fields can also be overridden, but in this case the binding of an access is based on the static type, not the dynamic type. Both of these are illustrated by the following:

```
class A {
    String name = "class A";
    public void print() {
        println("class A");
        }
    }

class B extends A {
    String name = "class B";
    public void print() {
        println("class B");
        }
    }

class test {
    public void test() {
        Class B b = new B();
        Class A a = b;
        println(a); // produces class A
        println(b); // produces class B
        a.print(); // produces class B, not class A
        b.print(); // produces class B
        }
    }
```

Although Java confuses subtypes and subclasses by making the assumption that all subclasses are subtypes, of all the strongly typed languages we are considering it goes the farthest in separating the two concepts through the idea of *interface*.

Interfaces provide a hierarchical organization similar to but independent of classes. As noted in Chapter 7, interfaces define only the protocol for their operations, not an implementation. By use of the extends clause, new interfaces can be built on top of existing interfaces, as classes are. In this way one can generate a subtype hierarchy that is completely independent of the subclass hierarchy.

Interfaces can be used to define variables, which can hold values of any type that declares that it implements the interface. Thus, the static type is an interface type, while the dynamic type is a class type. Method binding is based on the dynamic type.

For example, in the design of an iterator system for data structures in Java (see Chapter 16 for a discussion of iterators), one might imagine a hierarchy of forward-only, bi-directional, and random-access iterators. These might be defined by the following protocols:

```
interface forwardIterator {
    void advance();
    int currentValue();
    }

interface bidirectionalIterator extends forwardIterator {
    void moveBack();
    }

interface randomAccessIterator extends bidirectionalIterator {
    int at(int);
    }
```

Data structures can then define an iterator appropriate to the access that fits their implementation technique.

```
class listIterator implements forwardIterator {
    // ...
    }
```

10.3 Merits of Static versus Dynamic Binding

Arguments over the relative merits of static and dynamic typing, or static and dynamic binding invariably come down to the relative importance of efficiency and flexibility. To put these points in succinct form, static typing and static binding are more efficient; dynamic typing and dynamic binding are more flexible.

As we observed, dynamic typing implies that every object must keep track of its own type. If we take the "rugged individualist" view of objects (that every object must take care of itself and not depend on others for its actions or maintenance), dynamic typing seems to be the more "object-oriented" technique. Certainly, it greatly simplifies problems such as the development of general-purpose data structures, but the cost involved is a run-time search to discover the meaning (that is, the code to execute) every time an operation is used on a data value. Although there are techniques to reduce this cost, the expense cannot be eliminated altogether. Largely because these costs can be quite substantial, most programming languages use static typing.

Static typing simplifies a programming-language implementation, even if (as in Java, Object Pascal, and in some cases C++) dynamic binding is used to match a method to a message. When static types are known to the compiler, storage can be allocated for variables efficiently, and efficient code can be generated for ambiguous operations (such as addition). But there are costs associated with static typing. For example, often (although not necessarily, as we see in Object Pascal) objects lose their "self-knowledge." As we saw in the discussion of the container problem, this fact makes writing general-purpose data structure abstractions more difficult.

If static typing simplifies an implementation, static method binding simplifies it even more. If a match between method and message can be discovered by the compiler, message passing (regardless of the syntax used) can be *implemented* as a simple procedure call, with no run-time mechanism required to perform the method lookup. This is about as efficient as we can reasonably expect (although inline functions in C++ can even eliminate the overhead of procedure calling).

Dynamic binding, on the other hand, always requires the execution of at least some run-time mechanism, however primitive, to match a method to a message. In languages that use dynamic typing (and thus must use dynamic binding of messages to methods), it is generally not possible to determine in advance whether a message-passing expression will be understood by the receiver. When a message is not understood, there is no alternative but to generate a run-time error message. The advocates of static languages argue that many of these errors can be caught at compile time in a language that uses static method binding; this is disputed (as one might suspect) by supporters of dynamic languages.

Thus, we seem to be left to decide which is more important: efficiency or flexibility, correctness or ease of use. Brad Cox [Cox 1986] argues that these decisions depend both on what level of abstraction the software represents and on whether we are the producer or the consumer of the software system. Cox asserts that object-oriented programming will be the primary (although not the only) tool in the "software industrial revolution." Just as the nineteenth-century Industrial Revolution was made possible only after the development of interchangeable parts, the goal of the software industrial revolution is the construction of reusable, reliable, high-level, abstract software components from which software systems will be fabricated.

Efficiency is the primary concern at the lowest level of construction–what Cox refers to as the gate-level abstractions, using an analogy from electronic components. As the level of abstraction rises, through chip-level and card-level components, flexibility becomes more important.

Similarly, performance and efficiency are primary concerns for the developer of software abstractions. For a consumer interested in combining independently developed software systems in new and novel ways, flexibility may be much more important.

There is no single right answer to the question of which binding technique is more appropriate in a programming language. A variety of schemes are available, and each is useful in some situations.

Exercises

1. Object Pascal uses static typing, but also uses dynamic binding. Explain why the converse is not possible–that is, why it is not possible for a language to use dynamic typing and static binding of messages and methods.

2. Give an example that will illustrate why, in a statically typed object-oriented language (such as C++ or Object Pascal), the compiler is justified in not permitting a value associated with a variable declared as a parent class to be assigned to another variable declared as an instance of a subclass.

3. Discuss whether the error-checking facilities made possible by static typing are worth the loss in flexibility. How important is the container class problem?

4. Where does Cox's analogy between hardware and software systems break down? What prevents the development of interchangeable, reliable software components?

Chapter 11

Replacement and Refinement

Up to this point, our intuitive model of inheritance has been one in which the set of data values and methods associated with a child class is larger than the set associated with a parent class. That is, a subclass simply adds new data or new methods to those provided by the superclass. Clearly, however, this situation does not always hold. Remember Phyl and Phyllis, the platypuses described in Chapter 1? In our discussion there a basic bit of information we know about the class Mammal was that all mammals bear live young. Nevertheless Phyllis, while steadfastly claiming to be a loyal member of the family Mammal, continues to give birth by laying eggs.

We can say about this situation that the subclass (Platypus) does more than monotonically add to the set of information we know about the parent class (Mammal). Instead, the child class actually changes or alters some property of the parent class. To understand a subclass changing the meaning of a method defined in a parent class, we must examine the subtle notion of inheritance in greater detail.

11.1   Adding, Replacing, and Refining

We have assumed, up to this point, that data and methods added by a subclass to those inherited from a parent class are always distinct. In other words, the set of methods and data values defined by the child class is distinct from the set of values and methods defined by the parent (and ancestor) classes. To describe this situation, we say that such methods and data values are *added* to the protocol for the parent class.

It is different when a child class defines a method by the *same name* as that used for the method in the parent class: The method in the child class effectively hides, or *overrides*, the method in the parent class. For example, my

195

specific knowledge of the class Platypus overrides my more general knowledge from the class Mammal.

As described in Chapter 1, when a message is sent to an object, the search for a matching method always begins with an examination of the methods associated with the class of the object. If no method is found, the methods associated with the immediate parent class of the object are examined. If, once again, no method is found, the immediate parent class of *that* class is examined, and so on. Ultimately, either no further classes remain (in which case an error is reported) or an appropriate method is found.

A method in a class that has the same name as a method in a superclass is said to *override* the method in the parent class. During the search for a method to invoke in response to a message, the method in the child class will naturally be discovered before the method in the parent class. (For the most part, overriding is associated only with methods. Java is unique among the languages we discuss, and indeed nearly unique among object-oriented languages, in permitting a restricted form of overriding for data fields.)

11.1.1   American and Scandinavian Semantics

A method defined in a child class can override an inherited method in one of two ways. A method *replacement* totally replaces the method in the parent class during execution. That is, the code in the parent class is never executed when instances of the child class are manipulated. A method *refinement* includes, as part of its behavior, the execution of the method inherited from the parent class. Thus, the behavior of the parent is preserved and augmented.

The first override type is often called *American semantics*, because it is usually associated with languages of American origin (such as Smalltalk and C++). The second is known as *Scandinavian semantics*, because it is most frequently associated with Simula [Dahl 1966, Birtwistle 1979, Kirkerud 1989], the original object-oriented language, and with the later language Beta [Madsen 1993], both of Scandinavian origin.

In Chapter 7 we described the mechanics of adding a new method in a child class. The remainder of this chapter will be devoted to describing the mechanics of replacement and refinement in each of the languages we are considering, as well as describing some of the advantages and disadvantages of the two approaches.

11.2   Replacement

In Smalltalk, integers and floating-point numbers are objects; they are instances of class Integer and class Float, respectively. In turn, both of these classes are subclasses of a more general class, Number. Now suppose we have a variable, aNumber, that currently contains a Smalltalk integer, and we send to aNumber the square-root-generating message sqrt. There is no method corresponding to this name in class Integer, so class Number is searched, and the following method is discovered:

```
sqrt
        " covert to float "
        " then compute square root "

    ↑ self asFloat sqrt
```

This method passes the message asFloat to self, which, you will recall from Chapter 4, represents the receiver for the sqrt message. The asFloat message results in a floating-point value with the same magnitude as that of the integer number. The message sqrt is then passed to this value. This time, the search for a method begins with class Float. It so happens that class Float contains a different method named sqrt, which for floating-point values *overrides* the method in class Number. That method (which is not shown here), computes and returns the expected floating-point value.

The ability to override and totally *replace* the method sqrt means that many kinds of numbers can share the single default routine found in class Number. This sharing avoids the need to repeat this code for each of the different subclasses of Number (which includes not only integers and floats but infinite-precision integers and fractions). Classes, such as Float, that require a behavior different from the default can simply override the method and substitute the alternative code.

11.2.1   Replacement and the Principle of Substitutability

The major difficulty with using replacement as the fundamental model of inheritance is the assumption that subclasses are also subtypes. Recall that a linchpin of the argument for the principle of substitutability is that instances of a subclass behave in all important respects similarly to instances of the parent class. But if subclasses are free to replace methods with new methods that can perform any arbitrary action, what guarantees are there that the behavior of the child class will have any relationship to that of the parent class?

In the example just cited, the methods in both class Float and class Number were tied only by their conceptual relationship to the abstract concept "square root." Great havoc can ensue if the design of a subclass alters the behavior of an inherited method too radically–for example, by changing the sqrt method so that it computes logarithms.

Several possible ways to resolve the conflict between replacement and substitutability can be found in programming languages:

1. Simply ignore the problem and leave it to the programmer to ensure that subclasses do the right thing in any important situation. This is the approach used in all the languages we consider: Object Pascal, C++, Objective-C, Java, and Smalltalk.

2. In Eiffel [Meyer 1988a, Rist 1995], another well-known object-oriented language, a programmer can attach *assertions* to a method. These assertions

are Boolean expressions that test the state of an object at various points during execution, ensuring that certain conditions are satisfied. The assertions are automatically inherited and enforced by subclasses, even when the actual methods are overridden. Thus, they can be used to make certain the child class performs in an acceptable fashion.

3. Separate the concepts of subclass and subtype, as is partially done in Java. Subclasses can then use replacement semantics as an implementation technique, without necessarily implying that the resulting object is a subtype of the original class.

4. Abandon the semantics of replacement entirely, and use refinement semantics. This possibility will be investigated in a subsequent section.

11.2.2   Notating Replacement

Programming languages use several different approaches to document a method that is being overridden, either for replacement or refinement. Smalltalk, Java, and Objective-C require no indication that overriding is taking place. In C++, the base class (the parent class) must have a special indication of the possibility of overriding. In Apple Object Pascal this indication is provided, not in the parent class, but in the child class. In Delphi Pascal a marker must be placed in both classes.

The placement of some indication in the parent class generally makes the implementation easier, since, if overriding is not a possibility, message passing can be implemented by the more efficient process of procedure calling (that is, the dynamic lookup at run time can be avoided). Removing the requirement that this marking be present makes the language more flexible, since it permits any class to be subclassed even if the author of the parent class has not foreseen the possibility.

For example, one programmer may produce a class (say a List) for a particular application. Later, a second programmer may want to make a specialization of this class (for example, OrderedList), overriding many of the methods in the original. In languages such as C++, this could require textual changes to the original class to declare methods as virtual; in contrast, in a language such as Java or Objective-C, no change to the parent class description would be necessary.

11.3   Replacement in Various Languages

11.3.1   Replacement in C++

Overriding in C++ is complicated by the intertwining of overriding, overloading, virtual (or polymorphic) functions, and constructors. Overloading and virtual functions will be explored in more detail in subsequent chapters; here we will restrict ourselves to an explanation of simple replacement.

```
class CardPile {
public:
    CardPile(int, int);

    card & top();
    void pop();
    bool empty();
    virtual bool includes(int, int);
    virtual void select(int, int);
    virtual void addCard(card &);
    virtual void display(window &);
    virtual bool canTake(card &);


protected:
    Card * firstCard;
    int x;
    int y;
};

class SuitPile : public CardPile {
public:
    SuitPile(int, int);
    virtual bool canTake(card &);
};
```

Figure 11.1 – The Declaration of a class and subclass in C++.

Simple replacement occurs when the arguments in a child class match identically in type and number the arguments in the parent class, and the virtual modifier is used in the declaration of the method in the parent class.[1] We saw an example of this in the class CardPile, used in the solitaire game described in Chapter 8. If we were to translate the solitare program into C++, the declarations might look something like Figure 11.1, which shows the declaration of the class CardPile as well as a subclass–in this case SuitPile.

Here the method canTake, among others, is being declared in such a fashion that it overrides the method in the parent class. The method in the parent class is the "just say no" function–it always returns false when asked if the pile can take a new card.

---

[1]There is actually one special case where the return type declared in the child class need not match the return type in the parent class. We will describe this exception in Section 12.3.1 in the next chapter.

```
bool CardPile::canTake (card & c)
{    // just say no
    return false;
}
```

The method in the class SuitPile, on the other hand, will answer true if the
pile is empty and the card is an ace, or if the card matches the topmost card of
the pile in suit and is one larger in rank:

```
bool SuitPile::canTake (card & c)
{
        // can add ace to pile
    if (empty())
        return c.rank() == 0;
    card & topcard = top();
        // must match in suit and be next card
    if ((c.suit() == topcard.suit()) &&
        (c.rank() == 1 + topcard.rank()))
            return true;

    return false;
}
```

For this technique to work, it is imperative that the method in the child class
totally hide the method in the parent class.

There is a subtle difference in meaning for the C++ compiler depending upon
whether the method canTake is declared *virtual* in the class CardPile. Both are
legal. For the method to work in what we are describing as an object-oriented
fashion, it should be declared as virtual. The virtual modifier is optional as part
of the declarations in the child classes; once a method is declared as virtual it
remains so in all subclasses. However, for the sake of documentation it is usually
repeated in derived classes.

Were the virtual modifier not given, the method would still replace the similarly named method in the parent class; however, the binding of method to
message would be altered. Nonvirtual methods are static, in the sense described
in Chapter 10. That is, the binding of a call on a nonvirtual method is performed
at compile time, on the basis of the declared (static) type of the receiver, and
not at run time. If the virtual keyword were removed from the declaration of
canTake, variables *declared* as SuitPile would execute the method in class Suit-
Pile, whereas variables *declared* as CardPile would execute the default method
(regardless of the actual value held by the variable).

Another complicating factor in overriding functions in C++ is the interactions
between overloading and overriding. We will discuss this later in Chapter 17.
The complex semantics of method replacement in C++ is in keeping with the C++
philosophy that features should incur a run-time penalty only when they are

used. If virtual functions are not employed, then inheritance imposes absolutely no execution time overhead. This is not true for the other languages we examine. However, the fact that both virtual and nonvirtual forms are legal, but differ in their interpretations, is frequently a source of subtle errors in C++ programs.

Constructors in C++ always use refinement semantics, not replacement semantics. We will discuss these when we introduce refinement.

11.3.2 Replacement in Object Pascal

In the Apple version of Object Pascal, a method can replace another method in a superclass only if:

- The method name is spelled identically to the identifier of the method in the parent class.

- The order, types, and names of the parameters, and the type of function result, if any, match exactly.

- The description of the method in the child class is followed by the keyword override.

Figure 11.2 illustrates a method being replaced. Here, Employee is a general description for employees in a firm, and SalaryEmployee and HourlyEmployee are two subclasses. The function computePay in class Employee computes a value, which is the pay for a given period. This method is overridden in the subclasses, since the calculations used for the two types of employee are different.

Consider a variable emp declared as an instance of class Employee. As we noted, such a variable can hold a value that is either a SalaryEmployee or an HourlyEmployee (or any other employee type). Regardless of the value, a call on the procedure computePay will invoke the correct method for the employee type.

The syntax used by the Borland Delphi Pascal language is much closer to C++ syntax. In the Borland language a method allowed to be subclassed must be followed by the keyword virtual in the parent class, as in Figure 11.3.

11.3.3 Replacement in Smalltalk and Objective-C

In Smalltalk and Objective-C, a method having the same name as a method in a parent class will always override, and totally replace, the method inherited from the parent class. There is no need for the user to indicate explicitly that a method is being replaced. However, for good documentation, it is helpful for the programmer to indicate this fact in a comment.

11.3.4 Replacement in Java

In Java, as in Smalltalk and Objective-C, no syntax is necessary to indicate that replacement is permitted or is taking place other than that a method shares the same name, argument list, and return type as a method in a parent class.

```
type
  Employee = object
      name : alpha;

      function computePay : integer;
      function hourlyWorker : boolean;
      procedure create;
    end;

  SalaryEmployee = object (Employee)
      salary : integer;

      function computePay : integer; override;
      function hourlyWorker : boolean; override;
      procedure create; override;
    end;

  HourlyEmployee = object (Employee)
      wage : integer;
      hoursworked : integer;

      function computePay : integer; override;
      function hourlyWorker : boolean; override;
      procedure create; override;
    end;

function Employee.computePay : integer;
begin
    return 0; (* this is overridden by subclasses *)
end;

function HourlyEmployee.computePay : integer;
begin
    return hoursworked * wage; (* pay is hours times hourly wage *)
end;

function SalaryEmployee.computePay : integer;
begin
    return salary div 12; (* pay is salary divided by pay period *)
end;
```

Figure 11.2 – Overriding a method in Apple Object Pascal.

```
type
  Employee = class (TObject)
      name : string;

      function computePay : integer; virtual;
      function hourlyWorker : boolean; virtual;
      constructor create; virtual;
    end;

  SalaryEmployee = class (Employee)
      salary : integer;

      function computePay : integer; override;
      function hourlyWorker : boolean; override;
      constructor create; override;
  end;
```

Figure 11.3 – Notating replacement in Delphi Pascal.

As noted in Chapter 10, it is even possible in Java to replace data fields (something that is not permitted in any of our other languages). However, such replacements are not dynamic, and the data field selected will be determined by the declared (static) class of a variable, not its dynamic value. This situation is sometimes described as the variable name in the child class *shadowing* the variable of the same name defined in the parent class. This was illustrated in an example program in Chapter 10.

An interesting feature of the Java language is the keyword final. If applied to a method, this keyword specifies that the associated method is a leaf in the class hierarchy tree and cannot be further overridden in any fashion. If applied to an entire class, the keyword specifies that the class itself cannot be subclassed. A Java complier is permitted to optimize final methods by expanding them inline at the point of call. (The language Beta, which we will introduce in Section 11.4.1, has a similar facility).

11.4   Refinement

We earlier noted the conflict between overriding by replacement and the preservation of subclasses as subtypes. One way to mitigate this difficulty is to alter the semantics of overriding. Rather than totally replacing the code in the parent class, the actions described by code in the child class are *combined* with the actions described by the parent class, thus guaranteeing that the actions of the parent will in all cases be executed (and in this way ensuring a minimum level of functionality). The desirability of such behavior is most often observed during the initialization of a new object. In this case we want to perform the initialization specified by the parent class and then whatever additional initialization may be necessary for the child class.

Since, in most object-oriented languages, access to both data and methods is inherited in the child class, the addition of new functionality can be accomplished simply by copying the overridden code from the parent class. But this approach violates several important principles of good design; for example, it reduces code sharing, blocks information hiding, and lessens reliability since errors can occur in copying and errors corrected in the parent class may not be propagated to the child classes.

For this reason, it is useful to have some mechanism within an overriding method that invokes the same method in the parent class, and thus will "reuse" the code of the overridden method. When a method invokes the overridden method from a parent class like this, we say that the method *refines* that of the parent class.

11.4.1   Refinement in Simula and Beta

Refinement semantics occured in the earliest object-oriented language, Simula, which was developed in the early 1960s (see [Dahl 1966]). In Simula the initialization of a newly created object was specified by a statement block attached to the class description, as in the following:

```
class Employee
begin
    integer identificationNumber;

        ... class description omitted

    comment statements given here
        are executed to initialize
        each newly created object;

    identificationNumber :=
        prompt_for_integer("Enter idNumber:");

    inner;
end;
```

This initialization block is executed each time an instance of the class Employee is executed. The keyword inner in the initialization block specifies the point during initialization at which any actions specified by a subclass are executed. Imagine, for example, that we now construct a subclass of Employee that represents hourly workers. This class can also be given an initialization block. When an instance of class HourlyEmployee is created, the initialization block in the parent class Employee is first executed. When the inner statement is reached, the initialization block in the class HourlyEmployee is invoked. If desired this block can in turn execute its own inner statement, which triggers initializations of further subclasses, and so on to any depth. If no subclass is used, execution of an inner statement produces no effect.

```
Employee class HourlyEmployee
begin
    integer hourlyWage;

        ... class description omitted

    hourlyWage :=
        prompt_for_integer("Enter wage:");
    inner;
end;
```

Simula only used refinement and the inner keyword during initialization of new objects; overriding of ordinary methods was handled by replacement semantics. It remained for the language Beta [Madsen 1993] to systematically apply refinement semantics to all methods, through the unification of class, function, and method into one construct, called the *pattern* (not to be confused with *design patterns*, which we will discuss in Chapter 18).

To illustrate Beta-style patterns and refinement, let us first consider an example that uses simple functions rather than classes and methods. Suppose we want to create a series of functions to print HTML anchors for World Wide Web addresses. An anchor consists of some initial text, followed by an WWW URL (machine and file address), followed by some closing text. An example is the following:

```
<A HREF="http://www.cs.orst.edu/~budd/oop.html">
```

In Beta we might accomplish this by first writing a function to print only the beginning and ending text, but not the actual Web address.

```
printAnchor:
    (#
        do
            '<A HREF="http:'->puttext; INNER
            '">'->puttext
    #);
```

The command puttext displays textual output. The three statements in this function produce the beginning text, followed by the refinement action (if any), followed by the ending text.

A second function might specialize the actions of the first by restricting the

Web addresses to a specific site, for example, the Web server at Oregon State University. This is accomplished by defining a new function as a refinement of the first, and providing the actions that are to be executed in place of the INNER statement in the original.

```
printOSUAnchor : printAnchor
    (#
        do
            '//www.cs.orst.edu/'->puttext;
            INNER
    #);
```

When we execute this function, the code in the parent function (printAnchor) is executed first, since we specified that this function is a refinement of the earlier. When the statement INNER in the parent function is executed, the code for the new function is inserted. In this case this code prints a specific Web address, and then executes any further refinements.

Refinement can be extended to any depth. A third function, for example, might print out a Web address for a specific individual.

```
printBuddAnchor : printOSUAnchor
    (#
        do
            '~budd/'->puttext;
            INNER
    #);
```

Executing printBuddAnchor results in the text:

```
<A HREF="http://www.cs.orst.edu/~budd/">
```

In Beta, refinements can even be defined inline. Executing the statement

```
printBuddAnchor(# do 'oop.html/'->puttext #)
```

results in the following output:

```
<A HREF="http://www.cs.orst.edu/~budd/oop.html/">
```

In class descriptions, the effect we have been describing as refinement is achieved by a combination of function refinement and virtual methods (called *virtual pattern declarations* in Beta). As in our earlier example, we will create a class Employee that contains, among other items, a unique identification number and a function that will display employee information.

```
Employee :
    (#
        identificationNumber : @integer;

        display:<
            (#
                do 'Employee Number: '->puttext;
                identificationNumber->printInteger;
                INNER
            #);
    #);
```

A subclass, such as the following, extends the parent class, and virtual functions defined within the subclass can similarly extend methods defined in the parent class. In this case, execution of the display method has the effect of first executing the function in the parent class and then, when the INNER statement is encountered, executing the code from the child class.

```
HourlyEmployee : Employee
    (#
        wage : @integer;

        display::<
            (#
                do
                    ' wage: '->puttext;
                    wage->printInteger;
                    INNER
            #)
    #);
```

Upholding the principle of substitutability, an instance of HourlyEmployee may be associated with a reference to an Employee. If we then perform the display action on such a value, the statements in the method in the parent class are executed. When the INNER statement is reached, the statements in the display function, which is defined in the child class as an extension of the parent class, will be inserted.

The systematic use of refinement for overriding is conceptually elegant, in that it makes it almost impossible to write a subclass that is not also a subtype. On the other hand, many of the tricks useful in replacement semantics (such as the sqrt function in Smalltalk described earlier) are difficult to simulate in a language such as Beta. Most likely, only historical accident, perhaps coupled with the fact that refinement semantics are slightly more complex to implement than replacement semantics, accounts for the predominance of languages that use replacement.

11.4.2   Wrappers in CLOS

Another interesting variation on refinement semantics occurs in the Lisp dialect, CLOS [Keene 1989]. In CLOS a subclass may override a method in a parent class and specify a *wrapping method*. A wrapping method can be a *before method*, an *after method*, or an *around method*. According to the type, the method is executed before, after, or surrounding the method in the parent class. In the last case, a special statement, call-next-method, invokes the method in the parent class. This is similar to the way in which refinement is simulated in languages such as C++ and Object Pascal.

11.5   Refinement in Various Languages

Of the languages we are considering, only C++ uses refinement semantics, and even there it is only true for constructors. (C++ follows Simula in this regard, where refinement semantics are used only during initialization). However, in all the languages, the effect of refinement can be *simulated* by other mechanisms. How this is accomplished will be described in the following sections.

11.5.1   Refinement in Object Pascal

Refinement in Object Pascal is accomplished by the method in the child class explicitly invoking the overridden method inherited from the parent class. This is more or less the reverse of the Simula or Beta approach, in which the method in the parent class invokes the method in the child class. However, in most cases the effect is the same–both methods will be executed.

The keyword inherited is used within the child class to indicate the point during execution at which the method from the parent class should be invoked. Suppose, for example, that we wish to write a method named initialize that will prompt the user for values initializing the data fields in an object. The method for the parent class Employee might be written as follows:

```
procedure Employee.initialize;
begin
    writeln("enter employee name:");
    readln(name);
end;
```

The subclass might augment the initialization of the parent class data fields with code to initialize the data fields of the child class, as follows:

```
function SalaryEmployee.initialize;
begin
    inherited initialize;
    writeln("enter salary: ");
```

```
    readln(salary);
end;
```

In the Delphi Pascal language the inherited construct is used even in constructors. This is sometimes useful, since the point at which a constructor for
a parent class is invoked from within the constructor for the child class can be
determined by the programmer.

11.5.2 Refinement in C++

In C++ a method invocation can be augmented by a qualification to precisely
specify the class from which the method is to be derived, rather than by the
normal method lookup procedure. This qualification is written as a class name,
followed by a pair of colons, and finally the name of the method. The use of the
qualification removes the virtual message-passing mechanism and ensures that
the method will be taken from the named class.

The qualified name mechanism is used in C++ to simulate the mechanics of
refinement in overriding. In brief, the overridden method explicitly invokes the
method in the parent class, thereby ensuring that both will be executed.

We will once more use an example from our solitaire program, rewritten to
use C++ syntax. The method addCard in class CardPile takes care of the basic
actions of placing a new card on top of the card pile. The class DiscardPile must
in addition ensure that the new card being added to the stack is face up. It does
this by the following method:

```
void    DiscardPile::addCard (card & newCard)
{
        // make sure new card is face up
    if (! newCard.faceUp())
        newCard.flip();

        // then add to pile
    CardPile::addCard (newCard);
}
```

We noted earlier that one way in which a constructor differs from other
methods in C++ is that, in a child class, it *always* uses refinement rather than
replacement. That is, a constructor in a child class always invokes the constructor
for the parent class.

If no indication is provided in the constructor for the child class, and if the
parent class contains a default constructor (a constructor with no arguments),
the default constructor for the parent class is automatically invoked. Otherwise,
the arguments to be used with the constructor for the parent class must be
explicitly specified. A constructor for the parent class is explicitly invoked by
giving the name of the parent class followed by the arguments to be used in the

constructor in an initialization list following the method heading. An example is found in the class TablePile, which takes two of its arguments and uses them to invoke the constructor for the parent class:

```
TablePile::TablePile (int c, int x, int y)
    : CardPile(x, y)
{
    column = c;
}
```

Destructors in C++ use just the opposite approach. The destructor for the child class is invoked, followed by any destructors for data members or parent classes.

11.5.3   Refinement in Smalltalk, Java, and Objective-C

In Chapter 6 we encountered the pseudo-variable super. Almost the sole purpose for this variable, in Smalltalk, Java, and Objective-C, is to permit refinement in situations where a method has been overridden by a subclass. Sending a message to super indicates that the search for the associated method should begin with the parent class to the current class, instead of the class of the receiver (as it would normally or if the message were sent to self).

```
class A {
    private int a;
    public initialize()
        {
            a = 3;
        }
}

class B extends A  {
    private int b;
    public initialize()
        {
          b = 7;
            // execute method from parent class
          super.initialize();
        }
}
```

In Java a constructor invokes the constructor for a parent class with the keyword super.

```
class newClass extends oldClass {
    newClass(int a, int b, int c) {
        // call parent class constructor
        super(a, b);
        // ...
    }
}
```

Similar constructs are used for the same purpose in Smalltalk and Objective-C.

Exercises

1. If neither replacement nor refinement occurs, give an argument to demonstrate that a subclass must always be a subtype.

2. Give an example to illustrate that a subclass need not be a subtype if replacement occurs.

3. Although the systematic use of refinement semantics makes it more difficult to create subclasses that are not subtypes, it is still possible. Illustrate this by giving an example subclass that uses refinement but is nevertheless not a subtype of a base class.

4. Frequently while an instance of a subclass is being initialized, some code from the parent class must be executed, followed by some code from the child class, followed by more code from the parent class. In a windowing system, for example, the parent class might allocate some important data structures, the child class might then modify some fields in these data structures (such as the name of the window and the window size), and finally the parent class might map the window onto the display device. Show how this particular sequence of calls might be executed in an object-oriented language. (Hint: You will probably need to split the initialization process into two or more messages).

5. Not all uses of refinement can be easily simulated by replacement. To see this, write a series of classes that provide functionality similar to the WWW-address anchor routines described in Section 11.4.1. As with question 4, to accomplish this you will probably need to introduce a number of "hidden" methods.

Chapter 12

Implications of Inheritance

The introduction of inheritance has a subtle but pervasive impact on almost all aspects of a programming language. In this chapter, we will examine some of these effects, considering in detail the type system, the meaning of operations such as assignment, testing for equivalence, and storage allocation.

We have described the *is-a* relationship as a fundamental property of inheritance. One way to view the *is-a* relationship is as a means of associating a *type*, as in a type of a variable, with a set of *values*, namely, the values the variable can legally hold. If a variable win is declared as an instance of a specific class, say Window, certainly it should be legal for win to hold values of type Window. If we have a subclass of Window, say TextWindow, since a TextWindow *is-a* Window, it should certainly make sense that win can hold a value of type TextWindow. This is the principle of substitutability that we encountered in previous chapters.

While this principle makes intuitive sense, from a practical point of view there are difficulties associated with implementing object-oriented languages in such a manner that this intuitive behavior can be realized. These difficulties are not insurmountable, but the way in which various language designers have chosen to address them differs from language to language. An examination of these problems, and of how they affect the language, illuminates the reasons for obscure features of languages over which the unwary programmer is likely to stumble.

12.1   Memory Layout

Let us start by considering a seemingly simple question, the various answers to which will lead us in different directions: How much storage should we allocate to a variable that is declared to be of a specific class? To take a concrete example, how much storage should we allocate to the variable win that we earlier described as being an instance of class Window?

It is commonly believed that variables allocated on the stack as part of the procedure-activation process are more efficient than are variables allocated on

213

the heap (but see [Appel 1987] for a dissenting opinion). Accordingly, language designers and implementors go to great lengths to make it possible for variables to be stack-allocated. But there is a major problem with stack allocation–the storage requirements must be determined statically, at compile time or at the latest at procedure entry time. These times are well before the values the variable will hold are known.

The difficulty is that subclasses can introduce data not present in a super-class. The class TextWindow, for example, probably brings with it data areas for character buffers, locations of the current edit point, and so on. The following might be a typical declaration:

```
class Window {
      int height;
      int width;
      ...
   public:
      virtual void oops();
   };

class TextWindow : public Window {
      char *contents;
      int cursorLocation;
      ...
   public:
      virtual void oops();
   };
```

Window win;   // *declare a variable of type window*

Should the additional data values (contents and cursorLocation here) be taken into consideration when space for win is allocated? There are at least three plausible answers:

1. Allocate the amount of space necessary for the base class only. That is, allocate to win only those data areas declared as part of the class Window, ignoring the space requirements of subclasses.

2. Allocate the maximum amount of space necessary for any legal value, whether from the base class or from any subclass.

3. Allocate only the amount of space necessary to hold a single pointer. Allocate the space necessary for the value at run time on the heap, and set the pointer value appropriately.

All three solutions are possible, and two of them are found in the languages we are considering. In the following sections, we will investigate some of the implications of this design decision.

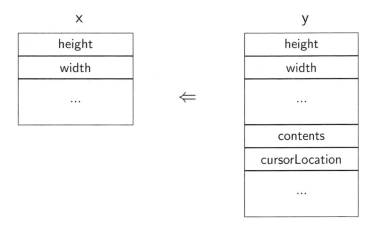

Figure 12.1 – Assigning a larger value to a smaller box.

12.1.1 Minimum Static Space Allocation

The language C was designed to be run-time efficient. Thus, given the widespread belief that stack-based allocation of memory locations results in faster execution times than are possible with dynamic variables, it is not surprising that its successor, C++, retains the concepts of both nondynamic and dynamic (run-time-allocated) variables.

In C++, the distinction is made in how a variable is declared and, accordingly, whether pointers are used to access the values of the variable. In the following, for example, the variable **win** is allocated on the stack. Space for it will be set aside on the stack when the procedure containing the declaration is entered. The size of this area will be the size of the base class alone. The variable tWinPtr, on the other hand, contains only a pointer. Space for the value pointed to by tWinPtr will be allocated dynamically when a **new** statement is executed. Since by this time the size of a TextWindow is known, there are no problems associated with allocating an amount of storage on the heap sufficient to hold a TextWindow.

```
Window win;
Window *tWinPtr;
...
tWinPtr = new TextWindow;
```

What happens when the value pointed to by tWinPtr is assigned to win? In other words, what happens when the user executes the statement

```
win = *tWinPtr;
```

The space allocated to win is only large enough to accommodate a Window, whereas the value pointed to by tWinPtr is larger (Figure 12.1). Clearly, not all of the values pointed to by tWinPtr can be copied. The default behavior is to copy only the corresponding fields. (In C++, the user can override the meaning of the assignment operator and provide any semantics desired. Thus, we refer here only to the default behavior observed in the absence of any alternative provided by the user.) Clearly, then, some information is lost (the information contained in the extra fields of tWinPtr). Some authors use the term *slicing* for this process, as the fields in the right side that are not found in the left side are sliced off during assignment.

Is it important that this information is lost? Only if the user can tell the difference. The question is therefore how the user might be able to notice.

The semantics of the language ensure that only methods defined in the class Window can be invoked with win, and no methods defined in TextWindow. Methods defined in Window and implemented in that class cannot access or modify data defined in subclasses, so no access is possible there. But what about methods defined in class Window but *overridden* in the subclass?

Consider, for example, the two procedures oops() shown below. If the user executed win.oops() and the method from class TextWindow was selected, an attempt would be made to display the data value win.cursorLocation, which does not exist in the storage assigned to win. This would either cause a memory violation or (more likely) produce garbage.

```
void Window::oops()
{
    printf("Window oops");
}

void TextWindow::oops()
{
    printf("TextWindow oops %d", cursorLocation);
}
```

The solution to this dilemma selected by the designer of C++ was to change the rules that are used to bind a procedure to the invocation of a virtual method. The new rules might be summarized as follows:

- For pointers (and references), when a message invokes a member function that could potentially have been overridden, the member function selected is determined by the dynamic value of the receiver.

- For other variables, the binding on a call of a virtual member function is determined by the static class (the class of the declaration) and not by the dynamic class (the class of the actual value).

More accurately, during the process of assignment the value is *changed* from the type representing the subclass to a value of the type represented by the parent class. This is analogous to the way an integer variable might be changed during assignment to a floating-point variable. With this interpretation, it is possible to ensure that, for stack-based variables, the dynamic class is *always* the same as the static class. Given this rule, it is not possible for a procedure to access fields that are not physically present in the object. The method selected in the call win.oops() would be that found in class Window, and the user would not notice the fact that memory was lost during the assignment.

Nevertheless, this solution is achieved only at the expense of introducing a subtle inconsistency. Expressions involving pointers bind virtual methods in the manner we described in earlier chapters. Thus, these values will perform differently from expressions using nondynamic values. Consider the following:

```
Window win;
TextWindow *tWinPtr, *tWin;
...
tWinPtr = new TextWindow;
win = * tWinPtr;
tWin = tWinPtr;

win.oops ( ) ;
( *tWin ).oops ( ) ;
```

Although the user is likely to think that win and the value pointed to by tWin are the same, it is important to remember that the assignment to win has transformed the type of the value. Because of this change, the first call on oops() will invoke the method in class Window, whereas the second will invoke that in class TextWindow.

12.1.2 Maximum Static Space Allocation

A different solution to the problem of deciding how much space to allocate to a declaration for an object is to assign the maximum amount of space used by any value the variable might hold, whether from the class named in the declaration or from any subclass. This approach is similar to the one used to lay out overlaid types in conventional languages, such as variant records in Pascal or union structures in C. On assignment, it is not possible to assign a value larger than what fits in the target destination, so the picture shown in Figure 12.1 cannot occur and the subsequent problems described in the last section do not arise.

This would seem to be an ideal solution were it not for one small problem: The size of any object cannot be known until an entire program has been seen. Not simply a module (unit in Object Pascal, File in C++), but the entire program must be scanned before the size of any object can be determined. Because this requirement is so restrictive, no major object-oriented language uses this approach.

12.1.3   Dynamic Memory Allocation

The third approach does not store the *value* of objects on the stack at all. When space for an identifier is allocated on the stack at the beginning of a procedure, it is simply large enough for a pointer. The values are maintained in a separate data area, the heap, that is not subject to the first-in last-out allocation protocol of the stack. Since all pointers have a constant fixed size, no problem arises when a value from a subclass is assigned to a variable declared to be from a superclass.

This is the approach used in Object Pascal, Smalltalk, Java, and Objective-C, which the user might already have guessed by the close similarity of objects and pointers in Object Pascal. For both pointers and objects, it is necessary to invoke the standard procedure new to allocate space before the object can be manipulated. Similarly, it is necessary for the user to call free explicitly to release space allocated for the object.

Besides the requirement for explicit user memory allocation, another problem with this technique is that it is often tied to the use of *pointer semantics* for assignment. When pointer semantics are used, the value transferred in an assignment statement is simply the pointer value rather than the value indicated by the pointer. Consider the program shown below, which implements a one-word buffer that can be set and retrieved by the user:

```
type
    intBuffer : object
        value : integer;
    end;
var
    x, y : intBuffer;

begin
    new(x);           { create a buffer }
    x.value := 5; writeln(x.value);
    y := x;           { y is same buffer as x }
    y.value := 7; writeln(x.value);
end;
```

Notice the two variables x and y declared to be instances of this class. In executing the program, the user might be surprised when the last statement prints out the value 7 rather than the value 5. The reason for this surprising result is that x and y do not just have the same value; they point to the same object. This situation is shown in Figure 12.2. The use of pointer semantics for objects in Object Pascal is particularly confusing because the alternative, *copy semantics*, is used for all other data types. If x and y were structures, the assignment of y to x would result in the copying of information from y to x. Since this would create two separate copies, changes to y would not be reflected in changes in x.

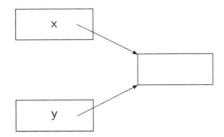

Figure 12.2 – Two object variables pointing to the same value.

12.2 Assignment

The memory-allocation strategies used in both C++ and Object Pascal have an effect on the meaning of assignment, so we will summarize the exact meaning of this operator in the various languages we are considering. As noted in the last section, there are two interpretations we can give to assignment.

Copy semantics. Assignment copies the entire value of the right side, assigning it to the left side. Thereafter, the two values are independent and changes in one are not reflected in changes in the other.

Pointer semantics. Assignment changes the reference of the left side to be the right side. (This approach is sometimes referred to as *pointer assignment*). Thus, the two variables not only have the same value but also refer to the same object. Changes in one will alter the value, which will be reflected in references obtained under either name.

(A compromise position between copy semantics and pointer semantics is found in some programming languages, although not in any of the languages we are considering in our case studies. The idea is to use pointer semantics for assignment but to convert a value into a new structure if it is ever modified. In this manner assignments are very efficient, but a value cannot be inadvertently modified by a change to an aliasing variable. This technique is often termed *copy on write*.)

Generally, if pointer semantics are used, languages provide some means for producing a true copy. Also, pointer semantics are generally more often used when all objects are allocated on a heap (dynamically) rather than on the stack (automatically). When pointer semantics are used, it is common for a value to outlive the context in which it is created.

Object-oriented languages differ in which of the two semantics they use, providing one, the other, or combinations of both.

12.2.1   Assignment in C++

The default algorithm used in C++ to assign a class value to a variable is to
copy corresponding data fields recursively. However, it is possible to overload
the assignment operator to produce any behavior desired. This technique is so
common that some C++ translators issue a warning if the default assignment rule
is used.

In assignment overloading the interpretation is that the assignment operator
is a method in the class of the lefthand side, with argument from the righthand
side. The result can be void if embedded assignments are not possible, although
more typically the result is a reference to the lefthand side. The following example shows assignment of a string data type, which redefines assignment so that
two copies of the same string share characters.

```
String & String::operator = (String& right)
{
    len = right.len;  // copy the length
    buffer = right.buffer;  // copy the pointer to values
    return (*this);
}
```

A common source of confusion for new C++ programmers is the use of the
same symbol for assignment and for initialization. In conventional C, an assignment used in a declaration statement is simply a syntactic shorthand. That is,
the effect of

```
int limit = 300;
```

is the same as

```
int limit;
limit = 300;
```

In C++ an assignment used in a declaration may select the constructors invoked and may not use the assignment operator at all. That is, a statement such
as

```
Complex x = 4;
```

is interpreted to mean the same as the declaration

```
Complex x(4);
```

Initialization is often used with reference variables and yields a situation
very similar to pointer semantics. If s is a valid String, for example, the following

makes t an alias for the value of s, so that any change in one will be reflected in
the other. As we have noted, declarations in C++ can be inserted into a program
at any point.

... // use of variable s

```
String & t = s;
```

... // t and s now refer to the same value

Reference variables are most often used to implement call-by-reference parameter passing. This use can be considered a form of pointer assignment, where
the parameter is being assigned the argument value. Of course, pointer semantics
in C++ can also be achieved through pointer variables.

Parameter passing is in part a form of assignment (the assignment of the
parameter values to the arguments), and so it is not surprising that the same
issues occur here as in assignment. For example, consider the definitions shown
below:

```
class Base {
public:
     virtual void see();
};

class Derived {
public:
     virtual void see();
};

void f (Base);
void g (Base &);

Derived z;
f(z); g(z);
```

Both the functions f and g take as argument a value declared as the base
type, but g declares the value as a reference type. If f is called with a value of
a derived type, the value is converted (*sliced*) to create a value of the base type
as part of the assignment of the arguments. Thus, if see is invoked from within
f, the virtual function from the base class will be used. On the other hand, this
conversion, or slicing, does not occur as part of the parameter passing to g; so if
see is invoked from within g, the procedure from the derived class will be used.
This difference in interpretation, which depends only on the one character in the
function header, is sometimes known as the *slicing problem*.

The overloading of the assignment symbol and the choice of parameter-passing mechanisms provided by value and reference assignment in C++ are powerful features, but they can also be quite subtle. For example, the assignment symbol used in initialization, although it is the same as the assignment symbol used in statements, is not altered by a redefinition of the assignment operator. A good explanation of the uses and power of assignment in C++ is given by Koenig [Koenig 1989a, Koenig 1989b].

Copies of values are frequently produced by the C++ run-time system as temporaries or arguments to procedures. The user can control this task by defining a *copy constructor*. The argument to a copy constructor is a reference parameter of the same type as the class itself. It is considered good practice to always create a copy constructor.

```
class Complex {
    ...
    Complex (const Complex & source)
        {
            // simply duplicate fields from source
            rl = source.rl;
            im = source.im;
        }
    ...
private:
    double rl;
    double im;
}
```

12.2.2   Assignment in Object Pascal and Java

Object Pascal and Java both use pointer semantics for assignment of objects. In Object Pascal there is no system-supplied mechanism for producing a copy of an object, so it is common to create a no-argument method, copy, which yields a copy of the receiver if this functionality is desired. In Java the class Object defines a method, clone, that produces a bit-wise clone of the receiver, and subclasses are free to redefine this method. The return type of this method is Object, so a cast expression must be used to convert it to the appropriate type.

```
newBall = (Ball) aBall.clone();
```

Notice that in Object Pascal pointer semantics are used only for objects. All other types, such as arrays and records, use copy semantics for assignment. This is often confusing to the novice programmer.

12.2.3   Assignment in Smalltalk

Smalltalk uses pointer semantics for assignment. The class Object, which is a superclass of all classes, implements two methods for copying objects; thus, copy assignment can use a combination of assignment and message passing. The statement

```
x <- y copy
```

creates a new instance just like y, in which the fields (instance variables) point to objects that are shared with the instance variables of the receiver. In contrast, the statement

```
x <- y deepCopy
```

creates a new instance just like y, in which the fields (instance variables) are initialized with copies of the fields of y.

Put another way, a copy (also called a shallowCopy) shares instance variables with the original, whereas a deepCopy also copies the instance variables. If y is an object that has three instance variables–named a, b, and c, for example–a copy (or shallowCopy) of y will look like this:

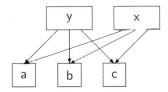

On the other hand, a deepCopy creates new copies of the instance variables, yielding a picture like this:

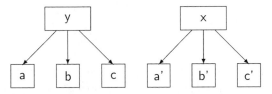

The instance variables are themselves created using the method copy. Classes are free to override any of the methods copy, shallowCopy, or deepCopy, so instances of some classes may exhibit different behavior.

12.2.4   Assignment in Objective-C

Objective-C uses pointer semantics for assignment of objects. A copy of an object can be obtained using any of the three methods copy, shallowCopy, or

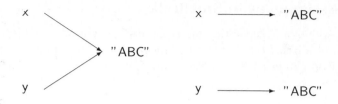

Figure 12.3 – Identity and equality for character strings.

deepCopy, which are analogous to the methods used in Smalltalk.

```
id x, y, z;

\\ ... some definition of y

x = [ y copy ];

z = [ y deepCopy ];
```

12.3   Equality

Like assignment, deciding whether one object is equivalent to another is more subtle than it might at first appear. In part, the difficulty in determining exactly what equality means is a reflection of similar confusion in spoken English. If a speaker asks "Is the morning star the evening star?" the answer can legitimately be either yes or no. If we see that the comparison requested is between the actual objects denoted by the two terms (that is, the planet Venus in both cases), then the answer is clearly yes. On the other hand, for someone just learning the language who wants to know whether the term "the morning star" refers to the object that appears in the evening sky, the answer is just as clearly no.

The study of reference, meaning, and equality in language is complex, and we will not pursue it further. The interested reader might wish to explore the episode of the white knight in *Alice in Wonderland* or some of the collected papers in Rosenberg, 1971 and Whorf, 1956. Fortunately, equality in programming languages is usually well defined, if not consistent among languages.

The most obvious dichotomy mirrors the distinction between the pointer semantics and copy semantics in assignment. Many languages use *pointer equivalence*, in which two references to objects are considered pointer equivalent if they point to the same object. If we consider "the morning star" to be a pointer to Venus, then "morning star" is equivalent to "evening star" under this interpretation. This form of equivalence is also sometimes known as object *identity*.

Often, a programmer is not as interested in whether two variables point to the identical object as in whether the two objects possess the same value. The latter is usually desired, for example, in comparing character strings (Figure 12.3). But how is equality of value to be determined? For numbers or character strings, the mechanism is usually *bit-wise equality*. Two objects are equivalent in this interpretation if their bit representations in memory are the same.

For composite objects, such as records in Pascal, bit-wise equality may not be sufficient. Often, the memory layout for such values can possess empty space, or padding, which is not related to the values held by the object. Since such padding should not be considered in determination of equality, a second mechanism, *member equality*, is used. In member equality, we test corresponding members for equality, recursively applying the rule until nonrecord members are found, where bit-wise equality is then applied. If all members agree, the two records are considered equal. If any disagree, the two records are unequal. Such a relation is sometimes known as *structural equivalence*.

Object-oriented programming techniques add their own twist to equality testing. For example, even if the static types of the two values being compared are equal, their dynamic types need not be. Should comparisons of equality take this into account? What if one type defines fields that are not found in the other? Another problem is the fact that the selection of an interpretation for a message is determined entirely by the receiver. There are no guarantees that such fundamental properties as communitivity will be preserved. If x and y are of different types, it can easily happen that "x = y" is true but "y = x" is false!

There is one sense in which the problem of equality is easier to solve than are the corresponding difficulties with assignment. Although assignment is usually considered part of the syntax and semantics of a language, and may not be changeable, the programmer is always free to provide his or her own methods (perhaps using slightly different syntax) for equality testing. Thus, there is no single consistent meaning for equality, and equality can mean something different for every class of objects.

12.3.1   Covariance and Contravariance

Equality testing is one area where it frequently seems useful for subclasses to alter the type signatures of inherited methods. Consider the class **Shape** and its two subclasses, **Triangle** and **Square**. It seems sensible that triangles should only be compared against other triangles, and squares against other squares. Thus, the programmer might be tempted to write class descriptions like the following:

```
class Shape {
public:
    boolean equals (Shape)
        { return false; }
    ...
};
```

```
class  Triangle : public Shape {
public:
    boolean equals (Triangle);
    ...
};

class  Square : public Shape {
public:
    boolean equals (Square);
    ...
};
```

Notice how the argument to the equality-testing function differs in each of the classes. In the parent class the argument is simply another shape, while in the subclasses it has been restricted to the more specialized type. There are two terms used for this form of redefinition:

- An argument that, in the child class, is enlarged to a *more* general class than that associated with the corresponding argument in the parent class is said to be *covariant*.

- An argument that, in the child class, is restricted to a *less* general class than that associated with the corresponding argument in the parent class is said to be *contravariant*.

In this example the argument to the equality-testing function is contravariant.

Covariant and contravariant arguments frequently appear to be a natural solution to a problem, but few languages, and none of those we are considering, permit them. In the following we will explore a few reasons for this restriction.

First, the principle of substitutability we discussed in earlier chapters, asserts that we can substitute an instance of a child class in situations were an instance of the parent class is expected. But this principle implies that the child class must be willing to accept, at the least, any argument value accepted by the parent class. This seems to imply that contravariant overriding is permitted (since the child class could then accept an even larger set of arguments than the parent) but that covariant overriding should be ruled out (since this child class would, in this case, be more restrictive than the parent). As this example illustrates, however, it is covariant overriding that occurs more commonly in actual problems. (A similar, but opposite, argument can be made with regard to function return types).

In the imaginary language we envision here, consider what meaning might be assigned to an attempt to compare a triangle to a square. There are two possibilities:

- The search for a method is based solely on the receiver, a triangle, and yields the triangle method, which requires a triangle as argument. Thus, the use of a square as argument results in a compiler error.

- The search for a method is based both on the receiver and on the argument type signatures. Since the argument does not match the method in class Triangle, the method in class Shape is then invoked.

Most programmers would agree that the second interpretation seems the more natural (although it complicates the task of the compiler). This can lead to some curious situations, as demonstrated by the possibility of the polymorphic variable–the variable of type Shape–that can hold either a square or a triangle. Imagine first that this polymorphic variable is used as an argument, as in the following:

```
Triangle aTriangle;
Shape aShape;

aShape := aTriangle;
if aTriange.equals(aTriangle) ... // returns true
if aTriangle.equals(aShape)) ... // returns false!
```

The first call on equals in the example is bound to the method in class Triangle and, as expected, returns true. The second class is bound to the method in class Shape, since the argument is not explicitly a triangle. This returns false, despite the fact that the actual value is really an equivalent (indeed, identical) triangle.

A similar incongruity occurs if the polymorphic variable is used as a receiver. Since the only reasonable method to use is the one defined in the parent class, the following test yields an unexpected false value.

```
if aShape.equals(aTriangle) ... // returns false
```

Both because the implementation of either covariant or contravariant overriding is complex and because the semantics are cloudy, almost all object-oriented languages prohibit any modification of argument types in overridden methods. Such a policy might be termed *novariance*. To get around this restriction, programmers most often resort to explicit tests and casts, as in the following.

```
    boolean Triangle.equals (Shape & aShape)
    {      Triangle & right = dynamic_cast<Triangle>(aShape);
        if (right) {
            ... do triangle comparison
            }
        else
            return false;
    }
```

There is one small way in which C++ permits contravariant overriding, and this is that the return type of an overridden function can be a subclass of the parent class. Thus, a member function in class Shape could be declared as returning a Shape value, while the subclass Triangle overrides the same function, and declares the return type as Triangle. The relaxation of the novariance rule in this fashion eliminates a large number of cast operations, while not introducing any possibilities of type errors. For example, variables declared as type Shape will indeed return a shape value, even if they are polymorphic variables that are holding a triangle (in this case, the value will just happen to be a triangle).

Programming languages that permit covariance and/or contravariance include Eiffel [Rist 1995] and Sather.

12.3.2   Equality in Objective-C, Java, and Object Pascal

In Objective-C, Java, and Object Pascal, objects are always (or almost always for Objective-C) represented internally by pointers. Thus, it is not surprising that the default meaning of the equality operator (= in Object Pascal; == in Objective-C and Java) is identity, or pointer, equality. Two object variables will test equal only if they point to exactly the same object.

Although it is not possible in either language to override the meaning of the built-in operator, it is common to define methods that provide alternative definitions of equality. The following illustrates an equality test as a method in class Card. Two cards are considered equal in this case if they have the same suit and rank, even if they are not the identical card.

```
function Card.equal ( aCard : Card ) : boolean;
begin
    if (suitValue = aCard.suit) and
       (rankValue = aCard.rank)
      then equal := true
    else equal := false
end;
```

None of these languages support either covariant or contravariant overriding, and compiler warnings will be generated if an attempt is made. In situations where covariant overriding might be useful, as in the equality-testing operator, explicit tests of the dynamic type for the argument must be performed. In Chapter 10 we described the mechanisms to perform such tests.

```
class Triangle extends Shape {
    boolean equals (Shape aShape) {
        if (aShape instanceOf Shape) {
            ... // test triangles
            }
        else return false;
        }
    }
```

12.3.3 Equality in Smalltalk

Smalltalk distinguishes between object identity and object equality. Object identity is tested by use of the operator formed as two equal signs (==). Object equality is tested by use of a single equal sign (=) and is considered a message passed to the left-side argument. The default meaning of this message is the same as the identity operator; however, any class is free to redefine the symbol arbitrarily. The class Array, for example, defines equality to hold when the righthand argument is an array of the same size and corresponding elements are equal.

That equality can be redefined arbitrarily means that there are no guarantees that it will always be symmetric or that the meaning of "x = y" will be related in any way to the meaning of "y = x."

Because Smalltalk is a dynamically typed language, the notions of covariant and contravariant overriding are less meaningful for programmers. Where necessary, explicit tests can be used to determine the actual type (class) of a value.

12.3.4 Equality in C++

C++ provides no default meaning for equality. Individual classes can provide their own meaning by overloading the == operator. The same rules used to disambiguate overloaded operators are used with other overloaded functions, giving the appearance of permitting covariance or contravariant overloading. In reality, such use is not permitted. For example, consider the class definitions shown below:

```
class A {
public:
    int i;
    A(int x) { i = x; }

    int operator== (A& x)
        { return i == x.i; }
};

class B : public A {
public:
    int j;
    B(int x, int y) : A(x) { j = y;}

    int operator== (B& x)
        { return (i == x.i) && (j == x.j); }
};
```

If a and b are instances of classes A and B, respectively, then both a == a and a == b will use the method found in class A, whereas b == b will use the method found in class B. The expression b == a generates a compiler error, since the argument fails to match the definition of the equality operator for instances of class B. (This was the first, and less intuitive, choice in our earlier discussion, where we tried to provide a meaning to a contravariant method).

More important, if a polymorphic variable (which in C++ must be either a pointer or a reference) of type A in fact contains a value of type B, the use of the equality operator is still bound to that in class A. This is because the two definitions shown in the above example are entirely different functions, and no overriding is taking place, which is true even if the keyword virtual is applied to the first definition.

12.4   Type Conversion

In statically typed object-oriented languages, such as C++ and Object Pascal, it is illegal to assign a value from a class to a variable declared as an instance of a subclass. A value known (to the compiler) only as an instance of class Window cannot be assigned to a variable declared to be of class TextWindow. The reasons for this restriction are perhaps already clear; if not, we explore them in Exercises 1 and 2.

Nevertheless, on rare occasions it is desirable to break this rule. Most often, this situation occurs when the programmer knows from further information that a value, despite being maintained in a variable of some superclass, is in reality an instance of a more specific class. In these circumstances, it is possible (although not encouraged) to circumvent the type system.

In C++ and Objective-C, we accomplish this circumvention using the C construct called the *cast*. The cast directs the compiler to convert a value from one type to another. Most often, this technique is used with pointers, in which case only a logical change is made and no physical transformation takes place.

We can illustrate this with a variation on our billiards game, which we will assume has been suitably translated into C++. Instead of making each instance of Ball maintain a linked-list pointer, we write a generalized Link class, as below:

```
class Link {
protected:
    Link *link;

    Link * next ();
    void    setLink (Link *ele);
};
```

```
void Link::setLink(Link *ele) ( link = ele; }

Link * Link::next() { return link; }
```

The class Ball can then be made a subclass of Link. Since the method setLink is inherited from the superclass, it need not be repeated. There is a problem with the inherited method next, however. The method next claims to return a pointer to an instance of Link, not Ball. Yet we know that the object is actually a Ball, since that is the only kind of object we are inserting in the list. We therefore rewrite the Ball class to override the method next and use a cast to change the return type:

```
class Ball : public Link
{
    . . .
    public:
    . . .
    Ball *  next ();
    . . .
};

Ball * Ball::next()
    { return dynamic_cast<Ball *>(Link::next()); }
```

Notice that the method next is *not* declared to be virtual; it is not possible to alter the return type of a virtual procedure. It is important to remember that, in C++, this cast is legal only with pointers and not with objects themselves (See Exercise 2). The dynamic_cast function is part of the RTTI (run-time typing information) system we described in Chapter 10. RTTI casts should be used instead of the older forms, since inappropriate casts are a common source of errors in programs.

In Object Pascal, the idea is similar. Since all objects are treated internally as pointers, this conversion can be applied to any type of object, not simply to pointers. Object Pascal permits a run-time test for the class of an object, so all such "questionable" coercions should be screened by an explicit test prior to the assignment.

```
var
    x : TextWindow;
    y : Window;

begin
    . . .
    if Member(y,TextWindow) then
        x := TextWindow(y)
```

```
    else
        writeln('illegal window assignment');
    ...
end;
```

In Java a variable holding a value from a subclass of the declared class can be cast to the lower class value, but such conversions are verified at run time and an exception will be thrown if the result is invalid. If the programmer does not want an exception to be thrown, the run-time type of a value can be tested with the operator instanceOf, as in the following:

```
    Ball aBall;
    WhiteBall wBall;

    if (aBall instanceOf WhiteBall)
        wBall = (WhiteBall) aBall;
    else
        ...
```

Exercises

1. Explain why, in statically typed object-oriented languages (such as C++ and Object Pascal) it is illegal to assign a value from a class to a variable declared as an instance of a subclass. That is, something like the following will result in a compiler error message:

```
    TextWindow X;
    Window Y:
    ...
    X = Y;
```

2. Assume that the C++ memory-allocation technique operates as described in Section 12.1. Explain what problems can arise if the user attempts to circumvent the problem of Exercise 1 using a cast–that is, writes the assignment as

```
    x = (TextWindow) Y;
```

3. Give an example, in either Object Pascal or C++, to illustrate why an entire program, not simply a file, must be parsed before the size of any object can be determined with the approach of Section 12.1.

4. Argue why, if the principle of substitutability is to be preserved, the return type associated with an overridden method can be no more general than that associated with the parent class.

5. Show that it is possible to define a language similar to Object Pascal that does not use pointer semantics for assignment. In other words, give an algorithm for assignment for a language that uses the approach to memory management described in Section 12.1, but that does not result in two variables pointing to the same location when one is assigned to the other. Why do you think the designers of Object Pascal did not implement assignment using your approach?

Chapter 13

Multiple Inheritance

In the discussion up to this point, we have assumed that a class will inherit from only one parent class. Although this situation is certainly common, there are nevertheless occasions when concepts are heir to two or more independent backgrounds. If you think of classes as corresponding to categories, as we did in Chapter 1, and you try to describe yourself in terms of the groups to which you belong, it is most likely you will encounter many nonoverlapping classifications. I am a parent, for example, as well as a professor, a male, and a North American. Not one of these categories is a proper subset of any other.

For example, *Beth* is a Potter. Her neighbor, *Margaret*, is a PortraitPainter, and the sort of painting she does is different from that of *Paul*, who is a House-Painter. Although we normally view single inheritance as a form of specialization (a Potter is an Artist), it is more common to view multiple inheritance as a process of *combination* (a PortraitPainter is an Artist *as well as* a Painter), as shown in Figure 13.1).

13.1   Incomparable Complex Numbers

A more concrete example will illustrate the difficulties resulting from having a single inheritance hierarchy. In Smalltalk, the class Magnitude defines a protocol

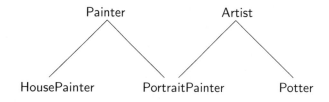

Figure 13.1 – Inheritance as a form of combination.

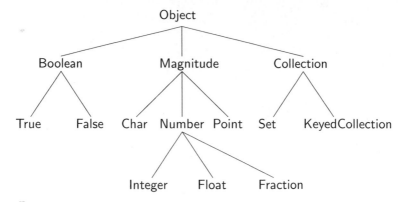

Figure 13.2 – A portion of the Smalltalk class hierarchy.

for objects that have measure–that is, that can be compared with one another. For example, individual characters (instances of class Char) can be compared if we use the underlying representation (such as ASCII) as a basis for measure. A more common class of objects that can be compared are numbers, such as instances of the class Number in Smalltalk. In addition to being measurable, instances of class Number support arithmetic operations–addition, multiplication, and so forth. These operations do not make sense for objects of class Char. There are various number types supported by Smalltalk; examples include the classes Integer, Fraction, and Float. A portion of the class hierarchy is shown in Figure 13.2.

Now suppose we add the class Complex, representing the complex number abstraction. The arithmetic operations are certainly well defined for complex numbers, and it is preferable to make the class Complex a subclass of Number so that, for example, mixed-mode arithmetic is provided automatically. The difficulty is that comparison between two complex numbers is ambiguous. That is, complex numbers are simply not measurable.

Thus, we have the following constraints:

- The class Char should be a subclass of Magnitude but not of Number.

- The class Integer should be a subclass of both Magnitude and Number.

- The class Complex should be a subclass of Number but not of Magnitude.

It is not possible to satisfy all of these requirements in a single inheritance hierarchy, but there are some alternative solutions to this problem:

1. Make Complex a subclass of Number, which is in turn a subclass of Magnitude, then redefine the methods relating to measure in class Complex to produce error messages if they are invoked. This is subtyping for limitation, as described in Chapter 7. Although not elegant, this solution

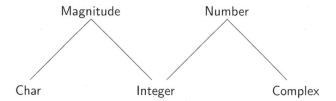

Figure 13.3 – A multiple inheritance hierarchy for complex numbers.

is sometimes the most expedient if your programming language does not support multiple inheritance.

2. Avoid the use of inheritance altogether, and redefine every method in each of the classes Char, Integer, Complex, and so on. This solution is sometimes called *flattening the inheritance tree*. Of course, it eliminates all the benefits of inheritance described in Chapter 7–for example, code reuse and guaranteed interfaces. However, in a statically typed language, such as C++ or Object Pascal, it also prevents the creation of polymorphic objects; thus, for example, it is not possible to create a variable that can hold an arbitrary measurable object or an arbitrary type of number.

3. Use part of the inheritance hierarchy and simulate the rest. For example, place all numbers under class Number, but have each measurable object (whether character or number) implement the comparison operations.

4. Make the two classes Magnitude and Number independent of each other and thus require the class Integer to use inheritance to derive properties from *both* of the parents (Figure 13.3). The class Float will similarly inherit from both Number and Magnitude.

An important point about options 2 and 3 is that they are much more attractive in a dynamically typed programming language, such as Objective-C and Smalltalk. In C++ or Object Pascal, the definition of which types are "measurable" might be phrased in terms of classes–an object is "measurable" if it can be assigned to a variable declared to be of class Magnitude. In Smalltalk and Objective-C, on the other hand, an object is measurable if it understands the messages relating to measure, regardless of where in the class hierarchy it is defined. Thus, techniques such as double-dispatching (see [Ingalls 1986] or Section 18.2.3) can be used to make complex numbers interact with other values even if they share no common ancestor classes.

A class that inherits from two or more parent classes is said to exhibit *multiple inheritance*. Multiple inheritance is a powerful and useful feature in a language, but creates many subtle and difficult problems for the language implementor. Of the languages we are considering, only C++ supports multiple inheritance,

```
┌──────────────────────────────────────────────────────┐
│                                                        │
│   Menu                                                 │
│                                                        │
│   ─────────────────────────────                        │
│                                                        │
│                                                        │
│     display–Draw entire menu.                          │
│     hilight–Highlight current selection,               │
│     unhighlight previous selection.                    │
│     select–Execute current menu item.                  │
│                                                        │
│                                                        │
│                                                        │
│                                                        │
│                                                        │
└──────────────────────────────────────────────────────┘
```

Figure 13.4 – A CRC card for class Menu.

although some research versions of Smalltalk do as well. In this chapter, we will explore some of the advantages, and some of the problems associated with this facility.

13.2   Walking Menus

A second example will illustrate many of the issues to keep in mind when you are considering the use of multiple inheritance. This example is inspired by the library for creating graphical user interfaces associated with an object-oriented language called Eiffel [Meyer 1988a, Meyer 1988b]. In this system, menus are described by a class Menu. Instances of Menu maintain features such as the number of menu entries, a list of menu items, and so on. The functionality associated with a menu includes the ability to be displayed on a graphical screen, and to select a menu item (Figure 13.4).

Each item in the menu is represented by an instance of class MenuItem; instances of which maintain their text, their parent menu, and the command to be executed when the menu item is selected (Figure 13.5).

A common facility in graphical user interfaces is known as a *walking menu* (sometimes called *cascading menu* in other systems), which is needed when the menu item has several alternative parts. For example, a menu item in a terminal-emulator program might simply indicate "set options." When that item is selected, a second menu–the walking menu–is displayed and permits the user to

```
┌──────────────────────────────────────────────────────────────┐
│                                                                │
│   MenuItem                                                      │
│   ─────────────────────────────────────                        │
│                                                                │
│                                                                │
│   text–Return title text.                                      │
│   execute–Execute associated action                            │
│                      (overridden in subclasses)                │
│                                                                │
│                                                                │
│                                                                │
│                                                                │
│                                                                │
│                                                                │
└──────────────────────────────────────────────────────────────┘
```

Figure 13.5 – A CRC card for class MenuItem.

select from a number of available options (visual bell, audio bell, dark background, light background, and so on).

The walking menu is clearly a Menu. It maintains the same information that a Menu does and it must perform like a Menu. On the other hand, it is also clearly a MenuItem; it must maintain a name and the ability to execute (by displaying itself) when the associated entry is selected on the parent menu. Important behavior can be obtained with little effort by allowing the class WalkingMenu to inherit from both parents. For example, when the walking menu is asked to execute its associated action (inherited from class MenuItem), it will display its entire menu (by executing the drawing method inherited from class Menu).

As with the use of single inheritance, it is important to remember the *is-a* relationship when using multiple inheritance. In this case, multiple inheritance is appropriate because clearly, both the assertions "a walking menu *is-a* menu" and "a walking menu *is-a* menuItem" make sense. When the *is-a* relationship is not satisfied, multiple inheritance can be misused. For example, it would not be appropriate to describe a class Automobile as a subclass of the two classes Motor and Body, or the class ApplePie as a subclass of the classes Pie and Apple. Clearly, an ApplePie *is-a* Pie, but it is not true that it is an Apple.

When multiple inheritance is properly used, a subtle but nevertheless important change in the view of inheritance takes place. The *is-a* interpretation, used in single inheritance, views a subclass as a more specialized form of another category, represented by the parent class. When multiple inheritance is used, a class is viewed as a *combination* or collection of several different characterizations, each providing a different protocol and some basic behavior, which is then specialized to the case at hand. Facilities for storing and retrieving objects from a permanent depository, such as a disk, is a common example. Often, this facility is implemented as part of a behavior associated with a specific class, say Persistence or Storable. To add this ability to an arbitrary class, we merely add the class Storable to the list of ancestors of the class.

Of course, it is important to distinguish being heir to independent backgrounds from being built out of independent components, as the example of an Automobile and a Motor illustrates.

13.3   Name Ambiguity

A frequent difficulty with multiple inheritance is that names can be used to mean more than one operation. To illustrate this, we consider once more a programmer developing a card-game simulation. Suppose that there is already a data abstraction CardDeck that provides the functionality associated with a deck of cards (such as shuffling and being able to draw a single card from the deck) but has no graphical capabilities. Suppose further that another set of existing classes implements graphical objects. Graphical objects maintain a location on a two-dimensional display surface. In addition, graphical objects must all know how to display themselves by means of the virtual method called draw.

The programmer decides that, to achieve maximum leverage from these two existing classes, he will have the class for the new abstraction, GraphicalDeck, inherit from both the classes CardDeck and GraphicalObject. It is clear that conceptually, the class GraphicalDeck *is-a* CardDeck, and is thus logically descendant from that class, and also that a GraphicalDeck *is-a* GraphicalObject. The only trouble is the clash between the two meanings of the command draw.

As Meyer points out [Meyer 1988a] the problem is clearly with the child and not with the parent classes. The meaning of draw is unambiguous and meaningful in each of the parent classes when taken in isolation. The difficulty is with the combination. Since the problem arises only in the child class, the solution should also be found in that class. In this case, the child class must decide how to disambiguate the overloaded term.

The solution usually involves a combination of *renaming* and *redefinition*. By *redefinition* we mean a change in the operation of a command, as happens when a virtual method is overridden in a subclass. By *renaming* we simply mean changing the name by which a method is invoked without altering the command's functionality. In our graphical deck of playing cards, the programmer might have draw mean the process of drawing the graphical image and rename the process of removing a card from the deck drawCard.

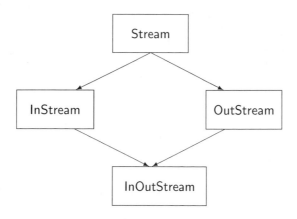

Figure 13.6 – An inheritance graph.

13.3.1 Inheritance from Common Ancestors

A more difficult problem occurs if a programmer wishes to use two classes that both inherit from a common parent class. Suppose, for example, that a programmer is developing a set of classes to implement *streams* for input and output. A stream is a generalization of a file, except that its elements can have more structure. We can have a stream of integers, for example, or a stream of reals. The class InStream provides a protocol for input streams. A user can open an input stream by attaching it to a file, retrieve the next element in the stream, and so on. The class OutStream provides similar functionality for output streams. Both classes inherit from a single parent class, Stream. The information that points to the actual underlying file is maintained in the parent class.

Now suppose the user wants to create a combined input-output stream. It makes sense to claim that an input-output stream is a descendant of both an input stream and an output stream. Renaming, such as we described in the last section, can resolve the meaning of any functions defined in both InStream and OutStream. But what about features inherited from the common grandparent? The difficulty is that the inheritance tree is a directed graph rather than a simple tree (Figure 13.6). If all that is inherited from the common parent class is behavior (methods), the resolution technique described previously can be used. But if the parent class also defines data fields, such as a file pointer, there are two choices. Do we want two copies of the data values or only one copy? A similar problem occurs if the grandparent class uses constructors or other initialization routines that should be invoked only once. In the next section, we will describe how this problem is handled in C++.

```
class LinkedList {
public:
  Link *elements;

  LinkedList()
    { elements = (Link *) 0; }

  void add(Link *n)
    { if (elements) elements->add(n); else elements = n; }

  void onEachDo(void f(Link *))
    {if (elements) elements->onEachDo(f); }
};

class Link {
public:
  Link *next;

  Link()
    { next = (Link *) 0; }

  void setLink(Link *n)
    { next = n; }

  void add(Link *n)
    { if (next) next->add(n); else setLink(n); }

  void onEachDo(voidf(Link *))
    { f(this); if (next) next->onEachDo(f); }
};
```

Figure 13.7 – Classes to implement linked lists.

```
class IntegerLink: public Link {
  int value;
public:
  IntegerLink(int i) : Link()
    { value = i; }

  print()
    { printf("%d\n", value); }
};
void display(IntegerLink *x)
  { x->print(); }

main() {
  LinkedList list;

  list.add(new IntegerLink(3));
  list.add(new IntegerLink(17));
  list.add(new IntegerLink(32));

  list.onEachDo(display);
}
```

Figure 13.8 – Specializing the Link class.

13.4 Multiple Inheritance in C++

We will illustrate the use of multiple inheritance in C++ by working through a small example. Suppose, in a previous project, a programmer developed a set of classes for working with linked lists (Figure 13.7). The abstraction has been divided into two parts: The class Link represents the individual links in the list, and the class LinkedList stores the head of the list. A basic function of linked lists adds a new element. Linked lists also provide the ability to execute a function on each element of the list, where the function is passed as an argument. Both of these activities are supported by associated routines in the class Link.

We form specialized links by subclassing class Link. For example, in Figure 13.8, the class IntegerLink maintains integer values associated with each link. The figure gives a short program illustrating how this data abstraction is used.

Now suppose that in the current project, this same programmer must develop a Tree data type. After pondering this a while, she discovers that a Tree can be thought of as a collection of linked lists. At each level of the tree, the link fields point to siblings (trees that are all at the same level). However, each node also points to a linked list that represents its children. Figure 13.9 illustrates this design, where angled arrows indicate child pointers and horizontal arrows indicate sibling connections.

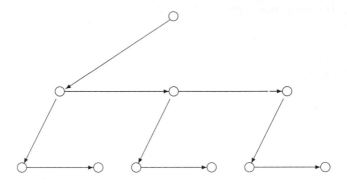

Figure 13.9 – A tree viewed as linked lists.

Thus, a node in the tree is both a LinkedList (because it maintains a pointer to its list of children) and a Link (because it maintains a pointer to its sibling). In C++ we indicate multiple inheritance such as this simply by listing the names of the superclasses, separated by commas, following the colon in the class description. As with single inheritance, each superclass must be preceded by a visibility keyword, either public or private. Figure 13.10 shows the class Tree publicly inheriting from both Link and LinkedList. In addition to maintaining pointers to the children, nodes in a tree also contain an integer value.

Now the problem of name ambiguity must be handled. First, the ambiguity in the name add is a reflection of the ambiguity in meaning. The two senses of the add operation on a tree are to add a child node and to add a sibling node. The first sense is that provided by the add operation in class LinkedList; the second is provided by the add function in class Link. After some reflection, our programmer decides to let add mean "add a child," but to provide two new functions as well that specifically name the intent.

Notice that all three of these functions are, in a sense, merely renamings. They provide no new functionality, but merely redirect the execution to a previously defined function. Some object-oriented languages (such as Eiffel) allow the user to specify such renamings without creating a new function.

The ambiguity of the method onEachDo is more complex. Here, the appropriate action is to execute a traversal of the tree in which the child nodes are visited first, followed by the current node, followed by the sibling nodes (which will, of course, recursively visit *their* children). Thus, execution is a *combination* of the actions provided by the underlying classes Link and LinkedList, as is shown in Figure 13.10.

Renaming is occasionally necessary because of a subtle interaction in C++ between inheritance and parametric overloading. When an overloaded name is used in C++, the inheritance mechanism is first used to find a name scope in which the function is defined. Parameter types are then used to disambiguate the function name *within that scope*. For example, suppose there are two classes

```
class Tree: public Link, public LinkedList {
  int value;

public:
  Tree(int i)
    { value = i; }

  print()
    { printf("%d\n",value); }

  void add(Tree *n)
    { LinkedList::add(n); }

  void addChild(Tree *n)
    { LinkedList::add(n); }

  void addSibling(Tree *n)
    { Link::add(n); }

  void onEachDo(void f(Link *))
    { /* first process children */
      if (elements) elements->onEachDo(f);
      /* then operate on self */
      f(this);
      /* then do siblings */
      if (next) next->onEachDo(f); }
};

main() {
  Tree *t = new Tree(17);
  t->add(new Tree(12));
  t->addSibling(new Tree(25));
  t->addChild(new Tree(15));

  t->onEachDo(display);
}
```

Figure 13.10 – An example of multiple inheritance.

```
class A {
  public:

  void virtual display(int i)
    { printf("in A %d\n", i); }
};

class B {
  public:

  void virtual display(double d)
    { printf("in B %g\n", d); }
};

class C: public B, public A
{
  public:
  void virtual display(int i)
    { A::display(i); }

  void virtual display(double d)
    { B::display(d); }
};

main() {
  C c;
  c.display(13);
  c.display(3.14);
}
```

Figure 13.11 – Inheritance and overloading interacting.

A and B that both define a method display, but that take different arguments (Figure 13.11). The user might be tempted to believe that because the two uses of display can be disambiguated by their parameter types, a child class can inherit from both parents and have access to both methods. Unfortunately, mere inheritance is not sufficient. When the user calls the method display with an integer argument, the compiler cannot decide whether to use the function in class A (which matches the argument more closely) or that in class B (which is the first method encountered in the method search and is applicable by performing an automatic conversion on the parameter value). Fortunately, the compiler *will* warn about this; however, the warning is produced at the point the ambiguous method is invoked, not at the point the class is declared.

The solution is to redefine both methods in the child class C, as shown in

```
class Stream {
  File *fid;
  ...
};

class InStream : public virtual Stream {
  ...
  int open(File *);
};

class OutStream : public virtual Stream {
  ...
  int open(File *);
};

class InOutStream: public InStream, public OutStream {
  ...
};
```

Figure 13.12 – An example of virtual inheritance.

Figure 13.11. By doing so we eliminate the contention between inheritance and overloading; both end up examining the class C, where it is clear to the compiler that the parametric overloading is indeed intentional.

In an earlier section we described a difficulty that occurs when a class inherits from two parent classes, both of which in turn inherit from a common grandparent class. This problem was illustrated with two classes, InStream and OutStream, which both inherited from a common class, Stream. If we want the derived class to inherit only one copy of the data fields defined in Stream, the intermediate classes (InStream and OutStream) must declare that their inheritance from the common parent class is virtual. The virtual keyword indicates that the superclass may appear more than once in descendant classes of the current class, but that only one copy of the superclass should be included. Figure 13.12 shows the declarations for the four classes.

An unfortunate consequence of the C++ approach is that, as Meyer points out, the name confusion is a problem only for the child class but the solution (making the common ancestor virtual) involves changes to the parent classes. It is the intermediate parent classes that give the virtual designation, not the final combined class.

Rarely, it *is* desirable to create two copies of the inherited data fields. For example, graphical objects and card decks might both be maintained on linked lists by each being subclassed from the class Link. Since the two types of links are independent, they should both be maintained in the combined class GraphicalDeck. In this situation the virtual keywords are omitted and the desired outcome will be

```
class D {
public:
  D() { ... }
  D(int i) { ... }
  D(double d) { ... }
};

class A : virtual D {
public:

  A() : D(7)  { ... }
};

class B : virtual D {
public:
  B() : D(3.14) { ... }
};

class C: public A, public B
{
public:
  C() : B(),A() { ... }
};
```

Figure 13.13 – Constructors in multiple inheritance.

obtained. It is important to ensure, however, that the resulting name conflicts do not cause erroneous interpretations.

The fact that visibility keywords can be attached to parent classes independently means that it is possible for a virtual ancestor class to be inherited in different ways–for example, as both **public** and **protected**. In this case, the lesser level of protection (for example, **protected**) is ignored and the more general category used.

When more than one parent class defines a constructor, the order of execution of the various constructors, and hence initialization of their data fields, may be important. The user can control this by invoking the constructors for the base classes directly in the constructor for the child class. For example, in Figure 13.13, the user explicitly directs that when an instance of class C is initialized, the constructor for B is to be invoked first, before the constructor for A. Reversing the order of invocations of the constructor in class C has the effect of reversing the order of initialization.

An exception to this rule occurs with virtual base classes. A virtual base class is always initialized once, before any other initialization takes place, by the constructor (provided by the system if not by the user), which takes no arguments. Thus, in Figure 13.13 the order of initialization when a new element of type C is constructed is first class D with the no-argument constructor, then class B, then class A. The two seeming calls on the constructor for class D that appear in the constructors for classes A and B actually have no effect, since the parent class is marked as virtual.

If it is imperative that arguments for the virtual base class be provided with the constructor, class C may legally provide these values even though D is not an immediate ancestor for C (this is the only situation in which it is legal for a class to provide a constructor for another class that is not an immediate ancestor). That is, the constructor for class C could have been written as follows:

```
C()  :  D(12), B(),  A() { . . . }
```

Constructors for virtual base classes must be invoked first, before the constructors for nonvirtual ancestors.

Virtual methods defined in virtual superclasses can also cause trouble. Suppose that each of the four classes shown in Figure 13.12 defines a method named initialize(). This method is defined as virtual in the class Stream and redefined in each of the other three classes. The initialize methods in InStream and OutStream each invoke Stream::initialize and, in addition, do some subclass-specific initialization.

Now consider the method InOutStream. It cannot call both the inherited methods InStream::initialize and OutStream::initialize without invoking the method Stream::initialize twice. The repeated invocation of Stream::initialize may have unintended effects. The way to avoid this problem is to rewrite Stream::initialize so that it detects whether it has been initialized, or to redefine the methods in the subclasses InStream and OutStream so that they avoid the invocation of the method from class Stream. In the latter case, the class InOutStream must then invoke the initialization procedures explicitly for each of the three other classes.

13.5   Multiple Inheritance in Java

Java does not support multiple inheritance of classes, but it does include multiple inheritance of interfaces. A class can indicate that it supports several different forms of interface. For example, one interface might support storage of values on a disk while a second defines the protocol for objects that can display themselves. A storable graphical object would support both of these.

```
class graphicalObject implements Storable, Graphical {
    // ...
}
```

While classes cannot inherit (extend) from two or more classes, interfaces can. We can define an interface for graphical, storable objects as follows:

```
interface GraphicalObject extends Storable, Graphical {
    // ...
}
```

Further Reading

A critique of multiple inheritance can be found in Sakkinen [Sakkinen 1988a], which is an abridgment and adaptation of a Ph.D. dissertation [Sakkinen 1992]. An explanation of multiple inheritance in C++ is given in Ellis [Ellis 1990].

Exercises

1. Cite two examples of multiple inheritance in non-computer-associated situations.

2. In [Wiener 1989], a "practical example of multiple inheritance in C++" is described that defines a class IntegerArray, which inherits from the two classes, Array and Integer. Do you think this example is a good use of multiple inheritance? Explain your answer.

3. Modify the Tree class definition so that it can be used as a binary tree. Provide facilities to retrieve or change the left or right child of any node. What assumptions do you need to make?

4. Extend your work in Exercise 3 to implement a binary search tree. A binary search tree maintains a list of integers with the property that, at every node, the values in the left subtree are less than or equal to the value associated with the node, and the values stored in the right subtree are larger than the node value.

5. Discuss virtual inheritance in C++ from the point of view of Parnas's principles on information hiding.

Chapter 14

Polymorphism

The term *polymorphic* has Greek roots and means roughly "many forms." (*poly* = many, *morphos* = form. Morphos is related to the Greek god Morphus, who could appear to sleeping individuals in any form he wished and hence was truly polymorphic.) In biology, a polymorphic species is one, such as *Homo sapiens*, that is characterized by the occurrence of different forms or color types in individual organisms or among organisms. In chemistry, a polymorphic compound is one that can crystallize in at least two distinct forms, such as carbon, which can crystallize both as graphite and as diamond.

14.1 Polymorphism in Programming Languages

In programming languages, a polymorphic object is any entity, such as a variable or function argument, that is permitted to hold values of different types during the course of execution. Polymorphic functions are those that have polymorphic arguments.

14.1.1 Polymorphic Functions in Dynamic Languages

Polymorphic functions are relatively easy to write in dynamically typed languages, such as Lisp or Scheme in the functional paradigm, or Smalltalk in the object-oriented paradigm. The following illustrates a Smalltalk method, named silly, that takes as argument a value, x, and returns the value x + 1 if x is an integer, the reciprocal of the value if x is a fraction, the reversal if x is a string, and the special value nil otherwise.

```
silly: x       " a silly polymorphic method "
    (x isKindOf: Integer) ifTrue: [ ↑ x + 1 ].
    (x isKindOf: Fraction) ifTrue: [ ↑ x reciprocal ].
    (x isKindOf: String) ifTrue: [ ↑ x reversed ].
    ↑ nil
```

Polymorphism can also occur in more strongly typed languages. Its most common form in conventional programming languages is *overloading*, such as the overloading of the + symbol to mean both integer and real addition. We will discuss this form of polymorphism in a subsequent section.

Recent functional languages, such as ML [Milner 1990], permit a style of strongly typed polymorphism referred to as *parametric polymorphism*, in which a parameter can be characterized only partially, such as "list of T," where T is left undefined. This permits list operations to be performed on the value, and such functions to be applied to lists of different types. Similar features are available in a few object-oriented languages through the use of *generics* or *templates*.

In general, polymorphism in object-oriented languages reflects the principle of substitutability. That is, a polymorphic object-oriented variable is permitted to hold a value of its expected (declared) type or of any subtype of the expected type.

14.1.2   Low-Level and High-Level Abstractions

One way to view polymorphism is in terms of high-level and low-level abstractions. A low-level abstraction is a basic operation, such as on a data structure, that is built on top of only a few underlying mechanisms. A high-level abstraction is a more general plan, such as a sorting algorithm or the description of a window-resizing operation, that gives the general approach to be followed but does not specify the details.

Algorithms are usually described in a high-level fashion, whereas the actual implementation of a particular algorithm must be a high-level abstraction that is built on top of a specific low-level data structure. A simple example, a high-level recursive algorithm to compute the length of a list, might be written as follows:

```
function length (list) -> integer
begin
    if list.link is nil
    then
        return 1
    else
        return 1 + length(list.link)
end
```

An actual implementation in a conventional language like Pascal would require exact type specifications not only for the portion of the data being manipulated (here, the link fields) but also for features that are part of the data structure but not used in this algorithm. Thus, the algorithm might be rewritten as follows in Pascal:

```
type
    intlist : record
        value : integer;
        link :  ^  intlist;
    end;

function length ( x :  ^ intlist) : integer;
begin
    if x^.link = nil then
        length := 1
    else
        length := 1 + length(x^.link);
end;
```

This algorithm can be used to compute the length of a linked list of integer values but not to compute the length of a linked list of reals. Computing the length of any type of list other than integers requires complete rewriting of the data structure code.

Most programs will consist of both high-level and low-level abstractions. A programmer familiar with the precepts of structured programming and data abstraction will more or less automatically recognize low-level abstractions and design a software system, such as a new data structure, independently of any particular application. Thus, low-level abstractions are tools in that they can be carried from one project to another. In a conventional language, a high-level abstraction, on the other hand, must be grounded in a specific type of data structure. Therefore, it is difficult to carry a high-level abstraction from one project to another so only the design is reused. For this reason even simple high-level abstractions, such as computing the length of a list or searching a table for a specific value, tend to be rewritten for each new application.

One of the greatest powers of polymorphism is that it permits high-level algorithms to be written once and reused repeatedly with *different* low-level abstractions. Even relatively complex structured algorithms can be collected as *frameworks* or *patterns* and reused in multiple applications. We will discuss both frameworks and patterns in subsequent chapters, once we have introduced the mechanics of polymorphism.

14.2   Varieties of Polymorphism

In object-oriented languages, polymorphism is a natural result of the *is-a* relationship and of the mechanisms of message passing, inheritance, and substitutability. One of the great strengths of the OOP approach is that these devices can be combined in a variety of ways, yielding a number of techniques for code sharing and reuse.

Pure polymorphism occurs when a single function can be applied to arguments of a variety of types. In pure polymorphism, there is one function (code body) and a number of interpretations. The other extreme occurs when we have a number of different functions (code bodies) all denoted by the same name–a situation known as *overloading* or sometimes *ad hoc polymorphism*. Between these two extremes are *overriding* and *deferred methods.*[1]

14.3   Polymorphic Variables

With the exception of overloading, polymorphism in object-oriented languages is made possible only by the existence of *polymorphic variables*. A polymorphic variable is one with many faces; that is, it can hold values of different types. Polymorphic variables embody the principle of substitutability. In other words, while there is an expected type for any variable the actual type can be from any value that is a subtype of the expected type.

In dynamically bound languages (such as Smalltalk and Objective-C), all variables are potentially polymorphic–any variable can hold values of any type. In these languages the expected type is defined by a set of expected behaviors. For example, an algorithm may make use of an array value, expecting the subscripting operations to be defined for a certain variable; any type that defines the expected behavior is suitable. Thus, the user could define her own type of array (for example, a sparse array) and, if she defined the operations using the same names, use this new type with the existing algorithm.

In statically typed languages (C++, Java, Object Pascal, and Objective-C when used with static declarations), the situation is slightly more complex. We noted how these languages treat subclassing like subtyping. Polymorphism occurs in these languages through the difference between the declared (static) class of a variable and the actual (dynamic) class of the value the variable contains. As we noted in Chapter 10, in many languages this distinction is defined by the subclass relationship. A variable can hold a value of the same type as that of the declared class of the variable, or of any subclasses of the declared class.

In Object Pascal and Java, this is true for all variables declared as object type. In C++, and in Objective-C when static declarations are used, polymorphic variables occur only through the use of pointers and references. Again, we noted in Chapter 10, when pointers are not used the dynamic class of a value is always coerced into being the same as the static class of a variable.

A good example of a polymorphic variable is the array allPiles in the solitare

---

[1]Once again we note that there is little agreement regarding terminology in the programming language community. In [Horowitz 1984], [Marcotty 1987], [MacLennan 1987], and [Pinson 1988] for example, *polymorphism* is defined in a manner roughly equivalent to what we are here calling *overloading*. In [Sethi 1989] and [Meyer 1988a] and in the functional programming languages community (such as [Wikström 1987, Milner 1990]), the term is reserved for what we are calling *pure polymorphism*. Other authors use the term for one, two, or all of the mechanisms described in this chapter. Two complete, but technically daunting, analyses are [Cardelli 1985] and [Danforth 1988].

game presented in Chapter 8. The array was declared as maintaining a value of type CardPile, but in fact it maintains values from each of the different subclasses of the parent class. A message presented to a value from this array, such as display in the example code shown below, executes the method associated with the dynamic type of the variable and not that of the static class.

```
public class Solitaire extends Applet {
    ...
    static CardPile allPiles [ ];
    ...

    public void paint(Graphics g) {
        for (int i = 0; i < 13; i++)
            allPiles[i].display(g);
    }
    ...
}
```

14.4 Overloading

We say a function name is *overloaded* if there are two or more function bodies associated with it. Note that overloading is a necessary part of overriding, which we discussed in Chapter 11 (and will describe again in the next section,) but the two terms are not identical and overloading can occur without overriding.

In overloading, it is the function *name* that is polymorphic–it has many forms. Another way to think of overloading and polymorphism is that there is a single abstract function that takes various types of arguments; the actual code executed depends on the arguments given. The fact that the compiler can often determine the correct function at compile time (in a strongly typed language), and can therefore generate only a single code sequence are simply optimizations.

14.4.1 Overloading Names in Real Life

In Chapter 1 we saw an example in which overloading occurred without overriding, when I wanted to surprise my grandmother with flowers for her birthday. One possible solution was to send the message sendFlowersTo to my local florist; another was to give the *same* message to my wife. Both my florist and my wife (an instance of class Spouse) would have understood the message, and both would have acted on it to produce a similar result. In a certain sense, I could have thought of sendFlowersTo as being one function understood by both my wife and my florist, but each would have used a different algorithm to respond to my request.

Note, in particular, that there was no inheritance involved in this example. The first common superclass for my wife and my florist was the category Human. But certainly the behavior sendFlowersTo was not associated with all humans.

My dentist, for example, who is also a human, would not have understood the message at all.

14.4.2 Overloading and Coercion

As an example more closely tied to programming languages, suppose a programmer is developing a library of classes representing common data structures. A number of data structures can be used to maintain a collection of elements (sets, bags, dictionaries, arrays, and priority queues, for example), and these might all define a method, add, to insert a new element into the collection.

This situation–in which two totally separate functions are used to provide semantically similar actions for different data types–occurs frequently in all programming languages, not simply in object-oriented languages. Perhaps the most common example is the overloading of the addition operator, +. The code generated by a compiler for an integer addition is often radically different from the code generated for a floating-point addition, yet programmers tend to think of the operations as a single entity, the "addition" function.

In this example it is important to point out that overloading may not be the only activity taking place. A semantically separate operation, *coercion*, is also usually associated with arithmetic operations. It occurs when a value of one type is converted into one of a different type. If mixed-type arithmetic is permitted, the addition of two values may be interpreted in a number of different ways:

- There may be four different functions, corresponding to integer + integer, integer + real, real + integer, and real + real. In this case, there is overloading but no coercion.

- There may be two different functions for integer + integer and real + real. In integer + real and real + integer, the integer value is coerced by being changed into a real value. In this situation there is a combination of overloading and coercion.

- There may be only one function, for real + real addition. All arguments are coerced into being real. In this case there is coercion only, with no overloading.

14.4.3 Overloading Does Not Imply Similarity

There is nothing intrinsic to overloading that requires the functions associated with an overloaded name to have any semantic similarity. Consider a program that plays a card game, such as the solitaire game we examined in Chapter 8. The method draw was used to draw the image of a card on the screen. In another application we might also have included a draw method for the pack of cards, that is, to draw a single card from the top of the deck. This draw method is not even remotely similar in semantics to the draw method for the single card, and yet they share the same name.

Note that this overloading of a single name with independent and unrelated meanings should *not* necessarily be considered bad style, and generally it will not contribute to confusion. In fact, the selection of short, clear, and meaningful names such as add, draw, and so on, contributes to ease of understanding and correct use of object-oriented components. It is far simpler to remember that you can add an element to a set than to recall that to do so requires invoking the addNewElement method, or, worse, that it requires calling the routine Set_Module_Addition_Method.

All the object-oriented languages we are considering permit the occurrence of methods with similar names in unrelated classes. In this case the resolution of overloaded names is determined by observation of the class of the receiver for the message. Nevertheless, this does not mean that functions or methods can be written that take arbitrary arguments. The statically typed nature of C++ and Object Pascal still requires specific declarations of all names.

14.4.4 Parameteric Overloading

Another style of overloading, in which procedures (or functions or methods) in the same context are allowed to share a name and are disambiguated by the number and type of arguments supplied, is called *parameteric overloading*; it occurs in C++ and Java as well as in some imperative languages (such as Ada) and many functional languages. We have already seen examples of this style in the overloading of the constructor function. C++ permits any method, function, procedure, or operator to be overloaded parameterically, as long as the arguments are such that the selection of the routine intended by the user can be unambiguously determined at compile time. (When automatic coercions–for example, from character to integer or from integer to float–can occur, the algorithm used to resolve an overloaded function name becomes quite complex. More detailed information can be found in [Ellis 1990] and [Stroustrup 1986].)

Overloading is a necessary prerequisite to the other forms of polymorphism we will consider: overriding, deferred methods, and pure polymorphism. It is also often useful in reducing the "conceptual space," that is, in reducing the amount of information that the programmer must remember. Often, this reduction in programmer-memory space is just as significant as the reduction in computer-memory space permitted by code sharing.

14.5   Overriding

In Chapter 11 we described the mechanics of overriding (refinement and replacement) in the various object-oriented languages we are considering, so we will not repeat that discussion here. Recall, however, the following essential elements of the technique. In one class (typically an abstract superclass), there is a general method defined for a particular message that is inherited and used by subclasses. In at least one subclass, however, a method with the same name is defined, that hides access to the general method for instances of this class (or, in the case of

refinement, subsumes access to the general method). We say the second method
overrides the first.

Overriding is often transparent to the user of a class, and, as with overloading,
frequently the two functions are thought of semantically as a single entity.

14.5.1   Overriding in Class Magnitude

An interesting example of overriding occurs in the class Magnitude in the Little
Smalltalk system. Magnitude is an abstract superclass dealing with quantities
that possess at least a partial, if not a total, ordering. Numbers are perhaps the
most common example of objects that have magnitude, although time and date
can also be ordered, as can characters, points in a two-dimensional coordinate
plane, and words in a dictionary.

The six relational operators are defined in the class Magnitude as follows:

```
<= arg
    ↑ self < arg or: [ self = arg ]

>= arg
    ↑ arg <= self

< arg
    ↑ self <= arg and: [ self ~= arg ]

> arg
    ↑ arg < self

= arg
    ↑ self == arg

~= arg
    ↑ (self = arg) not
```

Note that the definitions appear to be circular, each one depending on some
number of the others. How then is an infinite loop to be avoided if any of them
are invoked? The answer is that subclasses of class Magnitude must override and
redefine at least one of the six relational messages. We leave it as an exercise for
the reader to show that if the message = and either < or <= are redefined, all
the remaining operators can be executed without a loop ensuing.

Overriding of a method contributes to code sharing, insofar as instances of
the classes that do *not* override the method can all share one copy of the original.
It is only in situations where this method is not appropriate that an alternative
code fragment is provided. Without overriding, it would be necessary for all

subclasses to provide their own method to respond to the message, even though many of these methods are identical.

Users of C++ should be aware of the subtle semantic difference between overriding a virtual method and overriding a nonvirtual method. We will discuss this in more detail in Section 14.9.

14.6 Deferred Methods

A *deferred method* (sometimes called an *abstract method*, and in C++ called a *pure virtual method*) can be thought of as a generalization of overriding. In both cases, the behavior described in a parent class is modified by the child class. In a deferred method, however, the behavior in the parent class is essentially null, a place holder, and *all* useful activity is defined as part of the code provided by the child class.

One advantage of deferred methods is conceptual, in that their use allows the programmer to think of an activity as associated with an abstraction at a higher level than may actually be the case. For example, in a collection of classes representing geometric shapes, we can define a method to draw the shape in each of the subclasses Circle, Square, and Triangle. We could have defined a similar method in the parent class Shape, but such a method cannot, in actuality, produce any useful behavior since the class Shape does not have sufficient information to draw the shape in question. Nevertheless, the mere presence of this method permits the user to associate the concept *draw* with the single class Shape, and not with the three separate concepts Square, Triangle, and Circle.

There is a second, more practical reason for using deferred methods. In statically typed object-oriented languages, such as C++ and Object Pascal, a programmer is permitted to send a message to an object only if the compiler can determine that there is in fact a corresponding method that matchs the message selector. Suppose the programmer wishes to define a polymorphic variable of class Shape that will, at various times, contain instances of each of the different shapes. Such an assignment is possible, according to our rule of substitutability; nevertheless, the compiler will permit the message draw to be used with this variable only if it can ensure that the message will be understood by any value that may be associated with the variable. Assigning a method to the class Shape effectively provides this assurance, even when the method in class Shape is never actually executed.

14.7 Pure Polymorphism

Many authors reserve the term *polymorphism* (or *pure polymorphism*) for situations where one function can be used with a variety of arguments, and the term overloading for situations where there are multiple functions all defined with a single name.[2] Such facilities are not restricted to object-oriented languages. In Lisp or ML, for example, it is easy to write functions that manipulate lists of arbitrary elements; such functions are polymorphic, because the type of the argument is not known at the time the function is defined. The ability to form polymorphic functions is one of the most powerful techniques in object-oriented programming. It permits code to be written once, at a high level of abstraction, and to be tailored as necessary to fit a variety of situations. Usually, the programmer accomplishes this tailoring by sending further messages to the receiver for the method. These subsequent messages often are not associated with the class at the level of the polymorphic method, but rather are *virtual methods* defined in the lower classes.

An example will help us to illustrate this concept. As we noted in Section 14.5 on overriding, the class **Magnitude** in Smalltalk is an abstract superclass that deals with quantities that possess at least a partial, if not a total, ordering. Consider the method called **between:and:** shown below:

```
between: low and: high
    " test to see if the receiver "
    " is between two endpoints "
    ↑ (low <= self) and: [ self <= high ]
```

This method occurs in the class **Magnitude** and presumably (according to the comment) tests whether the receiver is between two endpoints. It performs this test by sending the message <= to the lower bound with the receiver as argument and to the receiver with the upper bound as argument. (Remember, in Smalltalk all operators are treated as messages.) Only if both of these expressions yield true does the method determine that the receiver is between the two endpoints.

After this message has been sent to an object with a pair of arguments, what happens next depends on the particular meaning given to the message <=. This message, although defined in class **Magnitude**, is overridden in many of the subclasses. For integer values, the meaning is that of integer comparison; thus, **between:and:** can be used to test whether an integer value is between two other integer values. Floating-point values define < similarly, with similar results.

```
anInteger between: 7 and: 11
```

```
aFloat between: 2.7 and:  3.5
```

For characters, the relation <= is defined in terms of the underlying ASCII

---

[2]The extreme cases may be easy to recognize, but discovering the line that separates overloading from polymorphism can be difficult. In both C++ and ML a programmer can define a number of functions, each having the same name, but which take different arguments. Is it overloading in C++ because the various functions sharing the same name are not defined in one location, whereas in ML-style polymorphism they must all be bundled together under a single heading?

collating sequence; thus between:and: tests whether a character is between two other characters. To see whether a variable aChar contains a lowercase letter, for example, we can use the following expression ($a is the token denoting the literal character a in Smalltalk):

```
aChar between: $a and: $z
```

For Points, the relation $<=$ is defined as being true if the receiver is above and to the left of the argument (that is, both the first and second components of the point are less than or equal to their corresponding part in the other point). Point objects are a basic data type in Smalltalk; numbers respond to the @ operator by constructing a point with their own value as the first coordinate and the argument as the second coordinate. Note that the definition of $<$ for points provides only a partial order, as not all points are thereby commensurate. Nevertheless, the expression:

```
aPoint between: 2@4 and: 12@14
```

is true if aPoint is in the box defined by the coordinates (2,4) in the upper left and (12,14) in the lower right corner.

The important point here is that in all of these cases there is only *one* method being used for between:and:. This method is polymorphic; it works with a number of argument types. In each case, the redefinition of the messages involved in the polymorphic routine (in this case, the message $<=$) tailors the code to specific circumstances.

In Chapter 18 we will encounter many more examples of polymorphic routines when we discuss frameworks.

14.8 Generics and Templates

Yet another form of polymorphism is provided by the facility known as a *generic* (in C++ called a *template*). Generics provide a way of parameterizing a class or a function by use of a *type*, just as normal parameters to a function provide a way to define an abstract algorithm without identifying specific values. To illustrate this concept, we refer to the beginning of this chapter, where we noted that a problem with conventional strongly typed languages is that they do not permit the creation of a type such as the Linked List of X, where X is an unknown type. Generics provide this ability.

With generics, a variable is defined as a type parameter. This parameter can then be used within the class definition just as if it were a type, although no properties of the type are known when the class description is being parsed by the compiler. At some later point the type parameter is matched with a specific type and a value can then be declared. For example, a linked list can be declared in C++ in the following fashion:

```
template <class T> class List {
public:
    void add(T);
    T firstElement();
        // data fields
    T value;
    List<T> * nextElement;
};
```

In this example, T is being used as a type parameter. Each instance of class List holds a value of type T and a pointer to the next link. The add member function adds a new element to the list, while the value of the front of the list is returned by the function firstElement.

To create an instance of the class, the user must provide a type value for the parameter T. The following declares both a list of integer values and a list of floating-point values.

```
List<int> aList;
List<double> bList;
```

Functions, including member functions, can also have template definitions. Here is the definition of a function for determining the number of elements in a list regardless of the list type.

```
template <class T> int length(List<T> & aList)
{
    if (aList == 0)
        return 0;
    return
        1 + length(aList.nextElement);
}
```

In C++ template functions are used extensively in the standard template library, described in Chapter 16.

14.9   Polymorphism in the Various Languages

14.9.1   Polymorphism in C++

Polymorphic Variables

As we noted in Chapter 10, in C++ true polymorphic variables occur only through the use of pointers or references. When a true variable (that is, nonpointer and nonreference) is assigned a value derived from a subclass, the dynamic class of the value is always coerced into being the same as the static class of the variable.

When pointers (or references) are used, however, the value retains its dynamic type. To understand this, consider the following two classes One and Two.

```
class One {
public:
    virtual int value()
        { return 1; }
};

class Two : public One {
public:
    virtual int value()
        { return 2; }
};
```

Class One defines a virtual method value that yields the value 1. This method is replaced in class Two by a method that yields the value 2.

Next, three functions are defined:

```
void directAssign (One x)
    { printf("by assignment value is %d\n", x.value()); }

void byPointer (One * x)
    { printf("by assignment value is %d\n", x->value()); }

void byReference (One & x)
    { printf("by assignment value is %d\n", x.value()); }
```

These functions take as argument a value of type One, passing it by value, by pointer, and by reference, respectively. When executed by an argument of type Two, the value parameter will be converted into a value of type One and thus will produce the result "1." The other two functions, however, define arguments that are polymorphic. In both cases, the value passed will retain its dynamic type and the value printed will be "2."

Virtual and Nonvirtual Overriding

A potentially confusing aspect of overriding in C++ is the difference between overriding a virtual method and overriding a nonvirtual method. As we noted in Chapter 11, the virtual keyword is not necessary for overriding to take place. However, the semantic meaning is very different when it is used and when it is not used. If the virtual keyword is removed from the method declaration used in the class One in the earlier example (even if it is retained in the class Two), then the result "1" will be produced by all three functions.

Without the virtual keyword, the dynamic type of a variable (even a pointer or reference variable) is ignored when the variable is used as a receiver for the associated message.

An even more subtle confusion may occur if a programmer tries to redefine a virtual function in a subclass but declares (perhaps by mistake) a different argument signature. For example, the parent class might contain the declaration:

```
virtual void display (char *, int);
```

Whereas the subclass might define the method as:

```
virtual void display (char *, short);
```

Since the two argument signatures are distinct, the second is not recognized as being a redefinition of the first. This results in the virtual overloading of the method to be treated as if it were an "ordinary" (that is, a nonvirtual) redefinition. When invoked as the parent type, for example, the first method would be selected, not the second. Such errors are exceedingly subtle since both forms are legal, and thus the compiler will seldom generate a warning message.

Given this situation, one might legitimately ask why the two different forms are permitted and why all overriding isn't virtual. There are at least two plausible explantions. The first is that, on rare occasions, the nonvirtual form of overriding is exactly what the programmer wants to do, and without this mechanism it would be very difficult to simulate. The second and more compelling reason has to do with efficiency. Virtual inheritance is always more costly in execution time than nonvirtual inheritance. An underlying design tenent in C++ is that if a language feature is not needed or used in a particular problem, the programmer should not be required to pay (in execution time) for its existence. Therefore, if virtual inheritance is not needed or used in a particular case, no execution-time overhead is imposed. It is only when the programmer explicitly states that he needs a virtual function that the additional overhead required by the facility is imposed.

Parameteric Overloading

C++ permits multiple functions to share the same name in any context as long as the argument lists of the various functions are sufficiently distinct to permit the compiler to determine unambiguously which function is being intended. This most commonly occurs when there are multiple constructors for the same class, each taking a different set of argument values. However, any function, method, or operator can be so defined.

The rules for disambiguating overloaded functions are somewhat subtle, particularly when automatic coercions are possible. One of the more important principles to remember is that when searching for a function to match to a particular call, the compiler seeks the most enclosing name scope in which the function name has been defined, and then seeks to match the function in that scope on the basis of argument type. Thus, a function will effectively hide another function with the same name in a surrounding scope.

Deferred Methods in C++

In C++, a deferred method (here called a *pure virtual method*) must be declared explicitly, by use of the virtual keyword. The body of the deferred method is not given; instead, the value 0 is "assigned" to the function, as shown below.

```
class  Shape {
public:
    ...
    virtual void     draw     () = 0;
    ...
};
```

The compiler will not permit the user to instantiate an instance of a class that contains a pure virtual method, but only instances of subclasses that override the method. The redefinition of a pure virtual method must be handled by an immediate subclass.

Generic Classes and Functions

Generics in C++ are implemented by the template keyword. An example of a template class was presented earlier. Template classes and functions are used extensively in the Standard Template Library, which we will discuss in Chapter 16.

14.9.2   Polymorphism in Java

Java supports both the subclass hierarchy (through the keyword extends) and a separate subtype hierarchy (through the use of interfaces). Variables can be declared through either a class or an interface. All variables are polymorphic, in that a variable declared as a class can hold values from any subclass while a variable declared as an interface can hold values from any class that implements the interface.

Deferred methods are implemented in Java through the use of the keyword abstract. Methods declared as abstract do not have a method body, but instead are terminated with a semicolon. They must be overridden in a subclass. A class that includes an abstract method must itself be declared as abstract. It is not permitted to create an instance of an abstract class.

```
abstract class shape {
        // the following must be overridden
    public abstract draw();
    // ...
```

```
    }

class triangle extends shape {
    public draw() {
        // ... draw a triangle
        }
    // ...
    }
```

An interesting feature in Java is the modifier final, which is almost the opposite of an abstract class. A class or method that is declared as final cannot be subclassed or overridden.

14.9.3   Polymorphism in Object Pascal

Polymorphic Variables

In Object Pascal all variables are potentially polymorphic, with the implicit assumption that subclasses represent subtypes. Any variable can maintain a value either from the declared class for the variable or from a derived subclass.

Deferred Methods in Object Pascal

As we noted in Chapter 7, the Apple and Borland versions of Object Pascal differ in how they indicate that a method in a child class is overriding a method inherited from a parent class. In Apple Object Pascal, the indication (the keyword override) is placed on the description of the method in the child class; the Delphi language requires both the override keyword and the keyword virtual placed on the same method in the parent class.

Apple Object Pascal provides no support for deferred methods. Often a deferred method simply produces an error message, as the following shows:

```
type
    Shape = object
        corner : Point;
        procedure draw(); ...
        end;

    Circle = object (Shape)
        radius : integer;
        procedure draw(); override;   ...
        end;

procedure Shape.draw();
begin
    writeln('descendant should define draw');
```

```
      halt();
end;
```

In Delphi Pascal, a method can be declared as deferred by placement of the keyword **abstract** after the keyword **virtual** (or **dynamic**) in the parent class declaration. No method body is then defined for an abstract method. Unlike in C++, it is possible to create an object whose class has nonoverridden abstract methods. Thus, we can say that Delphi Pascal supports abstract methods but not abstract classes.

```
type
    class TShape
        procedure draw; virtual; abstract;
        ...
    end;

    class TTriangle (TShape)
        procedure draw; override;
        ...
    end;
```

14.9.4   Polymorphism in Objective-C

Polymorphic Variables

When declared as **id**, all variables in Objective-C are polymorphic, and thus can hold any value. When declared as a specific class, such variables have all the properties (good and bad) of C++ variables.

Deferred Methods in Objective-C

No special indication is needed to describe a deferred method in Objective-C. To aid in the creation of such methods, a message **subclassResponsibility** is defined in class **Object** (and therefore is accessible to all objects). This message simply prints a message indicating that an action was executed that should have been overridden in some subclass.

The method **draw** for class **Shape** could have been written, for example, as shown below:

```
@implementation Shape : Object

  ...

- draw { return [ self subclassResponsibility ]; }
```

```
  . . .
```

```
@ end
```

14.9.5   Polymorphism in Smalltalk

Polymorphic Variables

Because Smalltalk is a dynamically typed language, all variables are polymorphic; they can hold any value.

Deferred Methods in Smalltalk

No special indication is needed to describe a deferred method in Smalltalk. Nevertheless, to aid in the creation of such methods, a message subclasssResponsibility is defined in class **Object** (and therefore is accessible to all objects). This message simply prints a message indicating that an action was executed that should have been overridden in some subclass.

The method **draw** for class **Shape** could have been written, for example, as shown below:

```
draw
      " child classes should override this "

      ↑ self subclassResponsibility
```

14.10   Efficiency and Polymorphism

An essential point is that programming always involves compromises. In particular, programming with polymorphism involves compromises between ease of development and use, readability, and efficiency. In large part, efficiency has been already considered and dismissed; however, it would be remiss not to admit that it is an issue, however slight.

A function, such as the **between:and:** method described in the last section, that does not know the type of its arguments can seldom be as efficient as a function that has more complete information. A relational test may correspond to only a few assembly-language instructions if the arguments are integer, whereas much more extensive operations are necessary if the arguments are points. Nevertheless, the advantages of rapid development and consistent application behavior and the possibilities of code reuse usually more than make up for any small losses in efficiency.

Exercises

1. Do you think that the value nil in Pascal, or the value NULL in C, should be considered a polymorphic object? Explain your answer.

2. Other than the arithmetic operations, what operations are typically overloaded in conventional languages such as Pascal and C?

3. Trace the sequence of method invocations, and the classes in which method are found, in evaluating the expression:

   ```
   anInteger between: 7 and: 11
   ```

4. Suppose that in Smalltalk we have two classes, Apple and Orange, subclasses of class Fruit. Show the minimal amount of code we would need to compare apples and oranges.

Chapter 15

A Case Study: Container Classes

Simple data structures are found at the heart of almost all nontrivial computer programs. Examples include linked lists, stacks, queues, trees, sets, and dictionaries. Because such data structures are so common, one would expect them to be ideal for development as reusable components. Indeed, it *is* possible to create such components, but the complexity involved is often much greater than one would expect. An exploration of the problems in developing reusable container classes is for this reason a good illustration of how the features of a programming language influence the style of development, as well as a demonstration of some of the powers and some of the limitations of object-oriented techniques.

In the following discussions, we will consider three related questions:

- Is it possible to construct reusable general-purpose container abstractions that are independent of their element values and can therefore be carried from one project to the next?

- Can such containers maintain only one type of value (a so-called *homogeneous container*), or can one construct containers that will maintain values of different types (a *heterogeneous container*)?

- Is it possible to give users of the container access to the elements being held, without removing the elements and without exposing the internal implementation details of the container?

15.1   Using Conventional Techniques

To place the problem in perspective, we must first consider how data structures are usually implemented in a conventional language, such as C or Pascal. We will use a linked list of integers as our example abstraction. In Pascal a linked list might be formed out of two types of records. The first is the list header itself, which maintains a pointer to the first link:

```
type
    List = Record
            firstLink : ↑ Link;
        end;
```

A list header can be statically allocated, as the amount of storage it maintains (namely, one pointer) remains fixed throughout execution. The second record is used to maintain the actual values themselves. Each Link node maintains one integer value and a pointer to the next link:

```
type
    Link = Record
            value : integer;
            nextElement : ↑ Link;
        end;
```

Link nodes must be dynamically allocated and released, although such details can be largely hidden from the user of the list abstraction through the development of functions, such as one to add a new value to the front of the list, return and remove the first element in a list, and so on.

```
procedure addToList (var aList : List, newVal : integer);
var          (* add a new value to a list *)
    newLink : ↑ Link;
begin
        (* create and initialize a new link *)
    new (newLink);
    newLink.value = newVal;
        (* place it at the front of the list *)
    newLink.nextElement = aList.firstLink;
    aList.firstLink = newLink;
end;

function firstElement (var aList : List) : integer;
var          (* remove and return first element from a list *)
    firstNode : ↑ Link;
begin
    firstNode := aList.firstLink;
    firstElement := firstNode↑.value;
    aList.firstLink := firstNode↑.nextElement;
    dispose (firstNode);
end;
```

Our concern here is not with the details of how a linked list might be implemented (such details can be found in any data structure textbook) but with the question of reusability. Suppose our programmer has implemented the linked-list abstraction given above and now wishes to maintain, in addition to a linked list of integers, a linked list of real numbers.

The problem is that the programming language is *too* strongly typed. The data type integer used for the value being held by the link is an intrinsic part of the definition. The only way it can be replaced by a different type is through the creation of a totally new data type, for example RealLink, as well as a totally new list header, RealList, and totally new routines for accessing and manipulating the data structures.

Now, it is true that something like a variant record (called a *union* in C) could be used to permit a single list abstraction to hold both integers and real numbers. Indeed, a variant record would permit one to define a heterogeneous list that contains both integers *and* real numbers. But variant records solve only part of the problem. It is not possible to define a function that returns a variant record, for example, so one still needs to write separate functions for returning the first element in a list. Furthermore, a variant record can have only a finite number of possible alternatives. What happens when the next project requires a totally new type of list, such as a list of characters?

Now let us turn to the problem of accessing the underlying elements without removing them from the container. A typical loop that prints the values in a list might be written similarly to the following:

```
var
    aList : List;    (* the list being manipulated *)
    p : Link;    (* a pointer for the loop *)

begin
    ...
    p := aList.firstLink;
    while (p <> nil) do begin
        writeln (p.value);
        p := p↑.nextElement;
    end;
```

Note that to create a loop it was necessary to introduce an extraneous variable, here named p. Furthermore, this variable had to be of type Link, a data type we were taking pains to hide, and the loop itself required access to the link fields in the list, which we were also attempting to hide.

So we see that a conventional strongly typed language does not provide the facilities necessary to create and manipulate truly reusable container abstractions.

15.2   Containers in Dynamic Languages

Producing reusable container abstractions is considerably easier in a dynamically typed language, such as Smalltalk or Objective-C. Indeed, such languages usually come with a large collection of data abstractions already developed, thus freeing the programmer from having to solve the container problem. As we saw in our earlier discussion on binding times, in dynamically typed languages it is a value itself that retains knowledge of its type, not the variable by which it is accessed. So, for example, our linked-list abstraction might be defined by the following Objective-C structures:

```
@ interface List : Object
{
    id      firstLink;
}
- (void) addToList: value
- id firstElement
@end

@ interface Link : Object
{
    id      Value
    id      NextElement
}
+
- id      value
- id      nextElement
@ end
```

A value placed in such a structure is simply known as an id, that is, as an object type. Similarly, a value removed from the list is also known as an id, but it can be assigned to any object variable, as all variables can hold any object type.

To create a new list, the programmer uses the new message on the factory object for the class List:

```
id aList;
  ...
aList = [ List new ];
```

To place a value in the list, the programmer uses the appropriate member function:

```
[ aList addToList: aValue ];
```

The implementations of the list operations need not concern themselves with the type of values they are maintaining, other than that they represent an object.

```
@ implementation List

- (void) addList: newElement
        /* add new element to list */
{    id newLink;
    newLink = [ Link new ];
    [ newLink setValue: newElement link: firstLink ];
    firstLink = newLink;
}


- id firstElement
        /* remove and return first element from list */
{    id result;
    result = [ firstLink value ];
    firstLink = [ firstLink nextElement ]
    return result;
}
@ end
```

Iteration can be similarly handled in dynamically typed languages without exposing the internal structure of the containers. We will describe two techniques; one used in Smalltalk and the other more widely applicable to a variety of languages.

We noted earlier how Smalltalk permits statements to be bundled together into a type of object called a block, which is in many ways similar to a function. Like a function, a block can possess an argument list. The normal way that iteration is performed in Smalltalk is to pass a block as argument with a message to the structure being accessed. For simple iteration this message is by convention called do:. A loop to print the values of a list might therefore be written as follows:

```
aList do: [ :ele | ele print ]
```

The list class simply passes the block to the link class. Each element of the link class invokes the block using the current value, and then passes the block on to the next element.

```
linkDo: aBlock
        " execute block, pass on to next link "
    aBlock value: value.
    nextLink notNil
        ifTrue: [ nextLink linkDo: aBlock ]
```

```
@ implementation ListIterator {
    currentLink : id;
    }

+ newIterator: aList {
    self = [ ListIterator new ];
    currentLink = [ aList firstLink ];
    return self; }

- id value
    { return [ currentLink value ] }

- int atEnd
    { return currentLink == nil; }

- void advance
    { if (! [ self atEnd] )
        currentLink = [ currentLink nextElement ]; }
@end
```

Figure 15.1 – An iterator in Objective-C.

In this fashion a wide variety of iteration styles are made possible, all without exposing the structure of the list.

In Objective-C and other object-oriented languages the solution to the iteration problem is slightly more complicated, because of the absence of blocks. A common alternative is to introduce a type of assistant, called an iterator. This is an object provided by the developer of a container class, such as the list; its sole purpose is to provide access to the elements in a container, one at a time, without exposing the list's inner structure. Typically an iterator maintains a pointer into the structure and manipulates this pointer value using various operations. Figure 15.1 illustrates how an iterator for our linked-list abstraction might be defined.

The iterator is normally constructed by the list itself in response to a message. A loop over the elements of a list might be constructed as follows:

```
id aList;      /* declaration for list */
id itr;           /* declaration for iterator */

for (itr = [aList iterator]; ! [ itr atEnd]; [itr advance])
    print( [itr value ] );
```

Notice that although the loop required the declaration of an extra iterator variable, making use of this variable did not require knowing the internal structure of the linked list.

The ease with which data abstractions can be constructed and manipulated is one of the major selling points of dynamically typed languages. These collections are completely general and can even maintain heterogeneous collections of many different types of values. Unfortunately, such benefits are not without cost. As we noted previously, there is a trade-off between ease of use and efficiency of execution, and dynamic languages can seldom execute as efficiently as can more strongly typed languages.

15.3   Containers in Strongly Typed Languages

We now move on to considering how container classes might be constructed in strongly typed languages, such as Object Pascal and C++. It is tempting to think that substitutability by itself can solve the container class problem for strongly typed languages. Recall from Chapter 6 that the principle of substitutability claims that a variable declared as maintaining some object type can, in fact, be assigned a value derived from a subclass of the variable's declared class. Indeed to a limited extent the principle of substitutability *does* help solve some of our problems, but not nearly as many as we would like.

To use substitutability, we first need to create a class that will be a parent class to everything we want to store in our data structures. We will call this hypothetical class ListElement. We then create a list abstraction that holds a set of element values. The declaration shown in Figure 15.2 illustrates how this is performed in Object Pascal.

Objects that we want to hold in such a list structure must all be declared as subclasses of the class ListElement. Thus, for instance, we cannot maintain a list of integers or a list of floating-point values, but must first subclass ListElement to create a new type of integer value. Often this is not a serious problem. In fact, we are even free to maintain a heterogeneous list of different types of values in the same list, as long as all values are subclasses of the base class ListElement.

The real problem comes when we try to do something with a value we have removed from a list. The strong typing that bound the result type to the parent class ListElement gets in our way, as we need to "undo" the substitution of the child value for the ListElement type. Suppose, for example, we created two subclasses of ListElement, one representing a black ball (class BlackBall) and one representing a white ball (class WhiteBall). We have a list of ball values, and we wish to remove the first value in a list and assign it to a variable declared as holding a WhiteBall.

We say in our earlier discussion on binding that there are actually two issues here, and different object-oriented languages may or may not keep them separate. They are: Can we determine the type of value we have extracted from the list, and, if so, will the compiler let us perform the assignment in a type-safe fashion.

Recall that Object Pascal resolves the first issue through the use of the

```
type
    List = object
        firstLink : ↑ ListElement;

        procedure addToList (var newValue : ListElement);
        function  firstValue : ListElement;
    end;

    ListElement = object
        next    : ↑ ListElement;
    end;

procedure List.addToList (var newValue : ListElement);
    (* add a value to the front of a list *)
begin
        (* set link field to point to current link *)
    newValue.next = firstLink;
        (* change first link value *)
    firstLink := newValue;
end;

function firstValue : ListElement;
        (* remove and return the first element in a list *)
var
    first : ListElement;
begin
    first := firstLink;
    firstValue := firstLink;
    firstLink := first.next;
end;
```

Figure 15.2 – A container declaration in Object Pascal.

Boolean function **Member**, which tells us whether or not a variable holds a value from a given class. If the **Member** function indicates that a conversion is legal, a *cast* can be used to convert the element into the appropriate type.

```
var
    aBall : WhiteBall;
    aList : List;
    aValue : ListElement;
  ...
        (* extract element from list *)
    aValue := aList.firstElement;
        (* first see if type is ok *)
    if Member(aValue, WhiteBall) then
            (* then cast in order to do assignment *)
        aBall := WhiteBall(aValue);
```

Thus, retrieving a value from our data structure can involve several steps, but this is essentially the technique used in many commercially available data structure classes. The annoying difficulty with its use has led many programmers to consider alternative arrangements.

Loops are often created by defining iterator-like structures, similar to the objective-C solution presented earlier. However, just as with the firstElement function, these can only yield a value of type ListElement. It is up to the programmer to cast this to a different type:

```
var
    aList : List;
    aValue : ListElement;
    itr : ListIterator;
...
    itr := aList.iterator;
    while (not itr.atEnd) do begin
        aValue := itr.current;
        if Member(aValue, WhiteBall) then
            ...
        itr.advance;     (* move iterator to next value *)
    end;
```

Prior to the introduction of RTTI, values in C++ did not normally know their own dynamic type. This difficulty compounded the problem of containers because in this case the programmer needed not only to perform the cast but also had to provide her own mechanism for determining, at run time, the dynamic type of a value. The recent introduction of the dynamic_cast function has addressed this problem.

15.4   Hiding the Cast with Subclassing

The principal difficulties in the technique described in the previous section are
the following:

- Only values that are subclasses of the class ListElement can be held by the
  data structure.

- The language must support the principle of substitutability.

- Objects must know their own dynamic type.

- Both an explicit test and a cast are required when values re extracted.

Casts are a notoriously dangerous programming construct and should be
avoided whenever possible. In addition, the second difficulty is important when
creating data abstractions in C++. Recall that C++ does *not* support substitutability for regularly declared object values but only for pointers or references.
For this reason many data structures in C++ are designed to store not values
themselves but pointers to values.

A commonly suggested programming technique uses subclassing and inheritance to hide the necessity to perform a cast in this situation. Suppose, for
example, that we have already defined a data abstraction with the following
interface:

```
class GenericList { // list of generic void * pointers
public:
    void     addToList    (void * newElement);
    void *   firstElement   ();

private:
    GenericLink *      firstLink;
};

class GenericLink {
public:
    void *         value;
    GenericLink *    nextLink;
};
```

That is, our generic list class will hold void pointers–pointers that can refer
to anything. In theory, such a collection can even be heterogeneous, having
pointers to many different types of objects. Now, suppose we want to create a
list of window pointers, where Window is some structure. It is only necessary
to subclass the generic list class and change the argument types and the result
type of the extraction method; doing either simply invokes the function from the
parent class to do the actual work.

```
class WindowList : public GenericList
{
public:
    void         addToList (Window * newElement)
        { GenericList::addToList (newElement); }
    Window *    firstElement
        { return (Window *) GenericList::firstElement; }
};
```

It is even possible to create data structures in this fashion that will maintain nonpointer values, such as floating-point values or integers. But doing so requires subclassing both the list and link classes and possibly even creating new forms of iterator classes.

We have achieved a certain amount of reusability, but only by forcing the programmer to create new subclasses whenever he wishes to make use of the data abstractions. Many programmers reject such a solution simply because it is almost as much trouble as recoding the data structures from scratch.

15.5 Parameterized Classes

The bottom line in the discussion above is that, at least for strongly typed languages, inheritance alone is not sufficient for the creation of easily reusable container classes. Instead, a new mechanism must be introduced. This is the ability to define classes that are *parameterized* by type arguments. Such classes are called *templates* in C++, and *generics* in some other languages.

A class template gives the programmer the ability to define a data type in which some type information is purposely left unspecified, to be filled in at a later time. One way to think of this is that the class definition has been parameterized in a manner similar to a procedure or function. Just as several different calls on the same function can all pass different argument values through the parameter list, different instantiations of a parameterized class can fill in the type information in different ways.

A parameterized class definition for a linked list abstraction might be written in C++ in the following way:

```
template<class T>
class List {
public:
    void    addElement (T newValue);
    T    firstElement ();
    ListIterator<T> iterator();
private:
    Link<T> * firstLink;
};
```

```
template<class T>
class Link {
public:
    T     value;
    Link *    nextLink;

    Link (T, Link *);
};
```

Within the class template, the template argument (T, in this case) can be used as a type name. Thus, one can declare variables of type T, have functions return values of type T, and so on.

Member functions that define template operations must also be declared as template:

```
template<class T>
void List< T>::addElement (T newValue)
{
    firstLink = Link new (newValue, firstLink);
}
```

```
template<class T>
T List< T>::firstElement ()
{
    Link first = firstLink;
    T result = first.value; ⎯
    firstLink = first->nextLink;
    delete first;
    return result;
}
```

```
template<class T>
Link<T>::Link(T v, Link * n) : value(v), nextLink(n)
{ }
```

The user creates different types of lists by filling in the parameterized type values with specific types. For example, the following creates a list of integer values as well as a list of real numbers.

```
List<int>     listOne;
List<double>    listTwo;
```

In this fashion, homogeneous lists of any type can be created.

A template is an elegant solution to the container class problem. It allows truly reusable, general-purpose components to be created and manipulated with a minimum of difficulty and yet still retain the type safety, which is the goal of strongly typed languages.

There are drawbacks to the use of templates. They do not permit the definition of heterogeneous lists, as all elements must match the declared type. (This problem can often be overcome by storing pointers to values rather than values themselves). More important, implementations of the template mechanism vary greatly in their ease of use and the quality of code they generate. Most implementations act as little more than sophisticated macros, generating for each new type of element an entirely new class definition as well as entirely new method bodies. Needless to say, if several different element types are used in the same program, this can result in a considerable growth in code size.

Nevertheless, because templates free the programmer from so much conceptual drudgery (namely, rewriting data structure classes in every new program), their appeal is widespread. In the next chapter we will examine one such library.

15.5.1   Loops and Iteration in C++

The existence of the template mechanism for both classes and individual functions permits the introduction of not one but two different mechanisms for iteration in C++. Both of these forms are found, for example, in the recent standard C++ library that we will examine in more detail in Chapter 16.

The first form uses an iterator. The container class defines a type for the iterator as well as functions that return iterator values. An iterator for our linked-list class, for example, could be written as follows:

```
template<class T>
class List {
public:
    typedef ListIterator<T> iterator;
    ...
    iterator begin()
        // return starting iterator to myself
        { return ListIterator<T>(firstLink); }
    iterator end()
        // return ending iterator marker
        { return ListIterator<T>(0); }
};

template<class T>
class ListIterator {
public:
    ListIterator (Link<T> * sl)
        : currentLink(sl) { }
    void    operator ++ ()      // advance to next element
        { currentLink = currentLink->nextLink; }
```

```
    T           operator * ()     // return current element
        { return currentLink->value; }
    bool      operator == (ListIterator<T> & right)
        { return currentLink == right.currentLink; }
private:
    Link<T>    * currentLink;
};
```

An iterator can then be declared as initialized with a given list. Looping over elements in the list can be performed without the internal structure of the list being known:

```
    List<int>::iterator start = aList.begin();
    List<int>::iterator end = aList.end();
    for (; start != end ; itr++)
        cout << (*itr) << endl;
```

A second form of iteration, sometimes termed *apply iteration*, is in some ways similar to the way in which Smalltalk creates loops. In this technique the container is given a function as argument and the container itself applies the function to each element of the collection. These two forms are combined in the function for_each, which executes the function passed as argument on each element of a collection:

```
void printOut (int n)
{
    cout << "the collection contains a " << n << "\n";
}

...

for_each (aList.begin(), aList.end(), printOut);
```

A problem with apply iteration is that it requires the creation or use of a function that can be passed as argument. If the container is a purely local value, it may be difficult to create. In such cases iterator looping may be easier to use.

Exercises

1. Argue whether container classes represent a success or a failure of object-oriented programming techniques.

2. Data structures can be divided into those that are characterized by their implementation (linked lists, trees) and those that are characterized by their purpose (stacks, sets). Describe how object-oriented programming

techniques can be used to simplify the latter, hiding the implementation details. Give an illustration of a data structure with one interface and two very different implementations.

3. Give an example application of a heterogeneous container–that is, one with many different types of values.

4. The Smalltalk approach to iteration is to bundle the action to be performed and hand it to the data structure; in contrast, an iterator is a data structure that hands values one by one back to a statement performing a certain action. Would it be possible to implement the Smalltalk approach in a different programming language, such as Object Pascal or C++? Does strong typing get in the way?

5. Give an example application for templates that is not associated with container classes.

Chapter 16

A Case Study: The STL

A rich collection of template data structures was recently added to the definition of the C++ standard library. These data structures include classes for vectors, lists, sets, maps (dictionaries), stacks, queues, and priority queues. As implementations of this standard become more widespread, the C++ programmer will become increasingly free from the need to constantly redefine and reimplement the standard set of data structure classes. (Further information on the Standard Template Library can be found in [Musser 1996, Glass 1996]).

The design of the Standard Template Library (STL) is the result of many years of research conducted by Alexander Stepanov and Meng Lee of Hewlett-Packard, and David Musser of Rensselaer Polytechnic Institute. STL development drew inspiration not only from previous object-oriented libraries but from the creators' many years of experience in functional and imperative programming languages such as Scheme and Ada.

One of the more unusual design ideas in STL, *generic algorithms*, deserves discussion because it seems to fly in the face of the object-oriented principles we have been describing and yet it is the source of a great deal of STL's power. The implementation of generic algorithms in STL uses the ability not only to create a template container *class* but also to make template definitions of individual *functions*. To understand the concept of generic algorithms, we must first describe how encapsulation is used in most object libraries.

Object-oriented programming holds *encapsulation* as a primary ideal. A well-designed object will try to encapsulate all the state and behavior necessary to perform whatever task it is designed for, and, at the same time, hide as many of the internal implementation details as possible. In many previous object-oriented libraries, this philosophical approach was manifested by container classes with exceedingly rich functionality and, consequently, with large interfaces.

The designers of STL moved in an entirely different direction. The behaviors provided in their standard components are minimal, almost spartan. Instead, each component is designed to operate in conjunction with a rich collection of *generic algorithms*, also provided. These generic algorithms are independent of the containers and can therefore operate with many different container types.

By separating the functionality of the generic algorithms from the container classes themselves, the STL realizes a great savings in size, in both the library and the generated code. Instead of duplication of algorithms in each of the dozen or so different container classes, a single definition of a library function can be used with any container. Furthermore, the definition of these functions is so general that they can be used with ordinary C-style arrays and pointers as well as with other data types.

An example will illustrate some of the basic features of the standard template library. A generic algorithm, find, finds the first occurrence of a given value in a collection. Iterators in the standard library consist of *pairs* of values, marking the beginning and end of a structure. The find algorithm takes an iterator pair and searches for the first occurrence. It is defined as follows:

```
template<class InputIterator, class T >
InputIterator
    find (InputIterator first, InputIterator last, const T& value)
{
    while (first != last && *first != value)
        ++first;
    return first;
}
```

The algorithm will work with any type of structure, even regular C-style arrays. To find the location of the first 7 value in a vector of integers, for example, the user executes the following:

```
int data[100];
    ...
int * where;
where = find(data, data+100, 7);
```

Finding the first value in a list of integers is hardly more difficult:

```
list<int> aList;
    ...
list<int>::iterator where;
where = find(aList.begin(), aList.end(), 7);
```

In a single chapter we can only describe the most basic features of the STL. The following sections present two basic concepts used by the library, namely iterators and function objects. Then three case studies will illustrate the STL's use of containers and generic algorithms.

16.1 Iterators

Iterators are fundamental to the use of the container classes and the associated algorithms provided by the standard library. Abstractly, an iterator is simply a pointer-like object used to cycle through all the elements stored in a container.

Just as pointers can be used in a variety of ways in traditional programming, iterators are also used for a number of purposes. An iterator can denote a specific value, just as a pointer can reference a specific memory location. On the other hand, a *pair* of iterators can describe a *range* of values, analogously to two pointers describing a contiguous region of memory. In the case of iterators, however, the values being described are not necessarily physically in sequence but rather logically in sequence. This is because they derive from the same container and the second follows the first in the order in which elements are maintained by the container.

Conventional pointers can sometimes be *null*–that is, they point at nothing. Iterators as well can fail to denote any specific value. Just as it is a logical error to dereference and use a null pointer, it is an error to dereference and use an iterator that is not denoting a value.

When two pointers that describe a region in memory are used in a C++ program, conventionally the ending pointer is *not* considered part of the region. For example, an array named x of length 10 is sometimes described as extending from x to x+10, even though the element at x+10 is not part of the array. Instead, the pointer value x+10 is the *past-the-end* value–the element that is the next value *after* the end of the range being described. Iterators describe a range in the same manner. The second value is not considered part of the range denoted, but is a *past-the-end* element, describing the next value in sequence after the final value of the range.

Just as with conventional pointers, the fundamental operation that modifies an iterator is the increment operator (operator ++). When the increment operator is applied to an iterator that denotes the final value in a sequence, it is changed to the past-the-end value. The dereference operator (operator *) accesses the value being denoted by an iterator.

Ranges can describe the entire contents of a container by constructing an iterator to the initial element and a special "ending" iterator. They can also describe subsequences within a single container by using two iterators to specific values. In the standard containers, the beginning iterator is returned by the function begin(), and the ending iterator is returned by the function end().

16.2 Function Objects

A number of the generic algorithms provided in the STL require functions as arguments. A simple example is the generic algorithm for_each(), which invokes a function, passed as argument, on each value held in a container. The following, for example, might be used to produce output describing each element in a list of integer values:

```
void printElement (int value)
{
    cout << "The list contains " << value << endl;
}

main () {
    list<int> aList;
        . . .
    for_each (aList.begin(), aList.end(), printElement);
}
```

Functions have been generalized to include *function objects*. A function object is an instance of a class that defines the parenthesis operator as a member function. There are a number of situations where it is convenient to substitute function objects for functions. When a function object is used as a function, the parenthesis operator is invoked whenever the function is called.

To illustrate, we will consider the following class definition:

```
class biggerThanThree {
    public:
        bool operator () (int v )
            { return v > 3; }
};
```

If we create an instance of the class biggerThanThree, every time we reference this object using the function call syntax, the parenthesis operator member function will be invoked. The next step is to generalize this class by adding a constructor and a constant data field, which is set by the constructor:

```
class biggerThan {
    public:
        biggerThan (int x) : testValue(x) { }
        const int testValue;
        bool operator () (int val)
            { return val > testValue; }

};
```

The result is a general "bigger than X" function, where the value of X is determined when we create an instance of the class, which we can do, for example, as an argument to one of the generic functions that require a predicate function. In this manner the following will find the first value larger than 12 in a list:

```
list<int>::iterator firstBig =
    find_if (aList.begin(), aList.end(), biggerThan(12));
```

16.3 Example Program–An Inventory System

Our first example uses a simple inventory management system to illustrate the creation and manipulation of containers in the STL. We will assume that a business named WorldWideWidgetWorks requires a software system to manage its widget supply. Widgets are simple devices, distinguished by different identification numbers:

```
class  Widget {
public:
    Widget(int a) : id(a) { }
    Widget() : id(0) { }
    int id;
};

ostream & operator << (ostream & out, Widget & w)
    { return out << "Widget " << w.id; }

bool operator -- (const Widget & lhs, const Widget & rhs)
    { return lhs.id == rhs.id; }

bool operator < (const Widget & lhs, const Widget & rhs)
    { return lhs.id < rhs.id; }
```

The state of the inventory is represented by two lists. One represents the stock of widgets on hand; the other represents the type of widgets that customers have back-ordered. The first is a list of widgets, and the second is a list of widget identification types. To handle our inventory we have two commands; the first, order(), processes orders, and the second, receive(), processes the shipment of a new widget.

```
class inventory {
public:
    void order (int wid);     // process order for widget type wid
    void receive (int wid);    // receive widget of type wid
private:
    list<Widget> on_hand;
    list<int> on_order;
};
```

When a new widget arrives in shipment, we compare its identification number with the list of widget types on back order. We use find() to search the back-order list, immediately shipping the widget if necessary. Otherwise, it is added to the stock on hand.

```
void inventory::receive (int wid)
{
    cout << "Received shipment of widget type " << wid << endl;
    list<int> ::iterator weNeed =
            find (on_order.begin(), on_order.end(), wid);
    if (weNeed != on_order.end()) {
        cout << "Ship " << Widget(wid)
            << " to fill back order" << endl;
        on_order.erase(weNeed);
        }
    else
        on_hand.push_front(Widget(wid));
}
```

When a customer orders a new widget, we scan the list of widgets in stock, using the function find_if(), to determine if the order can be processed immediately. To do so we need a unary function that takes as its argument a widget and determines whether the widget matches the type requested. We write this as a function object as follows:

```
class WidgetTester {
public:
    WidgetTester (int t) : testid(t) { }
    const int testid;
    bool operator () (const Widget & wid)
        { return wid.id == testid; }
};
```

The widget order function is then as follows:

```
void inventory::order (int wid)
{
    cout << "Received order for widget type " << wid << endl;
    list<Widget>::iterator weHave =
        find_if(on_hand.begin(), on_hand.end(), WidgetTester(wid));
    if (weHave != on_hand.end()) {
        cout << "Ship " << *weHave << endl;
        on_hand.erase(weHave);
        }
    else {
        cout << "Back order widget of type "  << wid  << endl;
        on_order.push_front(wid);
        }
}
```

```
typedef map<string, int> stringVector;
typedef map<string, stringVector> graph;

string pendleton("Pendleton");
string pensacola("Pensacola");
string peoria("Peoria");
string phoenix("Phoenix");
string pierre("Pierre");
string pittsburgh("Pittsburgh");
string princeton("Princeton");
string pueblo("Pueblo");

graph cityMap;

cityMap[pendleton][phoenix] = 4;
cityMap[pendleton][pueblo] = 8;
cityMap[pensacola][phoenix] = 5;
cityMap[peoria][pittsburgh] = 5;
cityMap[peoria][pueblo] = 3;
cityMap[phoenix][peoria] = 4;
cityMap[phoenix][pittsburgh] = 10;
cityMap[phoenix][pueblo] = 3;
cityMap[pierre][pendleton] = 2;
cityMap[pittsburgh][pensacola] = 4;
cityMap[princeton][pittsburgh] = 2;
cityMap[pueblo][pierre] = 3;
```

Figure 16.1 – Statements initializing a graph.

16.4   Example Program–Graphs

The second and third example programs both use the map data type. A map is
an indexed dictionary, a collection of key and value pairs.

A map in which elements are themselves maps is a natural representation for
a directed graph. For example, suppose we use strings to encode the names of
cities, and we wish to construct a map where the value associated with an edge
is the distance between two connected cities. We could create such a graph in
the fashion shown in Figure 16.1.

The type stringVector is a vector of integers indexed by strings. The type
graph is, in effect, a two-dimensional sparse array, indexed by strings and holding
integer values. The sequence of assignment statements initializes the graph. The
statements shown in Figure 16.1 represent the graph shown in Figure 16.2.

A number of classic algorithms can be used to manipulate graphs represented

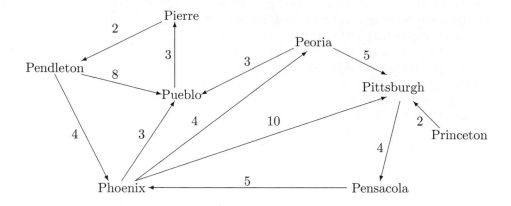

Figure 16.2 – A weighted graph.

in this form. One example is Dijkstra's shortest-path algorithm; which begins from a specific city given as an initial location. A *priority queue* of distance/city pairs is then constructed and initialized with the distance to the starting city (zero). This priority queue maintains values in order from nearest to farthest. The definition for the distance pair data type is as follows:

```
struct DistancePair {
    unsigned int first;
    string second;
    DistancePair() : first(0) { }
    DistancePair(unsigned int f, string & s)
        : first(f), second(s) { }
};

bool operator < (DistancePair & lhs, DistancePair & rhs)
    { return lhs.first < rhs.first; }
```

On each iteration around the loop we pull a city from the queue. If we have not yet found a shorter path to the city, the current distance is recorded, and by examining the graph we can compute the distance from this city to each of the adjacent cities. This process continues until the priority queue becomes exhausted.

```
void shortestDistance(const graph & cityMap,
        const string & start, stringVector & distances)
{
    // process a priority queue of distances to cities
    priority_queue<DistancePair, vector<DistancePair> ,
        greater<DistancePair> > que;
    que.push(DistancePair(0, start));

    while (! que.empty()) {
            // pull nearest city from queue
        int distance = que.top().first;
        string city = que.top().second;
        que.pop();
            // if we haven't seen it already, process it
        if (0 == distances.count(city)) {
                // then add it to shortest distance map
            distances[city] = distance;
                // and put values into queue
            stringVector::iterator start, stop;
            start = cityMap[city].begin();
            stop = cityMap[city].end();
            for (; start != stop; ++start)
                que.push(DistancePair(distance + (*start).second,
                            (*start).first));
        }
    }
}
```

16.5   Example Program–A Concordance

The final example program is a concordance. The program makes use of linked
lists as well as the multimap data type. A multimap is a form of map that permits
multiple values to be indexed with the same key.

A concordance is an alphabetical listing of words in a text that shows the
line numbers on which each word occurs. The data values are maintained in
the concordance by a multimap, indexed by strings (the words) and holding
integers (the line numbers). A multimap is employed because the same word
often appears on multiple lines; indeed, discovering such connections is one of
the primary purposes of a concordance.

The concordance data type can be defined as follows:

```
class concordance {

    typedef multimap<string, int> wordDictType;

public:
    concordance() : wordMap() { }

    void addWord (string, int);
    void readText (istream &);
    void printConcordance (ostream &);

private:
    wordDictType wordMap;
};
```

The creation of the concordance is divided into two steps: First the program generates the concordance (by reading lines from an input stream) and then prints the result on the output stream. This is reflected in the two member functions readText() and printConcordance(). The first of these, readText(), is written as follows:

```
void concordance::readText (istream & in)
    // read text from istream
    // placing words into concordance
{
    string line;

        // read each line from input
    for (int i = 1; getline(in, line); i++) {
        allLower(line);      // convert into lowercase
        list<string> words;
        split(line, " ,.;:", words); // split line into words
        list<string>::iterator wptr; // enter words into collection
        for (wptr = words.begin(); wptr != words.end(); ++wptr)
            addWord(*wptr, i);
    }
}
```

Lines are read from the input stream one by one. The text of the line is first converted into lowercase; then the line is split into words via the function split().

The split() function breaks a line of text into individual words. The set of separator characters as well as the original text are passed as arguments. This function illustrates some of the string-processing features that have been added by the STL.

```
void split
    (string & text, string & separators, list<string> & words)
{
    int n = text.length();
    int start, stop;

        // find first character that is not a separator
    start = text.find_first_not_of(separator);
    while ((start >= 0) && (start < n)) {
            // find end of current word
        stop = text.find_first_of (separators, start);
        if ((stop < 0) || (stop > n)) stop = n;
            // add word to list of words
        words.push_back (text.substr(start, stop-start));
            // find start of next word
        start = text.find_first_not_of (separators, stop+1);
        }
}
```

Following the call on split, each word is entered into the concordance, using the following method:

```
void concordance::addWord (string word, int line)
{
        // see if word occurs in list
        // first get range of entries with same key
    wordDictType::iterator low = wordMap.lower_bound(word);
    wordDictType::iterator high = wordMap.upper_bound(word);
        // loop over entries, see if any match current line
    for ( ; low != high; ++low)
        if ((*low).second == line)
            return;
        // didn't occur, add now
    wordMap.insert(make_pair(word, line));
}
```

The major portion of addWord() is taken up with ensuring that values are not duplicated in the word map should the same word occur twice on the same line. It does so by examining the range of values matching the key, each value is tested and if any match the line number no insertion is performed. It is only if the loop terminates without discovering the line number that the new word/line number pair is inserted.

The final step is to print the concordance. This is performed in the following fashion:

```
void concordance::printConcordance (ostream & out)
{
    string lastword("");
    wordDictType::iterator pairPtr;
    wordDictType::iterator stop = wordMap.end();
    for (pairPtr = wordMap.begin(); pairPtr != stop; ++pairPtr)
            // if word is same as previous, just print line number
        if (lastword == (*pairPtr).first)
            out << " " << (*pairPtr).second;
        else {    // first entry of word
            lastword = (*pairPtr).first;
            cout << endl << lastword << ": " << (*pairPtr).second;
            }
    cout << endl; // terminate last line
}
```

An iterator loop cycles over the elements being maintained by the word list. Each new word generates a new line of output, and thereafter line numbers appear separated by spaces. If, for example, the input is the text:

```
It was the best of times,
it was the worst of times.
```

The output, from "best" to "worst," is:

```
best: 1
it: 1 2
of: 1 2
the: 1 2
times: 1 2
was: 1 2
worst: 1
```

16.6   The Future of OOP

We have noted that in many ways the design of the STL is not object-oriented at all, drawing inspiration instead from techniques used in functional programming languages. Does the introduction of the STL into the standard C++ library imply that OOP is now out-moded and obsolete?

Absolutely not. Object-oriented design and programming techniques are almost without peer as guideposts in the development of large complex software. For the majority of programming tasks, OOP techniques will remain the preferred approach, but the development of software such as the STL indicates a welcome realization within the object-oriented community that not *all* ideas should be expressed in object-oriented fashion, nor all problems solved with purely object-oriented techniques.

Exercises

1. Assume a straight forward implementation of a linear data structure class, such as the linked-list class we described in Chapter 15. Outline the major features of an iterator class for this structure. What information does your iterator need to maintain?

2. Consider next a nonlinear data structure, for example, a binary tree. What information does an iterator need to maintain to traverse the elements being held in the container?

Chapter 17

Visibility and Dependency

In Chapter 1, we identified the interconnected nature of software conventionally created as a major obstacle in the development of reusable software components. This fact has long been recognized in the software engineering community, where a large body of literature deals with various ways of characterizing connections and there are rules for avoiding harmful connections (see, for example [Gillett 1982, Fairley 1985]). In this chapter, we will explore some of these issues in the context of object-oriented programming.

We can express interconnections in terms of visibility and dependency. The software engineering term *visibility* describes a characterization of *names*–the handles by which objects are accessed. An object is visible in a certain context if its name is legal and denotes the object. A related term frequently used to describe visibility is the *scope* of an identifier.

Visibility is related to connectedness in the sense that, if it is possible to control and reduce the visibility of names for an identifier, we can more easily characterize how the identifier is being used. In Smalltalk, for example, instance variables have their visibility restricted to methods; they cannot be accessed directly except within a method. This does not mean that such values cannot be accessed or modified outside of the class; all such uses, however, must be mediated by at least one method. In Apple Object Pascal, on the other hand, instance variables are visible wherever a class name is known. Thus, the language provides no mechanisms to ensure that instance variables are modified only by methods; instead, we must rely on the appropriate conduct of users.

The concept of *dependency* relates one portion of a software system to another. If a software system (such as a class or a module) cannot meaningfully exist without another system, it is said to be *dependent* on that system. A child class is almost always dependent on its parent, for example. Dependencies can also be much more subtle, as we will discover in the next section.

17.1   Coupling and Cohesion

The concepts of *coupling* and *cohesion* were introduced by Stevens, Constantine, and Myers (in [Stevens 1981]) as a framework for evaluating effective use of modules. We will discuss these with regard to a language that supports modules and then will describe their counterparts in an object-oriented language.

Coupling describes the relationships *between* modules, and cohesion describes the relationships *within* them. A reduction in interconnectedness between modules (or classes) is therefore achieved via a reduction in coupling. On the other hand, well-designed modules (or classes) should have some purpose; all the elements should be associated with a single task. This means that in a good design, the elements within a module (or class) should have internal cohesion.

17.1.1   Varieties of Coupling

Coupling between modules can arise for different reasons, some of which are more acceptable, or desirable, than others. A ranked list might look something like the following:

- Internal data coupling

- Global data coupling

- Control (or sequence) coupling

- Parameter coupling

- Subclass coupling[1]

Internal data coupling occurs when one module (or class) modifies the local data values (instance variables) in another module (class). This activity makes understanding and reasoning about programs difficult and should be avoided whenever possible. In a later section, we will explore one heuristic used to reduce internal data coupling in object-oriented systems.

Global data coupling occurs when two or more modules (classes) are bound together by their reliance on common global data structures. Again, this situation frequently complicates the understanding of modules taken in isolation, but it is sometimes unavoidable.

In practice, it is important to distinguish between two varieties of global variables. In multifile programs some global variables have *file scope*, which means they are used only within one file. Other global variables have *program scope*, which means they can potentially be modifed anywhere in a program. Understanding the use of global variables that possess program scope can be much more difficult than understanding the manipulation of variables that have only file scope.

---

[1]This list is adapted from the presentation by Fairley [Fairley 1985], although he does not discuss subclass coupling, and other terms have been changed slightly to make them more language independent.

In an object-oriented framework, a possible alternative to global data coupling is to make a new class that is charged with "managing" the data values, and to route all access to the global values through it. (This approach is similar to our use of access functions to shield direct access to local data within an object.) This technique reduces global data coupling to parameter coupling, which is easier to understand and control. In Java there are no global variables, and all values must be managed by some class.

Control or sequence coupling occurs when one module must perform operations in a certain fixed order, but the order is controlled by another module. A database system might go through, in order, the stages of performing initialization, reading current records, updating records, deleting records, and generating reports; however, each stage is invoked by a different routine and the sequencing of the calls can be dependent upon code in a different module. The presence of control coupling indicates that the designer of a module was following a lower level of abstraction than was necessary (each of the various steps versus a single directive, "process a database") Even when control coupling is unavoidable, prudence usually dictates that the module being sequenced assure itself that it is being processed in the correct order, rather than rely on the proper handling of the callers.

Parameter coupling occurs when one module must invoke services and routines from another, and the only relationships are the number and type of parameters supplied and the type of value returned. This form of coupling is common, easy to see, and easy to verify statically (with tools that check parameter calls against definition, for example); therefore, it is the most benign option.

Subclass coupling is particular to object-oriented programming. It describes the relationship a class has with its parent class (or classes in the case of multiple inheritance). Through inheritance, an instance of a child class can be treated as though it were an instance of the parent class. As we have seen in several case studies in this book, this feature permits the development of significant software components (such as windowing systems) that are only loosely related, via subclass coupling, to other portions of an application.

17.1.2 Varieties of Cohesion

The internal cohesion of a module is a measure of the degree of binding of the various elements within the module. As with coupling, cohesion can be ranked on a scale of the weakest (least desirable) to the strongest (most desirable) as follows:

- Coincidental cohesion

- Logical cohesion

- Temporal cohesion

- Communication cohesion

- Sequential cohesion

- Functional cohesion

- Data cohesion

Coincidental cohesion occurs when elements of a module are grouped for no apparent reason–often the result of someone "modularizing" a large program by arbitrarily segmenting it into several small modules. It is usually a sign of poor design. In an object-oriented framework, we say that coincidental cohesion occurs when a class consists of methods that are not related.

Logical cohesion occurs when there is a logical connection among the elements of the module (or methods in a class) but no actual connection in either data or control. A library of mathematical functions (sine, cosine, and so on) might exhibit logical cohesion if each of the functions is implemented separately without reference to any of the others.

Temporal cohesion occurs when elements are bound together because they all must be used at approximately the same time. A module that performs program initialization is a typical example. Here, a better design would distribute the various initialization activities over the modules more closely charged with subsequent behavior.

Communication cohesion occurs when elements of a module, or methods in a class, are grouped because they all access the same input/output data or devices. The module or class acts as a "manager" for the data or the device.

Sequential cohesion occurs when elements in a module are linked by the necessity to be activated in a particular order. It often results from an attempt to avoid sequential coupling. Again, a better design can usually be found if the level of abstraction is raised. (Of course, if it is necessary for actions to be performed in a certain order, this sequentiality must be expressed at some level of abstraction; the important principle is to hide this necessity as much as possible from all other levels of abstraction.)

Function cohesion is a desirable type of binding in which the elements of a module or the methods in a class all relate to the performance of a single function.

Finally, data cohesion in a module occurs when the module internally defines a set of data values and exports routines that manipulate the data structure. Data cohesion occurs when a module is used to implement a data abstraction.

One can often estimate the degree of cohesion within a module by writing a brief statement of the modules purpose and examining the statement (similar to the CRC card description we used in Chapter 2). The following tests are suggested by Constantine:

1. If the sentence that describes the purpose of a module is a compound sentence containing a comma or more than one verb, the module is probably performing more than one function; therefore, it probably has sequential or communicational binding.

2. If the sentence contains words relating to time, such as "first," "next," "then," "after," "when," or "start," the module probably has sequential or temporal binding. An example is "Wait for the instant teller customer to insert a card, then prompt for the personal identification number."

3. If the predicate of the sentence does not contain a single, specific object following the verb, the module is probably logically bound. For example, "Edit all data" has logical binding; "Edit source data" may have functional binding.

4. If the sentence contains words such as "Initialize" or "Clean up," the module probably has temporal binding.

17.1.3 Coupling and Cohesion in Object-Oriented Systems

In Chapter 1, we noted the many ways in which a class can be viewed as a logical extension of a module–as a "module in the small," as it were. Thus, design rules for modules carry over easily to design rules for objects. Objects from distinct classes should have as little coupling as possible, not only to make them more understandable but also so that they may be easily extracted from a particular application and reused in new situations. On the other hand, each object should have some definite purpose, and each method should further that purpose in some manner. That is to say, the object must form a cohesive unit.

17.1.4 The Law of Demeter

Style guidelines for program coding range from the abstract, such as the directive "Modules should exhibit internal cohesion and minimize external coupling," to the concrete, such as "No procedure should contain more than 60 lines of code." Concrete guidelines are easy to understand and apply, but often they lull programmers (and managers) into a false sense of security and may direct attention away from the real problem. As an aid in reducing complexity, the rule banning all procedures of more than 60 lines is an approximation at best; a short procedure with complicated control flow may be much more difficult to understand and code correctly than a far longer sequence of straight-line assignment statements.

Similarly, the fanatical attempt some people made a few years back to ban goto statements was often misguided. The goto itself was merely a symptom of a disease, not the disease itself. The assertion was not that goto statements are intrinsically bad and programs that avoid them are uniformly improved, but rather that it is more difficult to produce an easily understood program using goto statements. It is the understandability of programs that is important, not the use or nonuse of goto statements. Nevertheless, we cannot overlook the utility of a simple rule that is easy to apply and that is effective *most* of the time in achieving some desirable end, and we may ask whether any such guidelines might be developed specifically for object-oriented programs.

One such guideline has been proposed by Karl Lieberherr as part of his work on an object-oriented programming tool called Demeter; it is called the Law of Demeter [Lieberherr 1989a, Lieberherr 1989b]. There are two forms of the law, strong and weak. Both strive to reduce the degree of coupling between objects by limiting their interconnections.

The Law of Demeter. In any method, M, attached to a class, C, only methods defined by the following classes may be used:

- The instance-variable classes of C.

- The argument classes of method M (including C); note that global objects or objects created inside the method M are considered arguments to M.

If we rephrase the law in terms of instances (or objects) instead of methods, we arrive at the following:

The Law of Demeter (weak form). Inside a method, data can be accessed in and messages can be sent to only the following objects:

1. The arguments associated with the method being executed (including the self object).

2. Instance variables for the receiver of the method.

3. Global variables, both with file scope and with program scope.

4. Temporary variables created inside the method.

The strong form of the law restricts access to instance variables only to those variables defined in the class in which the method appears. Access to instance variables from superclasses must be mediated through accessor functions.

The Law of Demeter (strong form). Inside a method it is permitted to access or send messages only to the following objects:

1. The arguments associated with the method being executed (including the self object).

2. Instance variables defined in the class containing the method being executed.

3. Global variables.

4. Temporary variables created inside the method.

It is instructive to consider what forms of access are ruled out by the law of Demeter and to relate the law to the concepts of coupling and cohesion described earlier. The major style of access eliminated by programs that satisfy the rule is the direct manipulation of instance variables in another class. Permitting access in this form creates a situation where one object is dependent on the internal representation of another–a form of internal data coupling. On the other hand, satisfaction of this rule means that classes generally can be studied and understood in isolation from one another, since they interact only in simple, well-defined ways. Wirfs-Brock and Wilkerson go even further than the Law of Demeter, arguing that even references to instance variables from within a method should always be mediated by accessor functions [Wirfs-Brock 1989a]. Their argument is that direct references to variables severely limit the ability of programmers to refine existing classes.

17.1.5 Class-Level versus Object-Level Visibility

The idea that a class can have multiple instances introduces a new dimension in the control of coupling. Two general models are used in object-oriented languages to describe the visibility of names. These can be described as *class-level visibility* and *object-level visibility*. The distinction can be summarized as the answer to a simple question: Is an object allowed to examine the inner state of a sibling object?

Languages that control visibility on the class level, such as C++, treat all instances of a class in the same manner. As we will see shortly, C++ permits a wide range of possibilities in controlling the visibility of identifiers, yet even in the most restrictive case–so-called "private" data fields–an instance of a class is always permitted access to the data fields of other instances of the same class. In short, objects are permitted complete access to their sibling objects' internal state.

Object-level control of visibility, on the other hand, treats the individual object as the basic unit of control. Languages that exhibit object-level control include Smalltalk, in which no object is permitted access to the inner state of another object, even if both are instances of the same class.

17.1.6 Active Values

An active value [Stefik 1986], is a variable for which we want to perform some action each time its value changes. An active-value system illustrates why parameter coupling is preferable to other forms of coupling, particularly in object-oriented languages. Suppose a simulation of a nuclear power plant includes a class Reactor that maintains various pieces of information about the reactor state. Among these values is the temperature of the heat mediator–(the water that surrounds the cooling rods). Further suppose that this value is modified, in good object-oriented fashion, via a method, setHeat; and access is achieved through the function getHeat. This class is pictured below:

```
@interface Reactor : Object
{ ...
    double heat; ...
}
- (void)  setHeat: (double) newValue;
- (double) getHeat;
```

Imagine the program has been developed, and is working, when the programmer decides it would be nice to have a visual display that continuously shows the current temperature of the moderator as the simulation progresses. It is desirable to do this as noninvasively as possible; in particular, the programmer does not want to change the Reactor class. (This class may have been written by another programmer, for example, or it may be used in other applications where this new behavior is not desired.)

A simple solution is to make a new subclass of Reactor–say, GraphicalReactor–which does nothing more than override the setHeat method, updating the graphical output before invoking the superclass methods (see below). The programmer thus needs only to replace the creation of new Reactor objects with the creation of GraphicalReactor objects. This creation probably takes place once during initialization. As long as all changes to the Reactor value are mediated through the method setHeat, the gauge will reflect the value accurately.

```
@implementation GraphicalReactor : Reactor
- (void) setHeat: (double) newValue
    {
        /* code necessary to */
        /* update gauge */
        [ super setHeat: newValue ];
    }
@end
```

Smalltalk and Objective-C both support a more generalized concept called *dependency*. We will discuss this in Section 17.4.

17.2   Subclass Clients and User Clients

We have noted several times that an object, like a module, has both a public and a private face. The public side encompasses all features, such as methods and instance variables, that can be accessed or manipulated by code outside the module. The private face includes the public face, as well as methods and instance variables accessible only within the object. The user of a service provided by a module (the client) needs to know the details only of the public side of a module. Details of implementation, and other internal features not important module utilization, can be hidden from view.

Alan Snyder [Snyder 1986] and other researchers noted that inheritance in an object-oriented languages means that classes have yet a third face–namely, those features accessible to subclasses but not necessarily to other users. The designer of a subclass for a given class will probably need to know more internal implementation details of the original class than will an instance-level user, but may not need as much information as the designer of the original class.

We can think of both the designer of a subclass and a user of a class as "clients" of the original class, since they use the facilities it provides. Because these two groups have different requirements, however, it is useful to distinguish them as *subclass clients* and *user clients*. User clients create instances of the class and pass messages to these objects. Subclass clients create new classes based on the class.

In the classes we developed as part of our solitaire game in Chapter 8, the class Card declares to be private the variables r and s, which maintain the rank and suit of the card. Only methods associated with class Card can access or modify these values. The data associated with class CardPile, on the other hand, are divided into the three categories: private, protected, and public. The private variable firstCard can be accessed only within the class CardPile, while the protected fields x and y can be accessed either in this class or by subclasses. The only public interface is through methods; there are no publicly accessible instance variables. By eliminating publicly accessible instance variables, the language ensures that no data coupling is permitted between this class and other software components. (However, the language only provides the mechanism. It is still the responsibility of the programmer to use the features properly–for example, by declaring all data members as private or protected.)

We can think of software evolution and modification in terms of user and subclass clients. When a class designer announces the public features of a class, he is making a contract to provide the services described. He can consider and implement changes in the internal design freely as long as the public interface remains unchanged (or perhaps only grows). Similarly, although perhaps less common and less obvious, the designer of a class is specifying an interface to subclasses. A common and subtle source of software errors is created when the internal details of a class are changed and subclasses cease to operate. By dividing the private internal details of a class from the various levels of public interface, if only by convention, the programmer sets the boundaries for acceptable change and modification. The ability to make changes to existing code safely is critical in the maintenance of large and long-lived software systems.

The notion of a subclass client may strike some readers as odd, since when an instance of the subclass is created, the class and the subclass are melded into one object. Nevertheless, the notion makes good sense when we consider the creators or designers of the class. Often, the designer of a subclass and the designer of the original class are not the same. It is thus good OOP practice for the designer of any class to consider the possibility that, at some future point, the class may be subclassed, and to provide adequate documentation and software connections to facilitate this process.

17.3 Control Of Access and Visibility

In this section, we briefly outline the various information-hiding features of the object-oriented languages we are considering, and we note how each language supports the concepts discussed in earlier sections of this chapter.

17.3.1   Visibility in Smalltalk

The Smalltalk system provides few facilities for the protection and hiding of either data or methods. Instance variables are always considered private and are accessible only within the methods associated with the class in which the variables are defined, or in subclasses. Access to them from outside the object must be accomplished indirectly through access functions.

Methods, on the other hand, are always considered public, and can be accessed by anybody. Just as there are no facilities for making instance variables public, there are no facilities for enforcing the hiding of methods. It is common, however, for certain methods to be labeled "private," meaning that they should be used only by the class itself and should not be invoked by user clients. It is good practice to respect these suggestions and to avoid using private methods.

17.3.2   Visibility in Object Pascal

Apple Object Pascal provides weak facilities for managing the visibility of object fields. All fields–data and methods–are public and are accessible to both user and subclass clients. It is only by convention or agreement that data fields are restricted to subclass clients and that methods are open to user clients. Even though style guidelines such as the Law of Demeter cannot be strictly enforced by the system, they are still valuable and should be respected by programmers. It is helpful, too, if programmers use comments to indicate those methods in a class that they expect to be overridden in subclasses.

The Borland version of the language is slightly more powerful. Delphi supports the keywords public, protected, and private in a fashion very similar to that in C++. However, within the implementation section of a unit, all fields are treated as public. This allows sibling instances to access the private data fields of sister objects.

17.3.3   Visibility in C++

Of the languages we are considering, C++ provides by far the most complete range of facilities for controlling access to information. As we noted in earlier chapters, these facilities are provided through three new keywords, public, protected, and private.

When these keywords are used in the field-definition part of class descriptions, their effect can be described almost directly in terms of the concepts from Section 17.2. The data that follow the public: access specifier are available to subclass and user clients alike. The data that follow the protected: access specifier are accessible only within the class and subclasses, and so are intended for subclass clients not for user clients. Finally, the private: designator precedes fields that are accessible only to instances of the class itself and not to subclass or user clients. In the absence of any initial designation, fields are considered private.

Philosophically, the C++ access-control mechanisms are intended to protect against accident, not to guarantee security from malicious users. There are several ways to defeat the protection system. Probably the most direct involves the use of functions that return pointer or reference values. Consider the class shown below:

```
class Sneaky
{
    private:
        int safe;
    public:
            // initialize safe to 10
        Sneaky() { safe = 10; }
        int &sorry() { return safe; }
}
```

Although the field safe is declared private, a reference to the value is returned by the method sorry. Thus, in an expression such as

```
Sneaky x;
x.sorry() = 17;
```

the value of the data member safe will be changed from 10 to 17, even if the call to sorry takes place in user (client) code.

A more subtle point is that access specifiers in C++ control not visibility, but the access of members. The classes shown below illustrate this:

```
int i;    // global variable

class A {
private:
    int i;
};

class B : public A {
    void f();
};

B::f()
{ i++;}      // error - A::i is private
```

An error occurs because the function f attempts to modify the variable i, which is inherited from class A, although it is inaccessible (because it is declared private:). If the access modifiers controlled visibility, rather than accessibility, the variable i would be invisible and the global variable i would have been updated.

Sibling Instances

Access modifiers define properties of a class, not of instances. Thus, private fields
in C++ do not correspond exactly to the concept developed in our earlier general
discussion of visibility. In that discussion, private data were accessible only to
an object itself, whereas, in C++ the private fields are accessible to any object of
the same class. That is, in C++, an object is permitted to manipulate the private
members of another instance of the same class.

As an example, consider the class declaration shown below. Here the rp and
ip fields, representing the real and imaginary parts of a complex number, are
marked as private.

```
class Complex {
private:
    double rp;
    double ip;
public:
    Complex (double a, double b) { rp = a; ip = b; }
    Complex operator + ( Complex & x)
        { return Complex(rp + x.rp, ip + x.ip); }
};
```

The binary operation + is overridden to provide a new meaning for the
addition of two complex numbers. Despite the private nature of the rp and ip
fields, the operator function is permitted to access these fields in the argument
x, because the argument and the receiver are of the same class.

Constructor and destructor functions, such as the constructor function Complex shown above, are usually declared public. Declaring a constructor as protected implies that only subclasses or *friends* (see the subsequent discussion) can
create instances of the class, while declaring it as private restricts creation only
to friends or other instances of the class.

The weak form of the Law of Demeter can be enforced in part by declaration
of all data fields as protected. The strong form is enforced by declaration of such
fields as private. A more detailed analysis of the Law of Demeter for C++ can be
found in [Sakkinen 1988b].

While the access modifiers in C++ provide power and flexibility far in excess
of the other languages we are considering, making effective use of these features
requires foresight and experience. As with the question of whether to make
a method virtual, one serious problem with the degree of control provided by
C++ or Delphi Pascal is that the ease with which a subclass can be formed is
often dependent upon how much thought the designer of the original class gave
to the possibility of subclassing. Being overly protective (declaring information
private that should be protected) can make subclassing difficult. Problems arise
if the subclass designer cannot modify the source form of the original class–for
example, if the original is distributed as part of a library.

Private Inheritance

The keywords public and private also preface the name of a superclass in a class definition. When they are used in this fashion, the visibility of information from the superclass is altered by the modifier. A subclass that inherits publicly from another class corresponds to the notion of inheritance we have used up to this point–namely, that a subclass is also a subtype. If a subclass inherits privately, the public features of the superclass are reduced to the level of the modifier. In effect, this indicates that inheritance is being used only for construction, and the resulting class should not and cannot be considered a subtype of the original class.

When a class inherits publicly from another class, instances of the subclass cannot be assigned to identifiers of the superclass type, as is possible with public inheritance. An easy way to remember this limitation is in terms of the *is-a* relationship. Public inheritance is an overt assertion that the *is-a* relationship holds and thus an instance of the subclass can be used when the superclass is called for. A Dog *is-a* Mammal, for example, and so a Dog can be used in any situation in which a Mammal is called for. Private inheritance does not maintain the *is-a* relationship, since instances of a class that inherits in such a manner from a parent class cannot always be used in place of the parent class. Thus, it would not make sense to use a SymbolTable where an arbitrary type of Dictionary was required. If a variable is declared to be a type of Dictionary, we cannot assign a value of type SymbolTable to it (whereas we could if the inheritance were public).

Friend Functions

Another aspect of visibility in C++ is a *friend function*. This is simply a function (not a method) that is declared by the friend modifier in the declaration of a class. Friend functions are permitted to read and write the private and protected fields within an object.

Consider the class declaration that follows, which extends the earlier complex-number class description:

```
class Complex {
private:
    double rp;
    double ip;

public:
    Complex(double, double);
    friend double abs(Complex&);
};
```

```
Complex::Complex(double a, double b)
{
    rp = a; ip = b;
}

double abs(Complex& x)
{     return sqrt(x.rp * x.rp + x.ip * x.ip); }
```

The fields rp and ip of the data structure representing complex numbers are declared to be private and thus are generally not accessible outside of methods associated with the class. The function abs–which incidentally overloads a function of the same name defined for double precision values–is not a method; it is simply a function. However, since the function has been declared a friend of the complex class, it is permitted to access all fields of the class, even private fields.

It is also possible to declare classes, and even individual methods in other classes, as friends. The most common reasons for using friend functions are that they require access to the internal structure of two or more classes, or that it is necessary for the friend function to be invoked in a functional, rather than a message-passing, style (that is, as abs(x) instead of as x.abs()).

Friend functions are a powerful tool, but they are easy to abuse. In particular, they introduce exactly the sort of data couplings that we identified in the beginning of this chapter as detrimental to the development of reusable software. Whenever possible, more object-oriented encapsulation techniques (such as methods) should be preferred over friend functions. Nevertheless, there are times when no other tool can be used, such as when a function needs access to the internal structure of two or more class definitions. In these cases, friend functions are a useful abstraction [Koenig 1989c].

Name Spaces

Yet another recent change in C++ is the introduction of *name spaces*. The namespace facility helps reduce the poliferation of global names. While the static keyword can limit the scope of a name to a single file, previously if a name needed to be shared between two or more files the only choice was to make the name global. Such values can now be enclosed within a name-space definition.

```
namespace myLibrary {
    int x;
    class A {
        ...
        };
    class B : public A {
        ...
        };
}
```

The variables defined within the name space are not global. If a programmer wishes to include the name space, she issues an explicit directive, which then places all top-level names defined in the name space in the current scope.

```
using namespace myLibrary;
```

Individual items can also be imported from a specific name space, either by explicity naming the space or by importing just the single item.

```
myLibrary::A anA; // explicitly name the name space
```

```
using myLibrary::B;   // import only the class B
B aNewB;          // B is now a type name
```

Constant Members

In C++, the keyword const is used to indicate a quantity that is unchanging during the life of the object. Global variables that are so declared become global constants. Constant variables that are declared local to a procedure are accessible only within the procedure and cannot be modified except in the initialization statement that creates them.

Data members often act as constants, but their initial value cannot be deter mined until the object is created. For example, the data members representing the real and imaginary fields in the Complex number class shown earlier should never be altered once the complex number is created. In Chapter 3 we called such fields *immutable*. They can be created by the const keyword.

Although it is not permitted to assign to constant data members, they can be initialized in C++ with the same syntax used to invoke parent class constructors as part of the constructor process (see Chapter 7 for a discussion of invoking parent class constructors). Consider the class definition shown below:

```
class Complex {
public:
    const double rp;
    const double ip;
    Complex(double, double);
};
```

```
Complex::Complex(double a, double b) : rp(a), ip(b)
{
/* empty statement */
}
```

Here the fields rp and ip have been declared constant, so there is no danger in making them public as they cannot be modified. To provide an initial value the constructor seems to invoke rp and ip as if they are superclasses. This is the only way that constant data members can be assigned. Once the body of the constructor starts executing, the value of the constant data member cannot be altered.

Data members declared as reference variables can be initialized in the same manner. The const keyword can be applied to function or procedure members as well; however, a discussion of that topic is beyond the scope of this book.

Interaction between Overloading and Overriding

Another confusing aspect of the visibility rules in C++ is the interaction of overloading and overriding. Function names, including member functions, can be overloaded with two or more definitions as long as their argument lists are sufficiently different that the compiler can tell them apart. This is shown in the following class description, which overloads the function name test, by use of an integer argument with one and a double-precision argument with the second.

```
class A {
public:
    void test (int a)
        { cout << "This is the integer version\n"; }
    void test (double b)
        { cout << "This is the floating point version\n"; }
};
```

In attempting to match a message to a corresponding method, C++ first searches for a name space in which the message selector is defined and then searches for the most appropriate function *defined* in that name space. Even if a more appropriate function is inherited from another name space, it will not be considered. This is illustrated in the following class descriptions.

```
class A {
public:
    void test (double b)
        { cout << "This is the floating point version\n"; }
};

class B : public A {
public:
    void test (int a)
        { cout << "This is the integer version\n"; }
};
```

An attempt to send the message test with a floating-point value to an instance of class B will result in a compiler warning, since in the name space in which the compiler first finds a method named test (namely, the class B) there is no function defined that can handle a floating-point argument. This is despite the fact that an appropriate function can be inherited from class A. The result is the same whether or not the function is declared as virtual. To get around this the programmer needs to define both versions in class B, one of which simply invokes the corresponding function in the parent class.

```
class B : public A {
public:
    void test (double b)
        { A::test(b); }
    void test (int a)
        { cout << "This is the integer version\n"; }
    };
```

17.3.4   Visibility in Java

As we have seen in the examples of Java code in this book, in Java the modifiers public and private are placed individually on each data field and member function.

Java introduces an interesting new modifier named final. A final class cannot be subclassed, a final method cannot be overridden, and a final instance variable cannot be assigned to. Use of the final keyword permits the compiler to perform a number of optimizations.

As in C++, the private modifier in Java refers to classes, not instances. Sibling members of the same class are permitted access to each other's private data fields.

Another name-scoping facility provided by Java is the *package*–a group of classes and interfaces that serve as a tool for managing large name spaces and avoiding conflicts. A package is specified by the package statement, which must be the first statement in a file.

```
package packageName;
```

Code in one package can specify classes or interfaces from another package either by explicitly naming the package in which the object is found or by importing one package into another. The following illustrates the first mechanism:

```
// get type foo from package bar
bar.foo newObj = new bar.foo();
```

The importing of a package makes the names of all its public classes and interfaces available, just as if they were defined in the present file.

```
    // import all objects and interfaces
    // from package named bar
import bar.*;
```

If desired, individual objects or interfaces can be specified by use of a name in place of the wild-card character.

```
    // import the name foo
    // from the package bar
import bar.foo;
```

17.3.5   Visibility in Objective-C

In Objective-C, instance-variable declarations must appear in the interface description of a class. It is not possible to define new fields in the implementation section, even though such values are not part of the interface, since they are accessible only within methods (they are protected, to use the C++ terminology). The visibility of instance-variable fields can be modified through the @public keyword, which makes all fields following the keyword publicly accessible to users. For example, the following shows an interface definition for a class, Ball, representing a graphical ball object. The location of the ball, represented by the coordinates in the x and y fields, are publicly accessible whereas the direction and energy of the ball are protected.

```
@interface Ball : Object
{
    double direction;
    double energy;
@public
    double x;
    double y;
}
```

Unlike in instance-variable fields, it is possible to define methods in the implementation section of a class that are not declared in the interface section. Such methods are visible, and can be invoked, only within that portion of the program that follows the definition of the new method.

There is no way to create a method that can be invoked by subclass clients but not by user clients, and there is no way to create truly private instance-variable values.

17.4   Intentional Dependency

Although most often programmers attempt to avoid dependency in their code, there are situations where it is an essential component. A simulation, for example, might include a model that changes over time as the simulation progresses. Features of the model might be displayed graphically in one or more windows, and as the model changes, the windows should be continuously updated.

Yet a concern for reducing the coupling within the program should lead the programmer to avoid making too tight a connection between the model and the windows. In particular, there is no reason for the model to know the type or even the number of views in which it might be displayed. (There may be more than one view–for example, both a numeric or a graphical representation of a variable numeric quantity). How can the model alert the views to update their displays without an explicit connection between the two?

One way to avoid a tight interconnection between dependent components is to use a *dependency manager*. Such a feature is a standard part of the Smalltalk and Objective-C run-time library, but can be easily constructed in other languages, such as C++. The basic idea is for the dependency manager to act as the intermediary, maintaining a list of objects and the other components that depend upon them. The model need know only about the dependency manager. The view objects "register" themselves with the dependency manager by indicating that they depend upon the model object. Subsequently, when the model object changes it sends a single message to the dependancy manager, saying that it has changed and that all of its dependents should be notified. The dependents will then receive a message, sent by the dependency manager, indicating that the model has been modified and they should take appropriate action.

The dependency system works well at isolating components from each other, reducing the number of explicit links within a program. However, unlike the scheme described in Section 17.1.6, it works only when dependents know that someone may be waiting on their change. This scheme will not work when, as in the Reactor example, it is necessary to be as noninvasive of the original code as possible.

Exercises

1. Design a tool that can examine programs written in your favorite object-oriented language and report violations of the Law of Demeter.

2. The strong form of the Law of Demeter prevents access to inherited instance variables. Describe the advantages and disadvantages of this restriction. Consider issues such as the coupling between classes and the effect on the understandability of code.

3. Do you think the strong form of the Law of Demeter also should have restricted access to global variables? Support your opinion by well-reasoned arguments. You might want to look at the article by Wulf and Shaw [Wulf 1973] in preparing your answer.

4. What other concrete rules, similar to the Law of Demeter, can you think of in which (1) the satisfaction of the law usually leads to systems with

320   *CHAPTER 17.   VISIBILITY AND DEPENDENCY*

fewer interconnections and more cohesion and (2) exceptions in which the rule must be violated are rare. In particular, the Law of Demeter addresses coupling between different objects. Can you think of a guideline that encourages greater cohesion within an object?

5. There is an alternative level of visibility that, like protected (subclass client) data, is also more restrictive than public information and less restrictive than information to which access is permitted only inside an object. Under this alternative, instances of the same class have access to the internal state of an object even when such access is denied to all others. In C++, for example, an object can access any field in another instance of the class, even if those fields are private or protected. In other languages, such as Smalltalk, this style of access is not permitted. Discuss the advantages and disadvantages of each approach.

6. Another possible variation on visibility rules for subclass clients is to permit access to an immediate ancestor class but not to more distant ancestors. Discuss the advantages and disadvantages of this rule. (This issue is presented in [Snyder 1986]).

7. Of the languages we are considering, only C++ and Delphi Pascal have explicit facilities for distinguishing features accessible to subclass clients from those accessible to user clients. Nevertheless, all languages have some mechanism for describing the programmer's intent through the use of comments. Often, structured comments, such as compiler directives, are used to provide optional information to a language system. Describe a commenting convention that could denote levels of visibility. Then outline an algorithm that could be used by a software tool to enforce the visibility rules.

Chapter 18

Patterns and Frameworks

A *class* is a mechanism for encapsulating the solution to a specific problem. It embodies a certain service, providing data and behavior that is useful to other classes working together to implement an application. But, while a major utility of the class mechanism is that it concisely defines a software component, allowing it to be analyzed and described in isolation, single classes by themselves are seldom the complete solution to any problem.

Given this fact, there has been a growing interest in the past several years in describing the manner in which collections of classes work *together* in the solution of problems. This interest can be seen in two important ideas that have become popular, **application frameworks** and **design patterns**. In subsequent sections we will describe each of these in more detail.

18.1 Application Frameworks

A *application framework* is a set of classes that cooperate closely with each other and together embody a reusable design for a general category of problems. The most common use of application frameworks is in the creation of graphical user interfaces, or GUI applications, and we will examine one such framework in detail in Chapter 19. However, the concept has applicability beyond the development of user interfaces. For example, frameworks exist that are geared to building editors for various domains, for compiler construction, and for financial modeling applications [Gamma 1995, Deutsch 1989, Weinand 1988].

Although we might abstract and discuss the design elements that lie behind a framework, a framework is nevertheless always a set of specific classes that are typically implemented only on a specific platform. An example might be the Model-View-Controller framework in Smalltalk or the OWL graphical user interface framework for PCs.

The framework dictates the overall structure of the application. It describes how responsibilities are partitioned between various components, and how these components must interact with each other. The benefit of a framework then is that the designer of a new application need only concentrate on the specifics of the problem at hand. Previous design decisions embodied in the structure of the framework need not be reexamined, nor does the code provided by the framework need to be rewritten.

For example, the Little Application Framework (LAF) to be discussed in Chapter 19 consists of about a dozen classes. The central class, application, implements the behavior we expect for graphical interface windows, such as the ability to move and be resized, but does not implement any application-specific behavior. Instead, the user of the framework is expected to create a new class that inherits from the class application and in this class redefine certain methods (such as those that respond to a mouse event or that repaint the window). The following is the class description from a solitaire game similar to the one we developed in Chapter 8, written with the LAF.

```
class cardApp : public application {
public:
        // constructor
    cardApp();

        // application-specific behavior
    virtual void mouseButtonDown(int x, int y);
    virtual void paint();

private:
    CardPile * piles[13];
};
```

By simply creating an instance of this class, the user of the framework can produce a graphical window for his application. The developer need not worry about how to write all the window-handling code, but instead can concentrate on the application-specific behavior.

However, the fact that the overall design has already been laid out by the creator of the framework is also a weakness, because in providing the structure of an application the framework severely constrains the way in which new applications are allowed differ from each other. The LAF, for example, simplifies the development of applications that use a single window, buttons, menus, and text areas, but it restricts the application to a single window. This restriction cannot be lifted easily without major revision to the framework (thereby eliminating the reason for using the framework in the first place).

The use of a application framework usually leads to an inversion of control between the new application-specific code and the library-supplied code. In a traditional application, application specific code defines the overall flow of execution through the program, occasionally invoking library routines in order to execute some specific function (such as an a mathematical routine or an input/output operation).

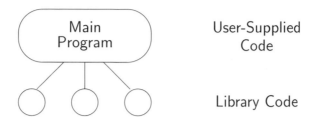

In a application framework, on the other hand, the flow of control is dictated by the framework and is the same from application to application. The creator of a new application merely changes the routines invoked by the framework, but does not change the overall structure. Thus, the framework has the dominant position and the application-specific code is reduced to a secondary position.

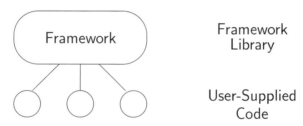

Because a framework inverts this relationship between application-developer-defined code and library code, it is sometimes described as an *upside-down library* [Wilson 1990].

18.1.1 The Java API

Another example of a framework is the Java Application Programming Interface (API), which consists of a number of classes that programmers use to construct new Java applications (called *applets*). As with the LAF, the creation of new class that inherits from an API base class is a primary mechanism for incorporating new behavior into an application.

The fundamental class for every Java application is the class Applet. This class defines the overall structure of the application through a method, main, that is normally not overridden by programmers. This method invokes a number of other methods, which are overridden to provide application-specific behavior. A few of these methods are summarized here:

init()	Invoked when the applet is initialized.
start()	Invoked when the application is started.
paint(Graphics)	Invoked when window is to be redrawn.
mouseDown(Event, int, int)	Invoked when the mouse is pressed.
keyDown(Event, int)	Invoked when key is pressed.
stop()	Invoked when the window is removed.

In addition, the framework provides a rich collection of classes for constructing items such as buttons and menus, displaying text in a variety of fonts, dealing with colors, mathematical operations, and much more.

18.1.2   A Simulation Framework

To illustrate that not all frameworks need be associated with user interfaces, we will sketch the design of a framework that can be used to drive simulations such as the billiard ball illustration presented in Chapter 6. As described in the latter part of that chapter, we might start by defining all objects in the simulation as subclasses of a general class for graphical objects, such as the following:

```
GraphicalObject = object
        (* data fields *)
    link : GraphicalObject;
    region : Rect;

        (* initialization function *)
    procedure setRegion (left, top,  right, bottom : integer);

        (* operations that graphical objects perform *)
    procedure draw;
    procedure erase;
    procedure update;
    function intersect (anObj : GraphicalObject) :  boolean;
    procedure hitBy (anObj : GraphicalObject);
end;
```

Graphical objects have a region, know how to draw themselves, and can tell when they intersect. Thus, the framework for the simulation can be provided by a general-purpose class for managing graphical objects, such as the following:

```
GraphicalUniverse = object
        (* data fields *)
    moveableObjects : GraphicalObject;
    fixedObjects : GraphicalObject;
    continueUpdate : boolean;
        (* methods *)
    procedure initialize;
    procedure installFixedObject (newObj : GraphicalObject);
    procedure installMovableObject (newObj : GraphicalObject);
    procedure drawObjects;
    procedure updateMoveableObjects;
    procedure continueSimulation;
end;
```

The heart of the framework is the routine to update all moveable objects. This procedure simply cycles through the list of movable objects, asking each to update itself. If any object requests that the update cycle continue (by invoking the routine continueSimulation), the update cycle continues; otherwise, the simulation halts.

```
procedure GraphicalUniverse.updateMoveableObjects;
var
    currentObject : GraphicalObject;
begin
    repeat
        continueUpdate := false;
        currentObject := moveableObjects;
        while currentObject <> nil do begin
            currentObject.update;
            currentObject := currentObject.link;
        end
    until not continueUpdate
end;
```

The resulting framework knows nothing of the particular application in which it will be used and therefore can be used for the simulation of billiard balls, the simulation of fish in a fish tank, an ecological simulation of rabbits and wolves, and many other applications.

Another sort of simulation is "event-driven," where "events" are stored in a priority queue ordered by their "time" of execution. Values are removed from the queue and executed one by one. Each event may spawn new events, which are then added to the queue. A framework for this type of application is described in [Budd 1994].

18.2 Design Patterns

Whereas an application framework is a set of specific classes designed to help create applications for a specific set of problems on a specific platform (or set of platforms), a *design pattern* is much more amorphous. A design pattern simply captures the salient characteristics of a solution to a problem that has been observed to occur repeatedly in many different problem domains. Usually these patterns involve the interactions between several objects or classes. By examining patterns in a systematic fashion, the student becomes aware of the wide range of possible approaches to any particular problem and can hopefully recognize circumstances where the same pattern may be applicable when encountered in future situations.

18.2.1   The Intermediary Pattern

An example will help clarify the concept. A general design pattern might be described as *"standing in place of."* In this pattern, there is one object, the *client*, that "thinks" it is interacting with another object, the *intermediary*. However, in truth the intermediary is not performing the requested services but they are being handled by a third object, the *worker*. This simple concept can appear in many different guises; we will cite only a few.

Proxy. The intermediary is a transmission agent, sending requests along some pathway such as a network. The actual servicing of the request is handled by a server at the other end of the network, and the responses sent back. The use of the intermediary hides the details involved in transmission, giving the appearance of a simple message.

Facade. The actual work involved in servicing requests from the client is not done by a single object but rather by a collection of interacting objects. The intermediary acts as a focus point, handing off requests to the appropriate handler. It hides the need to remember all the objects performing the actual service by providing a single simple interface.

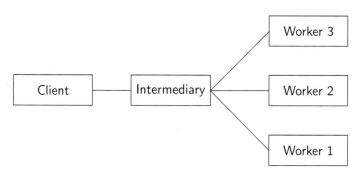

Translator (or Adapter). The actual work is being performed by a single object, but the protocol used by this object differs from that used by the client. The intermediary simply acts as a translator, changing the name of messages from the form understood by the client to the form understood by the worker.

Decorator (or Wrapper or Filter). While the worker is performing the bulk of the activity, the intermediary adds some additional behavior without necessarily changing the interface. For example, the wrapper might produce a border (or scroll bars) around a window while the worker performs the task of rewriting the window contents. The client interacts with the wrapper as if it were the worker, although the major part of the work is actually performed elsewhere. In this fashion, the wrapper may be entirely transparent to the client. A wrapper is often a low-cost and more flexible alternative to subclassing, since it can be easily added and removed at run time.

Bridge (or State). Once again, the intermediary defines the interface for a task but not an implementation. There may be several different implementations, perhaps changing over time. The intermediately selects and executes an appropriate one. The use of the intermediary provides a single point of interface, while the actual implementation may vary over time or depending upon certain conditions.

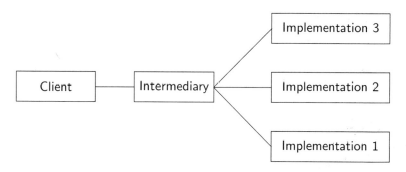

The intermediary pattern most often refers to the situation where the middleman is relatively "light weight," meaning that it does almost no work itself but instead simply passes commands on to others for completion. The interpreter pattern described in the next section, for example, might in one sense be viewed as a form of intermediary, inasmuch as the client interacts with a single object that is in fact a facade for a much more complex structure. But the interpreter by nature must be relatively heavy weight, requiring a lot of information about the structure over which it is cycling. In this fashion the interpreter differs from the rest of the design patterns described here.

18.2.2 Traversal Patterns

Another common pattern occurs when data values are organized into a hierarchical composite structure, such as a binary tree. A common task is for an object to visit every node in the tree. Variability can occur in the client that is doing the visiting, in the nodes of the tree themselves, or in both.

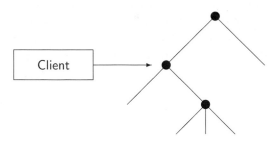

Visitor. In the first example, the node values in the hierarchy are all the same, but there are many different visitors who might traverse the tree. An example might be a binary tree where each node has the following class structure:

```
template <class T> class TreeNode {
public:
    TreeNode (T & initial);
    void visit (Visitor & v);
private:
    T value;
    TreeNode<T> * left;
    TreeNode<T> * right;
};
```

That is, each node contains a value and a right and left pointer, either of which might be a null pointer.

Visitors to the tree must all be subclasses of a general class named Visitor, which redefines a virtual method named action. The visit method in the class TreeNode performs a preorder traversal of the structure, carrying out the action on each node. (An alternative might be to encode the actual traversal of the tree on the client side, but it is usually easier and more object oriented for the tree itself to perform the traversal).

```
TreeNode::visit (Visitor & v)
{
    v.action(value);
    if (left != NULL) left->visit (v);
    if (right != NULL) right->visit (v);
}
```

Variability comes about through the deferred method action. The routine visit has no knowledge of exactly what behavior is being executed by this routine. On the other hand, this pattern requires that all visitors be subclasses of the general abstract class Visitor.

Interpreter. A pattern that is superficially similar occurs when the composite structure is still hierarchical but no longer uniform. A common example is an abstract-syntax tree. A tree might represent the structure of a regular expression, which is composed of alternation nodes, repetition nodes, and literals. Alternation and repeition nodes maintain as part of their state subtrees, which represent the various alternatives or the structure being repeated.

This pattern differs from the first in that the action to be performed is usually encoded as part of the tree rather than as an action outside of the data structure. For example, our abstract syntax tree might be passed a sample input (a string, for instance) and be asked whether or not the input matches the regular expression. To determine this, each node in the expression performs a different series of actions. A literal node will match only exact values, while an alternation node will try each alternative in turn to see if any match, and so on. The client hands the string to be matched to the root of the tree, then receives the response after it has been processed.

The pattern also differs from the first in that the data structure itself has no interaction with the client other than receiving input values and returning a result. Once a method defined by the root of the tree is invoked by the client, the tree itself performs a series of actions leading to the result.

Iterator. One problem with the first visitor pattern is that the client and the tree structure are too tightly connected. Either the client performed the traversal, which implies that the client had intimate knowledge of the tree structure, or the tree itself performed the traversal, which implies that the action to be performed must be known to the tree (at least as a deferred method). This coupling can be greatly reduced by placing a mediator between the client and the data values themselves.

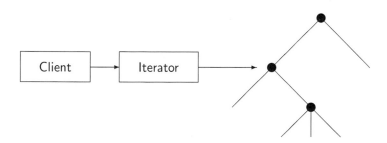

This mediator, called an *iterator*, performs the traversal of the tree structure, offering values one by one to the client. The client is then presented with a flat, linear structure rather than the hierarchical collection actually used to store the values. The interface to an iterator is typically something like the following:

initialize	Initialize iterator to root of tree.
current	Return current value.
atEnd	Return true if no further values.
advance	Advance to next value.

Using the iterator, the client performs a loop such as the following:

```
itr.initialize();
while not itr.atEnd() do begin
    ... some action with itr.current() ...
    itr.advance();
end;
```

The iterator effectively separates the client and the actual data structure. The data structure need not know how its values are being used, and the client need not know the internal representation of the data structure.

18.2.3   The Double-Dispatching Pattern

The double-dispatching pattern occurs when there are two or more sources of variation in an exchange. This might be during a visit, as described in the previous pattern, where both the client and the nodes of the hierarchical structure vary. However, many other situations involve the same idea.

Suppose, for example, that we have a variety of polygon shapes represented by a general class Shape and various subclasses (Triangle, Square, and the like). We also have two types of output device, say a printer and a terminal, represented by subclasses of Device. The graphics commands necessary to perform printing operations for these devices are sufficiently different that no general interface is possible. Instead, each shape itself encapsulates information concerning how to display on a printer and how to display on a terminal.

```
class Triangle : public Shape {
public:
    Triangle (Point, Point, Point);
        // ...
    virtual void displayOnPrinter (Printer);
    virtual void displayOnTerminal (Terminal);
        // ...
private:
    Point p1, p2, p3;
};
```

The question is how to handle two polymorphic variables: one a Shape (which could be any subclass of class Shape) and the other a Device. The clue to this pattern is that message passing can be used to "tie down" one of the two values. To determine both, we simply make each value a receiver for a message in turn. (The extension of the idea to three or more variables is then obvious–simply make each unknown a receiver in turn).

For example, we first pass the device a command, and pass the shape as argument. This command is deferred and redefined in each of the subclasses of

Device. Message passing therefore selects the right function to be executed. An example might be the following:

```
function Printer.display (Shape aShape)
begin
    aShape.displayOnPrinter (self);
end;

function Terminal.display (Shape aShape)
begin
    aShape.displayOnTerminal (self);
end;
```

Note that the display method has no idea what type of form is being generated. But each of the methods displayOnPrinter and displayOnTerminal is itself deferred: defined in class Shape and redefined in every subclass. Suppose that the shape is indeed a triangle. By the time the method in class Triangle is executed both sources of variation, the shape and the printing device, have been bound to specific quantities.

```
void Triangle.displayOnPrinter (Printer p)
{
    // printer-specific code to
    // display triangle
    // ...
}

void Triangle.displayOnTerminal (Terminal t)
{
    // terminal-specific code to
    // display triangle
    // ...
}
```

The major difficulty with this technique is the large number of methods it requires. Notice, for example, that every shape must have a different method for every printing device. Nevertheless, it is very efficient for handling variability in two or more quantities ([Ingalls 1986, Budd 1991, LaLonde 1990a, Hebel 1990]).[1]

---

[1] Double dispatching was first described by Dan Ingalls [Ingalls 1986], who called the technique *multiple polymorphism*. The alternative term *double dispatching* has come to be more widely used, to avoid confusion with multiple inheritance.

18.2.4   Classifying Design Patterns

As illustrated by these examples, an important aspect of design patterns is that they provide a vocabulary for discussing solutions to problems. This common vocabulary allows groups of programmers to share ideas in an application-independent fashion, and it provides a means by which to codify and pass on knowledge and tradition from one project to the next.

While individual patterns may be relatively easy to describe, a more complicated problem is to develop a categorization technique that can be used to record and recall patterns in later projects. Much of the current work in this area involves creating such knowledge bases [Gamma 1995, Coplien 1995, Pree 1995].

Note that patterns operate at a different level of granularity than do frameworks. A framework embodies the complete design of an entire application. A pattern, on the other hand, is just the outline of a solution to a small and specific problem. Actual applications are often pieced together with a number of different patterns.

Finally, it should be emphasized that though patterns may be useful in exposing the developer of an application to many alternative design possibilities, selecting a pattern is not a substitute for developing a solution. That is, the pattern simply lays out the broad outlines of a solution; filling in the details may still require considerable effort.

Exercises

1. Describe the role played by inheritance and deferred methods in the creation of a application framework. Would it be possible to create a framework in a non-object-oriented programming language?

2. Describe another application that could be created with the graphical simulation framework described in Section 18.1.2.

3. Can you think of other example uses that fit the "mediator" pattern?

4. Explain why encapsulation is better served in the visitor design pattern by having the data structure, rather than the client, perform the traversal of the tree.

5. Explain how, in an untyped language such as Smalltalk, the technique of double-dispatching can be used to perform mixed-type arithmetic, such as the addition of two numbers that could be either integers or floating-point values.

Chapter 19

A Case Study: The LAF

As we noted in Chapter 18, an *application framework* is a collection of classes that together define a structure for solving a particular problem. Probably the most commonly used application frameworks are those for developing graphical user interfaces for software systems. Indeed, a great deal of the popularity of object-oriented techniques can be attributed to the success of GUI application frameworks in simplifying the creation of user interfaces, thereby making computer applications accessible to a much wider range of users.

In this chapter we will examine one very simple application framework, the *Little Application Framework*, or LAF. The LAF is purposely much simpler than most commercial application frameworks, being intended only for trivial programs and for explaining the framework concept. For example, the LAF has fewer than a dozen classes in all, whereas many commercial application frameworks have well over a hundred. Nevertheless, the LAF is complete enough to demonstrate most of the important concepts found in graphical user application frameworks.

The LAF is also designed to permit applications to be ported easily to different platforms. While the implementation details differ considerably, the interface to the LAF between platforms is constant. Versions of the LAF exist for the Macintosh, for PCs, and for UNIX systems.

19.1 Components of a Graphical User Interface

The components of a graphical user interface constructed by the LAF include a single window, menus, buttons, text boxes, and the ability to respond to mouse and key presses.

The principle way in which a programmer specializes the appearance of a component, such as a button, a menu, or the window itself, is through inheritance. There is a generic class, button, for example, which is subclassed to form a specific type of button. The same holds with menus, menu items (the individual lines of a menu), and windows.

Before explaining the structure of these components in the LAF, we should first have an overall understanding of the structure of event-driven programs, such as user interfaces.

19.2   Event-Driven Execution

The first conceptual hurdle a programmer must overcome in attempting to understand the techniques for developing graphical user interfaces is structuring programs around event-driven execution.

A conventional program proceeds on its own agenda. We can think of execution as something like a finger that is moving through the program from beginning to end. At various points the program may interact with the user, but the responses the program is willing to deal with are very proscribed. For example, a program may ask questions of the user and respond only to simple yes/no answers typed at a keyboard.

In an event-driven program the user is in control. The program is largely *reactive* to the user rather than *proactive*, and execution is largely confined to a single loop. The following describes, in pseudo-code, the main program for almost all event-driven applications. The initialization and cleaning-up stages start and terminate the application, and between the two the program simply loops, waiting for the user to do something such as moving the mouse, hitting the keyboard, or inserting a floppy disk into a disk drive. When the user acts, the application reacts and then goes back to waiting for the next action.

```
program main;
begin
    initialize application;
    while not finished do
        begin
            if user has done something interesting
                respond to it
        end;
    clean up application;
end
```

The "interesting things" the user can do are called *events*. Since the flow of control is directed by the sequence of events, this is called event-driven execution. Not all events need to correspond to user-initiated activities. Actions like inserting a disk can cause a sequence of internally generated events, and the program will respond to these in the same way as it does to user-generated events.

Object-oriented programming fits naturally with event-driven execution because the flow of control is so highly structured. It is relatively easy to create a library of classes that go through the motions of an event-driven application but perform no actual work. By subclassing from this library and changing the meaning of just a few methods, we can add the "work" part of an application to this library without needing to rewrite the "control" portions. This is exactly what is done by an GUI application framework.

Steve Burbeck of Apple has described a typical event-driven application as being constructed with an "upside-down library" [Wilson 1990]. In a traditional program a software library may provide bits and pieces of code, but it is the job of the programmer to write the "glue" that holds everything together. In a GUI system the library provides the glue and the programmer merely specializes pieces of the library, using subclassing and overriding, to obtain application-specific behavior.

19.3   Using Inheritance to Customize

The primary means by which an application framework is customized to create a new program is inheritance. The application framework provides one or more abstract superclasses–classes that will be overridden by the programmer. To explain the mechanism for customization, we can divide the methods defined in these classes into three categories:

1. Base methods. These provide certain essential functionality that is useful to the customization process but will probably not be overridden by the programmer. An example might be methods to draw circles and lines and other graphical images on a window.

2. Algorithm methods. These describe an abstract algorithm, for which the specific details are left to other methods. An example might be a method that implements the event loop described earlier. These methods provide the structure for the application framework without doing any of the actual work. As with base methods, algorithm methods are not usually overridden in a new application.

3. Abstract methods. These methods do the actual work of the application. In the application framework an abstract method is often simply a dummy procedure that performs nothing. By the overriding of the abstract methods, actions specific to a new application are provided.

When building a new program using an application framework the programmer simply creates several new classes as subclasses of those provided by the application framework, overriding abstract methods to create application-specific behavior. The application framework plays the role of the main program (the "top" part of an application) and often provides certain base functionality (the "bottom" part), leaving it to the programmer to fill in the details in the middle.

19.4   Classes in the LAF

There are seven main classes provided by the LAF, three of which are used mainly as a basis for subclassing. These seven classes are application, button, menu, menuItem, staticText, and editText. The three classes normally subclassed are application, button, and menuItem. These will all be described in more detail.

Fundamentally, we create an application by subclassing the class application and overriding certain methods. The main event loop is started by invocation of the method run, inherited from class application. This method implements the event loop described earlier. Execution is terminated when the user selects the quit menu item, closes the application window, or invokes the quit() method inherited from class application.

The simplest application possible is shown below. Notice that creating it consists of (a) defining the application class, (b) creating an instance of the class, and (c) invoking the run method for the instance of the application class.

```
class simpleApp : public application {
public:
    simpleApp() : application("simple application") { }
};

void main() {
    simpleApp theApp;

    theApp.run();
};
```

In this case the application does nothing more than display a window on the user's screen and wait for the user to quit the application.

19.5   The Class application

The functionality provided by the class application is described by Figure 19.1. The function, run, normally is the last function called in the procedure main. The function does not return. The method quit can halt the running application.

The methods update() or clearAndUpdate() are invoked whenever the user schedules a screen refresh. Most often this is necessary following a response to an event, such as a mouse-down or a key-press event. The clear method first clears the screen before the refresh. To perform the refresh, the application paint() method is invoked. The user typically does not invoke the paint() method directly.

The method paint() redraws the screen image. It is usually overridden in application classes to provide application-specific behavior. This function should not be directly called by the user; instead, the method is invoked in response to a call on the method update() or clearAndUpdate().

Function	Purpose
run	Begin execution for application
quit	Halt application
update	Schedule window for updating
clearAndUpdate	Clear window, schedule for updating
paint	Redisplay screen
mouseButtonDown	Respond to mouse-down event
keyPressed	Respond to character key being pressed
top	Return coordinate of top of window
bottom	Coordinate of bottom of window
left	Coordinate of left of window
right	Coordinate of right of window
height	Return height of window
width	Return width of window
circle	Draw circle centered at x,y with radius r
point	Draw point (small filled circle)
line	Draw line from point to point
rectangle	Draw rectangle
print	Print text at given position
setPen	Set pen characteristics

Figure 19.1 – Methods defined for class application.

When the mouse button is pressed the method mouseButtonDown() is invoked. The two integer arguments represent the coordinates of the cursor, relative to the application window, at that time. The default behavior associated with this method is to do nothing. This method must be subclassed by the application class to perform any action.

The mouse-down event usually does not perform any actions that directly modify the image on the screen. Instead, it typically records whatever information may be necessary and then invokes either update() or clearAndUpdate() in order to force a screen redrawing.

When the user presses a key the method keyPressed() is invoked. This method takes as argument the character representing the key.

The methods top(), bottom(), left(), and right() return the screen coordinates of the application window, expressed in pixels. Note that these values are given in the global coordinate system, where 0,0 is the upper lefthand portion of the screen. Almost all other functions that use coordinates use the application-relative number, where 0,0 is the upper lefthand portion of the window.

A number of simple printing and drawing routines are available as methods in class application. Normally calls on graphics functions are executed during screen update. If clearAndUpdate() is used, any graphics actions performed before the update procedure is called will be lost. This means that calls on the graphics routines are usually made from the paint() method or from a method invoked by it. The coordinates for drawing are the same as for mouse-down events; thus, the value 0,0 represents the upper left corner and x-axis values increase as one moves right while y-axis values increase as one moves *down*. The latter is often counterintuitive to the beginning programmer.

19.5.1   The Class button

A new form of button is created by subclassing the class button and redefining the virtual method pressed. Once a button has been attached to the window, this method is invoked automatically when the button is pressed.

```
class quitButtonClass : public button {
public:
    quitButtonClass (window * win)
        : button(win, "Quit", 5, 5, 20, 50) { }
protected:
    pressed (window * win) { ... }
};
```

The application window is passed as argument to the constructor for the button. As part of initialization, the button then coordinates with the window to ensure that the button will be properly displayed. Most often, the button is declared as part of the state of a new application class and initialized as part of the constructor for the application class, as shown in the following:

```
class newApplication : public application {
public:
    newApplication : application("new program"),
        quitButton(this) { }
    ...
private:
    quitButtonClass quitButton;
};
```

It is common that when a button is pressed the response is simply to invoke a member function of the application class. We can define a single general-purpose class that supports this and thereby avoid the need to define new classes for each type of button. Because the C++ language is strongly typed, this new class must use a template and be parameterized by the new application class.[1] The template definition for this is as follows:

---

[1] The classes tbutton and tmenu require the ability to make a pointer to a member function for a class described as a template parameter. Although legal, not all compilers permit this use. Where it is not available, the programmer must define a new class for each button or menu item.

```
template <class T>
class tbutton : public button {
public:
    tbutton (window * win, char * t,
        int x, int y, int h, int w, void (T::*f)() )
        : button(win, t, x, y, h, w), fun(f) { }
protected:
    void (T::* fun)();
    virtual void pressed (window * win)
        { (((T *) win)->*fun)(); }
};
```

The final argument, f, is a pointer to a member function and must match
some method defined in class T. The syntax used to describe a pointer to a
member function is admittedly obtuse. This function is stored in the variable
fun and is then invoked when the button is pressed. By use of this class an
application with two buttons can be created as follows:

```
class helloApp : public application {
public:
    helloApp() :
        application("hello world"),
        quitButton (this, "quit", 5, 5, 50, 20, quit),
        clearButton (this, "clear", 5, 30, 50, 20, clearAndUpdate)
            { };
    virtual void mouseButtonDown(int, int);
private:
    tbutton <helloApp> quitButton;
    tbutton <helloApp> clearButton;
};
```

19.5.2   The Classes menu and menuItem

Menus are in many ways similar to buttons. There are two menu classes supplied
with the LAF, menu and menuItem. The first represents a category on the menu
bar and the second represents a specific item from the category. When the user
points to a menu, the associated menu items are displayed. When a menu item
is selected by the mouse, the selected method for the menu item is executed.
Thus, in a manner similar to the way in which behavior for buttons is specialized, application specific behavior for menu items is provided by subclassing the
menuItem class and redefining the method selected.

Just as with buttons, menus are typically declared as data fields in an application class and are initialized by the constructor. The following illustrates
this:

```
class clearMenuItem : public menuItem {
public:
    clearMenuItem (menu & m, char * t) : menuItem(m, t) { }

protected:
    virtual void selected (window *);
};

class helloApp : public application {
public:
    helloApp() :
        application("hello world")
        clearMenu (this, "Clear"),
        clearItem (clearMenu, "clear/C")
        { };
    virtual void mouseButtonDown(int, int);
private:
    menu clearMenu;
    clearMenuItem clearItem;
};

void clearMenuItem::selected (window * w)
    { w->clear(); }
```

The class **tmenuItem** is similar to the class **tbutton**. In the same way that the class **tbutton** eliminates the need to create a new button class when all a button does is invoke a member function, the class **tmenuItem** inherits from the class **menuItem** and adds an addition argument, which must be a member function. This function will be invoked when the associated menu item is selected.

```
template <class T>
class tmenuItem : public menuItem {
public:
    tmenuItem (menu & m, char * t, void (T::* f)() )
        : menuItem(m, t), fun(f) { }
protected:
    void (T::* fun)();
    virtual void selected (window * win)
        { (((T *) win)->*fun)(); }
};
```

Other classes in the LAF permit the programmer to place boxes of text, editable or not, in the window. These features are not described here, but more complete documentation on the LAF as well as sources, can be found at the address ftp://ftp.cs.orst.edu/pub/budd/laf.

19.6 Summary

The importance of the LAF is not so much in the functionality it provides (although it is an easy-to-use framework for creating simple graphical user interfaces) but in the way in which the system is typical of application frameworks. We can summarize these as follows:

- An application framework is designed to help solve a narrow range of problems. In the case of the LAF the problems involve the creation of simple one-window applications with buttons and menus.

- An application framework provides the execution (run-time) structure of the solution, but omits many essential execution details. In the case of the LAF, the framework defines the event-driven execution loop but omits how the program will respond to mouse-down events or key presses.

- An application framework provides a set of general-purpose low-level tools with which the programmer can construct solutions to specific problems. The LAF, for example, provides general graphics primitives, the ability to display boxes of text within a window, and so on.

- Inheritance is the primary technique used by the programmer to specialize an application framework in creating a new application. In the LAF the programmer uses inheritance to redefine the meaning of the mouse-down and key-press methods as well as the response to button presses and menu selections.

Exercises

1. Show how a simple application that has three types of buttons is implemented with the LAF.

2. What are the three types of methods found in an application framework? Give an example of each from the methods described for the class application in the LAF.

3. Trace the flow of control through the various classes from the time the user presses a button on the screen until the program returns to wait for the next event. Assume that the programmer issues an update at the end of the mouse-down routine to force the screen to be repainted.

Chapter 20

A Second Look at Classes

Up to this point, we have relied largely on an intuitive sense of what constitutes a *class*. Unfortunately, intuition differs from person to person. Some people think of a class as a template, a cookie-cutter with which multiple different instances can be stamped out or a factory assembly line spewing out objects; other people think of a class as a generalized sort of record, a structure with both data and function fields, and so on. In this chapter, we investigate some of the more subtle issues brought about by classes in programming language.

What exactly is a class? The answer to this question depends, in part, on what language you are considering. Broadly speaking, there are two general schools of thought on the issue. Some languages, such as C++ and Object Pascal, consider a class to be a *type*, similar to an integer or a record type. Other languages, such as Smalltalk and Objective-C, consider a class to be an *object*. In the next two sections we consider some of the ramifications of these different points of view.

20.1   Classes as Types

To understand the idea that a class is simply a type, we must first try to understand the meaning of the term *type* in programming languages. Unfortunately, the concept of type is used for a great many purposes. The following list, adapted from [Wegner 1986], illustrates a few of the many answers that could be given to the question "What is a type?"

- Application programmer's view: Types partition values into equivalence classes with common attributes and operations.

- System evolution (object-oriented) view: Types are behavior specifications that may be composed and incrementally modified to form new behavior specifications. Inheritance is a mechanism for incrementally modifying behavior, permitting a more natural form of system evolution.

- Parser view: A type implies the syntax that can be used with a particular expression. For example, subscripts can only be used with arrays, dot operators only with records or objects, parenthesis only with functions.

- Type-checking view: Types impose semantic constraints on expressions so that operators and operands of composite expressions are compatible. A type system is a set of rules for associating a type with every semantically meaningful subexpression of a programming language.

- Verification view: Types determine behavioral invariants that instances of the type are required to satisfy.

- System programming and security view: Types are a suit of armor that protects raw information (bit strings) from unintended interpretations.

- Implementation view: Types specify a storage mapping for values.

The list is not intended to be complete; nevertheless, it is sufficient as a starting point for a discussion of classes as types.

Programming languages such as C++ and Object Pascal treat classes as an extension of the idea of the structure (or record). Like a record, a class defines fields; and each instance of the class maintains its own values for these fields. Unlike a record, a class can also have fields that represent functions or procedures (and, unlike the data fields, there is only one copy of each such function, shared by all instances of the class).

This interpretation of classes fits nicely with most of the views listed. From the vantage point of the application programmer and of system evolution, all instances of a type have common fields, and they at least respond to the same set of commands. Certainly object-oriented techniques are even better than conventional methods for protecting raw bits from direct manipulation by the programmer.

However, as soon as we add inheritance to our concept of classes, a type becomes somewhat more complex. In one sense, we can think of inheritance simply as a means of extending an existing record type; but this interpretation is not entirely accurate for a number of reasons.

20.1.1   How Inheritance Complicates the View of Types

An overridden method is not simply replacing a field in a record, but rather is altering the behavior of the object in a potentially arbitrary fashion. Consider the effect of this change on the process of verification. A programmer may develop a set of classes and, by associating input and output conditions with each method, prove the correctness of a particular program. A second programmer may then create subclasses of the original classes, overriding some of the methods. If our view of subclasses corresponds to the *is-a* relation, then, since an instance of the subclass *is-a* instance of the superclass, we should be able to substitute instances of the subclass for instances of the superclass in the program and still hope that the resulting program will remain correct. This is the *principle of substitutability* discussed in Chapter 10.

While common programming practice (and common sense) dictate that an overridden method should not deviate too radically from the parent method, there is generally no guarantee that the behavior or effect of an overridden method will have any relationship to the behavior of the method in the superclass. (Indeed, it usually will not have the same behavior or there would be no need for overriding.) Thus, we are *not* in general assured that the same input-output conditions will hold for the two methods. If one of these conditions is violated, the basis for our belief in the correctness of the program is invalidated, and the program probably will fail. A common source of the yo-yo problem (Chapter 7) is a programmer replacing, perhaps unintentionally, one method with a different method that does not preserve some important behavior.

Playing Card Example

If we argue for the correctness of the solitaire program presented in Chapter 8, part of that argument involves an explanation of the routine draw in class TablePile, which displays one row of the tableau. To create this drawing, this routine simply loops over the cards from bottom to top, erasing the board under each card and redrawing the card image. Thus, the underlying cards are drawn and then partially erased as the stack is drawn.

Suppose that the application has been developed, and we argue, formally or informally, for its correctness. A new programmer now decides that she can improve the efficiency of the drawing routines using parallelism. Since drawing operations are somewhat time consuming, when a card is asked to draw itself it will simply fork off a process to perform the drawing operation and continue execution in parallel. Techniques such as we described in Chapter 7 make this change easy to program. All that is necessary is to make a new class–for example, ParallelCard–that inherits from class Card and overrides the single method draw. A class description for this class is shown below. The programmer can then change the references to class Card in the initialization portion of the program to use ParallelCard instead.

```
class ParallelCard : public Card
{
    // inherit everything, but change drawing
public:
    void draw()

        { if (! fork()) { Card::draw(); exit(0); }
};
```

Unfortunately, the result of this change is to remove the certainty that, by the time we are drawing a card, all the cards in the pile below will have been

drawn. Thus, it is possible–indeed, likely–that a random order of drawing will
be produced, leading to a mangled display such as that shown in Figure 20.1.

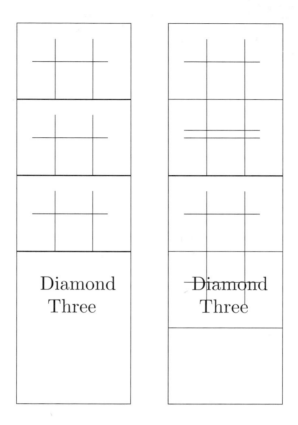

Figure 20.1 – A proper and a mangled pile of cards.

   The important point is that the interface to the method has not changed,
nor has the effect of the method in large part (both the original and the revised
methods still draw the card), but there has been a change in some small portion
of the behavior we associated with the method draw. Since our arguments for
the correctness of the program depended on the assumption that there would be
no change, the altered program fails.

   This example also illustrates that even the testing of programs can be altered
by inheritance. The original program can be developed and thoroughly tested,
and a later programmer might be tempted to think that as long as the *is-a*
relationship is maintained, an alteration will not invalidate the earlier testing.
Unfortunately, this assumption is, in general, not valid, and any change should
be verified through regression testing [Perry 1990].

Using Assertions

The object-oriented language Eiffel [Meyer 1988a, Rist 1995] overcomes at least some aspects of this problem in an interesting way. Assertions can be attached to methods and are inherited by, and cannot be overridden in, subclasses (although they can be extended). The compiler will generate code to check, at run time, the veracity of the assertions. Thus, a minimum degree of functionality can be ensured for a method, irrespective of any overriding that may take place. Of course, some assertions may be difficult to phrase in terms of executable code, such as the assertion that the card is completely drawn before the program returns from the method.

Note that Java introduces an interesting twist on this idea through the modifier final. A class that is declared as final cannot be subclassed, and thus the programmer is guaranteed that the behavior specified by the class will be maintained.

20.1.2 Inheritance and Storage

Finally, consider the relationship between types and storage mappings. Here, too, inheritance results in subtle problems that are not present in the types, such as records and arrays, found in more conventional languages. Since, in the "classes as records" view, an instance of a subtype for a class is an extension of an instance of the original class, it can, of course, take up more space. As we saw in Chapter 12, however, this change in size complicates such seemingly trivial issues as assignment. Recall that either of the following is required in assigning a value that is an instance of a subclass to a variable that is an instance of the parent class:

- That the assignment slice off the fields in the subclass that will not fit in the target storage area.

- That the storage for object values be maintained on a heap, not in the activation record stack.

In summary, the concept of class as a type fits nicely with much of our intuitive understanding of the idea of "typeness," but the fit is not exact. The second view–that of classes as objects–eliminates some of these problems by avoiding a discussion of type altogether.

20.2 Classes as Objects

We have emphasized from the beginning that the basic philosophy in object-oriented programming is the delegation of authority to an individual object. Every object is responsible for its own internal state and makes changes to that state according to a few fixed rules of behavior. Alternatively, every activity must be the responsibility of some object, or it will not be performed. Certainly, the creation of new instances of a given class is an activity. The question is, *who* (that is, which object) should have the responsibility for this behavior?

20.2.1   Object Creation Factories

One model is to have a centralized "object-creation" object. A request for the dynamic creation of a new object is translated into a call to this object, passing to it as arguments the size of the requested object and the list of methods to which the new object will respond. Although this mechanism is workable, it has the unfortunate property of placing the responsibility for remembering internal class information (that is, size and methods) with the individual creating the instance, not the class itself.

A better solution encapsulates this information, placing a layer of management between the user who desires the creation of a new object and the code that performs the allocation of the memory. Responsibility for knowing the size of objects and the methods to which they will respond is placed with the intermediate management level and thus need not be known by either the user or the allocation code.

Working in this manner, we arrive at a scheme in which we have one new object for each class in the system. The major responsibility of this object is simply to create new instances of the class. To do this, it must maintain information about the size of the class it represents and the methods to which instances of this class will respond. In a practical sense, this object *is* the class.

20.2.2   The Class Class

Every object must be an instance of some class, and this object is no exception. Of what class is this object an instance? The answer, in Smalltalk, Objective-C, Java, and similar systems, is that it is an instance of a class called Class. Figure 20.2 shows a CRC card (both front and back) for the class Class in the Little Smalltalk system. By convention, the value of this object is maintained in a variable that has the same name as the class itself. That is, the variable Set contains as a value the object, with a structure similar to that shown in Figure 20.3, that is responsible for creating new instances of the class.

Creation is accomplished by the message new, which is defined as a method in class Class. Every created object is an instance of some class and maintains a pointer back to the object representing that class. During message passing, this pointer is used to find a method that matches the selector for the message being evaluated.

To understand this structure, you must differentiate between the *subclass* relationship and the *instance* relationship. The class Class is a subclass of the class Object; thus, the object Class points to the object Object as its superclass. On the other hand, the object Object is an instance of the class Class; thus, Object points back to Class. Class Class is itself a class and thus an instance of itself. If we examine a typical class, say class Set, the object Set is an instance of class

Class Class of all classes

---

new Make new instance of class.

addSubclass:super:instanceVariables:
   Add a new subclass.

method: Return method by given
   name.

Class Data values maintained

---

name Name of the class as string.

instanceSize Number of instance variables.

methods Dictionary containing all the
   methods.

superClass Superclass object.

variables Names of variables.

Figure 20.2 – A CRC card for class Class.

Class but a subclass (indirectly) of class Object. A particular set is an instance of the class Set. These relationships are illustrated in Figure 20.3, where solid lines represent the instance relationship and dashed lines represent the subclass relationship.

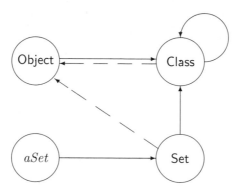

Figure 20.3 – Instance and subclass relationships.

20.2.3   Metaclasses and Class Methods

We noted that initialization is often an important part of object creation. Since objects are responsible for maintaining their own state, it would be useful if the object in charge of creating new instances of a class could also ensure that the object was properly initialized. The meaning of "initialize," however, is different from class to class. If all class objects are instances of the same class, we cannot specialize their behavior; that is, they must all execute the same method and thus perform in the same manner.

A related problem is that creation and initialization often require more information than simply the values shown in Figure 20.2. To create an array, for example, we need to know the number of positions to allocate to it. Other classes may require even further information.

Both of these problems require that we *specialize* the behavior of the class object, so it is not surprising that the same mechanism is used in both solutions. We have always insisted that behavior be associated with classes, not with individual objects (all instances of a class will share the same behavior). If we want the class variables to have their own behavior, the only solution is to make them instances of their own classes.

A *metaclass* is a class of a class. In Smalltalk-80 a metaclass is implicitly and automatically constructed for each class defined by the user. Each metaclass has only one instance, which is the class object itself. Metaclasses are organized into a class-subclass hierarchy that mirrors the class-subclass hierarchy of the original class, but that has metaclasses and has class Class at the root–instead of class Object.

To illustrate, the following shows a portion of the class hierarchy in Smalltalk-80:

> Object – *The superclass of all objects*
> > Collection – *The abstract superclass of all collections*
> > > Bag – *A class for multi-set data objects*

The following presents the corresponding metaclass hierarchy:

> Object – *The superclass of all objects*
> > Class – *Behavior common to all classes*
> > > Metaclass-Object – *Initialization of all objects*
> > > > Metaclass-Collection – *Initialization of collections*
> > > > > Metaclass-Bag – *Initialization of bags*

Code specific to a single class can be associated with the metaclass for that class. For example, instances of the class Bag maintain a dictionary that is used to hold the actual values. The metaclass for Bag overrides the method new to perform default initialization of this dictionary when new instances are created. This behavior is accomplished by a method new being defined in class Metaclass-Bag that overrides the method from class Class. That method is shown below.

```
new
      " create and initialize a new instance"
    ↑ super new setdictionary
```

Since class Bag is an instance of class Metaclass-Bag, the method shown will respond to the message new. The method first passes the message on to the superclass, which performs an action similar to that shown on the CRC cards presented earlier. In this fashion the superclass creates the new object. Once the new object is returned, the message setDictionary is sent to it. This method, shown below, sets the instance field contents to a newly created dictionary.

```
setDictionary
      " set a new dictionary in the contents variable"
    contents <- Dictionary new
```

If you find this discussion confusing, you are not alone. The concept of meta-classes has a reputation for being one of the more arcane aspects of Smalltalk-80. Nevertheless, it serves a useful purpose, by permitting us to specialize behavior for the initialization of individual classes without leaving the pure object-oriented framework. Given the confusing nature of metaclasses, however, most programmers are grateful that the systems in which metaclasses are used largely prevent programmers from being aware of them. In Smalltalk-80, for example, class methods are created as part of browsing the base class, not the metaclass. Clicking the "class" or "instance" box in the second pane indicates whether the metaclass or the actual class is being described. Similarly, in Objective-C, methods that are preceded by a plus sign in the first column (so-called factory methods) are associated with the metaclass, whereas those that begin with a minus sign are class methods.

Further information on metaclasses and metaprogramming in general can be found in [Kiczales 1991].

20.2.4   Object Initialization

We have shown how class methods, which are defined by means of metaclasses, can be used to solve one of the problems outlined at the beginning of this section: specializing initialization. We now return to the second problem: the initialization of objects when more information than simply the size of the object is required. We will show how class methods can be used to solve this problem, and more.

As our example we will use the Smalltalk-80 class Date, instances of which represent a given date in a given year. Each instance of Date does its task by maintaining two values: the year number and a number between 1 and 366, which represents the day number. A new instance of Date can be created in a variety of ways. The message "Date today," for example, yields an instance of Date representing the current date. Dates can also be explicity defined by the user giving a year and day value. The code shown in Figure 20.4 is then invoked. This code performs a small amount of error checking, making certain the day number is positive and not larger than the number of actual days in the year, modifying both the day number and year number accordingly. When it is certain that legal values are known, it uses the method new to create a new object and initializes the object with the given values.

The message daysInYear:, invoked in the method shown in Figure 20.4, illustrates another use for class methods–as a way to provide functionality associated with the general idea of the class but not necessarily with any specific instance. The object Date can be asked for the number of days in any specific year and will return an integer without actually building a new instance of the class. It does this using the same mechanism of defining a class method, except that in this case the class method returns an integer rather than a new value. The method daysInYear, and the method leapYear:, which it calls, are shown in Figure 20.5.

20.2.5   Posing in Objective-C

An interesting artifact of the "classes as objects" view is the concept of *posing* in Objective-C. We have often seen situations where the programmer wishs to substitute one class with another in an existing application. Usually, the new class

```
newDay: daycount year: referenceYear
    " Answer with a Date which is dayCount days after "
    " the beginning of the year referenceYear."
    | day year daysInYear |
    day <- dayCount.
    year <- referenceYear.
    [day > (daysInYear <- self daysInYear: year)]
        whileTrue:
            [year <- year + 1
             day <- day - daysInYear].
    [day <= 0]
        whileTrue:
            [year <- year - 1
             day <- day + (self daysInYear: year)].
    ↑ self new day: day year: year
```

Figure 20.4 – The class method newDay:year: in class Date.

```
daysInYear: yearInteger
    " Answer the number of days in the year, yearInteger"
    ↑ 365 + (self leapYear: yearInteger)
```

```
leapYear: yearinteger
    " Answer 1 if the year yearInteger is a leap year; "
    " answer 0 if it is not."
    (yearInteger \\ 4 ~= 0 or:
        [yearInteger \\ 100 = 0 and:
        [yearInteger \\ 400 ~= 0]])
            ifTrue: [ ↑ 0]
            ifFalse: [ ↑ 1]
```

Figure 20.5 – The class method daysInYear: in class Date.

inherits from the original class and modifies only a small portion of the behavior. Examples are the GraphicalReactor class of Chapter 12 and the ParallelCard class described earlier in this chapter. In both cases, it would be necessary to change the creation messages to use the new class in place of the original.

Objective-C provides a unique alternative to this technique that is much less invasive of the original code. Any class can be instructed to pose as another class. In effect, the *poser object* takes the place of the original class object. For example, the user can write the following statement:

```
[ GraphicalReactor poseAs: [ Reactor class ]];
```

All subsequent references to the class Reactor, including messages to create new instances of the class, will be sent to the class GraphicalReactor. Most often, the object doing the posing is a class object that represents a subclass of the class being replaced; thus, the majority of messages will be passed back to the original class (now the superclass).

20.3   Class Data

Regardless of which view of classes we take, it is frequently desirable to have a data area that is shared by all instances of a class. All Windows might be maintained on a common linked list, for example, or all Cards in a single deck.

The conventional solution makes use of a global variable. Such a variable is certainly accessible to and shared by all instances of the class, since it is accessible to and shared by all objects. However, this broad accessibility flies in the face of the object-oriented philosophy, which is one of limiting access and of centralizing responsibility for activities in specific individuals. So the object-oriented view requires us to seek another alternative. That alternative is to create values that are accessible to instances of a class but not accessible to objects of different types. Such values are know as *class variables*.

A subtle problem is the initialization of class variables. In a certain sense, all instances of a class are equal: in that they all share the same behavior, yet there is only one copy of any class variable. The difficult aspect of class variables is avoiding two problems: (1) not initializing the class data at all and (2) initializing data fields more than once. In both Smalltalk and Objective-C, the system ensures that the class method initialize is sent to each class before any other message. The response to the initialize method can then be used to set the values of any class variables. This message is taken care of implicitly, and there should be no reason for the user ever to invoke the initialize method directly. Java has a similar facility, only the initialization block is not even named.

The implementation of class variables is not possible in all the languages we are considering. And, in the languages that do support them, the mechanisms vary. In the following sections, we describe how class variables are created in the languages that support the concept.

20.3.1 Class Variables in Smalltalk

We create class variables simply by listing them by name when we create a
new class. The following, for example, shows the declaration of the class Date.
As noted in Section 20.2.4, instances of Date are used to represent calendar
days. The class variables maintain several arrays of information that are useful
when manipulating dates, including the number of days in non-leap-year months,
the names of the months, the days of the week, and so on. Internally, such
variables are treated as instance variables of the metaclass associated with the
class. Initialization of class variables can be accomplished as part of the class
method initialize.

```
Magnitude subclass: #Date
    instanceVariableNames: 'day year'
    classVariableNames:
'DaysInMonth FirstDayOfMonth MonthNames SecondsInDay WeekDayNames'
    poolDictionaries: ''
    category: 'Numeric-Magnitudes'
```

20.3.2 Class Variables in C++

C++ redefines the keyword static when the latter is used in a class description.
In this fashion, the word implies that one copy of the value is created and this
value is shared by all instances of the class. Such values, which we are calling
class variables, are called static members in C++. The normal visibility rules
(indicated by the keywords private, protected, or public) can be used with static
members to limit accessibility outside the methods associated with the class.

A static member is initialized outside the class definition in a manner similar
to global variables, the class name disambiguation serving to tie the declaration
to the proper class (Figure 20.6). As with global variables, only one initialization
of a static data member can occur within a program.

Because there is only one copy of a static member in a class, a publicly
accessible static member can be accessed directly. For example, the class CardPile
can display a pile of cards using the code shown:

```
void CardPile::display()
{
    if (top == nilLink)
        game->clearArea(x, y, x+Card::CardWidth,
                              y+Card::CardHeight);
    else
        top->draw();
}
```

```
//
//  ————————————-     class Card
//
class Card
{
    public:
        // constructor
    Card(int s, int c);

        // constants
    static const int CardWidth;
    static const int CardHeight;

...
};

const int Card::CardWidth = 68;
const int Card::CardHeight = 75;
```

Figure 20.6 – A class description showing a static field.

By declaring the fields CardWidth and CardHeight in the class Card, we avoid the creation of separate constants in each instance of the class.

Note that static members need not be public; if they are not, the accessibility of the data follows the normal visibility rules. C++ also permits methods to be declared static. Static methods can access only static data and are in many ways similar to class methods described earlier for Smalltalk and Objective-C.

20.3.3   Class Variables in Java

Java follows C++ in using the keyword static to indicate a class variable. Data fields and methods declared in a stack can be marked as static, and in both cases the result is to make them apply to the class itself rather than to instances of the class.

Static variables can have initializers, which are executed in order when the class definition is loaded. In addition, a block of code can be labeled as static and will be similarly executed at load time. The following example illustrates this. Here a static array of values is declared and initialized with the values 1 to 12.

```
class statTest {
    static final size = 12;
    static int arr[] = new int[size]; // declare array
    static { // these statements executed at class load time
```

```
        for (int i = 0; i < arr.length; i++) {
            arr[i] = i + 1;
        }
    }
}
```

The combination of static and final creates an initialized field that cannot be subsequently reassigned.

Both static variables and static methods are normally accessed by the class name. However, for convenience they can also be accessed by an instance of the class.

20.3.4   Class Variables in Objective-C

There is no explicit support for class variables in Objective-C. We can create something similar by declaring simple C static variables in the implementation portion of a class. Such values are accessible only within the file containing the implementation, and cannot be accessed in subclasses or by users. For example, methods in the class Date in the following can reference the static array day-Names. (This trick also works in C++, as long as all functions accessing the data reside in the same file.)

```
# import "Date.h"

static char *dayNames[ ] = {"Sunday", "Monday", "Tuesday",
    "Wednesday", "Thursday", "Friday", "Saturday"};

@implementation Date
...
@end
```

20.4   Are Classes Necessary?

Given the subtle issues involved in objects, instances, classes, metaclasses, and the like, we might wonder whether an object-oriented language can be constructed without classes. The surprising answer is yes, although it is not yet clear whether programming in such classless object-oriented languages is any easier or faster than is programming in class-based languages or whether the resulting programs are any more efficient.

20.4.1   What is Knowledge?

The object-oriented approach is related to a view of understanding that asserts that people categorize information by appealing to an abstract idealization of a concept. Plato claimed, for example, that our understanding of the concept of "chair" was not grounded in any specific chair, but was instead derived from an idealized abstraction of the notion of "chairness." All physical objects are only approximations to this more perfect abstraction; they are mere shadows of the ideal.

An alternative view of understanding asserts that people acquire information by learning from specific instances and then slowly discard incidental specifics to build a more general abstraction. A person's understanding of the concept of "elephant," for example, may be grounded in a specific elephant he encountered at a particular zoo when he was young. He then understands a second elephant by relating it to the earlier example. The new elephant may have smaller ears, for example, so the learner decides that the size of the ear is not an essential characteristic of elephantness. By repeating this relating process a number of times, the person develops a general characterization. Each characterization is simply a thread that leads back to specific instances on which the characterization is based.

20.4.2   Delegation

In programming languages, this idea of relating specific instances is known as *delegation* [Lieberman 1986]. In delegation, there are no classes; instead, a programmer creates specific instances of objects, and behavior is associated with individual objects. Whenever an object is similar to an existing object, the program can delegate a portion of its behavior to the original. Any message not understood by the new object will be passed on to the delegated object. This object in turn may have delegated its behavior to another object, and so on.

Thus, we can build a language out of *objects*, which possess variables and methods, and *delegation*, by which an object can defer responsibility for any unrecognized methods to another object. Sharing takes place in such languages by the use of common delegates.

As an illustration, let us build a simple graphics system. Suppose we are provided with a line-drawing object, which can respond to only one message: drawFromTo(a, b, c, d). In response to this message, the object will draw a solid line from the coordinates (a,b) to (c,d).

We first build a *pen*, which is a drawing instrument that remembers its coordinates. The pen object encapsulates two variables, x and y, and defines a suite of methods for setting and retrieving them: getX(), getY(), setX(a), setY(b). Next, the pen object defines two methods for drawing with the pen nib–namely, moveTo(a,b), which merely moves the pen without drawing, and drawTo(a,b), which draws a line. These methods can be defined by the following pseudo-code:

```
method moveTo(a, b)
    self setX(a)
    self setY(b)
end
```

```
method drawTo(a, b)
    self drawFromTo(self getX(), self getY(), a, b)
    self moveTo(a, b)
end
```

The pen object delegates responsibility for the drawFromTo method to the line object (Figure 20.7).

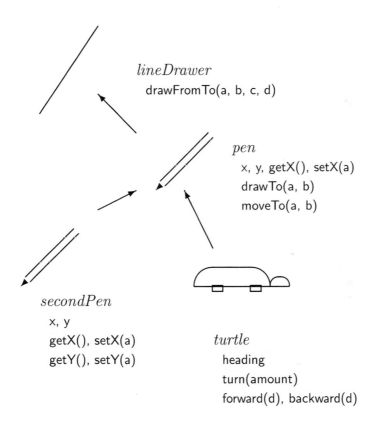

Figure 20.7 – Patterns of delegation.

Suppose the programmer wants to create a second pen. Using the delegation technique, she first provides a description of the object, relating it (if possible) to existing objects. One description might be "the second pen should behave exactly like the first pen, only it should maintain its own coordinates." From this description, it is clear that the second pen should maintain its own variables and should define methods for setX and the rest. Because it delegates to the first pen, however, these are the *only* methods that need to be defined; all other behavior can be inherited from the first pen. When a message is sent to the second pen, the receiver (the second pen) is sent as part of the message along the delegation path. When subsequent messages are sent to the "self" object (called the *client* in Lieberman's terminology), the search commences once more with the original receiver. Thus, the messages setX and getX–used, for example, in the drawTo method–will be matched to those in the second pen and not to those in the first pen. This process of matching is similar to the way in which method binding always begins with the base class of the receiver; it results in the delegation equivalent of the yo-yo problem.

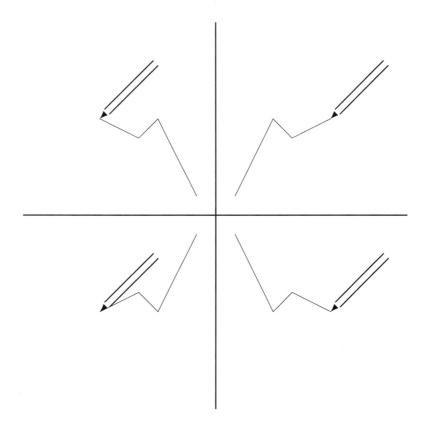

Figure 20.8 – Output of a kaleidoscope pen.

It is not necessary for delegating objects to redefine their variables. Suppose we want to create a kaleidoscope pen, which reflects every line around both the x and y axis, drawing four lines for each single line of the original pen (Figure 20.8). We can create an object that redefins only the single method drawTo; all other behavior can be delegated to the original pen. Since the x and y variables are those of the original pen, changes to the kaleidoscope pen result in changes to the original pen. The new drawTo method is as follows:

```
method    drawTo(a, b)
    self    drawFromTo(self getX(), self getY(), a, b)
    self    drawFromTo(- self getX(), self getY(), - a, b)
    self    drawFromTo(self getX(), - self getY(), a, - b)
    self    drawFromTo(- self getX(), - self getY(), - a, - b)
    self    moveTo(a, b)
end
```

Now suppose the programmer wants to define a *turtle*–a pen that maintains not only a location but also an orientation [Abelson 1981]. In addition to drawing, a turtle can be instructed to turn and to move forward or backward in the direction of its current orientation. If we use an existing pen to hold the turtle coordinates, the turtle needs to define only the single variable heading, as well as the methods turn(amount), forward(amount), and backward(amount).

An interesting feature of delegation-based systems is the ability to change delegates dynamically. Once the turtle facility has been constructed, if the user changes the delegate from a pen to a dashedPen, the turtle suddenly develops the ability to draw not only straight but also dashed lines. (Of course, changing to a delegate that does not understand all the messages required by an object can cause operational code to break down).

In a certain sense, the object-delegate relationship is similar to the instance-class relationship, with the exception that there are no longer two types of entities–the delegate is simply another object. Nevertheless, it is common to create class-like factory objects, which do nothing more than create copies of an existing object. For example, it is possible to generate a turtle factory that will, when requested, return a new turtle that is independent of all other turtles.

The primary reference for delegation is [Lieberman 1986]. His paper shows that by using delegation we can simulate inheritance. The reverse–that by using inheritance we can simulate delegation–has also been demonstrated [Stein 1987]. A delegation-based language, Self, has been described by Ungar [Ungar 1987], and Tomlinson provides a good analysis of the time and space requirements of delegation and inheritance [Tomlinson 1990], concluding that inheritance is generally faster and, surprisingly, requires less space.

Exercises

1. What aspects of the notion of *type* are not covered by Wegner's categories? Define new views to reflect these aspects.

2. Study the techniques of verification in conventional programming languages (good explanations are given in [Gries 1981, Dijkstra 1976]). What problems do you run into when you attempt to apply these techniques to object-oriented languages?

3. The message new passed to the object Dictionary in the method shown in Section 20.2.3 will actually be interpreted in the class MetaclassDictionary, whicy may override it to provide default initialization for dictionaries. Draw the metaclass hierarchy Dictionary, similar to the hierarchy for class Bag. Then trace the actual method invoked by the new message in creating a new bag.

4. Discuss some of the advantages and disadvantages of class methods. Is the increased flexibility provided by class methods offset by the complexity incurred by the introduction of metaclasses?

5. Give a pseudo-code description of a second turtle, that shares behavior but no data with the first turtle created in Section 20.4.2.

6. Using delegation, create an object called twoPen that draws parallel lines with two pens that are held a fixed distance from each other.

7. By making use of class objects, sketch the proof that delegation can be used to simulate inheritance.

8. In Smalltalk, an attempt to pass a message to an object that does not understand it results in the message doesNotUnderstand:. This method can in fact be overridden by the programmer. Using this technique, sketch an implementation of delegation in Smalltalk.

Chapter 21

Implementation

It is not the intent of this book to provide a detailed introduction to programming language implementation. Nevertheless, a general understanding of the problems encountered in implementing object-oriented languages, and the various ways to overcome them can in many cases help the reader better understand object-oriented techniques. In particular, this will help clarify the way in which object-oriented systems differ from more conventional systems. In this chapter, we provide an overview of some of the more important implementation techniques, as well as pointers to the relevant literature for the reader who desires further information.

21.1   Compilers and Interpreters

Broadly speaking, there are two major approaches to programming language implementation: compilers and interpreters. A *compiler* translates the user's program into native machine code for the target machine and is invoked as a separate process independent of execution. An *interpreter*, on the other hand, is present during execution, and is the system that runs the user program.[1]

Generally, a program that is translated by a compiler will execute faster than will a program that is run under an interpreter. But the time between conception, entering text, and execution in a compiled system may be longer than the corresponding time in an interpreter. Furthermore, when errors occur at run time, the compiler often has little more than the generated assembly language to offer as a marker to the probable error location. An interpreter will usually relate the error to the original text the user entered. Thus, there are advantages and disadvantages to both approaches.

---

[1] As is true of most distinctions, while the endpoints are clear there are large gray areas in the middle. There are compilers that compile interactively even during executing (at least during the debugging stages). These compilers gain some of the advantages of the interpreter while giving the execution-time advantage of the compiler technique. Similarly, some interpreters can translate into either an intermediate representation or native code.

Although some languages are usually compiled and others are usually interpreted, there is nothing intrinsic in a language that forces the implementor to always select one over the other. C++ is usually compiled, but there are C++ interpreters. On the other hand, Smalltalk is almost always interpreted, but experimental Smalltalk compilers have been produced.

21.2   Compilers

A typical characteristic of compilers is that a certain amount of information is lost during the translation from source program to machine code–most notably in the translation from symbolic names to numerical addresses. Variables that are local to a procedure, for example, are addressed in the compiled code not by their names but rather by a fixed offset relative to the activation record created at procedure entry.[2] Similarly, fields in a record are described by their offset from the start of the record, not by their names.

Suppose a procedure contains a variable x and a record d, which in turn has a data field y. Assume that x is stored in location 20 of the activation record, and d begins at location 28. Finally, assume that data field y begins at the eighth byte of record d. With these assumptions, an assignment statement, such as:

```
x := d.y;
```

might be translated into a single assembly-language statement that moves the word stored at the thirty-sixth byte after the activation record into the location given by the twentieth byte after the activation record.

```
move AR+36, AR+20
```

Notice that the assembly-language statement does not use the symbolic names for the variables but only their offsets into an activation record.

As we noted in earlier chapters, an object has certain similarities to a *record* or *structure* in a more conventional language. Like those in a record, the data fields (instance variables) in an object can be allocated fixed locations relative to the beginning of the object. Subclasses can only *extend* this memory area–they cannot reduce it–so the memory layout of a descendant class is strictly larger than that of the ancestor class, and the offsets of the data items from the superclass must match the locations of the corresponding fields in the subclass (see Figure 21.1).

Consider the classes GraphicalObject and Ball from the billiards simulation described in Chapter 6. GraphicalObject maintains the instance variable fields link and region, and Ball adds to this the fields direction and energy, but maintains

---

[2]The activation record is a portion of the run-time stack set aside at procedure entry to hold parameters, local variables, and other information. Further details on the run-time environment of programs can be found in a compiler-construction textbook, such as [Aho 1985, Fischer 1988].

An instance of Wall

link
region
convertFactor

An instance of Ball

link
region
direction
energy

Figure 21.1 – Fields in child classes matched to those in parent classes.

the fields of the earlier class in exactly the same offsets. That the offsets of the fields from the parent class are preserved in the child class is important; it permits methods defined in the parent class to manipulate the instance data using fixed offsets, and thus such routines will execute correctly regardless of the classes of the arguments. For example, the moveTo method defined in class GraphicalObject will perform as intended regardless of the class of the receiver, since it manipulates only the region portion of the object.

21.2.1 The Slicing Problem

That a child class can only *extend* the data fields defined by a parent class nicely solves the problem described in a previous section. That is, it gives the compiler a way to generate code for procedure defined in a parent class so that it will nevertheless work on objects of a child class. But this same property introduces another problem.

As we discussed in earlier chapters, a *polymorphic variable* is one that is declared as representing one type, but which in fact holds values from another type. In object-oriented languages the values usually must come from a subclass of the parent class.

When a compiler sets aside space in an activation record, it generally knows only the declared type for a variable, not the run-time type. The question is therefore how much memory should be allocated in the activation record. As we discussed in Chapter 12, most programming languages elect one of two solutions to this problem:

- The activation record holds only pointers, not values themselves

- The activation record holds only the data fields declared in the parent, slicing off any data fields from the child class that will not fit.

There are merits to both alternatives, so we will not comment on which technique seems "better." However, as a programmer it is important that you understand the technique used by the system on which you work.

21.2.2   Matching Methods to Messages

The most novel feature of object-oriented programming, from the implementation point of view, is that the *interpretation* of a message can depend on the type (class) of the receiver. That is, different classes of objects may execute different procedures while responding to the same message. In our graphical simulation, a Wall will respond to the message draw in a different fashion than will a Ball.

For this reason, each object must somehow maintain a way to determine which procedure is to be invoked for each possible message that it understands. Furthermore, we want the mechanism that is used to bind a method to a procedure to execute as fast as possible. In compiled programming languages, the technique most commonly used to achieve this speed is called a *virtual method table*.

21.2.3   Virtual Method Tables

One possible solution to the problem of matching methods and messages is to allocate fields in an object for methods, exactly the way space is allocated for data fields. The values in these fields are pointers to the appropriate function, as shown in Figure 21.2.

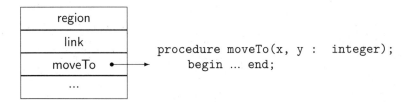

Figure 21.2 – Methods implemented as data fields.

For a method to be invoked, it suffices to take the value found at the correct offset in an object, dereference it to yield a procedure, and then call the procedure. However, this approach, although efficient in terms of execution speed, is wasteful of another important resource, space. Each object needs to maintain space (one pointer) for each method. Furthermore, the creation of such an object involves initializing all the method fields, which is unnecessarily costly. A compromise between speed and space is possible, based on the observation that all instances of the same class can *share* the same methods. In this fashion, a *single* table, called a *virtual method table*, can be created for each class, and all instances of the class will contain one pointer to it (see Figure 21.3). Initialization of a new instance includes the setting of this *virtual method table pointer*.

The values in the virtual method table are pointers to procedures. If we assume that these procedures are known to the compiler and do not change during execution, the table can be created statically at compile time. To execute

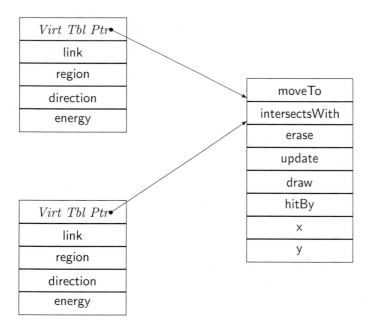

Figure 21.3 – Two balls sharing a virtual method table.

a method, we need to know only the offset of the method in the virtual method table.

As with the data areas, the virtual method table of an ancestor class will be a subset of the virtual method table of a descendant class, and offsets in the former will be appropriate for the latter. A class that inherits methods from a superclass merely copies the common portion of the virtual method table into the table for the subclass. When a method is overridden in a subclass, it is necessary to alter only the entry for that method. Figure 21.4 shows the virtual method tables for the two classes Ball and Wall, which are both descendants of the class GraphicalObject. Notice that they share pointers to the methods inherited from the parent class, and that the order of the entries is that given in the parent class, not the one given in the child class.

Once a compiler knows how to access the pointer to a method, the method can be invoked as a conventional procedure. The receiver is treated as though it were the first parameter in the argument list, so it is available as the value of the variable self (this, in C++). Assume, for example, that vtab is the internal field name used to represent the virtual method table in the class of an object, x, and that the offset of the method hitBy in that table is location 12. Then, a method invocation, such as

```
x.hitBy (y)
```

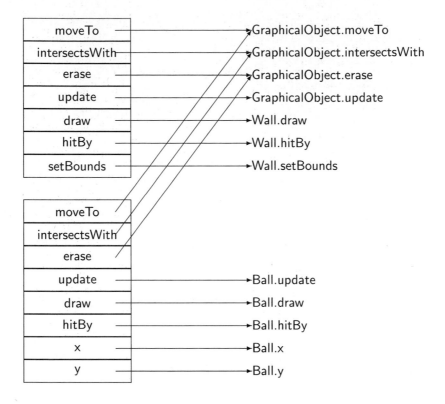

Figure 21.4 – Virtual tables for classes Wall and Ball.

is translated internally into something similar to the following:

```
(*(*(x.vtab))[12]) (x, y)
```

Notice that the method name does not appear in the final generated code, and that this code will select the appropriate method whether x is a Ball, a Wall, or any other graphical object. In terms of execution time, the overhead for a message send is simply two levels of pointer indirection and one subscript operation.

21.2.4   Name Encoding

We noted that since methods are all known at compile time and cannot change at run time, the virtual tables are simply static data areas established by the compiler. These data areas consist of pointers to the appropriate methods. Because linkers and loaders resolve references on the basis of symbols, some mechanism must be provided to avoid name collisions when two or more methods have the same name. The typical scheme combines the names of the class and the method. Thus, the draw method in class Ball might become Ball::draw internally. Usually, the user need never see this name, unless he is forced to examine the assembly-language output of the compiler.

In languages such as C++ that allow methods to be further overloaded with disambiguation based on parameter type, even more complicated Gödel-like[3] encodings of the class name, method name, and argument types are required. For example, the three constructors of class Complex described in an earlier chapter might be known internally as Complex::Complex, Complex::Complex_float, and Complex::Complex_float_float, respectively. Such internal names, referred to as *mangled*, can become very long. As we have seen, this internal name is not used during message passing but merely in the construction of the virtual tables and to make unique procedure names for the linker.

Multiple inheritance somewhat complicates the use of using virtual method tables; however, the details are beyond the scope of this book. Interested readers can find a more complete description in [Ellis 1990].

21.2.5 Dispatch Tables

Because languages such as C++ and Object Pascal are statically typed, they can determine at compile time at least the parent class type of any object-oriented expression. Thus, a virtual method table needs to be only large enough to accommodate those methods actually implemented by a class. In a dynamically typed language, such as Objective-C, a virtual method table has to include *all* messages understood by any class, and this table needs to be repeated for every class. If an application has 20 classes, for example, and they each implement 10 methods on average, we need 20 tables, each consisting of 200 entries. The size requirements quickly become exorbitant, and a better technique is called for.

An alternative technique is to associate with every class a table that, unlike the virtual method table, consists of selector-method pairs. This is called a *dispatch table.* The selectors correspond only to those methods actually implemented in a class. Inherited methods are accessed through a pointer in this table, which points to the dispatch table associated with a superclass (see Figure 21.5).

As in a system using virtual method tables, when dispatch tables are used every object carries with it an implicit (that is, not declared) pointer to the dispatch table associated with the class of the value it represents. This implicit pointer is known as the isa link (not to be confused with the *is-a* relation between classes). A message expression in Objective-C, such as the following expression from the eight-queens problem:

---

[3]The term "Gödel-like" refers to the technique of encoding a large amount of information (such as an entire computer program) as a single quantity. The technique was first described by the German computer scientist Kurt Gödel in a paper in 1931 [Gödel 1931]. Its use in a linker was, to my knowledge, first described by Richard Hamlet [Hamlet 1976].

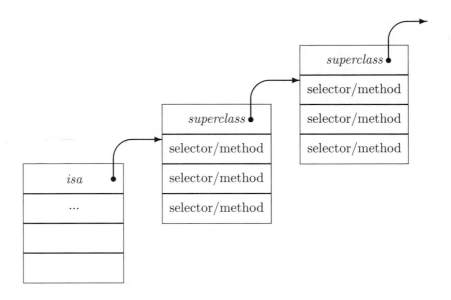

Figure 21.5 – An object and its dispatch table.

```
[neighbor checkrow: row column: column]
```

is translated by the Objective-C compiler[4] into:

```
objc_msgSend(neighbor,"checkrow:column:", row, column)
```

The function objc_msgSend, called the *messaging function*, follows the *isa* link of the first argument to find the appropriate dispatch table. The messaging function then searches the dispatch table for an entry that matches the selector. If such an entry is found, the associated method is invoked. If no such method is found, the dispatch table of the superclass is searched. If the root class (class Object) is finally searched and no method is found, a run-time error is reported.

A Method Cache

Although, for dynamically typed languages, the dispatch table is more economical in space than the virtual method table, the time overhead is considerably greater. Furthermore, this overhead is proportional to the depth of inheritance. Unless this penalty can be overcome, the latter point might lead developers to abandon inheritance, trading the loss in power for the gain in efficiency.

---

[4]The Objective-C system is actually a translator that produces conventional C code. In addition, the strong form of the selector is not actually used; instead, selectors are hashed into a numeric value.

Fortunately, we can largely circumvent this execution-time loss by means of a simple technique. We maintain a single system wide *cache* of methods that have been recently accessed. This cache is indexed by a hash value defined on the method selectors. Each entry in the cache is a triple, consisting of a pointer to a class (the dispatch table itself can serve this purpose), a selector value, and a pointer to a method.

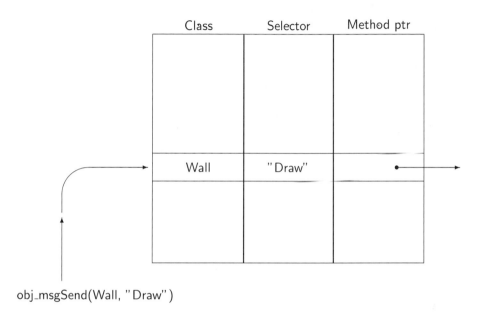

Figure 21.6 – The messaging function checking the method cache.

When the messaging function is asked to find a method to match to a selector class pair, it first searches the cache (see Figure 21.6). If the entry in the cache at the hash-table location corresponds to the requested selector and class, the associated method can be executed directly. If not, the search process described earlier is performed. Following this search, immediately before executing the method the cache is updated, overwriting whatever entry it contained previously at the hash location given by the message selector. Note that the value stored for the class entry in the cache is the class where the search began, not the class in which the method was eventually discovered.

By appropriate selection of hash functions and cache sizes, one can achieve cache hit ratios in the range of 90 to 95 percent, which reduces the overhead involved in a messaging expression to slightly over twice that of a conventional procedure call [Cox 1986]. This figure compares favorably with the overhead incurred with the virtual method table technique.

21.3   Interpreters

Interpreters are usually preferred over compilers if the amount of variation in a program is larger than can be accommodated easily in fixed code sequences. This variation can come from a number of sources; in a dynamically typed language, for example, we cannot predict at compile time the type of values that a variable can possess (although Objective-C is an example of a dynamically typed language that is nevertheless compiled). Another source of variation can occur if the user can redefine methods at run time.

A commonly used approach in interpreters is to translate the source program into a high-level "assembly language," often called a *bytecode* language (because typically each instruction can be encoded in a single byte). Figure 21.7 shows, for example, the bytecode instructions used in the Little Smalltalk system. The high-order four bits of the instruction are used to encode the opcode, and the low-order four bits are used to encode the operand number. If operand numbers larger than 16 are needed, the extended instruction is used and the entire following byte contains the operand value. A few instructions, such as "send message" and some of the special instructions, require additional bytes.

The heart of the interpreter is a loop that surrounds a large switch statement. The loop reads each successive bytecode, and the switch statement jumps to a code sequence that performs the appropriate action. We will avoid a discussion of the internal representation of a program (interested readers are referred to [Budd 1987]) and will concentrate solely on the processing of message passing.

```
while (timeslice-- > 0) {
  high = nextByte();  // get next bytecode
  low = high & 0x0F;  // strip off low nybble
  high >>= 4;      // shift left high nybble
  if (high == 0) {  //check extended form
    high = low;  // if so use low for opcode
    low = nextByte();  // get real operand
    }

  switch(high) {
    case PushInstance: ...
    ...
    case PushArgument: ..
    ...
    }
}
```

Just as objects in the compiled system presented earlier all contain a pointer to a virtual table, objects in the Smalltalk system all contain a pointer to their class. The difference is that, as we saw in Chapter 20, the class is itself an object. Among the fields maintained in the class object is a collection containing all the

0000xxxx	Extended instruction with opcode xxxx
0001xxxx	Push instance variable xxxx on stack
0010xxxx	Push argument xxxx on stack
0011xxxx	Push literal number xxxx on stack
0100xxxx	Push class object number xxxx on stack
0101xxxx	Push system constant xxxx
0110xxxx	Pop into instance variable xxxx
0111xxxx	Pop into temporary variable xxxx
1000xxxx	Send message xxxx
1001xxxx	Send message to super
1010xxxx	Send unary message xxxx
1011xxxx	Send binary message xxxx
1100xxxx	send arithmetic message xxxx
1101xxxx	Send ternary message xxxx
1110xxxx	Unused
1111xxxx	Special instruction xxxx

Figure 21.7 – Bytecode values in the Little Smalltalk system.

methods corresponding to messages that instances of the class will understand (Figure 21.8). Another field points to the superclass for the class.

When a message is to be sent, the interpreter must first locate the receiver for the message. By examining the class pointer for the receiver, it can find the object corresponding to the class of the receiver. It then searches the methods collection for a method that matches the name of the message being sent. If no such method is found, it follows the superclass chain, searching the classes in the superclass until either an appropriate method is found or the chain is exhausted. In the latter case, the interpreter reports an error. This is exactly the same sequence of steps as performed by the messaging function used in the dispatch table technique. As with that technique, a cache can be used to speed up the process of method search.

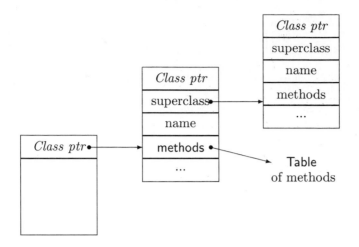

Figure 21.8 – The internal structure of a class.

Java uses a similar bytecode interpreter, although the actual bytecodes are somewhat different from those described here.

Further Reading

For the reader interested in learning more about the implementation of object-oriented languages, Cox [Cox 1986] contains a detailed analysis of the time-space trade-offs involved in various schemes. The implementation of multiple inheritance in C++ is sketched in [Ellis 1990], which is based on an earlier algorithm for Simula [Krogdahl 1985]. A detailed description of C++ implementation techniques is provided by Lippman [Lippman 1996].

The Smalltalk-80 interpreter is described in [Goldberg 1983]. [Krasner 1983] contains several papers that describe techniques for improving the efficiency of the Smalltalk-80 system. A simplfied Smalltalk interpreter is detailed in [Budd 1987]. Kamin [Kamin 1990] presents a good general overview of the issues involved in the implementation of nontraditional languages.

Exercises

1. Extend the dispatch table technique to permit multiple inheritance.

2. The Objective-C compiler permits optional declarations for object variables. Explain how a compiler might make use of such declarations to speed processing of messages involving such values. Consider what needs to occur on assignment and how messaging can be made more efficient.

3. Explain why methods that are not declared virtual in C++ can be invoked more efficiently than can virtual methods. How do you make measurements to determine whether the difference is significant?

4. Review the cache technique described in Section 21.2. Explain why the class stored in the cache is the one where the search for a method begins and not the one where the method is eventually found. Explain how the cache lookup algorithm would need to be changed if the latter value were used. Do you think the new algorithm would be faster or slower? Explain your answer.

5. Sketch the outline of a Smalltalk interpreter based on the bytecodes given in the text.

Appendix A

Source for the Eight-Queens Puzzle

This appendix gives the full programs for the eight-queens puzzle discussed in Chapter 5.

A.1   Eight-Queens in Apple Object Pascal

```
(*
    Eight-Queens Puzzle in Object Pascal
    Written by Tim Budd, Oregon State University, 1996
*)
Program EightQueen;

type
    Queen = object
        (* data fields *)
        row : integer;
        column : integer;
        neighbor : Queen;

            (* initialization *)
        procedure initialize (col : integer; ngh : Queen);
            (* operations *)
        function canAttack
            (testRow, testColumn : integer) : boolean;
        function findSolution : boolean;
        function advance : boolean;
        procedure print;
    end;
```

```
var
    neighbor, lastQueen : Queen;
    i : integer;

procedure Queen.initialize (col : integer; ngh : Queen);
begin
        (* initialize our column and neighbor values *)
    column := col;
    neighbor := ngh;

        (* start in row 1 *)
    row := 1;
end;

function Queen.canAttack
    (testRow, testColumn : integer) : boolean;
var
    can : boolean;
    columnDifference : integer;
begin
        (* first see if rows are equal *)
    can := (row = testRow);

        (* then test diagonals *)
    if not can then begin
        columnDifference := testColumn - column;
        if (row + columnDifference = testRow) or
            (row - columnDifference = testRow) then
                can := true;
        end;

        (* finally, test neighbors *)
    if (not can) and (neighbor <> nil) then
        can := neighbor.canAttack(testRow, testColumn);
    canAttack := can;
end;

function queen.findSolution : boolean;
var
    done : boolean;
begin
    done := false;
    findSolution := true;
```

```
        (* seek a valid position *)
    if neighbor <> nil then
        while not done and neighbor.canAttack(row, column) do
            if not self.advance then begin
                findSolution := false;
                done := true;
                end;
end;

function queen.advance : boolean;
begin
    advance := false;

        (* try next row *)
    if row < 8 then begin
        row := row + 1;
        advance := self.findSolution;
    end
    else begin

            (* cannot go further *)
            (* move neighbor to next solution *)
        if neighbor <> nil then
            if not neighbor.advance then
                advance := false
            else begin
                (* start again in row 1 *)
                row := 1;
                advance := self.findSolution;
            end;
    end;
end;

procedure queen.print;
begin
    if neighbor <> nil then
        neighbor.print;
    writeln('row ', row , ' column ', column);
end;

begin
    neighbor := nil;
    for  i := 1 to 8 do begin
            (* create and initialize new queen *)
        new (lastqueen);
```

```
        lastQueen.initialize (i, neighbor);
        if not lastQueen.findSolution then
            writeln('no solution');
            (* newest queen is next queen neighbor *)
        neighbor := lastQueen;
    end;

    lastQueen.print;

    for i := 1 to 8 do begin
        neighbor := lastQueen.neighbor;
        dispose (lastQueen);
        lastQueen := neighbor;
    end;
end.
```

A.2   Eight-Queens in C++

```
//      Eight-Queens Puzzle in C++
//      written by Tim Budd, Oregon State University, 1996
//

# include <iostream>

class queen {
public:
        // constructor
    queen (int, queen *);

        // find and print solutions
    bool findSolution();
    bool advance();
    void print();

private:
        // data fields
    int row;
    const int column;
    queen * neighbor;

        // internal method
    bool canAttack (int, int);
};
```

```cpp
queen::queen(int col, queen * ngh)
    : column(col), neighbor(ngh)
{
    row = 1;
}

bool queen::canAttack (int testRow, int testColumn)
{
        // test rows
    if (row == testRow)
        return true;

        // test diagonals
    int columnDifference = testColumn - column;
    if ((row + columnDifference == testRow) ||
        (row - columnDifference == testRow))
            return true;

        // try neighbor
    return neighbor && neighbor->canAttack(testRow, testColumn);
}

bool queen::findSolution()
{
        // test position against neighbors
    while (neighbor && neighbor->canAttack (row, column))
        if (! advance())
            return false;

            // found a solution
    return true;
}

bool queen::advance()
{
    if (row < 8) {
        row++;
        return findSolution();
        }

    if (neighbor && ! neighbor->advance())
        return false;
    row = 1;
    return findSolution();
}
```

```
void queen::print()
{
    if (neighbor)
        neighbor->print();
    cout << "column " << column << " row " << row << '\n';
}

void main() {
    queen * lastQueen = 0;

    for (int i = 1; i <= 8; i++) {
        lastQueen = new queen(i, lastQueen);
        if (! lastQueen->findSolution())
            cout << "no solution\n";
    }

    lastQueen->print();
}
```

A.3   Eight-Queens in Java

```
/*
    Eight-Queens Puzzle in Java
    Written by Tim Budd, Oregon State University, January 1996
*/

import java.awt.*;
import java.applet.*;

class Queen {
        // data fields
    private int row;
    private int column;
    private Queen neighbor;

        // constructor
    Queen (int c, Queen n) {
            // initialize data fields
        row = 1;
        column = c;
        neighbor = n;
        }
```

```java
public boolean findSolution() {
    while (neighbor != null &&
            neighbor.canAttack(row, column))
        if (! advance())
            return false;
    return true;
}

public boolean advance() {
    if (row < 8) {
        row++;
        return findSolution();
    }
    if (neighbor != null) {
        if (! neighbor.advance())
            return false;
    }
    else
        return false;
    row = 1;
    return findSolution();

}

private boolean canAttack(int testRow, int testColumn) {
    int columnDifference = testColumn - column;
    if ((row == testRow) ||
        (row + columnDifference == testRow) ||
        (row - columnDifference == testRow))
            return true;
    if (neighbor != null)
        return neighbor.canAttack(testRow, testColumn);
    return false;
}

public void paint (Graphics g) {
        // first draw neighbor
    if (neighbor != null)
        neighbor.paint(g);
        // then draw ourself
        // x, y is upper left corner
    int x = (row - 1) * 50;
    int y = (column - 1) * 50;
    g.drawLine(x+5, y+45, x+45, y+45);
    g.drawLine(x+5, y+45, x+5, y+5);
```

```
        g.drawLine(x+45, y+45, x+45, y+5);
        g.drawLine(x+5, y+35, x+45, y+35);
        g.drawLine(x+5, y+5, x+15, y+20);
        g.drawLine(x+15, y+20, x+25, y+5);
        g.drawLine(x+25, y+5, x+35, y+20);
        g.drawLine(x+35, y+20, x+45, y+5);
        g.drawOval(x+20, y+20, 10, 10);
        }
}

public class QueenSolver extends Applet {

    private Queen lastQueen;

    public void init() {
        int i;
        lastQueen = null;
        for (i = 1; i <= 8; i++) {
            lastQueen = new Queen(i, lastQueen);
            lastQueen.findSolution();
            }
        }

    public void paint(Graphics g) {
            // draw board
        for (int i = 0; i <= 8; i++) {
            g.drawLine(50 * i, 0, 50*i, 400);
            g.drawLine(0, 50 * i, 400, 50*i);
            }
            // draw queens
        lastQueen.paint(g);
        }

    public boolean mouseDown(java.awt.Event evt, int x, int y) {
        lastQueen.advance();
        repaint();
        return true;
        }

}
```

A.3.1   HTML File for the Java Application

```
<html>
<title>Eight-Queens Puzzle</title>
```

```
<body>
<H1>Eight-Queens Puzzle in Java</h1>
<h2>From Chapter 5 of</h2>
<h2>Introduction to Object-Oriented Programming (2nd Ed)</h2>
<h2>By Timothy Budd</h2>
<hr>
<applet code=QueenSolver.class width=500 height=500>
If you see this text, your web browser does not support the
execution of Java applets.
</applet>
<hr>
<p>
The application will initially display one solution.
After each mouse-down a new solution will be presented.
<p>
<a href="QueenSolver.java">The source.</a>
</body>
</html>
```

A.4   Eight-Queens in Objective-C

Note that both the classes **Queen** and **SentinelQueen** define implementation sections without prior interface definitions. This will produce a warning from the compiler but no error.

```
/*
    Eight-Queens Puzzle in Objective-C
    Written by Tim Budd, Oregon State University, 1996
*/


# include <stdio.h>
# include <objc/Object.h>


/*
    A sentinel queen sits
    to the left of the leftmost queen
*/

@implementation SentinelQueen : Object
- (int) advance
{
    /* do nothing */
    return 1;
}
```

```
- (int) findSolution
{
    /* do nothing */
    return 1;
}

- (void) print
{
    /* do nothing */
}

- (int) canAttack: (int) testRow column: (int) testColumn;
{
    /* cannot attack */
    return 0;
}
@end

@interface Queen : Object
{    /* data fields */
    int row;
    int column;
    id neighbor;
}

    /* methods */
- (void) initialize: (int) c neighbor: ngh;
- (int)   advance;
- (void) print;
- (int)   canAttack: (int) testRow column: (int) testColumn;
- (int)   findSolution;
@end

@implementation Queen : Object

- (void) initialize: (int) c neighbor: ngh
{
    /* set the constant fields */
    column = c;
    neighbor = ngh;
    row = 1;
}
```

```objc
- (int) advance
{
    /* first try next row */
    if (row < 8) {
        row = row + 1;
        return [ self findSolution ];
        }

    /* cannot go further, move neighbors */
    if ( ! [ neighbor advance ] )
        return 0;

    /* begin again in row 1 */
    row = 1;
    return [ self findSolution ];
}

- (void) print
{
    if (neighbor)
        [ neighbor print ];
    printf("column %d row %d\n", column, row);
}

- (int) canAttack: (int) testRow column: (int) testColumn
{    int columnDifference;

    /* can attack same row */
    if (row == testRow)
        return 1;

    columnDifference = testColumn - column;
    if ((row + columnDifference == testRow) ||
        (row - columnDifference == testRow))
            return 1;

    return [ neighbor canAttack:testRow column: testColumn ];
}

- (int) findSolution
{
    /* if neighbor can attack, then move on */
    while ( [ neighbor canAttack:row column: column ] )
        if ( ! [ self advance ] )
            return 0;
```

```
    /* otherwise we're safe for now */
    return 1;
}
@end

main() {
    id lastQueen, neighbor;
    int i;

    // create and initialize queens
    neighbor = [ SentinelQueen new ];
    for (i = 1; i <= 8; i++) {
        lastQueen = [ Queen new ];
        [ lastQueen initialize: i neighbor: neighbor ];
        [ lastQueen findSolution ];
        neighbor = lastQueen;
        }

    // then print out solution
    [ lastQueen print ];
}
```

A.5   Eight-Queens in Smalltalk

The class SentinelQueen in the Smalltalk solution has no instance variables. It uses the following methods:

```
advance
    ↑ false
```

```
canAttack: row column: column
    ↑ false
```

```
result
    ↑ List new
```

The class Queen has three instance variables, corresponding to the values of the row, column, and neighbor. It defines the following methods:

```
setColumn: aNumber neighbor: aQueen
        " initialize the data fields "
    column <- aNumber.
```

```
    neighbor <- aQueen.
        " find first solution "
    row <- 1.

canAttack: testRow column: testColumn | columnDifference |
    columnDifference <- testColumn - column.
    (((row = testRow) or:
        [ row + columnDifference = testRow]) or:
        [ row - columnDifference = testRow])
            ifTrue: [ ↑ true ].
    ↑ neighbor canAttack: testRow column: testColumn

advance
        " first try next row "
    (row < 8)
        ifTrue: [ row <- row + 1. ↑ self findSolution ].
        " cannot go further, move neighbor "
    (neighbor advance)
        ifFalse: [ ↑ false ].
    row <- 1.
    ↑ self findSolution

findSolution
    [ neighbor canAttack: row column: column ]
        whileTrue: [ self advance
            ifFalse: [ ↑ false ] ].
    ↑ true

result
    ↑ neighbor result; addLast: row
```

To find a solution, the following method is executed:

```
run     | lastQueen |
    lastQueen <- SentinelQueen new.
    1 to: 8 do: [:i | lastQueen <- (Queen new)
        setColumn: i neighbor: lastQueen.
        lastQueen findSolution ].
    'got a result' print.
    lastQueen result do: [:x | x print. ' ' print ].
    Char newline print.
```

Appendix B

Source for the Billiards Game

This appendix lists the complete source for the billiards simulation described in Chapter 6.

B.1   The Version without Inheritance

```
(*
    Billiard Simulation Program
    To demonstrate features of OOP in Object Pascal
    Written by Tim Budd, Oregon State University, September 1995
*)

Program billiards;

USES
  Windows;

type
    Ball = object
            (* data values maintained by balls *)
        link : Ball;
        region : Rect;
        filler : integer;
        direction : real;
        energy : real;

            (* initialization routine *)
        procedure initialize (x, y : integer);
```

```
        (* common methods *)
    procedure draw;
    procedure erase;
    procedure update;
    procedure hitBy (aBall : Ball);
    procedure setCenter (newx, newy : integer);
    procedure setDirection (newDirection : real);

        (* return x, y coordinate center of ball *)
    function x : integer;
    function y :integer;
end;

Wall = object
            (* data fields *)
        link : Wall;
        region : Rect;
            (* factor used to reflect striking balls *)
        convertFactor : real;

            (* initialization function *)
        procedure initialize
            (left, top, right, bottom : integer; cf : real);

            (* draw wall *)
        procedure draw;

            (* notify wall that a ball has struck *)
        procedure hitBy (aBall : Ball);
    end;

Hole = object
            (* data fields *)
        link : Hole;
        region : Rect;

            (* initialize location of hole *)
        procedure initialize (x, y : integer);

            (* draw the hole *)
        procedure draw;

            (* notify hole that it has received a ball *)
        procedure hitBy (aBall : Ball);
    end;
```

```
      var
          cueBall : Ball;
          saveRack : integer;
          ballMoved : boolean;
          listOfHoles : Hole;
          listOfWalls : Wall;
          listOfBalls: Ball;

          theWindow : windowPtr;

procedure Wall.initialize
    (left, top, right, bottom : integer; cf : real);
begin
        (* initialize conversion factor *)
    convertFactor := cf;

        (* set up region for wall *)
    SetRect (region, left, top, right, bottom);
end;

procedure Wall.draw;
begin
    PaintRect (region);
end;

procedure Wall.hitBy (aBall : Ball);
begin              (* bounce the ball off the wall *)
    aBall.setDirection(convertFactor - aBall.direction);
end;

procedure Hole.initialize (x, y : integer);
var left, top, bottom, right : integer;
begin
        (* identify region centered around x, y *)
    left := x - 5;
    top := y - 5;
    right := x + 5;
    bottom := y + 5;
    SetRect (region, left, top, right, bottom);
end;

procedure Hole.draw;
begin
    PaintOval (region);
end;
```

```
procedure Hole.hitBy (aBall : Ball);
begin
        (* drain energy from ball *)
    aBall.energy := 0.0;
    aBall.erase;

        (* move ball *)
    if aBall = CueBall then
        aBall.setCenter(50, 100)
    else begin
        saveRack := saveRack + 1;
        aBall.setCenter (10 + saveRack * 15, 250);
    end;

    (* redraw ball *)
    aBall.draw;
end;

procedure Ball.setCenter (newx, newy : integer);
var left, top, bottom, right : integer;
begin
        (* identify region centered around x, y *)
    left := newx - 5;
    top := newy - 5;
    right := newx + 5;
    bottom := newy + 5;
    SetRect (region, left, top, right, bottom);
end;

procedure Ball.initialize (x, y : integer);
begin
    setCenter(x, y);
    setDirection(0.0);
    energy := 0.0;
end;

procedure Ball.setDirection (newDirection : real);
begin
    direction := newDirection;
end;

procedure Ball.erase;
begin
    EraseRect (region);
end;
```

```
procedure Ball.draw;
begin
    if self = CueBall then
            (* draw open circle *)
        FrameOval (region)
    else
            (* draw filled circle *)
        PaintOval (region)
end;

procedure Ball.update;
var
    hptr : Hole;
    wptr : Wall;
    bptr : Ball;
    dx, dy : integer;
    theIntersection : Rect;
    i : integer;
begin
    if energy > 0.5 then begin
        ballMoved := true;
            (* erase ball *)
        erase;
            (* decrease energy *)
        energy := energy - 0.05;
            (* move ball *)
        dx := trunc(5.0 * cos(direction));
        dy := trunc(5.0 * sin(direction));
        offsetRect(region, dx, dy);
            (* redraw ball *)
        for i := 1 to 25 do
        draw;

            (* see if we hit a hole *)
        hptr := listOfHoles;
        while (hptr <> nil) do
            if SectRect(region, hptr.region, theIntersection) then
            begin
                hptr.hitBy(self);
                hptr := nil;
            end
            else
                hptr := hptr.link;

            (* see if we hit a wall *)
```

```
            wptr := listOfWalls;
            while (wptr <> nil) do
                if SectRect(region, wptr.region, theIntersection) then
                begin
                    wptr.hitBy(self);
                    wptr := nil;
                end
                else
                    wptr := wptr.link;

                (* see if we hit a ball *)
            bptr := listOfBalls;
            while (bptr <> nil) do
                if (bptr <> self) and
                    SectRect(region,bptr.region,theIntersection) then
                begin
                    bptr.hitBy(self);
                    bptr := nil;
                end
                else
                    bptr := bptr.link;
        end;
    end;

    function Ball.x :integer;
    begin
        x := (region.left + region.right) div 2;
    end;

    function Ball.y : integer;
    begin
        y := (region.top + region.bottom) div 2;
    end;

    function hitAngle (dx, dy : real) : real;
        const
            PI = 3.14159;
        var
            na : real;
    begin
        if (abs(dx) < 0.05) then
            na := PI / 2
        else
            na := arctan (abs(dy / dx));
        if (dx < 0) then
```

```
        na := PI - na;
    if (dy < 0) then
        na := - na;
    hitAngle := na;
end;

procedure Ball.hitBy (aBall : Ball);
var
    da : real;
begin
        (* cut the energy of the hitting ball in half *)
    aBall.energy := aBall.energy / 2.0;

        (* and add it to our own *)
    energy := energy + aBall.energy;

        (* set our new direction *)
    direction := hitAngle(self.x - aBall.x, self.y - aBall.y);

        (* and set the hitting ball's direction *)
    da := aBall.direction - direction;
    aBall.setDirection(aBall.direction + da);

        (* continue our update *)
    update;
end;

procedure mouseButtonDown (x, y : integer);
var
    bptr : Ball;
begin
        (* give the cue ball some energy *)
    cueBall.energy := 20.0;
        (* and a direction *)
    cueBall.setDirection(hitAngle (cueBall.x - x, cueBall.y - y));

        (* then loop as long as called for *)
    ballMoved := true;
    while ballMoved do begin
        ballMoved := false;
        bptr := listOfBalls;
        while bptr <> nil do begin
            bptr.update;
            bptr := bptr.link;
            end;
```

```
        end;
end;

procedure createGlobals;
var
    i, j : integer;
    newBall : Ball;
    newWall : Wall;
    newHole : Hole;
begin
    saveRack := 0;
    listOfWalls := nil;
    listOfHoles := nil;
    listOfBalls := nil;

            (* create walls *)
    new (newWall);
    newWall.initialize(10, 10, 300, 15, 0.0);
    newWall.link := listOfWalls;
    listOfWalls := newWall;
    new (newWall);
    newWall.initialize(10, 200, 300, 205, 0.0);
    newWall.link := listOfWalls;
    listOfWalls := newWall;
    new (newWall);
    newWall.initialize(10, 10, 15, 200, 3.14159);
    newWall.link := listOfWalls;
    listOfWalls := newWall;
    new (newWall);
    newWall.initialize(300, 10, 305, 205, 3.14159);
    newWall.link := listOfWalls;
    listOfWalls := newWall;

            (* create holes *)
    new(newHole);
    newHole.initialize(15, 15);
    newHole.link := listOfHoles;
    listOfHoles := newHole;
    new(newHole);
    newHole.initialize(15, 200);
    newHole.link := listOfHoles;
    listOfHoles := newHole;
    new(newHole);
    newHole.initialize(300, 15);
    newHole.link := listOfHoles;
```

```
        listOfHoles := newHole;
        new(newHole);
        newHole.initialize(300, 200);
        newHole.link := listOfHoles;
        listOfHoles := newHole;

                (* create balls *)
        new (cueBall);
        cueBall.initialize(50, 96);
        listOfBalls := cueBall;

        for i := 1 to 5 do
            for j := 1 to i do
                begin
                    new(newBall);
                    newBall.initialize(190 + i * 8,
                        100 + 16 * j - 8 * i);
                    newBall.link := listOfBalls;
                    listOfBalls := newBall;
                end;
end;

procedure drawBoard;
var
    aWall : Wall;
    aBall : Ball;
    aHole : Hole;
begin
    SetPort (theWindow);

    aWall := listOfWalls;
    while (aWall <> nil) do begin
        aWall.draw;
        aWall := aWall.link;
    end;

    aHole := listOfHoles;
    while (aHole <> nil) do begin
        aHole.draw;
        aHole := aHole.link;
    end;

    aBall := listOfBalls;
    while (aBall <> nil) do begin
        aBall.draw;
```

```
            aBall := aBall.link;
        end;

        cueBall.draw;

end;

procedure createWindow;
var
    name : STR255;
    winType : integer;
    windowRect : Rect;
begin
    name := 'billiards game';
    SetRect (windowRect, 50, 70, 500, 400);
    winType := DocumentProc;
    theWindow :=
        NewWindow(nil, windowRect, name,
            TRUE, winType, WindowPtr(-1),
            True, LongInt(09));
    SelectWindow(theWindow);
    showWindow(theWindow);
end;

procedure eventLoop;
var
    ignore : boolean;
    event : eventRecord;
    localPoint : Point;
    done : boolean;
begin
    done := false;
    while not done do begin
        systemTask;
        ignore := GetNextEvent(everyEvent, event);
        case event.what of
            keyDown:
                done := true; (* return and quit *)
            mouseDown:
                begin
                    localPoint := event.where;
                    GlobalToLocal(localPoint);
                    mouseButtonDown(localPoint.h, localPoint.v);
                end;
            updateEvt:
```

```
                    drawBoard;
            end;
        end;
end;

begin
    MaxApplZone;
     InitGraf(@qd.thePort);
    InitWindows;
    InitCursor;

    createGlobals;
    createWindow;

    eventLoop;
end.
```

B.2   The Version with Inheritance

Only those sections of the program that differ from the original are presented.

```
(*
    Billiard Simulation Program
    To demonstrate features of OOP in Object Pascal
    Written by Tim Budd, Oregon State University, September 1995
*)

Program billiards;

USES
  Windows;

type
    GraphicalObject = object
            (* data fields *)
        link : GraphicalObject;
        region : Rect;

            (* initialization function *)
        procedure setRegion (left, top, right, bottom : integer);

            (* operations that graphical objects perform *)
        procedure draw;
```

```
     procedure erase;
     procedure update;
     function intersect (anObj : GraphicalObject) : boolean;
     procedure hitBy (aBall : GraphicalObject);
end;

Ball = object (GraphicalObject)
        (* data values maintained by balls *)
     direction : real;
     energy : real;

           (* initialization routine *)
     procedure initialize (x, y : integer);

           (* common methods *)
     procedure draw; override;
     procedure update; override;
     procedure hitBy (aBall : GraphicalObject); override;
     procedure setCenter (newx, newy : integer);

           (* return x, y coordinate center of ball *)
     function x : integer;
     function y :integer;
end;

CueBall = object (Ball)
        (* changes only the draw routine *)
     procedure draw; override;
end;

Wall = object (GraphicalObject)
             (* factor used to reflect striking balls *)
         convertFactor : real;

             (* initialization function *)
         procedure initialize
             (left, top, right, bottom : integer; cf : real);

             (* draw wall *)
         procedure draw; override;

             (* notify wall that a ball has struck *)
         procedure hitBy (aBall : GraphicalObject); override;
     end;
```

```
    Hole = object (GraphicalObject)
                (* initialize location of hole *)
           procedure initialize (x, y : integer);

                (* draw the hole *)
           procedure draw; override;

                (* notify hole that it has received a ball *)
           procedure hitBy (aBall : GraphicalObject); override;
        end;

    var
        cueBall : Ball;
        saveRack : integer;
        ballMoved : boolean;
        listOfObjects : GraphicalObject;

        theWindow : windowPtr;

procedure GraphicalObject.setRegion
        (left, top, right, bottom : integer);
begin
    SetRect (region, left, top, right, bottom);
end;

procedure GraphicalObject.draw;
begin
end;

procedure GraphicalObject.erase;
begin
    EraseRect (region);
end;

procedure GraphicalObject.update;
begin
end;

procedure GraphicalObject.hitBy (aBall : GraphicalObject);
begin
end;

function GraphicalObject.intersect
        (anObject : GraphicalObject) : boolean;
var
```

```
        theIntersection : Rect;
begin
    intersect :=
        SectRect(region, anObject.region, theIntersection);
end;


procedure Wall.hitBy (anObj : GraphicalObject);
var
    aBall : Ball;
begin
    if Member(anObj, Ball) then begin
        aBall := Ball(anObj);
            (* bounce the ball off the wall *)
        aBall.setDirection(convertFactor - aBall.direction);
    end;
end;


procedure Hole.hitBy (anObj : GraphicalObject);
var
    aBall : Ball;
begin
    if Member(anObj, Ball) then begin
        aBall := Ball(anObj);
            (* drain energy from ball *)
        aBall.energy := 0.0;
        aBall.erase;

            (* move ball *)
        if aBall = CueBall then
            aBall.setCenter(50, 100)
        else begin
            saveRack := saveRack + 1;
            aBall.setCenter (10 + saveRack * 15, 250);
        end;

        (* redraw ball *)
        aBall.draw;
    end;
end;


procedure Ball.update;
var
    gptr : GraphicalObject;
    dx, dy : integer;
    i : integer;
```

```
begin
    if energy > 0.5 then begin
        ballMoved := true;
            (* erase ball *)
        erase;
            (* decrease energy *)
        energy := energy - 0.05;
            (* move ball *)
        dx := trunc(5.0 * cos(direction));
        dy := trunc(5.0 * sin(direction));
        offsetRect(region, dx, dy);
            (* redraw ball *)
        for i := 1 to 25 do
        draw;
            (* see if we hit anything *)
        gptr := listOfObjects;
        while gptr <> nil do begin
            if gptr <> self then
                if self.intersect(gptr) then
                    gptr.hitBy(self);
            gptr := gptr.link;
        end;
    end;
end;

procedure Ball.hitBy (anObj : GraphicalObject);
var
    aBall : Ball;
    da : real;
begin
    if Member(anObj, Ball) then begin
        aBall := Ball(anObj);
            (* cut the energy of the hitting ball in half *)
        aBall.energy := aBall.energy / 2.0;

            (* and add it to our own *)
        energy := energy + aBall.energy;

            (* set our new direction *)
        direction := hitAngle(self.x - aBall.x, self.y - aBall.y);
            (* and set the hitting ball's direction *)
        da := aBall.direction - direction;
        aBall.setDirection(aBall.direction + da);
    end;
end;
```

```
procedure Ball.draw;
begin
        (* draw filled circle *)
    PaintOval (region)
end;

procedure CueBall.draw;
begin
        (* draw open circle *)
    FrameOval (region);
end;

procedure mouseButtonDown (x, y : integer);
var
    gptr : GraphicalObject;
begin
        (* give the cue ball some energy *)
    cueBall.energy := 20.0;
        (* and a direction *)
    cueBall.setDirection(hitAngle (cueBall.x - x, cueBall.y - y));

        (* then loop as long as called for *)
    ballMoved := true;
    while ballMoved do begin
        ballMoved := false;
        gptr := listOfObjects;
        while gptr <> nil do begin
            gptr.update;
            gptr := gptr.link;
        end;
    end;
end;

procedure drawBoard;
var
    gptr : GraphicalObject;
begin
    SetPort (theWindow);

    gptr := listOfObjects;
    while gptr <> nil do begin
        gptr.draw;
        gptr := gptr.link;
    end;
end;
```

Appendix C

Source for the Solitaire Game

The solitaire game described in Chapter 8 is built on top of the standard Java API.

```
/*
    Simple Solitaire Card Game in Java
    Written by Tim Budd, Oregon State University, 1996
*/

import java.awt.*;
import java.applet.*;

class Card {
        // constructor
    Card (int sv, int rv) {
        s = sv;
        r = rv;
        faceup = false;
        }

        // access attributes of card
    public int          rank ()      { return r; }

    public int          suit()       { return s; }

    public boolean      faceUp()     { return faceup; }

    public void         flip()       { faceup = ! faceup; }
```

```java
public int          color()     {
   if (suit() == heart || suit() == diamond)
      return red;
   return black;
   }

public void         draw (Graphics g, int x, int y) {
   String names[] = {"A", "2", "3", "4", "5", "6",
      "7", "8", "9", "10", "J", "Q", "K"};
      // clear rectangle, draw border
   g.clearRect(x, y, width, height);
   g.setColor(Color.black);
   g.drawRect(x, y, width, height);
      // draw body of card
   if (faceUp()) {
      if (color() == red)
         g.setColor(Color.red);
      else
         g.setColor(Color.blue);
      g.drawString(names[rank()], x+3, y+15);
      if (suit() == heart) {
         g.drawLine(x+25, y+30, x+35, y+20);
         g.drawLine(x+35, y+20, x+45, y+30);
         g.drawLine(x+45, y+30, x+25, y+60);
         g.drawLine(x+25, y+60, x+5, y+30);
         g.drawLine(x+5, y+30, x+15, y+20);
         g.drawLine(x+15, y+20, x+25, y+30);
         }
      else if (suit() == spade) {
         g.drawLine(x+25, y+20, x+40, y+50);
         g.drawLine(x+40, y+50, x+10, y+50);
         g.drawLine(x+10, y+50, x+25, y+20);
         g.drawLine(x+23, y+45, x+20, y+60);
         g.drawLine(x+20, y+60, x+30, y+60);
         g.drawLine(x+30, y+60, x+27, y+45);
         }
      else if (suit() == diamond) {
         g.drawLine(x+25, y+20, x+40, y+40);
         g.drawLine(x+40, y+40, x+25, y+60);
         g.drawLine(x+25, y+60, x+10, y+40);
         g.drawLine(x+10, y+40, x+25, y+20);
         }
      else if (suit() == club) {
         g.drawOval(x+20, y+25, 10, 10);
         g.drawOval(x+25, y+35, 10, 10);
```

```
                  g.drawOval(x+15, y+35, 10, 10);
                  g.drawLine(x+23, y+45, x+20, y+55);
                  g.drawLine(x+20, y+55, x+30, y+55);
                  g.drawLine(x+30, y+55, x+27, y+45);
                  }
            }
      else { // face down
            g.setColor(Color.yellow);
            g.drawLine(x+15, y+5, x+15, y+65);
            g.drawLine(x+35, y+5, x+35, y+65);
            g.drawLine(x+5, y+20, x+45, y+20);
            g.drawLine(x+5, y+35, x+45, y+35);
            g.drawLine(x+5, y+50, x+45, y+50);
            }
      }

      // data fields for colors and suits
   final static int width = 50;
   final static int height = 70;
   final static int red = 0;
   final static int black = 1;
   final static int heart = 0;
   final static int spade = 1;
   final static int diamond = 2;
   final static int club = 3;
      // data fields
   private boolean faceup;
   private int r;
   private int s;
   public Card link;
}

class CardPile {

   CardPile (int xl, int yl) {
      x = xl;
      y = yl;
      firstCard = null;
      }

      // access to cards are not overridden

   public Card top() { return firstCard; }

   public boolean empty() { return firstCard == null; }
```

```java
public Card pop() {
    Card result = null;
    if (firstCard != null) {
        result = firstCard;
        firstCard = firstCard.link;
        }
    return result;
    }

    // the following are sometimes overridden

public boolean includes (int tx, int ty) {
    return x <= tx && tx <= x + Card.width &&
        y <= ty && ty <= y + Card.height;
    }

public void select (int tx, int ty) {
    // do nothing
    }

public void addCard (Card aCard) {
    aCard.link = firstCard;
    firstCard = aCard;
    }

public void display (Graphics g) {
    g.setColor(Color.black);
    if (firstCard == null)
        g.drawRect(x, y, Card.width, Card.height);
    else
        firstCard.draw(g, x, y);
    }

public boolean canTake (Card aCard) {
    return false;
    }

    // coordinates of the card pile
protected int x;
protected int y;
private Card firstCard;
}
```

```
class DeckPile extends CardPile {
    DeckPile (int x, int y) {
            // first initialize parent
        super(x, y);
            // then create the new deck
            // first put them into a local pile
        CardPile pileOne = new CardPile(0, 0);
        CardPile pileTwo = new CardPile(0, 0);
        int count = 0;
        for (int i = 0; i < 4; i++)
            for (int j = 0; j <= 12; j++) {
                pileOne.addCard(new Card(i, j));
                count++;
                }
            // then pull them out randomly
        for (; count > 0; count--) {
            int limit = ((int)(Math.random() * 1000)) % count;
                // move down to a random location
            for (int i = 0; i < limit; i++)
                pileTwo.addCard(pileOne.pop());
                // then add the card found there
            addCard(pileOne.pop());
                // then put the decks back together
            while (! pileTwo.empty())
                pileOne.addCard(pileTwo.pop());
            }
        }

    public void select(int tx, int ty) {
        if (empty()) return;
        Solitare.discardPile.addCard(pop());
        }
}

class DiscardPile extends CardPile {
    DiscardPile (int x, int y) { super (x, y); }

    public void addCard (Card aCard) {
        if (! aCard.faceUp()) aCard.flip();
        super.addCard(aCard);
        }
    public void select (int tx, int ty) {
        if (empty())
            return;
        Card topCard = pop();
```

```
        for (int i = 0; i < 4; i++)
            if (Solitare.suitPile[i].canTake(topCard)) {
                Solitare.suitPile[i].addCard(topCard);
                return;
                }
        for (int i = 0; i < 7; i++)
            if (Solitare.tableau[i].canTake(topCard)) {
                Solitare.tableau[i].addCard(topCard);
                return;
                }
        // nobody can use it, put it back on our list
        addCard(topCard);
        }
}


class SuitPile extends CardPile {
    SuitPile (int x, int y) { super(x, y); }

    public boolean canTake (Card aCard) {
        if (empty())
            return aCard.rank() == 0;
        Card topCard = top();
        return (aCard.suit() == topCard.suit()) &&
            (aCard.rank() == 1 + topCard.rank());
        }
}


class TablePile extends CardPile {
    TablePile (int x, int y, int c) {
        super(x, y); // initialize the parent class
            // then initialize our pile of cards
        for (int i = 0; i < c; i++) {
            addCard(Solitare.deckPile.pop());
            }
            // flip topmost card face up
        top().flip();
        }

    public boolean canTake (Card aCard) {
        if (empty())
            return aCard.rank() == 12;
        Card topCard = top();
        return (aCard.color() != topCard.color()) &&
            (aCard.rank() == topCard.rank() - 1);
        }
```

```
public boolean includes (int tx, int ty) {
        // don't test bottom of card
    return x <= tx && tx <= x + Card.width &&
        y <= ty;
    }

public void select (int tx, int ty) {
    if (empty())
        return;

        // if face down, then flip
    Card topCard = top();
    if (! topCard.faceUp()) {
        topCard.flip();
        return;
        }

        // else see if any suit pile can take card
    topCard = pop();
    for (int i = 0; i < 4; i++)
        if (Solitare.suitPile[i].canTake(topCard)) {
            Solitare.suitPile[i].addCard(topCard);
            return;
            }
        // else see if any other table pile can take card
    for (int i = 0; i < 7; i++)
        if (Solitare.tableau[i].canTake(topCard)) {
            Solitare.tableau[i].addCard(topCard);
            return;
            }
        // else put it back on our pile
    addCard(topCard);
    }

private int stackDisplay(Graphics g, Card aCard) {
    int localy;
    if (aCard == null)
        return y;
    localy = stackDisplay(g, aCard.link);
    aCard.draw(g, x, localy);
    return localy + 35;
    }
```

```java
    public void display (Graphics g) {
        stackDisplay(g, top());
        }


}

public class Solitare extends Applet {
    static DeckPile deckPile;
    static DiscardPile discardPile;
    static TablePile tableau[];
    static SuitPile suitPile[];
    static CardPile allPiles[];

    public void init() {
            // first allocate the arrays
        allPiles = new CardPile[13];
        suitPile = new SuitPile[4];
        tableau = new TablePile[7];
            // then fill them in
        allPiles[0] = deckPile = new DeckPile(335, 5);
        allPiles[1] = discardPile = new DiscardPile(268, 5);
        for (int i = 0; i < 4; i++)
            allPiles[2+i] = suitPile[i] =
                new SuitPile(15 + 60 * i, 5);
        for (int i = 0; i < 7; i++)
            allPiles[6+i] = tableau[i] =
                new TablePile(5 + 55 * i, 80, i+1);
        }

    public void paint(Graphics g) {
        for (int i = 0; i < 13; i++)
            allPiles[i].display(g);
        }

    public boolean mouseDown(Event evt, int x, int y) {
        for (int i = 0; i < 13; i++)
            if (allPiles[i].includes(x, y)) {
                allPiles[i].select(x, y);
                repaint();
                return true;
                }
        return true;
        }
}
```

Glossary

Object-oriented programming techniques introduce many new ideas and terms that may not be familiar to the novice, even if he or she has had extensive experience with other programming languages. More problematic is that among the various object-oriented languages, several terms are often used for the same idea. Such terms are listed as synonyms in the following glossary. Also indicated are situations where a term is given a particular meaning in one language that is not shared with other languages.

abstract class Syn. *deferred class*, *abstract superclass*. A class that is not used to make direct instances, but rather is used only as a base from which other classes inherit. In C++, the term is often reserved for classes that contain at least one *pure virtual* method, while in Java the term refers to a class that is explicitly declared as abstract.

abstract method (Java) A method that is explicitly declared as abstract. Such methods must be overridden by subclasses before an instance can be created.

abstraction A technique in problem solving in which details are grouped into a single common concept. This concept can then be viewed as a single entity and nonessential information ignored.

access specifier (C++, Delphi Pascal) A keyword (private, protected, or public) that controls access to data members and methods within user-defined classes.

accessor function A function that is used to access the values of an instance variable. By restricting access through a function, the programmer can ensure that instance variables will be read but not modified (see *mutator*).

ad hoc polymorphism Syn. *overloading*. A procedure or method identifier that denotes more than one procedure.

agent Syn. *object, instance*. A nontechnical term sometimes used to describe an object in order to emphasize its independence from other objects, and the fact that it is providing a service to other objects.

allocated class Syn. *dynamic class*. See *static class*.

ancestor class Syn. *base class, superclass.* (Object Pascal) A type from which an object type inherits. The type named in an object type definition statement is called the *immediate ancestor.*

ancestor type See *ancestor class.*

argument signature (C++) An internal encoding of a list of argument types; the argument signature is used to disambiguate overloaded function invocations, with that function body being selected that matches most closely the signature of the function call. See *parameteric overloading.*

automatic storage management A policy in which the underlying run-time system is responsible for the detection and reclamation of memory values no longer accessible, and hence of no further use to the computation. Among the object-oriented languages discussed in this book, only Smalltalk and Java provide automatic storage management. See *garbage collection.*

automatic variable A variable that is allocated space automatically when a procedure is entered. Contrast to a *dynamic variable*, which must have space allocated by the user.

base class Syn. *ancestor type, superclass, parent class.* (C++) A class from which another class is derived.

binding The process by which a name or an expression is associated with an attribute, such as a variable and the type of value the variable can hold.

binding time The time at which a binding takes place. *Early* or *static binding* generally refers to binding performed at compile time, whereas *late* or *dynamic binding* refers to binding performed at run time. Dynamically bound languages, such as Smalltalk and Objective-C, do not bind a variable and the type of value the variable can hold at compile time. Message passing is a form of procedure calling with late binding.

block (Smalltalk) An object that represents a sequence of statements to be executed at a later time. In this sense a block is similar to a nameless function. Blocks are values, and can be passed as arguments or (less frequently) assigned to variables. A block executes its associated statements in response to the message value.

browser A software tool used to examine the class hierarchy and methods associated with different classes. Originally developed as part of the Smalltalk programming environment, class browsers are now found in many programming environments. A different sort of browser is used to access information on the World Wide Web. More recent WWW browsers have included interpreters for the Java programming language, allowing Java programs to be very efficiently executed in during the reading of WWW pages.

cascaded message (Smalltalk) a shorthand way of sending multiple messages to a single receiver.

cast A unary expression that converts a value from one type to another.

child class Syn. *subclass, derived class.* (C++) A class defined as an extension of another class, which is called the *parent class.*

class Syn. *object type.* An abstract description of the data and behavior of a collection of similar objects. The representatives of the collection are called *instances* of the class.

Class (Smalltalk, Java) The class that maintains behavior related to class instance and subclass creation. See *metaclass.*

class description protocol The complete definition of all properties, features, and methods that are descriptive of any object that is an instance of a class.

class hierarchy A hierarchy formed by listing classes according to their class-subclass relationship. See *hierarchy.*

class object Syn. *factory object.* (Smalltalk) The single special object, and instance of class Class, that is associated with each class. New instances of the class are created by the message new being sent to this object.

class method (C++) A method declared with the keyword static. Class methods are not permitted to access instance variables but can access only class variables. They can be invoked independently of receivers using explicit name qualification.

class variable A variable shared by all instances of a class. (C++) A data member declared as static. (Smalltalk) A variable declared as a class variable in the class-construction message.

client-side computing In a network environment, a program that is executed on the client side rather than on the server side of the network. The Java programming language is intended to perform client-side computing and so is more efficient than programs that must wait for execution on the (generally more overloaded) server machine.

cohesion The degree to which components of a single software system (such as members of a single class) are tied together. Contrast with *coupling.*

collaborator Two classes which dependend upon each other for the execution of their behaviors are said to be collaborators.

collection classes See *container classes.*

constructor A method used to create a new object. The constructor handles the dual tasks of allocating memory for the new object and ensuring that this memory is properly initialized. The programmer defines how this initialization is performed. In C++ and Java a constructor is simply a method with the same name as the class in which it appears, while in Delphi Pascal a constructor is declared with a special keyword.

container classes Classes used as data structures that can contain a number of elements. Examples include lists, sets, and tables. The STL provides a number of standard container classes for C++.

contravariance A form of overriding in which an argument associated with a method in the child class is restricted to a less general category than the corresponding argument in the parent class. Contrast with *covariance*. Neither covariant nor contravariant overriding is common in object-oriented languages.

composition The technique of including user-defined object types as part of a newly defined object, as opposed to using inheritance.

copy constructor (C++) A constructor that takes as argument an instance of the class in which the constructor is being declared. The copy constructor is used to produce a copy, or clone, of the argument.

coupling The degree to which separate software components are tied together. Contrast with *cohesion*.

covariance A form of overriding in which an argument associated with a method in the child class is enlarged to a more general category than the corresponding argument in the parent class. Contrast with *contravariance*. Neither covariant nor contravariant overriding is common in object-oriented languages.

CRC card An index card that documents the name, responsibilities, and collaborators for a class, used during the process of system analysis and design.

data hiding An encapsulation technique that seeks to abstract away the implementation details concerning what data values are maintained for an object to provide a particular service.

data member (C++) See *instance variable*.

default constructor (C++) A constructor with no arguments. Such a constructor is often used to initialize temporary variables.

deferred class See *abstract class*.

deferred method A method that defines an interface (that is, argument and result types) but not implementation. Implementation is provided by subclasses that override the deferred method, preserving the interface. See *pure virtual method*.

delegation An alternative to class-based organization. Using delegation, objects can defer the implementation of behavior to other objects, called *delegates*. This technique permits sharing of behavior without the necessity to introduce classes or inheritance.

derived class Syn. *descendant type, subclass, child class.* (C++) A class that is defined as an extension or a subclass of another class, which is called the base class.

descendant type Syn. *subclass, child class.* See *derived class*.

destructor (C++) A method that is invoked immediately before memory is released for an object. The destructor can perform any actions required for the management of the object. The name of the destructor is formed by a tilde being prepended to the name of the class.

dispatch table (Objective-C) A table of method selectors and associated methods. Created when a class is compiled, the dispatch table is searched as part of the message-passing operation.

domain (Object Pascal) When used to refer to variables of object types, the set of object types that represent legal values for the variable. The domain consists of the declared type, and all of the descendant types.

dynamic binding The binding of a name to an attribute that occurs at run time rather than compile time. See *binding time*.

dynamic class See *static class*.

dynamic variable A variable for which space must be allocated explicitly by the user. Contrast to an *automatic variable*, which has space allocated for it automatically when a procedure is entered.

dynamic type The type associated with the value currently being held by a variable, which need not be the same as the *static type* given by the declaration for the variable. In object-oriented languages the dynamic type is frequently restricted to being a subclass of the static type.

dynamically typed language A programming language in which types are associated with values, not variables, and variables can hold any type of value. Smalltalk is one example of a dynamically typed language.

early binding See *binding time*.

ECOOP The European Conference on Object-Oriented Programming, the major conference in Europe in which object-oriented techniques and tools are discussed.

encapsulation The technique of hiding information within a structure, such as the hiding of instance data within a class.

exported name An identifier (variable, type name, function, or method) available for use outside of the context in which it is defined. (Objective-C) A variable, type, function, or method that is global or is defined in an interface (*.h) file. (Object Pascal) A variable, type, function, or method defined within the interface section of a unit. (Java) A class that is declared as public within the package in which it is defined.

extends (Java) A keyword used in forming a new class as a subclass of an existing class, or a new interface as an extension of an existing interface.

factory method (Objective-C) A method recognized only by the class object for a class. Contrast to an *instance method*, which is recognized by instances of the class.

factory object Syn. *class object*. (Objective-C) The unique object, associated with each class, used to create new instances of the class. Each factory object is an instance of class Class. New instances of the class are created by the message new being sent to this object.

final class (Java) A class declared using the keyword final. This keyword indicates that the class cannot be used as a base class for inheritance.

final method (Java) A method declared using the keyword final. This keyword indicates that the method cannot be overridden in subclasses.

finalizer (Java) A method with the name finalize, no arguments, and no return type. This method will be invoked automatically by the run-time system prior to the object in which it is declared being recycled by garbage collection.

friend function (C++) A function that is permitted access to the otherwise private or protected features of a class. Friend functions must be explicitly declared as such by the class that is protecting the features to which the friend is being given access. Friend classes and friend methods also can be defined.

function member (C++) See *method*.

garbage collection A memory management technique whereby the run-time system determines which memory values are no longer necessary to the running program, and automatically recovers and recycles the memory for different use. Garbage collection is found in Smalltalk and Java.

generic method Syn. *virtual method.*

global variable A variable that potentially can be accessed in any portion of a program.

has-a **relation** The relation that asserts that instances of a class possess fields of a given type. See *is-a* relation.

heap-based memory allocation Memory allocation performed at run-time and not tied to procedure entry and exit. Contrast with *stack-based memory allocation.*

hierarchy An organizational structure with components ranked into levels of subordination according to some set of rules. In object-oriented programming the most common hierarchy is that formed by the class-subclass relationship.

hybrid language A language the incorporates features of more than one programming style. C++ and Object Pascal are hybrid languages, as they support both imperative and object-oriented programming. Smalltalk is a *pure* object-oriented language, as it supports only object-oriented programming.

immediate superclass The closest parent class from which a class inherits. The superclass relationship is a transitive closure of the immediate superclass relationship.

immutable value A value that is not permitted to change once it has been set. Variables that hold such values are sometimes called "single-assignment" variables. In C++ immutable values can be identified via the const keyword.

information hiding The principle that users of a software component (such as a class) need to know only the essential details of how to initialize and access the component, and do not need to know the details of the implementation. By reducing the degree of interconnectedness between separate elements of a software system, the principle of information hiding helps in the development of reliable software.

inheritance The property of objects by which instances of a class can have access to data and method definitions contained in a previously defined class, without those definitions being restated. See *ancestor class.*

inheritance graph An abstract structure that illustrates the inheritance relationships with a collection of classes.

inherited (Object Pascal) A keyword used to activate the execution of an overridden procedure.

initialize (Objective-C, Smalltalk) A special message sent to the class object before the class receives instances of any other message. Can be redefined as a factory method to set up the appropriate run-time environment before instances of a class are used.

inline function A function that can be expanded directly in-line at the location it is called, thereby avoiding the overhead associated with a function call. Inline functions can be defined by the directive inline in C++ or the directive final in Java.

instance Syn. *object*. (C++) A variable of a class type. (Object Pascal) A variable of an object type. (Smalltalk) A specific example of the general structure defined by a *class*.

instance variable An internal variable maintained by an instance. Instance variables represent the state of an object.

instance method Syn. *method*. (Objective-C) A method recognized by instances of a class. See *factory method*.

interaction diagram A diagram that documents the sequence of messages that flow between objects participating in a scenario.

Internet A world-wide collection of machines that have agreed to communicate with each other using a common protocol.

is-a **relation** The relation that asserts that instances of a subclass must be more specialized forms of the superclass. Thus, instances of a subclass can be used where quantities of the superclass type are required. See *has-a relation*.

isa link (Objective-C) An implicit pointer, contained in every object, that references to the dispatch table for the object. Since objects are characterized only by their behavior, this pointer in effect encodes the class of the object.

iterator A class that is used mainly to provide access to the values being held in another class, usually a container class. The iterator provides a uniform framework for accessing values, without compromising the encapsulation of the container.

late binding See *binding time*.

Member (Object Pascal) A system-provided Boolean function that can be used to determine whether the value (dynamic type) of a variable is a member of the specific object type.

member (C++) A general term for the attributes associated with instances of a class. Instance variables are called *data members* in C++; methods are called *procedure* or *function* members.

message Syn. *message selector, method designator, method selector, selector.* The textual string that identifies a requested action is a message-passing expression. During message passing, this string is used to find a matching method as part of the method-lookup process.

message passing The process of locating and executing a method in response to a message. See *method lookup.*

message selector Syn. *method designator, method selector, selector.* The textual string that identifies a message in a message-passing expression. During message passing, this string is used to find a matching method as part of the method-lookup process.

message expression (Objective-C) A Smalltalk-like expression enclosed in a pair of square braces, [...]. The braces are used to differentiate message-passing code from normal C code.

metaclass (Smalltalk) The class of a class object. For each class, there is an associated metaclass. The class object is typically the only instance of this metaclass. Metaclasses permit the specialization of class behavior. Without them, all classes would need to behave in the same way.

metaprogramming A style of programming that makes extensive use of metaclasses, and in which the programming language itself can be used to control the semantics and meaning of different constructs. Smalltalk is one language that uses metaprogramming.

method A procedure or function associated with a class (or object type) and invoked in a message-passing style.

method declaration The part of a class declaration specific to an individual method.

method designator Syn. *message selector.* A method name identifier used as a procedure or function name in a message-passing expression. The method designator is used to search for the appropriate method during message sending. In general, you cannot determine from the program text which method a method designator will activate during execution.

method lookup The process of locating a method matching a particular message, generally performed as part of the message-passing operation. Usually, the run-time system finds the method by examining the class hierarchy for the receiver of the message, searching from bottom to top until a method is found with the same name as the message.

method selector See *message selector.*

multiple inheritance The feature that allows a subclass to inherit from more than one immediate superclass. Multiple inheritance is not supported by all object-oriented languages.

mutator A method that is used to modify the value of an instance variable. By requiring such modifications to be mediated through a function, a class can have greater control over how its internal state is being modified.

name space (C++) A mechanism for restricting the accessibility of global names. Globals can be declared as being part of a specific name space and are only accessible to portions of a program that explicitly include that name space. See *scope*.

native method (Java) A method that is implemented in another language, such as C or assembly language. See *primitive*.

object See *instance*. (Object Pascal) A keyword used to indicate the definition of an object type.

object field designator (Object Pascal) A (perhaps qualified) identifier that denotes the field within an object.

object hierarchy Syn. *class hierarchy*. (Object Pascal) A group of object types all related through inheritance.

object-oriented programming A style of design that is centered around the delegation of responsibilities to independent interacting agents, and a style of programming characterized by the use of message passing and classes organized into one or more inheritance hierarchies.

object type Syn. *class*. (Object Pascal) A data structure, similar to a Pascal record type definition, that can contain fields (methods) of procedures and functions, as well as data fields.

OOPSLA The annual conference on Object-Oriented Programming Systems, Languages and Applications, sponsored by the Association for Computing Machinery.

overload Used to describe an identifier that denotes more than one object. Procedures, functions, methods, and operators can all be overloaded. A virtual method, or a method that is overridden, can also be said to be overloaded. See *parameteric overloading*.

override The action that occurs when a method in a subclass with the same name as a method in a superclass takes precedence over the method in the superclass. Normally, during the process of binding a method to a message (see *message passing*), the overriding method will be the method selected. (Object Pascal) A keyword used to indicate that a method is to override the similarly named method in an ancestor type.

paradigm An illustrative model or example, which by extension provides a way of organizing information. The object-oriented paradigm emphasizes organization based on behaviors and responsibilities.

parameterized classes Classes in which some types are left unbound at the time of class definition. These bindings are filled in, resulting in qualified classes, before instances of the class are created.

parameteric overloading Overloading of function names in which two or more procedure bodies are known by the same name in a given context, and are disambiguated by the type and number of parameters supplied with the procedure call. (Overloading of functions, methods, and operators can also occur).

parent class Syn. *superclass, ancestor class.* An immediate superclass of a class.

Parnas's principles Principles that describe the proper use of modules, originally developed by the computer scientist David Parnas.

persistent object An object that continues to exist outside of the execution time of programs that manipulate the object.

polymorphic Literally "many shapes." A feature of a variable that can take on values of several different types, or when used with functions that describe a function that has at least one polymorphic argument. The term is also used for a function name that denotes several different functions. See *pure polymorphism, ad hoc polymorphism.*

polymorphic variable A variable that can hold many different types of values. Object-oriented languages often restrict the types of values to being subclasses of the declared type of the variable.

primitive (Smalltalk) An operation that cannot be performed in the programming language and must be accomplished with the aid of the underlying run-time system.

private inheritance (C++) Inheritance used for the purpose of implementation, which does not preserve the *is-a* relation, and thus, creates subclasses which are not subtypes. The inheriting class is permitted access to the features of the parent class, but instances of the child class cannot be assigned to variables declared as the parent class.

private method A method that is not intended to be invoked from outside an object. More specifically, the receiver for the message that invokes a private method should always be the receiver for the method in which the invocation is taking place (see self). Contrast with public method. In Smalltalk private methods are established only by convention, whereas C++, Java, and Delphi Pascal can guarantee the behavior of private methods.

procedure call The transfer of control from the current point in execution to the code associated with a procedure. Procedure calling differs from *message passing* in that the selection of code to be transferred to is decided at compile time (or link time) rather than run time.

protocol See *class description protocol.*

prototype (C++) A declaration for a function that lists the function name, return type, and argument types, but does not provide the function definition (or body).

pseudo-variable A variable that is never declared but can nevertheless be used within a method, although it cannot be directly modified (a pseudo-variable is therefore by definition read-only). The most common pseudo-variable is used to represent the receiver of a method. See *self, this,* and *super.*

public class (Java) A class that is global and can be accessed from other packages. One public class may be declared in each compilation unit.

public method A method that can be invoked at any time from outside an object.

pure polymorphism A feature of a single function that can be executed by arguments of a variety of types. See *ad hoc polymorphism.*

pure virtual method (C++) A *virtual method* without a body, created by the value 0 being assigned to the function in the class definition. Pure virtual methods provide specification for subclasses. See *deferred method.*

qualified name (C++) A name of a method or instance variable that indicates explicitly the class in which the method is located. In C++, the class name and method name are separated by two colons (class::method); in Java and Object Pascal, a period is used. Since the class of the method is named explicitly, a call on a qualified name can be performed by procedure calling in place of message passing.

rapid prototyping A style of software development in which less emphasis is placed on creation of a complete formal specification than on rapid construction of a prototype pilot system, with the understanding that users will experiment with the initial system and suggest modifications or changes, probably leading to a complete redevelopment of a subsequent system. See *exploratory programming.*

receiver The object to which a message is sent. In Smalltalk and Objective-C, the receiver is indicated as the object to the left of the message selector. In C++ and Object Pascal, the receiver is the object to the left of the field qualifier (period). Within a method, the current receiver is indicated in various ways: In C++, the variable this is a pointer to the current receiver; in Objective-C, Object Pascal, and Smalltalk, the pseudo-variable self contains the current receiver.

redefinition The process of changing an inherited operation, to provide different or extended behavior.

reference variable (C++) A variable declared by the address-of (&) modifier. The variable points to another value, and is an alias for this value. Changes to the reference variable will be reflected in changes in the object to which the reference has been assigned.

refinement A style of overriding in which the inherited code is merged with the code defined in the child class.

renaming The process of changing the name for an inherited operation without changing its behavior. Contrast with *redefinition*.

replacement A style of overriding in which the inherited code is completely replaced by the code defined in the child class.

responsibility-driven design A design technique that emphasizes the identification and division of responsibilities within a collection of independent agents.

RTTI (C++) The *Run-Time Type Identification* system. A set of values and functions that permit the identification of the dynamic type of a variable, as well as other associated information.

reverse polymorphism An attempt to undo an assignment to a polymorphic variable. That is, to take a value being held by a polymorphic variable and assign it to another variable that matches the dynamic type of the value, not the static type.

scope When applied to a variable identifier, the (textual) portion of a program in which references to the identifier denote the particular variable.

selector See *message selector*.

self (Objective-C, Object Pascal, Smalltalk) When used inside a method, refers to the receiver for the message that caused the method to be invoked. See *this*.

shadowed name A name that matches another name in a surrounding scope; the new name effectively makes the surrounding name inaccessible. An example is a local variable with the same name as that of a global or instance variable. Within the procedure, the local variable will be attached to all references of the name, making references to the surrounding name difficult. In C++ and Java access to such values can be provided by a fully qualified name.

single-assignment variable A variable the value of which is assigned once and cannot be redefined. (C++) Single-assignment variables can occur by use of either the const modifier or the definition of a reference variable (in the latter case, the reference is single assignment; the variable to which the reference points, on the other hand, can be modified repeatedly). A single-assignment variable can also be created by assigning a data member in a constructor and then not permitting any other method to modify the value.

slicing (C++) The process by which an argument of a derived type is passed to an parameter declared as a base type. In effect, the fields and methods of the derived type are sliced off from the base fields.

specification class An abstract superclass used only to define an interface. The actual implementation of the interface is left to subclasses.

stack-based memory allocation An implementation technique where memory is allocated for variables when the procedure in which the variables are declared is entered, and freed with the procedure is exited. Stack based allocation is very efficient, but does not work if either the lifetime of values is not tied to procedure entry/exit, or the size of values is not determined at compile time. Contrast with *heap-based memory allocation*.

static (C++ and Java) A declaration modifier that, when applied to global variables and functions, means that the variables are not accessible outside of the file in which they are declared; when applied to local variables, means that they continue to exist even after the procedure in which they are declared has exited; and when applied to class declaration fields, indicates that the fields are shared by all instances of the class. (Object Pascal) A variable that is allocated space automatically when a procedure is entered. Contrast to dynamic variables, which must have space allocated by the user.

static method a method that can be called by early binding. The method body can be determined uniquely at compile time, and thus no message passing is required to process a message to a static method.

static class In statically typed object-oriented languages, such as C++ and Object Pascal, the declared class of a variable. It is legal, however, for the value of the variable to be an instance of either the static class or any class derived from the static class. The class of the value for the variable is known as the *dynamic class*.

static type See *static class*.

statically typed language A language in which every variable must have a declared type. Such languages are often, although not necessarily, strongly typed. Object-oriented languages may bend static type rules by permitting variables to hold any value that is a subtype (or subclass) of the declared type.

statically typed object (Objective-C) A variable that is declared by class name, as opposed to simply being declared by the type id. Statically typing an object permits certain errors to be detected at compile time, rather than at run time, and permits certain optimizations.

strongly typed language A language in which the type of any expression can be determined at compile time.

subclass Syn. *descendant type, derived class, child class.* (Smalltalk) A class that inherits from another class.

subclass client A class that makes use of the facilities of a superclass to implement its own functionality.

subclass coupling The connection formed between a parent and child class. Subclass coupling is a very weak form of coupling, since instances of the subclass can be treated as though they were simply instances of the parent class. See *coupling* and *cohesion.*

substitutability, principle of The principle that asserts one should be able to substitute an instance of a child class in a situation where an instance of the parent class is expected. The principle is valid if the two classes are subtypes of each other, but not necessarily in general.

subtype A type A is said to be a subtype of a type B if an instance of type A can be substituted for an instance of type B with no observable effect. For example, a sparse array class might be defined as a subtype of an array type. Subclasses need not be subtypes, nor must subtypes be subclasses.

super (Objective-C, Smalltalk, Java) When used inside a method, a synonym for *self*. However, when used as the receiver for a message, the search for an appropriate method will begin with the parent class of the class in which the current method is defined.

superclass Syn. *ancestor class, base class.* (Smalltalk) A class from which another class inherits attributes.

symbol (Smalltalk) A value that is characterized only by its unique value. Similar to an enumerated value in C or Pascal, with the exception that symbols can print themselves textually at run time.

this (C++) When used inside a method, a pointer to the receiver for the message that caused the method to be invoked. Note that the pointer must be dereferenced to obtain the value of the receiver–for example, to send further messages to the receiver. See *self.*

type signature See *argument signature.*

user client a class that makes use of the facilities provided by another distance object. See *subclass client.*

virtual method (C++) A method that can be called with late binding. The method body to be invoked cannot be determined at compile time, and thus a run-time search must be performed to determine which of several methods should be invoked in response to a message. See *pure virtual method*.

virtual method pointer (C++) A pointer, maintained by every object that uses virtual methods, that points to the virtual method table associated with the type of the value currently contained in the variable.

virtual method table (C++) A table of pointers to methods, constructed for each class. All instances of the class point to this table.

void (C++, Java) A type name used to indicate a function returning no value–that is, a procedure.

World Wide Web A collection of machines on the Internet that have agreed to distribute information according to a common protocol. This information is usually accessed with a *browser*.

yo-yo problem Repeated movements up and down the class hierarchy may be required when the execution of a particular method invocation is traced.

Bibliography

[Abelson 1981]   Harold Abelson and Andrea diSessa, *Turtle Geometry: The Computer as a Medium for Exploring Mathematics*, MIT Press, Cambridge, MA, 1981.

[Actor 1987]   *Actor Language Manual*, The Whitewater Group, Inc., Evanston, IL, 1987.

[Aho 1985]   Alfred V. Aho, Ravi Sethi, and Jeffrey D. Ullman, *Compilers: Principles, Techniques, and Tools*, Addison-Wesley, Reading, MA, 1985.

[Appel 1987]   Andrew W. Appel, "Garbage Collection Can Be Faster Than Stack Allocation," *Information Processing Letters*, 25(4): 275–279, 1987.

[Atkinson 1988]   Malcolm P. Atkinson, Peter Buneman, and Ronald Morrison (Eds.), *Data Types and Persistence*, Springer-Verlag, New York, 1988.

[Beck 1989]   Kent Beck and Ward Cunningham, "A Laboratory for Teaching Object-Oriented Thinking," *Proceedings of the 1989 OOPSLA—Conference on Object-Oriented Programming Systems, Languages and Applications*; Reprinted in *Sigplan Notices*, 24(10): 1–6, 1989.

[Berztiss 1990]   Alfs Berztiss, *Programming with Generators*, Ellis Horwood, New York, 1990.

[Birtwistle 1979]   Graham M. Birtwistle, Ole-Johan Dahl, Bjørn Myhrhaug, and Kristen Nygaard, *Simula Begin*, Studentlitteratur, Lund, Sweden, 1979.

[Böhm 1966]   Corrado Böhm and Giuseppe Jacopini, "Flow Diagrams, Turing Machines and Languages with Only Two Formation Rules," *Communications of the ACM*, 9(5):366–371, May 1966.

[Borland 1995]   Borland International, *Object Pascal Language Guide*, Scotts Valley, CA, 1995.

[Brooks 1975]   Frederick P. Brooks, Jr., *The Mythical Man-Month: Essays on Software Engineering*, Addison-Wesley, Reading, MA, 1975.

[Brooks 1987]   Frederick P. Brooks, Jr., "No Silver Bullet: Essence and Accidents of Software Engineering," *IEEE Computer*, April 1987, pp. 10-19.

[Budd 1987]   Timothy A. Budd, *A Little Smalltalk*, Addison-Wesley, Reading, MA, 1987.

[Budd 1991]   Timothy A. Budd, "Generalized Arithmetic in C++," *Journal of Object-Oriented Programming*, 3(6): 11–23, February 1991.

[Budd 1994]   Timothy A. Budd, *Classic Data Structures in C++*, Addison-Wesley, Reading, MA, 1994.

[Cardelli 1985]   Luca Cardelli and Peter Wegner, "On Understanding Types, Data Abstraction, and Polymorphism," *Computing Surveys*, 17(4): 471–523, 1985.

[Carroll 1995]   Martin D. Carroll and Margaret A. Ellis, *Designing and Coding Reusable C++*, Addison-Wesley, Reading, MA, 1987.

[Chirlian 1990]   Paul M. Chirlian, *Programming in C++*, Merrill, Columbus, OH, 1990.

[Church 1936]   Alonzo Church, "An Unsolvable Problem of Elementary Number Theory," *American Journal of Mathematics*, 58: 345–363, 1936.

[Cohen 1981]   Jacques Cohen, "Garbage Collection of Linked Data Structures," *ACM Computing Surveys*, 13(3): 341–367, 1981.

[Coplien 1995]   *Pattern Languages of Program Design*, edited by James A. Coplien and Douglas C. Schmidt, Addison-Wesley, Reading, MA, 1995.

[Cox 1986]   Brad J. Cox, *Object Oriented Programming: An Evolutionary Approach*, Addison-Wesley, Reading, MA, 1986.

[Cox 1990]   Brad J. Cox, "Planning the Software Industrial Revolution," *IEEE Software*, 7(6): 25–35, November 1990.

[Dahl 1966]   Ole-Johan Dahl and Kristen Nygaard, "Simula, An Algol-Based Simulation Language," *Communications of the ACM*, 9(9): 671-678, September 1966.

[Danforth 1988]   Scott Danforth and Chris Tomlinson, "Type Theories and Object-Oriented Programming," *ACM Computing Surveys*, 20(1): 29–72, 1988.

[Deutsch 1989]   L. Peter Deutsch "Design Reuse and Frameworks in the Smalltalk-80 System" In Ted J. Biggerstaff and Alan J. Perlis (Eds.), *Software Reusability, Volume II: Applications and Experience*, pages 57-71, Addison-Wesley, Reading, MA, 1989.

[Dijkstra 1976]   Edsger W. Dijkstra, *A Discipline of Programming*, Prentice-Hall, Englewood Cliffs, NJ, 1976.

[Eckel 1989]   Bruce Eckel, *Using C++*, McGraw-Hill, New York, 1989.

[Ellis 1990]   Margaret A. Ellis and Bjarne Stroustrup, *The Annotated C++ Reference Manual*, Addison-Wesley, Reading, MA, 1990.

[Fairley 1985]   Richard Fairley, *Software Engineering Concepts*, McGraw-Hill, New York, 1985.

[Fischer 1988]   Charles N. Fischer and Richard J. LeBlanc, Jr., *Crafting A Compiler*, Benjamin Cummings, Menlo Park, CA, 1988.

[Floyd 1979]   Robert W. Floyd, "The Paradigms of Programming," *Communications of the ACM*, 22(8): 455–460, August 1979.

[Gamma 1995]   Erich Gamma, Richard Helm, Ralph Johnson, and John Vlissides, *Design Patterns: Elements of Reusable Object-Oriented Software*, Addison-Wesley, Reading, MA, 1995.

[Gibbs 1994]   Wayt Gibbs, "Software's Chronic Crisis," *Scientific American*, 271(3): 86-95, September 1994.

[Gillett 1982]   Will D. Gillett and Seymour V. Pollack, *An Introduction to Engineered Software*, Holt, Rinehart & Winston, New York, 1982.

[Glass 1996]   Graham Glass and Brett Schuchert, *The STL Primer*, Prentice-Hall, Englewood Cliffs, NJ, 1996.

[Gödel 1931]   Kurt Gödel, Über formal unentscheidbare Sätze der Principia Mathematica und verwandter Systeme, *Monatshefte für Mathematik und Physik*, 38: 173-198.

[Goldberg 1983]   Adele Goldberg and David Robson, *Smalltalk-80: The Language and Its Implementation*, Addison-Wesley, Reading, MA, 1983.

[Goldberg 1984]   Adele Goldberg, *Smalltalk-80: The Interactive Programming Environment*, Addison-Wesley, Reading, MA, 1983.

[Goldberg 1989]   Adele Goldberg and David Robson, *Smalltalk-80: The Language*, Addison-Wesley, Reading, MA, 1989.

[Goldberg 1995]   Adele Goldberg and Kenneth Rubin, *Succeeding with Objects* Addison-Wesley, Reading, MA, 1995.

[Gries 1981]   David Gries, *The Science of Programming*, Springer-Verlag, New York, 1981.

[Griswold 1983]   Ralph E. Griswold and Madge T. Griswold, *The Icon Programming Language*, Prentice-Hall, Englewood Cliffs, NJ, 1983.

[Halbert 1987]   Daniel C. Halbert and Patrick D. O'Brien, "Using Types and Inheritance in Object-Oriented Programming," *IEEE Software*, 4(5): 71–79, 1987.

[Hamlet 1976]   Richard G. Hamlet, "High-level binding with low-level linkers," *Communications of the ACM*, 19: 642-644, November 1976.

[Hanson 1981]   David R. Hanson, "Is Block Structure Necessary?" *Software Practice & Experience*, 1(8): 853–866, 1981.

[Hebel 1990]   Kurt J. Hebel and Ralph E. Johnson, "Arithmetic and Double Dispatching in Smalltalk-80," *Journal of Object-Oriented Programming*, 2(6): 40–44, 1990.

[Horowitz 1984]   Ellis Horowitz, *Fundamentals of Programming Languages*, Computer Science Press, Rockville, MD, 1984.

[Ingalls 1981]   Daniel H. H. Ingalls, "Design Principles Behind Smalltalk," *Byte*, 6(8): 286–298, 1981.

[Ingalls 1986]   Daniel H. H. Ingalls, "A Simple Technique for Handling Multiple Polymorphism," *Proceedings of the 1986 OOPSLA—Conference on Object-Oriented Programming Systems, Languages and Applications*; Reprinted in *Sigplan Notices*, 21(11): 347–349, 1986.

[Kaehler 1986]   Ted Kaehler and Dave Patterson, *A Taste of Smalltalk*, W.W. Norton & Company, New York, 1986.

[Kamin 1990]   Samuel N. Kamin, *Programming Languages: An Inter-preter Based Approach*, Addison-Wesley, Reading, MA, 1990.

[Kay 1977]   Alan Kay, "Microelectronics and the Personal Computer," *Scientific American*, 237(3): 230–244, 1977.

[Kay 1993]   Alan C. Kay, "The Early History of Smalltalk," The Second ACM SIGPLAN History of Programming Languages Conference (HOPL-II), *ACM SIGPLAN Notices* 28(3): 69-75, March 1993.

[Keene 1989]   Sonya E. Keene, *Object-Oriented Programming in Common Lisp*, Addison-Wesley, Reading, MA, 1989.

[Keller 1990]   Daniel Keller, "A Guide to Natural Naming," *Sigplan Notices*, 25(5): 95–102, May 1990.

[Kiczales 1991]   Gregor Kiczales, Jim des Rivières and Daniel G. Bobrow, *The Art of the Metaobject Protocol*, MIT Press, Cambridge, MA, 1991.

[Kim 1989]   Won Kim and Frederick H. Lochovsky (Eds.), *Object-Oriented Concepts, Databases, and Applications*, Addison-Wesley, Reading, MA, 1989.

[Kirkerud 1989]   Bjørn Kirkerud, *Object-Oriented Programming with Simula*, Addison-Wesley, Reading, MA, 1989.

[Kleene 1936]   Stephen C. Kleene, "λ-Definability and Recursiveness," *Duke Mathematical Journal*, 2: 340–353, 1936.

[Knolle 1989]   Nancy T. Knolle, "Why Object-Oriented User Interface Toolkits Are Better," *Journal of Object-Oriented Programming*, 2(4): 63–67, 1989.

[Koenig 1989a]   Andrew Koenig, "References in C++," *Journal of Object-Oriented Programming*, 1(6), 1989.

[Koenig 1989b]   Andrew Koenig, "Objects, Values, and Assignment," *Journal of Object-Oriented Programming*, 2(2): 37–38, 1989.

[Koenig 1989c]   Andrew Koenig, "What Are Friends For?" *Journal of Object-Oriented Programming*, 2(4): 53–54, 1989.

[Korienek 1993]   *A Quick Trip to ObjectLand*, Prentice-Hall, Englewood Cliffs, New Jersey, 1993.

[Krasner 1983]   Glenn Krasner, *Smalltalk-80: Bits of History, Words of Advice*, Addison-Wesley, Reading, MA, 1983.

[Krogdahl 1985]   Stein Krogdahl, "Multiple Inheritance in Simula-Like Languages," *BIT*, 25: 318–326, 1985.

[Kuhn 1970]   Thomas S. Kuhn, *The Structure of Scientific Revolutions*, 2nd ed., University of Chicago Press, Chicago, 1970.

[LaLonde 1990a]   Wilf LaLonde and John Pugh, "Integrating New Varieties of Numbers into the Class Library: Quaternions and Complex Numbers," *Journal of Object-Oriented Programming*, 2(5): 64–68, 1990.

[LaLonde 1990b]   Wilf LaLonde and John Pugh, *Inside Smalltalk*, Prentice-Hall, Englewood Cliffs, NJ, 1990.

[Lieberherr 1989a]   Karl J. Lieberherr and Ian M. Holland, "Assuring Good Style for Object-Oriented Programs," *IEEE Software*, 6(5): 38–48, 1989.

[Lieberherr 1989b]   Karl J. Lieberherr and Arthur J. Riel, "Contributions to Teaching Object-Oriented Design and Programming," *Proceedings of the 1989 OOPSLA—Conference on Object-Oriented Programming Systems, Languages and Applications*; Reprinted in *Sigplan Notices*, 24(10): 11–22, October 1989.

[Lieberman 1986]   Henry Lieberman, "Using Prototypical Objects to Implement Shared Behavior in Object-Oriented Systems," *Proceedings of the 1986 OOPSLA—Conference on Object-Oriented Programming Systems, Languages and Applications*; Reprinted in *Sigplan Notices*, 21(11): 214–223, 1986.

[Lippman 1996]   Stanley B. Lippman, *Inside the C++ Object Model*, Addison-Wesley, Reading, MA, 1996.

[Logan 1986]   Robert K. Logan, *The Alphabet Effect*, St. Martin's Press, New York, 1986.

[MacLennan 1987]   Bruce J. MacLennan, *Principles of Programming Languages*, Holt, Rinehart & Winston, New York, 1987.

[Madsen 1993]   Ole Lehrmann Madsen, Birger Møller-Pedersen, and Kristen Nygaard, *Object-Oriented Programming in the BETA Programming Language*, Addison-Wesley, Reading, MA, 1993.

[Marcotty 1987]   Michael Marcotty and Henry Ledgard, *The World of Pro-gramming Languages*, Springer-Verlag, New York, 1987.

[Markov 1951]   Andrei Andreevich Markov, "The Theory of Algorithms" (in Russian), *Trudy Mathematicheskogo Instituta immeni V. A. Steklova*, 38: 176–189, 1951.

[McGregor 1992]   John D. McGregor and David A. Sykes, *Object-Oriented Software Development: Engineering Software For Reuse*, International Thomson Computer Press, Albany, NY, 1992.

[Meyer 1988a]   Bertrand Meyer, *Object-Oriented Software Construction*, Prentice-Hall International, London, 1988a.

[Meyer 1988b]   Bertrand Meyer, "Harnessing Multiple Inheritance," *Journal of Object-Oriented Programming Languages*, 1(4): 48–51, 1988b.

[Meyer 1994]   Bertrand Meyer, *Reusable Software*, Prentice-Hall, Engle-wood Cliffs, NJ, 1994.

[Micallef 1988]   Josephine Micallef, "Encapsulation, Resuability and Ex-tensibility in Object-Oriented Programming Languages," *Journal of Object-Oriented Programming Languages*, 1(1): 12–35, 1988.

[Milner 1990]   Robin Milner, Mads Tofte, and Robert Harper, *The Defi-nition of Standard ML*, MIT Press, Cambridge, MA, 1990.

[Morehead 1949]   Albert H. Morehead and Geoffrey Mott-Smith, *The Com-plete Book of Solitaire and Patience Games*, Grosset & Dunlap, New York, 1949.

[Musser 1996]   David R. Musser and Atul Saini, *STL Tutorial and Ref-erence Guide*, Addison-Wesley, Reading, MA, 1996.

[O'Brian 1989]   Stephen K. O'Brian, *Turbo Pascal 5.5: The Complete Ref-erence*, McGraw-Hill, New York, 1989.

[Parnas 1972]   David L. Parnas, "On the Criteria to Be Used in Decom-posing Systems into Modules," *Communications of the ACM*, 15(12): 1059–1062, 1972.

[Perry 1990]   Dewayne E. Perry and Gail E. Kaiser, "Adequate Testing and Object-Oriented Programming," *Journal of Object-Oriented Programming*, 2(5): 13–19, 1990.

[Pinson 1988]   Lewis J. Pinson and Richard S. Wiener, *An Introduction to Object-Oriented Programming and Smalltalk*, Addison-Wesley, Reading, MA, 1988.

[Pohl 1989]   Ira Pohl, *C++ for C Programmers*, Addison-Wesley, Reading, MA, 1989.

[Post 1936]   Emil L. Post, "Finite Combinatory Processes Formulation, I," *The Journal of Symbolic Logic*, 1: 103–105, 1936.

[Pree 1995]   Wolfgang Pree, *Design Patterns for Object-Oriented Software Development* Addison-Wesley, Reading, MA, 1995.

[Pullum 1991]   Geoffrey K. Pullum, *The Great Eskimo Vocabulary Hoax*, The University of Chicago Press, Chicago, 1991.

[Rist 1995]   Robert Rist and Robert Terwilliger, *Object-Oriented Programming in Eiffel*, Prentice-Hall, Englewood Cliffs, NJ, 1995.

[Rogers 1967]   Hartley Rogers, Jr., *Theory of Recursive Functions and Effective Computability*, McGraw-Hill, New York, 1967.

[Rosenberg 1971]   Jay F. Rosenberg and Charles Travis (Eds.), *Readings in the Philosophy of Language*, Prentice-Hall, Englewood Cliffs, NJ, 1971.

[Sakkinen 1988a]   Markku Sakkinen, "On the darker side of C++," *ECOOP '88 Proceedings: European Conference on Object-Oriented Programming*, S. Gjessing and K. Nygaard, Eds., Springer-Verlag 1988.

[Sakkinen 1988b]   Markku Sakkinen, "Comments on 'the Law of Demeter' and C++," *Sigplan Notices*, 23(12): 38–44, 1988.

[Sakkinen 1992]   Markku Sakkinen, *Inheritance and Other Main Principles of C++ and Other Object-oriented Languages*, Ph.D. thesis, University of Jyväskylä, Jyväskylä, Finland, 1992.

[Sethi 1989]   Ravi Sethi, *Programming Languages: Concepts and Constructs*, Addison-Wesley, Reading, MA, 1989.

[Smith 1995]   David N. Smith, *IBM Smalltalk: The Language*, Addison-Wesley, Reading, MA, 1995.

[Snyder 1986]   Alan Snyder, "Encapsulation and Inheritance in Object-Oriented Programming Languages," *Proceedings of the 1986 OOPSLA—Conference on Object-Oriented Programming Systems, Languages and Applications*; Reprinted in *Sigplan Notices*, 21(11): 38–45, 1986.

[Stefik 1986]   Mark Stefik and Daniel G. Bobrow, "Object-Oriented Pro-
                     gramming: Themes and Variations," *AI Magazine*, 6(4):
                     40–62, 1986.

[Stein 1987]   Lynn Andrea Stein, "Delegation Is Inheritance," *Pro-
                     ceedings of the 1987 OOPSLA—Conference on Object-
                     Oriented Programming Systems, Languages and Appli-
                     cations*; Reprinted in *Sigplan Notices*, 22(12): 138–146,
                     1987.

[Stevens 1981]   W. Stevens, G. Myers, and L. Constantine, "Structured
                     Design," *IBM Systems Journal*, 13(2), 1974. Reprinted in
                     Edward Yourdon (Ed.) *Classics in Software Engineering*,
                     Prentice-Hall, Englewood Cliffs, NJ, 1979.

[Stroustrup 1986]   Bjarne Stroustrup, *The C++ Programming Language*,
                     Addison-Wesley, Reading, MA, 1986.

[Stroustrup 1988]   Bjarne Stroustrup, "What is 'Object-Oriented Program-
                     ming?' " *IEEE Software*, 5(3): 10–20, May 1988.

[Stroustrup 1994]   Bjarne Stroustrup, *The Design and Evolution of C++*,
                     Addison-Wesley, Reading, MA, 1994.

[Taenzer 1989]   David Taenzer, Murthy Ganti, and Sunil Podar, "Object-
                     Oriented Software Reuse: The Yoyo Problem," *Journal of
                     Object-Oriented Programming*, 2(3): 30 35, 1989.

[Tesler 1985]   Larry Tesler, "Object Pascal Report," Apple Computer,
                     Santa Clara, CA, 1985.

[Tomlinson 1990]   Chris Tomlinson, Mark Scheevel, and Won Kim, "Sharing
                     and Organization Protocols in Object-Oriented Systems,"
                     Journal of Object-Oriented Programming, 2(4): 25–36,
                     1989.

[Turbo 1988]   *Turbo Pascal 5.5 Object-Oriented Programming Guide*,
                     Borland International, Scotts Valley, CA, 1988.

[Turing 1936]   Alan Turing, "On computable numbers, with an applica-
                     tion to the Entscheidungsproblem," *Proceeds of the Lon-
                     don Mathematical Society*, Series 2, 42: 230–265; and 43:
                     544–546.

[Ungar 1987]   David Ungar and Randall B. Smith, "Self: The Power
                     of Simplicity," *Proceedings of the 1987 OOPSLA—
                     Conference on Object-Oriented Programming Systems,
                     Languages and Applications*; Reprinted in *Sigplan Notices*,
                     22(12): 227–242, 1987.

[Unger 1987]   J. Marshall Unger, *The Fifth Generation Fallacy*, Oxford University Press, New York, 1987.

[Usenix 1987]   *Proceedings of the C++ Workshop*, USENIX Association, Berkeley, CA, 1987.

[Webster 1989]   Bruce F. Webster, *The NeXT Book*, Addison-Wesley, Reading, MA, 1989.

[Wegner 1986]   Peter Wegner, "Classification in Object-Oriented Systems," *Sigplan Notices*, 21(10): 173–182, October 1986.

[Weinand 1988]   André Weinand, Erich Gamma, and Rudolf Marty. "ET++ –An Object-Oriented Application Framework in C++," in *Proceedings of the 1988 OOPSLA—Conference on Object-Oriented Programming Systems, Languages and Applications*; Reprinted in *Sigplan Notices*, 23(10): 46–57, October 1988.

[Weiskamp 1990]   Keith Weiskamp and Bryan Flamig, *The Complete C++ Primer*, Academic Press, New York, 1990.

[Wiener 1988]   Richard S. Wiener and Lewis J. Pinson, *An Introduction to Object-Oriented Programming and C++*, Addison-Wesley, Reading, MA, 1988.

[Wiener 1989]   Richard S. Wiener and Lewis J. Pinson, "A Practical Example of Multiple Inheritance in C++," *Sigplan Notices*, 24(9): 112–115, 1989.

[Wiener 1990]   Richard S. Wiener and Lewis J. Pinson, *The C++ Workbook*, Addison-Wesley, Reading, MA, 1990.

[Wikström 1987]   Åke Wikström, *Functional Programming Using Standard ML*, Prentice-Hall International, London, 1987.

[Wilson 1990]   David A. Wilson, Larry S. Rosenstein, and Dan Shafer, *Programming With MacApp*, Addison-Wesley, Reading, MA, 1990.

[Wirfs-Brock 1989a] Allen Wirfs-Brock and Brian Wilkerson, "Variables Limit Reusability," *Journal of Object-Oriented Programming*, 2(1): 34–40, May 1990.

[Wirfs-Brock 1989b] Rebecca Wirfs-Brock and Brian Wilkerson, "Object-Oriented Design: A Responsibility-Driven Approach," *Proceedings of the 1989 OOPSLA—Conference on Object-Oriented Programming Systems, Languages and Applications*; Reprinted in *Sigplan Notices*, 24(10): 71–76, October 1989.

[Wirfs-Brock 1990]   Rebecca Wirfs-Brock, Brian Wilkerson, and Lauren Wiener, *Designing Object-Oriented Software*, Prentice-Hall, Englewood Cliffs, NJ, 1990.

[Whorf 1956]   Benjamin Lee Whorf, *Language Thought & Reality*, MIT Press, Cambridge, MA, 1956.

[Wulf 1972]   William A. Wulf, "A Case Against the GOTO," *Proceedings of the Twenty-Fifth National ACM Conference*, 1972; Reprinted in Edward Yourdon (Ed) *Classics in Software Engineering*, Prentice-Hall, Englewood Cliffs, NJ, 1979.

[Wulf 1973]   William A. Wulf and Mary Shaw, "Global Variable Considered Harmful," *Sigplan Notices*, 8(2): 28–43, 1973.

Index